The Rights Retained by the People

A publication of the
Center for Constitutional Studies
of the Cato Institute

A Cato Institute book

THE RIGHTS RETAINED BY THE PEOPLE

THE HISTORY AND MEANING OF THE NINTH AMENDMENT

Edited by
Randy E. Barnett

George Mason University Press
Fairfax, Virginia

Copyright © 1989 by the

Cato Institute

George Mason University Press

4400 University Drive
Fairfax, VA 22030

Printed in the United States of America

British Cataloging in Publication Information Available

Distributed by arrangement with
University Publishing Associates, Inc.

4720 Boston Way
Lanham, MD 20706

3 Henrietta Street
London WC2E 8LU England

co-published by arrangement with the Cato Institute

Paperback edition first published in 1991

Library of Congress Cataloging-in-Publication Data

The Rights retained by the people : the history and meaning of the Ninth
Amendment / edited by Randy E. Barnett.
p. cm.
Bibliography: p. 399
1. United States—Constitutional law—Amendments—9th.   2. Civil
rights—United States.   I. Barnett, Randy E.
KF4558 9th.R54   1989
342.73'085—dc 20   89-16829 CIP
[347.30285]
ISBN 0-913969-22-2 (alk. paper)
ISBN 0-913969-37-0 (pbk.:alk paper)

All George Mason University Press books are produced on acid-free
paper which exceeds the minimum standards set by the National
Historical Publications and Records Commission.

Contents

FOREWORD   vii

INTRODUCTION: JAMES MADISON'S NINTH AMENDMENT
Randy E. Barnett   1

1. SPEECH TO THE HOUSE EXPLAINING HIS PROPOSED
AMENDMENTS WITH NOTES FOR THE AMENDMENTS SPEECH
James Madison   51

2. THE "HIGHER LAW" BACKGROUND OF AMERICAN
CONSTITUTIONAL LAW
Edward S. Corwin   67

3. THE NINTH AMENDMENT OF THE FEDERAL CONSTITUTION
Knowlton H. Kelsey   93

4. THE FORGOTTEN NINTH AMENDMENT
Bennett B. Patterson   107

5. ARE THERE "CERTAIN RIGHTS . . . RETAINED BY THE
PEOPLE"?
Norman Redlich   127

6. NATURAL RIGHTS AND THE NINTH AMENDMENT
Eugene M. Van Loan, III   149

7. THE NINTH AMENDMENT
John Hart Ely   179

8. THE NINTH AMENDMENT
Raoul Berger   191

9. ON READING THE NINTH AMENDMENT: A REPLY TO
    RAOUL BERGER
    Simeon C. R. McIntosh   219

10. THE HISTORY AND MEANING OF THE NINTH AMENDMENT
    Russell L. Caplan   243

11. FEDERALISM AND FUNDAMENTAL RIGHTS: THE NINTH
    AMENDMENT
    Calvin R. Massey   291

12. ON READING AND USING THE NINTH AMENDMENT
    Charles L. Black, Jr.   337

    APPENDIX A: Roger Sherman's Draft of the Bill of Rights   351

    APPENDIX B: Amendments to the United States
                 Constitution Proposed by State Ratifying
                 Conventions   353

    APPENDIX C: Justice Goldberg's Concurring Opinion in
                 Griswold v. Connecticut   387

    BIBLIOGRAPHY ON THE NINTH AMENDMENT   399

    CASE INDEX   405

    GENERAL INDEX   411

Foreword

The essays in this splendid book cannot fail to leave a reader with renewed awe at the mysteries of history. Consider: The topic is the meaning of the ninth of the ten brief amendments whose adoption, almost 200 years ago, was the sine qua non for the ratification of the Constitution itself. For all but the last quarter of a century the amendment lay dormant, rarely discussed and justifiably described as "forgotten" in the one book devoted to it. Then, in 1965, when Justice Goldberg relied on the Ninth Amendment in his concurring opinion in *Griswold v. Connecticut,* the world changed. Since then the Ninth Amendment has been cited in well over 1,000 cases and discussed in a wide array of scholarly works. It has become a legal, philosophical, and jurisprudential Rorschach test for the assessment of prospective judicial appointees.

Conservatives scrutinize candidates for the Supreme Court to ensure that they interpret the Ninth Amendment as embodying principles of federalism and little else. Anyone who would transform the Ninth Amendment into what Raoul Berger calls "a bottomless well in which the judiciary can dip for the formation of undreamed of 'rights' in their limitless discretion" need not apply. As for liberal judge-confirmers in the Senate (there are no liberal judge-nominators in the White House), they seek to ensure that nominees pay proper obeisance to *Griswold* and to Justice Goldberg's argument that a right of privacy is supportable by reference to the Ninth Amendment.

Once so awakened, will the Ninth Amendment ever sleep again? This book will diminish the prospect. It is the definitive study of the Ninth Amendment as well as a first-rate collection of essays on general principles of constitutional interpretation.

The essays raise both historical and philosophical questions: How should we use history in interpreting the Constitution? Which body of history should we use? Given that many of the Framers believed in natural rights, should those principles inform our constitutional adjudication, as Bennett B. Patterson argues? Might the rejection of natural law in our era have made it possible for us to ignore the Ninth Amendment altogether, as John Hart Ely suggests? And how can history help us specify the unenumerated rights protected by the Ninth Amendment when, as Charles Black, Jr., sagely informs us, "[t]he only hitch is . . . that the rights not enumerated are not enumerated"?

The differing historical interpretations reflected in these essays can only leave a reader with a sense of the limits of history in constitutional adjudication. So many scholars of such distinction and rectitude let loose on such a small body of history, and—lo and behold—they disagree with each other! Such discrepancies, of course, do not suggest that history is irrelevant to constitutional adjudication or that it may properly be ignored. The problem is that it is hard to decide what the most relevant history is, harder still to unearth that history, and hardest of all to decide how much weight to give it. The conflicting accounts of Ninth Amendment history set forth in these essays illustrate anew what a tortuous path we tread on when we seek to rely exclusively on the intentions of the Framers.

If history is problematic as a guide, what about language? The language of the Ninth Amendment suggests that at the very least it is a construction amendment. Whatever its ambiguities, the declaration that "[t]he enumeration in the Constitution, of certain rights, shall not be construed to deny or disparage others retained by the people" surely invalidates at least one construction of the Constitution: that the lack of an assertion of some right in the Bill of Rights necessarily means that the right does not exist. Chief Justice Burger found in *Richmond Newspapers, Inc. v. Virginia* (1979) that the absence of a specific constitutional guarantee of the right of the public to attend trials did not bar the Court from concluding that the right was protected. His finding is plainly consistent with the Ninth Amendment.

There are, of course, far more difficult Ninth Amendment issues. They are dealt with seriously and often passionately in the essays that follow. The Ninth Amendment, no longer forgotten, deserves such treatment.

FLOYD ABRAMS

Introduction: James Madison's Ninth Amendment

Randy E. Barnett

> It cannot be presumed that any clause in the constitution is intended to be without effect; and therefore, such a construction is inadmissible, unless the words require it.[1]

> I do not think you can use the Ninth Amendment unless you know something of what it means. For example, if you had an amendment that says "Congress shall make no" and then there is an inkblot, and you cannot read the rest of it, and that is the only copy you have, I do not think the court can make up what might be under the inkblot.[2]

Clearing a Path for the Ninth Amendment

The courts have long protected constitutional rights that are not listed explicitly in the Constitution,[3] but are they warranted in doing so? As scholars and commentators vigorously debate this and other questions about the appropriate role of judges in interpreting the Constitution, the Ninth Amendment has assumed increasing importance. Its declaration that "[t]he enumeration in the Constitution, of certain rights, shall not be construed to deny or disparage others retained by the people"[4] has suggested to many that the set of rights protected by the Constitution is not closed and that judges may be authorized to protect these "unenumerated" rights on occasion.

The purpose of this book is to make generally available the provocative—but largely unknown and inaccessible—body of Ninth Amendment scholarship that has appeared over the past fifty years.

---

[1]Marbury v. Madison, 5 U.S. (1 Cranch) 137, 174 (1803).

[2]Testimony of Robert Bork, as quoted in Wall St. J., Oct. 5, 1987, §A, at 22.

[3]For a list of judicially protected unenumerated rights, *see infra* note 98.

[4]U.S. Const. amend. IX.

By providing access to this rich literature, it is hoped that those who are now giving serious thought to the Ninth Amendment will be able to build on the base provided by others, rather than having to start each effort from scratch.

While much is controversial about the Ninth Amendment, the events that led to its adoption are generally agreed upon.[5] The Ninth Amendment was originally conceived by James Madison. A committee of the House of Representatives, on which Madison served, revised it. The House and the Senate debated and approved it, and the several states ratified it, along with the rest of the Bill of Rights.

Any provision that has survived this process must be presumed by interpreters of the Constitution to have some legitimate constitutional function, whether actual or only potential. Despite this long-respected presumption, the Supreme Court has generally interpreted the Ninth Amendment in a manner that denies it any role in the constitutional structure.[6] The Ninth Amendment's most important appearance in a Supreme Court case to date has been in a supporting role.[7] In his now-famous concurring opinion in *Griswold v. Connecticut*, Justice Goldberg stated:

> In interpreting the Constitution, real effect should be given to all the words it uses. . . . The Ninth Amendment to the Constitution may be regarded by some as a recent discovery, . . . but since 1791 it has been a basic part of the Constitution which we are sworn to uphold.[8]

[5]For discussions of the legislative history of the Ninth Amendment, see the following works, reprinted or excerpted in this book: B. Patterson, The Forgotten Ninth Amendment 6–18 (1955) (excerpts reprinted as chapter 4 of this book); Berger, *The Ninth Amendment*, 66 Cornell L. Rev. 1, 3–9 (1980) (ch. 8); Caplan, *The History and Meaning of the Ninth Amendment*, 69 Va. L. Rev. 223, 228–59 (1983) (ch. 10); Massey, *Federalism and Fundamental Rights: The Ninth Amendment*, 38 Hastings L.J. 305, 307–11 (1987) (ch. 11); Van Loan, *Natural Rights and the Ninth Amendment*, 48 B.U.L. Rev. 1, 4–16 (1968) (ch. 6).

[6]The singular exception to this is Richmond Newspapers, Inc., v. Virginia, 448 U.S. 555 (1980). There, the plurality based its opinion, in part, on the Ninth Amendment. *Id.* at 579 n.15.

[7]The judicial use of the Ninth Amendment is summarized in Redlich, *The Ninth Amendment*, in 3 The Encyclopedia of the American Constitution 1316–20 (L. Levy ed. 1982).

[8]381 U.S. 479, 491 (1965) (citations and quotation marks omitted) (reprinted as Appendix C of this book). Justice Goldberg relied on three scholarly works on the Ninth Amendment, each of which is reprinted or excerpted in this book: B. Patterson,

In this introduction, I hope to clear a path for a more fruitful and faithful interpretation of the Ninth Amendment by removing certain doctrinal and theoretical impediments to such an interpretation. This requires a critical appraisal of what I call the "rights-powers" conception of constitutional rights—a conception that the Court has applied exclusively to the Ninth Amendment, rendering it functionless. I then contrast this view with the very different "power-constraint" conception that the Court has used to interpret most other constitutional rights. If I accomplish nothing else in this introduction, I intend to show that the traditional rights-powers interpretation of the Ninth Amendment is untenable.

The rights-powers conception is, however, more a symptom than the real cause of the Ninth Amendment's past and current neglect. The principal obstacles in the path of a functional Ninth Amendment are certain views of constitutional structure and a deep-seated fear of letting judges base their decisions on unenumerated rights— a fear that stems in large part from a modern philosophical skepticism about rights. In this introduction, after laying the rights-powers conception to rest, I present the outlines of a power-constraint conception of the Ninth Amendment. In doing so, I discuss how the judicial protection of unenumerated rights is consistent with the structural features of the Constitution and why philosophical skepticism about the idea of "retained" rights should not operate as a bar to their recognition. Finally, I suggest a practical method of interpreting the rights retained by the people referred to in the Ninth Amendment.

My analysis relies heavily on the explanation of constitutional rights provided by James Madison in his speech before the House of Representatives.[9] I do this for two reasons. First, such a focus responds to the concern of some that giving the Ninth Amendment a genuine role to play in constitutional adjudication somehow conflicts with the intent of the Framers. As the Framer who conceived of the Ninth Amendment, Madison had a conception of constitutional rights that is the most pertinent to an understanding of the

---

supra note 5; Kelsey, *The Ninth Amendment of the Federal Constitution,* 11 Ind. L. J. 309 (1936) (ch. 3); Redlich, *Are There "Certain Rights . . . Retained by the People"?* 37 N.Y.U. L. Rev. 787 (1962) (excerpted in chapter 5).

[9]*See* 1 The Debates and Proceedings in the Congress of the United States 448 (J. Gales & W. Seaton ed. 1834) [hereinafter Annals of Cong.] (Speech of Rep. J. Madison) [hereinafter Madison] (reprinted as chapter 1 of this book).

Ninth Amendment's intended function. Whether or not the views Madison expressed to the House reflected a clear consensus of his contemporaries, if a robust theory of the unenumerated rights retained by the people is consistent with his vision, then it will be quite difficult to sustain an objection to such a theory on the ground that it violates original intent.

Second, I have great respect for Madison as a political theorist. For this reason, in deciding upon the best theory of the Ninth Amendment, I think it is useful to consult the opinion of the insightful person who conceived it and who also conceived a good deal of the Constitution's other important features. I view the Framers as teachers, not wardens, and consider their writings to be the best place to begin looking for a theoretical understanding of the text they wrote.

The theoretical issues raised by the Ninth Amendment are, in my view, extremely fundamental, and this article is in no way intended to be the last word on the subject.[10] A complete defense of allowing the Ninth Amendment a real constitutional function would require a much more extensive presentation than I attempt here. Indeed, a complete analysis of the rights "retained by the people" would require nothing short of a comprehensive theory of the Constitution.

Two Competing Conceptions of Constitutional Rights

Although the longstanding neglect of the Ninth Amendment is a product of basic concerns about grounding judicial review on unenumerated rights, this neglect would not have been possible without an interpretation that purports to give the amendment a meaning while denying it any functional role in constitutional disputes. Such an interpretation employs a rights-powers conception of constitutional rights, a view that can be traced to a Federalist argument against the addition of any bill of rights.

The Rights-Powers Conception of Constitutional Rights

The Federalists originally argued that a bill of rights was unnecessary because the Constitution granted the national government

---

[10]I discuss the relationship between the judicial protection of unenumerated rights and the ability of a constitution to impart legitimacy to enacted legislation in Barnett, *Foreword: The Ninth Amendment and Constitutional Legitimacy*, 64 Chi.-Kent L. Rev 37 (1988).

only enumerated powers. Any power that was not enumerated could not be exercised by the national government. A bill of rights, they argued, would be redundant and therefore unnecessary. Any rights enumerated in a bill of rights would be outside the powers of the national government and would need no further protection. As Alexander Hamilton wrote,

> [W]hy declare that things shall not be done which there is no power to do? Why, for instance, should it be said that the liberty of the press shall not be restrained, when no power is given by which restrictions may be imposed?[11]

James Wilson made the same argument:

> [E]very thing which is not given, is reserved. . . . [I]t would have been superfluous and absurd, to have stipulated with a federal body of our own creation, that we should enjoy those privileges, of which we are not divested either by the intention or the act that has brought that body into existence.[12]

In *United Pub. Workers v. Mitchell,* Justice Reed used this rights-powers conception of constitutional rights to interpret a Ninth Amendment claim. Writing for the Court, he stated:

> The powers granted by the Constitution to the Federal Government are subtracted from the totality of sovereignty originally in the states and the people. Therefore, when objection is made that the exercise of a federal power infringes upon rights reserved by the Ninth and Tenth Amendments, the inquiry must be directed toward the granted power under which the action of the Union was taken. If granted power is found, necessarily the objection of

---

[11]The Federalist No. 84, at 559 (A. Hamilton) (Mod. Lib. ed. 1937).

[12]Address by James Wilson to a Meeting of the Citizens of Philadelphia (1787), in 1 B. Schwartz, The Bill of Rights: A Documentary History 529 (1971). Both Hamilton and Wilson argued that an expressed protection of freedom of the press was unnecessary since the regulation of the press was beyond the powers of Congress. In the Federal Convention, Roger Sherman used the same example:

> Mr. Pinckney & Mr. Gerry, moved to insert a declaration "that the liberty of the Press should be inviolably observed—"
> Mr. Sherman—It is unnecessary—The power of Congress does not extend to the Press.

Federal Convention (Aug. 20, 1787), reprinted in 1 B. Schwartz, 437, 439 (1971).

invasion of those rights, reserved by the Ninth and Tenth Amendments, must fail.[13]

The rights-powers conception of the Ninth Amendment views delegated powers and constitutional rights as logically complementary. This approach has two important advantages. First, when rights are viewed as the logical obverse of powers, content can be given to unenumerated rights by exclusively focusing on the expressed provisions delegating powers. By avoiding the need to directly address the substance of unenumerated rights, the rights-powers conception appears to provide judges with a practical way of interpreting the otherwise open-ended Ninth Amendment. Second, the view that rights and powers are logically complementary seems to avoid any internal conflict or logical contradiction between constitutional rights and powers. In this way, the rights-powers conception has the apparent virtue of treating the Constitution as internally coherent. For these reasons, the rights-powers conception has continued to attract proponents.[14]

Nonetheless, the rights-powers conception amounts to a dubious interpretation of the Ninth Amendment for at least three reasons. First, this interpretation erroneously construes the Ninth Amendment to mean nothing more than what is stated in the Tenth. The Tenth Amendment reads: "The powers not delegated to the United States by the Constitution, nor prohibited by it to the States, are reserved to the States, respectively, or to the people."[15] The idea that animates the rights-powers conception—that powers not delegated are reserved—is expressed clearly here. There was absolutely no need for another amendment, confusingly written in terms

[13]United Pub. Workers v. Mitchell, 330 U.S. 75, 95–96 (1947). Calvin Massey reports that this case was one of only "seven Supreme Court cases prior to Griswold [that] dealt in any fashion with the ninth amendment. . . ." Massey, *supra* note 5, at 305 n.1.

[14]*See, e.g.*, Berger, *supra* note 5, at 3 (Ninth Amendment rights and Tenth Amendment powers "are two sides of the same coin."); Cooper, Limited Government and Individual Liberty: The Ninth Amendment's Forgotten Lessons, 4 J. Law & Pol. 63, 78 (1987) ("A ninth amendment claim against *federal* action . . . is determined by the extent of the federal government's enumerated powers. . . .").

[15]U.S. Const. amend. X. The Tenth Amendment explicitly incorporates the enumerated-powers theory of the national government. Although it is often thought of as a "states' rights" provision, the Tenth Amendment is entirely neutral as to which powers are "reserved to the states" and which "to the people"; therefore, it does not explicitly endorse any particular vision of state government.

of "rights" that are "retained by the people," to express exactly the same idea.[16]

Justice Reed's reference to *"those rights, reserved by the Ninth*

[16]*See, e.g.,* Kelsey, *supra* note 8, at 310 ("there was some distinction in the minds of the framers . . . between *declarations of right* and *limitations on* or *prohibitions of power* . . . [otherwise] the Ninth Amendment would have been unnecessary."); Kelly, *supra* note 5, at 832 ("Such a reading of the ninth amendment is clearly wrong; it is the tenth amendment that protects state powers against federal encroachment and that limits the federal government to the exercise of express and implied powers."). *Cf.* J. Ely, Democracy and Distrust 34–35 (1980) ("The Tenth Amendment . . . completely fulfills the function that is here being proffered as all the Ninth Amendment was about.") (excerpt reprinted as Chapter 1 of this book).

The distinct roles played by the Ninth and Tenth amendments are clarified by a draft of the Bill of Rights written by Roger Sherman (reprinted as Appendix A of this book). Sherman served with Madison as a member of the House committee that drafted the amendments and his working draft was recently discovered in the Library of Congress among Madison's papers. *See Handwritten Draft of Bill of Rights Found,* N.Y. Times, July 29, 1987, §A, at 1. The last paragraph of Sherman's eleventh amendment closely resembles what came to be the Tenth:

> And the powers not delegated to the Government of the United States by the Constitution, nor prohibited by it to the particular States, are retained by the States respectively, nor shall any [sic] the exercise of power by the Government of the United States particular instances herein enumerated by way of caution, be construed to imply the contrary.

In contrast, Sherman's second amendment reflects the sentiment that came to be expressed in the Ninth:

> The people have certain natural rights which are retained by them when they enter into Society. Such are the rights of Conscience in matters of religion; of acquiring property, and of pursuing happiness & Safety; of Speaking, writing and publishing their Sentiments with decency and freedom; of peaceably assembling to consult their common good, and of applying to Government by petition or remonstrance for redress of grievances. Of these rights therefore they Shall not be deprived by the Government of the united States.

Sherman's use of the phrase "Such are" indicates that those rights he lists—only some of which came to be enumerated—were merely examples of the rights retained by the people that "Shall not be deprived by the Government of the united States."

Moreover, Sherman's draft undermines the theory that the retained rights of the Ninth Amendment refer solely to a right of the people to revolt. Prior to his discussion of "natural rights which are retained by them when they enter into Society," his first amendment reads:

> The powers of government being derived from the people, ought to be exercised for their benefit, and they have an inherent and unalienable right to change or amend their political Constitution, whenever they judge such change will advance their interest & happiness.

and Tenth Amendments,"[17] illustrates the confusion that the rights-powers conception can cause. The Tenth Amendment does not speak of "rights," of course, but of reserved "powers." By contrast, the Ninth Amendment speaks only of rights, not of powers. Yet Charles Cooper states that "[t]he ninth amendment does not specify what rights it protects other than by its reference to the enumerated *powers* of the federal government."[18]

The second objection to the rights-powers conception follows from the first: This conception renders the Ninth Amendment effectively inapplicable to any conceivable case or controversy. On the assumption that rights and powers are logically complementary, rights begin at precisely the point where powers end. Thus, in principle, at least, there can never be a conflict between a right and a power. But because the focus of the rights-powers approach is entirely on the powers side, any claim that the national government had exceeded its enumerated powers would rely entirely upon the provisions enumerating the powers of the national government (to show the absence of a power) and the language of the Tenth Amendment (to show that those powers not delegated are reserved). The Ninth Amendment has absolutely no role to play in the analysis.

The problem is not that there would never be an occasion to use the Ninth Amendment. After all, there has been no occasion to enforce the rule requiring the President to be at least thirty-five years old, either. Rather, the problem is that a rights-powers conception deprives the Ninth Amendment of any potential application. It does not allow for even a hypothetical case that would require an independent Ninth Amendment analysis. Moreover, the rights-powers conception does not simply render the Ninth Amendment unenforceable by the judiciary. The Ninth Amendment is rendered irrelevant to any conceivable constitutional decision, regardless of which branch of government is the decision maker.

Of course, it is possible that Congress approved and the states ratified an amendment that was meant to be inapplicable to any conceivable circumstance. However, we cannot prefer such an interpretation of a constitutional enactment if one that contemplates

---

[17]United Pub. Workers v. Mitchell, 330 U.S. 75, 96 (1947) (emphasis added).

[18]Cooper, *supra* note 14, at 80 (emphasis added).

a potential role is also available.[19] Such an alternative interpretation, based on a power-constraint conception of constitutional rights, is suggested below. In sum, absent compelling evidence, we cannot presume any provision of the Constitution to be as superfluous as the rights-powers conception would render the Ninth Amendment.

The third objection to the rights-powers conception is that it cannot be limited to the Ninth Amendment. If it is correct, it must apply to the rights enumerated in the Constitution in the same manner as it does to the unenumerated rights referred to in the Ninth Amendment. Assuming that the rights of the people are the logical converse of the powers delegated to the government, the very enumeration of a particular power in the Constitution automatically ceded to the general government any potentially conflicting rights that might have existed prior to the adoption of the Constitution. If this conception is correct, however, then even an enumerated right should never constrain an enumerated power. In the words of Raoul Berger, "Thus viewed, the Bill of Rights added nothing, but was merely declaratory."[20] Of course, as noted below, this is not at all how courts have interpreted enumerated constitutional rights.[21] Legislative acts that fall within an enumerated power can violate an enumerated right.[22]

It is not surprising that a rights-powers conception denying the effect of unenumerated rights denies effect to enumerated rights as well. For the Federalists originally launched the rights-powers conception against the enumeration of any constitutional rights to defuse Anti-Federalist opposition to the Constitution. James Madison would have had no reason to devise a means of protecting unenumerated rights placed in jeopardy by an enumeration that he still opposed at that time. The problem that the Ninth Amendment was devised to solve simply had yet to arise.

---

[19]Cf. Massey, supra note 5, at 316 ("Construing the Ninth Amendment as a mere declaration of a constitutional truism, devoid of enforceable content, renders its substance nugatory and assigns to its framers an intention to engage in a purely moot exercise."). See supra note 1 and accompanying text.

[20]Berger, supra note 5, at 6 (footnote omitted).

[21]See infra notes 36–41 and accompanying text.

[22]See, e.g., Lamont v. Postmaster General, 381 U.S. 301 (1965) (congressional act regulating the receipt of "communist political propaganda" is violative of the first amendment and is unconstitutional).

The rights-powers conception reflects a losing argument against enumerating any constitutional rights. Notwithstanding the ultimate victory of the Federalists at the Constitutional Convention, their attempt to defend the absence of a bill of rights on the ground that such a declaration would be redundant was controversial when made,[23] and ultimately was rejected during the ratification process. No one denies that ratification of the Constitution depended upon the promise of a forthcoming bill of rights. It is odd indeed to insist that the best interpretation of the Bill of Rights is based on the theory used by its most vociferous opponents.

The rights-powers conception of constitutional rights is attractive both because it promises a practical way of interpreting unenumerated rights and because it appears to interpret the rights and powers provisions of the text in a logically consistent manner. Unfortunately, it achieves these objectives at the price of rendering the Ninth Amendment completely functionless and superfluous. Still, any alternative account of constitutional rights that contemplates unenumerated rights doing any serious work in constitutional analysis must show both the practicality of its method and the internal coherence of such a constitutional scheme.

In the balance of this article, I describe and defend another way to conceive of constitutional rights, including those rights retained by the people: the power-constraint conception. In the next two sections, I explain why conceiving constitutional rights as constraining the exercise of delegated powers is not a contradictory approach to rights and powers. Instead of viewing rights and powers as logically complementary, a power-constraint conception views rights and powers as functionally complementary. Moreover, this approach

---

[23]Thomas Jefferson, for example, rejected Wilson's argument that a bill of rights was unnecessary. In a letter to Madison, he wrote:

> To say, as Mr. Wilson does that a bill of rights was not necessary because all is reserved in the case of the general government which is not given, while in the particular ones all is given which is not reserved might do for the Audience to whom it was addressed, but is surely gratis dictum, opposed by strong inferences from the body of the instrument, as well as from the omission of the clause of our present confederation which had declared that in express terms.

Letter from Thomas Jefferson to James Madison (Dec. 20, 1787), *reprinted in* 1 B. Schwartz, *supra* note 12, at 606–07. Even Madison, who at one point accepted Wilson's argument that a declaration of rights was unnecessary, did not do so "in the extent argued by Mr. Wilson. . . ." Letter of James Madison to Thomas Jefferson (Oct. 17, 1788), reprinted in 1 B. Schwartz, *supra* note 12, at 615.

is truer than the rights-powers conception to the concerns expressed by some Federalists about the dangers of enumerating any rights. Finally, I examine the practicality of three methods of interpreting these power-constraining unenumerated rights.

Recasting the Original Debate over Constitutional Rights

The idea that constitutional rights are simply what is left over after the people have delegated powers to the government flies in the face of the amendments themselves. For example, it is impossible to find a right to "a speedy and public trial, by an impartial jury,"[24] a right against double jeopardy or self-incrimination,[25] or a right to be free from "unreasonable searches and seizures"[26] by closely examining the limits of the enumerated powers of the national government. The pivotal mistake of Justice Reed and those commentators who would neuter the Ninth Amendment is their exclusive concentration on only one of two Federalist arguments. Consequently, they fail to discern the distinct functions played by the Ninth and Tenth Amendments.[27]

The Federalists' argument that the enumeration of powers rendered a declaration of rights unnecessary is best viewed as a response to the criticism made by opponents of ratification that the Constitution was dangerous because it lacked a bill of rights. That response employed the theory that the federal government is one of limited and enumerated powers, a theory that eventually was incorporated in the Tenth Amendment. However, the Federalists not only responded to this criticism of the proposed Constitution, they also advanced a criticism of their own against the idea of a bill of rights. They attempted to turn the tables on the Anti-Federalists by arguing that a declaration of rights would be dangerous. In Hamilton's words, "I . . . affirm that bills of rights, in the sense and to the extent in which they are contended for, are not only unnecessary in the proposed Constitution, but would even be dangerous."[28]

---

[24]U.S. Const. amend. VI.

[25]U.S. Const. amend. V.

[26]U.S. Const. amend. IV.

[27]I thank David Mayer for emphasizing to me the importance of this separate strain of the Federalist argument for distinguishing the rationales of the Ninth and Tenth Amendments.

[28]The Federalist No. 84 (A. Hamilton), *supra* note 11, at 559.

Enumerating rights in the Constitution was seen as presenting two potential sources of danger. The first was that such an enumeration could be used to justify an unwarranted expansion of federal powers. As Hamilton explained, "They would contain various exceptions to powers which are not granted; and on this very account, would afford a colourable pretext to claim more than were granted."[29] The second potential source of danger was that any right excluded from an enumeration would be jeopardized. In his speech to the House explaining his proposed amendments, James Madison stressed this danger of enumerated rights:

> It has been objected also against a bill of rights, that, by enumerating particular exceptions to the grant of power, it would disparage those rights which were not placed in that enumeration; and it might follow by implication, that those rights which were not singled out, were intended to be assigned into the hands of the General Government, and were consequently insecure. This is one of the most plausible arguments I have ever heard urged against the admission of a bill of rights into this system; but, I conceive, that it may be guarded against.[30]

Madison's initial device for doing so was a provision that ran together both of these concerns:

> The exceptions here or elsewhere in the constitution, made in favor of particular rights, shall not be construed as to diminish the just importance of other rights retained by the people, or as to enlarge the powers delegated by the constitution; but either as actual limitations of such powers, or as inserted merely for greater caution.[31]

---

[29]Id.

[30]Madison, *supra* note 9, at 456. Contrast this expression of deep concern with Madison's passing reference, near the end of his speech, to the precursor of the Tenth Amendment:

> Perhaps words which may define this more precisely than the whole of the instrument now does, may be considered as superfluous. I admit they may be deemed unnecessary; but there can be no harm in making such a declaration. . . .

Id. at 458–59. This sharp dissimilarity of tone undermines the rights-powers theory that the Ninth and Tenth amendments were viewed as essentially the same and that the wording of the Tenth Amendment best captures what Madison was about in devising the Ninth.

[31]*Id.* at 452.

Eventually, the two ideas were unpacked. The danger of interpreting federal powers too expansively was handled by the Tenth Amendment, while the danger of jeopardizing unenumerated rights was addressed by the Ninth Amendment.

Thus, the Federalist position did not disparage as superfluous the rights retained by the people. Nor did it deny that retained rights operate as a genuine and enforceable constraint on government. To the contrary, the Federalists disparaged the idea of using a written declaration of rights in the Constitution precisely to protect the rights retained by the people. They expressed fear that an incomplete or inaccurate written declaration might well undermine the status of the unwritten retained rights. In sum, this Federalist objection to a bill of rights assumed the preeminent importance of the unwritten rights retained by the people.[32]

There is no reason to suppose that these Federalists did not share the then-prevailing beliefs in rights antecedent to government.[33] For example, the same James Wilson who used a rights-powers argument in his vocal opposition to a bill of rights was an ardent adherent to natural rights. In his lectures on jurisprudence, he explicitly rejected the views of both Edmund Burke and William Blackstone, contending that "[g]overnment, in my humble opinion, should be formed to secure and to enlarge the exercise of the natural rights of its members; and every government, which has not this in view, as its principal object, is not a government of the legitimate kind."[34] Nor were these mere "theoretical" or "philosophical" rights with no real bite:

> I go farther; and now proceed to show, that in peculiar instances, in which those rights can receive neither protection nor reparation

---

[32]Of course, some Federalists may have been motivated less by concerns about the efficacy and dangers of a bill of rights than by a concern that the absence of a bill of rights would jeopardize the ratification of the Constitution (which, in fact, it did until assurances of future amendments were made). Nonetheless, the analysis presented in the text assumes that the positions articulated by Hamilton, Wilson, and Madison were advanced in good faith. A contrary, more cynical, assumption can hardly be offered to bolster the case for a Federalist-style rights-powers conception.

[33]The beliefs are discussed in Corwin, *The "Higher Law" Background of American Constitutional Law*, 42 Harv. L. Rev. 149, 369 (1928–29) (excerpts reprinted as Chapter 2 of this book); Grey, *The Origins of the Unwritten Constitution*, 30 Stan. L. Rev. 843 (1978); Sherry, *The Founders' Unwritten Constitution*, 54 U. Chi. L. Rev. 1127 (1987).

[34]Wilson, *Of the Natural Rights of Individuals*, in 2 The Works of James Wilson 307 (J.D. Andrews ed. 1896).

from civil government, they are, notwithstanding its institution, entitled still to that defence, and to those methods of recovery, which are justified and demanded in a state of nature.

The defence of one's self, justly called the primary law of nature, is not, nor can it be abrogated by any regulation of municipal law.[35]

The Power-Constraint Conception of Constitutional Rights

A rights-powers conception of constitutional rights is untenable if a better account of constitutional rights is available. In fact, courts do not use a rights-powers conception to interpret enumerated or written constitutional rights. Enumerated rights need not be the logical mirror image of enumerated powers. Rather, enumerated rights can potentially limit in some manner the exercise of powers delegated by other provisions of the Constitution. A principal reason for this was voiced by Elbridge Gerry during the House debate concerning the proposed amendments:

> This declaration of rights, I take it, is intended to secure the people against the maladministration of the Government; if we could suppose that, in all cases, the rights of the people would be attended to, the occasion for guards of this kind would be removed.[36]

Constitutional rights can be conceived as power-constraints that regulate the exercise of power by Congress and the executive branch by constraining either their choice of means or their choice of ends. First, constitutional rights are means constraints. Although the enumeration of powers restricts Congress to pursuing only certain ends, constitutional rights further restrict the means by which these ends may be pursued.[37] In this way, in contrast with the rights-powers conception, the power-constraint conception contemplates a potential conflict between constitutional rights and enumerated powers.

[35]Id. at 335. Wilson's lectures, given between 1790 and 1792, also undermine the claim that by the time of the Constitution, Americans had lost their Lockean and revolutionary ardor for natural rights in favor of a more conservative Blackstonian positivism that favored legislative supremacy.

[36]1 Annals of Cong. 778 (Remarks of Rep. E. Gerry).

[37]See, e.g., S. Barber, On What the Constitution Means 113 (1984) ("Constitutional rights . . . remove certain means from those means available to the government for pursuing its authorized ends.").

Under this conception, it is possible that means chosen to pursue a constitutionally permissible end might infringe on a constitutional right.[38] Suppose, for example, that in pursuit of its enumerated power to "lay and collect Taxes" or to "raise and support Armies," Congress infringed on the enumerated rights of free speech and assembly. If so, Congress would not have violated the Tenth Amendment for it was acting within its delegated powers. But it may have violated the First Amendment because it exercised its power in a rights-violating manner.

The Supreme Court appears to have adopted a means-constraints approach when enumerated rights are at issue. As the Court stated in *Dennis v. United States:* "The question with which we are concerned here is not whether Congress has such a *power*, but whether the *means* which it has employed conflict with the First and Fifth Amendments to the Constitution."[39] On the floor of Congress, Madison made a very similar argument: "[T]he great object in view is to limit and qualify the powers of Government, by excepting out of the grant of power those cases in which Government ought not to act, *or to act only in a particular mode.*"[40] He then offered a similar example:

> The General Government has a right to pass all laws which shall be necessary to collect its revenue; the means for enforcing the collection are within the direction of the Legislature: may not general warrants be considered necessary for this purpose . . .? If there was reason for restraining the State Governments from exercising this power, there is like reason for restraining the Federal Government.[41]

---

[38]One might try to salvage the rights-powers theory by claiming that there can be no clash between powers and rights because Congress has no power to violate a constitutional right. Although this response maintains a formal distinction, it suggests an entirely different methodology for determining the content of constitutional rights than that described by Justice Reed in United Pub. Workers v. Mitchell. This formulation of the rights-powers distinction would require an inquiry into the substance of constitutional rights to determine the extent of congressional power. Moreover, this distinction does not provide an objection to including unenumerated rights in such an inquiry.

[39]341 U.S. 494, 501 (1951). *See also* Barenblatt v. United States, 360 U.S. 109, 112 (1959) ("Congress . . . must exercise its powers subject to the . . . relevant limitations of the Bill of Rights.").

[40]Madison, *supra* note 9, at 454 (emphasis added).

[41]*Id.* at 456.

Perhaps, then, John Ely judged Madison a bit too harshly when he attributed to him and others "a failure to recognize that rights and powers are not simply the absence of one another but that rights can cut across or 'trump' powers."[42] By the same token, Raoul Berger's response to Ely that "whether the Founders were mistaken in logic is of no moment if they acted on that mistaken view"[43] was premature, for at least one of the Framers was not mistaken in this regard.

Moreover, as Madison's example suggests, the Necessary and Proper Clause exacerbates the means-end problem within a scheme of delegated powers. After enumerating specific powers of Congress, the Constitution authorizes Congress "[t]o make all Laws which shall be necessary and proper for carrying into execution the foregoing Powers, and all other Powers vested in this Constitution in the Government of the United States, or in any Department or Officer thereof."[44] This open-ended language heightens the prospect that Congress or some department or officer of the general government may pursue a delegated end by means that infringe upon the rights of the people. Therefore, some regulation of the means employed to achieve enumerated government ends must supplement the device of enumerating powers. This is one way in which constitutional rights may functionally complement a scheme of delegated powers.

Even Madison, a strong proponent of the Necessary and Proper Clause, acknowledged that it was susceptible to abuse and consequently that there was a need for constitutional rights to constrain the means chosen by the general government:

> It is true, the powers of the General Government are circumscribed, they are directed to particular objects; but even if Government keeps within those limits, it has certain discretionary powers with respect to the means, which may admit of abuse to a certain extent, . . . because in the constitution of the United States, there is a clause granting to Congress the power to make all laws which shall be necessary and proper for carrying into

---

[42]J. Ely, *supra* note 16, at 36. The metaphor of "trump" suggests a power-constraint conception.

[43]Berger, *supra* note 5, at 21–22 (citation omitted).

[44]U.S. Const., art. I, § 8, cl. 18.

execution the powers vested in the Government of the United States, or in any department or officer thereof.[45]

The second power-constraining function of constitutional rights is to limit the permissible ends of government activity. Constitutional rights were adopted, in Madison's words, "as actual limitations of such powers, or . . . merely for *greater caution*."[46] This last phrase suggests that in addition to placing actual or additional limits on the means by which government can accomplish its legitimate ends, constitutional rights provide a "redundant," or cautionary, safeguard in the event that the acts of government exceed its proper ends. This function is also reflected in Madison's earlier quoted remark that "the great object in view is to limit and qualify the powers of Government, by excepting out of the grant of power *those cases in which the Government ought not to act*, or to act only in a particular mode."[47] In other words, the Bill of Rights was meant to constrain the powers of government in two ways: by reinforcing the limitations on the delegated powers or ends of government, and by placing additional restrictions on the means by which government may pursue its delegated ends.

The combination of two different strategies for limiting the powers of government—constitutional rights and expressed limitations on powers—creates an interesting dynamic. When government acts within a narrow construction of its powers, constitutional rights play only a minor role in constraining its activity. As the enumerated powers are given an increasingly expanded interpretation, however, constitutional rights assume a greater importance within the constitutional scheme. Even if no logical conflict initially existed between delegated powers and constitutional rights (whether enumerated or not), previously nonexistent conflicts between rights and powers might well emerge as the scope of government powers expands. As Justice Brennan has observed, "the possibilities for collision between government activity and individual rights will increase as the power and authority of government itself expands."[48]

---

[45]Madison, *supra* note 9, at 455.

[46]*Id.* at 452 (emphasis added).

[47]*Id.* at 454 (emphasis added).

[48]Brennan, *Construing the Constitution*, 19 U.C. Davis L. Rev. 1, 9 (1985).

If one concedes that the rights enumerated in the constitution were intended as "actual limitations of such [delegated] powers,"[49] the rights-powers conception becomes a dubious interpretation of the Ninth Amendment. For such an interpretation implies that a fundamentally different conception of constitutional rights applies to the "retained" rights of the Ninth Amendment than applies to the enumerated rights. This implication appears to conflict with Madison's claim that the enumerated rights also included retained rights:

> In some instances they [the enumerated rights] assert those rights which are exercised by the people in forming and establishing a plan of Government. In other instances, they *specify those rights which are retained when particular powers are given up to be exercised by the Legislature.* In other instances they specify positive rights, which may seem to result from the nature of the compact.[50]

The wording of the Ninth Amendment itself argues against such differential treatment. The Ninth Amendment declares that "[t]he enumeration in the Constitution, of certain rights, shall not be construed to deny *or disparage* others retained by the people."[51]

Supporters of a rights-powers interpretation of the Ninth Amendment rely heavily on a passage in a letter written by Madison to George Washington in 1789 in which Madison employed a rights-powers distinction as part of a defense of the Ninth Amendment:

> If a line can be drawn between the powers granted and the rights retained, it would seem to be the same thing, whether the latter

[49]Madison, *supra* note 9, at 452. The quotation is excerpted from the precursor to the Ninth Amendment that appears in full in the text accompanying note 31.

[50]*Id.* at 454 (emphasis added). Madison's characterization of the enumerated rights as including, among others, rights that were retained by the people also undermines Raoul Berger's claim that a judicial "power" to protect retained rights would undermine the Framers' intent to limit federal power:

> Madison made clear that the retained rights were not "assigned" to the federal government: to the contrary, he emphasized that they constitute an area in which the "Government ought not to act." This means, in my judgment, that the courts have not been empowered to enforce the retained rights against either the federal government or the states.

Berger, *supra* note 5, at 7. In fact, Madison speaks here of "particular powers . . . given up to be exercised *by the Legislature.*" He was most fearful of abuses in the legislative branch. *See infra* note 55 and accompanying text.

[51]U.S. Const. amend. IX (emphasis added).

to be secured by declaring that they shall not be abridged, or that the former shall not be extended. If no line can be drawn, a declaration in either form would amount to nothing.[52]

Madison's use of a rights-powers distinction to explain the Ninth Amendment, however, is not logically inconsistent with a robust power-constraining view of the Ninth Amendment. Indeed, it supports such a view.

Madison was distinguishing two conceptual strategies for accomplishing a single objective. An expressed declaration of "rights retained . . . that . . . shall not be abridged" has the same object in view as an expression that "powers granted . . . shall not be extended." The object of both strategies is that "the rights retained . . . be secure." Given this object, if one provision has teeth, so must the other. In stark contrast, the rights-powers conception specifies that the rights retained by the people automatically diminish as the powers of government expand—a construction that contradicts the stated purpose for declaring the existence of individual rights[53] and the very point Madison was making in his letter. Far from supporting a rights-powers conception of the Ninth Amendment, then, this quotation reveals a fundamental flaw in any interpretation that acknowledges the power-constraining function of enumerated powers while denying this same function to unenumerated rights.

The rights-powers conception gains its plausibility, in part, from the claim that the powers delegated by the Constitution provide sufficiently clear limitations on the scope of government activity. This claim was controversial when made and did not assuage proponents of a bill of rights. The ever-expanding scope of government power over the past two hundred years has confirmed their suspicions that more than delegated-powers provisions were needed to constrain the powers of government. We must now consider whether the safeguard provided by judicial review on the basis of enumerated constitutional rights alone is sufficient to this power-constraining task or whether unenumerated rights may also provide a basis for judicial review.

---

[52]Letter from James Madison to George Washington (Dec. 5, 1789), *reprinted in* 2 B. Schwartz, *supra* note 12, at 1190.

[53]*See supra* notes 36 and 40–47 and accompanying text.

Judicial Review of Unenumerated Rights

Should a power-constraint conception of unenumerated rights be enforced by judges, or must the protection of unenumerated rights be left to the political realm? To answer this question, it is useful to examine the principal dangers that Madison hoped a bill of rights would help avoid and one way he thought such a device would accomplish this objective. Considering both the contemplated end and the means envisioned for achieving it, I suggest that it is highly unlikely that the unenumerated rights were to be left entirely to the political process.

First, though, it is useful to note that there is no logical contradiction between the Federalist criticisms of a bill of rights and judicial review on the basis of unenumerated rights. True, one could argue that although the Framers attached great importance to protecting the rights retained by the people, they also believed judicial review to be an inefficacious means of accomplishing this end. There is nothing in the Federalist argument, however, to suggest that judicial review could be based only on enumerated rights. On the contrary, insofar as the Federalists believed in the judicial protection of rights, their fear that enumerating rights would diminish other, unenumerated rights suggests only that they wanted these unenumerated rights protected every bit as much as the enumerated rights. In other words, in the absence of a bill of rights, a Federalist who believed in the judicial protection of rights would have had to envision enforcing only the unenumerated rights retained by the people.[54]

The Equal Protection of Enumerated and Unenumerated Rights

The theory that the unenumerated rights retained by the people were to be protected exclusively by recourse to the political process or, perhaps, by recourse to popular insurrection seems untenable in light of the reasons given by Madison for needing a bill of rights. Madison, for one, believed that of the three branches of the national government, the legislature posed the greatest threat to liberty and to rights. In his speech to the House, he stated that

> the legislative [branch] . . . is the most powerful, and most likely to be abused, because it is under the least control. Hence, so far

---

[54]I thank Sheldon Richman for this point. *See* Sherry, *supra* note 33, at 1134–46 (discussing the practice of judicial review prevailing at the time of the framing).

as a declaration of rights can tend to prevent the exercise of undue power, it cannot be doubted but such declaration is proper.[55]

Although Madison viewed the legislature as the most dangerous branch of government, he saw the political power possessed by "the majority" of the people to be the ultimate source of the government threat to the rights and liberties of the people. In his speech explaining the need for a bill of rights, he said:

> [I]n a Government modified like this of the United States, the great danger lies rather in the abuse of the community than in the legislative body. The prescriptions in favor of liberty ought to be levelled against that quarter where the greatest danger lies, namely, that which possesses the highest prerogative of power. But this is not found in either the executive or legislative departments of Government, but in the body of the people, operating by the majority against the minority.[56]

This was hardly an argument made in passing. Madison had repeatedly expressed this view elsewhere in ways that amplified his conception of rights. In *The Federalist* No. 10, he wrote:

> By a faction I understand a number of citizens, whether amounting to a majority or minority of the whole, who are united and actuated by some common impulse of passion, or of interest, adverse to the rights of other citizens, or to the permanent and aggregate interests of the community.[57]

Later, in a letter to Thomas Jefferson, he wrote:

> Wherever the real power in a Government lies, there is the danger of oppression. In our Governments the real power lies in the majority of the Community, and the invasion of private rights is chiefly to be apprehended, not from acts of Government contrary to the sense of its constituents, but from acts in which the Government is the mere instrument of the major number of the Constituents.[58]

These passages not only reiterate the danger Madison saw in the political power of factious majorities, they also show that Madison

---

[55]Madison, *supra* note 9, at 454.

[56]*Id.* at 454–55. The omission of any reference to the judiciary here suggests that Madison saw the judicial department as little or no threat.

[57]The Federalist No. 10 (J. Madison), *supra* note 11, at 54.

[58]Letter from James Madison to Thomas Jefferson (Oct. 17, 1788), *reprinted in* 1 B. Schwartz, *supra* note 12, at 616.

did not view rights as a product of majoritarian will. Nor did he equate majority will with the common good. In the passage above from *The Federalist*, he allowed for the possibility that the interest of a majority can be "adverse" both to the "rights of other citizens" and to the "permanent and aggregate interests of the community."[59] In his letter to Jefferson, Madison said that the impetus for "invasion of private rights" is most likely to come from the "major number of the Constituents."

Given that the most dangerous branch of the national government was the legislature, it is unlikely that Madison would have envisioned the protection of the rights retained by the people being consigned exclusively to the legislature. Given that the government threat to the rights and liberties of the people was likely to be promoted by the majority seeking to operate against the minority, it is equally unlikely that Madison would have envisioned the protection of the rights retained by the people being consigned exclusively to the device of popular insurrection. How, then, was a bill of rights to help lessen this danger?

In his letter to Jefferson, Madison suggested several ways in which a bill of rights might prove useful, but he also expressed skepticism about the effectiveness of written bills of rights in addressing the bane of majoritarian abuses. "Repeated violations of these parchment barriers," he wrote, "have been committed by overbearing majorities in every State."[60]   Jefferson replied:

> In the arguments in favor of a declaration of rights, you omit one which has great weight with me, the legal check which it puts into the hands of the judiciary. This is a body, which if rendered independent, and kept strictly to their own department merits great confidence for their learning and integrity.[61]

---

[59]*Id*. In his letter to Jefferson, Madison may also be seen as implicitly distinguishing between the "rights of citizens" and the "permanent and aggregate interests of the community." The existence of such a distinction, however, does not entail an irreconcilable conflict between the two concepts. For example, one could view the protection of the rights of citizens as the best—or even the exclusive—means of advancing the permanent and aggregate interests of the community. In sum, protecting individual rights could be viewed as the best means of securing and even discovering the common good.

[60]*Id*.

[61]Letter from Thomas Jefferson to James Madison (Mar. 15, 1789), *reprinted in* 1 B. Schwartz, *supra* note 12, at 620.

After this correspondence, Madison used essentially the same argument on the floor of the House.[62] Immediately after emphasizing to the House the danger posed by "the abuse of the community," Madison stressed that "paper barriers" will favorably influence "public opinion in their favor, and rouse the attention of the whole community."[63] This was not, however, the only way a bill of rights could protect the rights and liberties of the people. Moments later, he added, in an often-quoted passage:

> If they are incorporated into the constitution, independent tribunals of justice will consider themselves in a peculiar mánner the guardians of those rights; they will be an impenetrable bulwark against every assumption of power in the legislative or executive; they will naturally be led to resist every encroachment upon rights expressly stipulated for in the constitution by the declaration of rights.[64]

In sum, Madison viewed a bill of rights as a means of constraining legislative and executive abuses, whether intended to benefit the officials or the majority of the community. The Bill of Rights accomplished this end, in part, by putting enforcement of the rights in the hands of independent tribunals of justice. In light of this purpose, it seems unlikely that Madison anticipated that the unenumerated rights retained by the people were to be left entirely to the will of the legislature or a majority of the community and that only enumerated rights would receive judicial protection.

The principal support for such a claim is Madison's use of the phrase "rights expressly stipulated" in the passage of his speech just quoted.[65] Seizing upon this phrase, Raoul Berger argued that judicial review was originally intended to be confined to the enumerated rights.[66] Although this passage is consistent with such an interpretation, it hardly compels it. The proposal under consideration at the time included an enumeration of expressly stipulated

---

[62]Bernard Schwartz suggests that it was Jefferson's letter that led Madison to this argument. *See* B. Schwartz, The Great Rights of Mankind 118 (1977).

[63]Madison, *supra* note 9, at 455. It is important to note that Madison was speaking here of the effectiveness of an entire bill of rights, including the enumerated-rights provisions. This passage in no way suggests that unenumerated rights were limited to this manner of protection.

[64]*Id.* at 457.

[65]*See supra* text accompanying note 64.

[66]*See* Berger, *supra* note 5, at 9.

rights, so naturally Madison would dwell on the advantages of such a strategy. This in no way requires, however, that expressly stipulated rights were to be the only rights receiving judicial protection.

Moreover, such an interpretation is implausible insofar as the quoted passage immediately follows Madison's explanation of the need for an express provision to deny any implication "that those rights which were not singled out, were intended to be assigned into the hands of the General Government, and were consequently insecure."[67] Without judicial review of government interference with the unenumerated rights retained by the people, the legislature would be the judge in its own case—something that is not permitted when enumerated rights are violated.[68] Madison saw the problem of legislative partiality quite clearly:

> No man is allowed to be a judge in his own cause, because his interest would certainly bias his judgment, and, not improbably, corrupt his integrity. With equal, nay with greater reason, a body of men are unfit to be both judges and parties at the same time; yet what are many of the most important acts of legislation but so many judicial determinations, not indeed concerning the rights of single persons, but concerning the rights of large bodies of citizens? And what are the different classes of legislators but advocates and parties to the causes which they determine?[69]

Thus, Madison viewed a written bill of rights, in part, as a means of constraining abuses by the legislature attempting to aggrandize its own interest or that of the majority. Essential to the success of such a strategy was the fact that such rights would be enforced by independent tribunals of justice. In light of this purpose and this strategy, it seems highly unlikely that Madison anticipated that only the enumerated rights would receive protection from independent tribunals of justice and that any right retained by the people that was otherwise omitted from the declaration would be protected from legislative and majoritarian abuse solely by means of legislative or majoritarian will.

---

[67]Madison, *supra* note 9, at 456.

[68]*See supra* notes 21 and 40 and accompanying text.

[69]The Federalist No. 10 (J. Madison), *supra* note 11, at 57. True, when he wrote this passage, Madison did not expect judicial review based on "parchment barriers" to be an important check on legislation. But by the time he proposed his amendments, he had been brought around to this view. *See supra* notes 60–64 and accompanying text.

An analysis that supports judicial review of legislative interference with enumerated rights while denying equal judicial protection to unenumerated rights is inherently suspect.[70] The words of the Ninth Amendment argue strongly against such a construction. As Charles Black has noted:

> [A]ffirmative settlement of the question (if, as I doubt, it was a real question in 1790) of the rightness of judicial review, on the basis of *any* right "enumerated" in the Constitution, would settle the rightness of judicial review on the basis of those rights not enumerated, though "retained by the people," because anything else would "deny or disparage" these latter, in a quite efficacious way.[71]

To concede that enumerated rights are judicially enforceable power constraints, but that unenumerated rights are not, is to "diminish" the "just importance" of and surely to "disparage" unenumerated rights, if not to "deny" them altogether. Denying judicial protection to the unenumerated rights effectively surrenders them up to the general government. As Calvin Massey has concluded:

> By assuming that the ninth amendment can be invaded by congressional action and that the first eight amendments cannot, Justice Reed made a distinction fatally disparaging to ninth amendment rights. Unless the text be ignored, the ninth amendment forbids the distinction.[72]

The Rights-Preserving Function of Unenumerated Rights

There is an understandable reluctance to open the Pandora's box of judicial review of such an open-ended provision as the Ninth Amendment. Some fear that giving any real effect to the Ninth Amendment would provide a "bottomless well in which the judiciary can dip for the formation of undreamed of 'rights' in their limitless discretion"[73] and would permit judges to impose their

---

[70]My use of "equal protection" here and elsewhere is not a reference to the Equal Protection Clause of the Fourteenth Amendment. While that clause refers to the equal protection of the laws to be afforded all persons within the jurisdiction of any state, I am referring to the equal protection of all rights protected by the Constitution.

[71]Black, *On Reading and Using the Ninth Amendment,* in Power and Policy in Quest of Law: Essays in Honor of Eugene Victor Rostow 188 (M. McDougal & W.N. Reisman ed. 1985) (reprinted as chapter 12 of this book).

[72]Massey, *supra* note 5, at 323 n.97.

[73]Berger, *supra* note 4, at 2.

purely subjective preferences on the people, and that judicial review would quickly become judicial supremacy and tyranny. How, then, does a power-constraining conception of the Ninth Amendment square with the separation of powers and the enforcement of enumerated rights?

The first line of the constitutional defense of individual rights and liberties was not the judicial protection of constitutional rights— rights that needed to be added by amendment.[74] Rather, the government structure and procedures established by the Constitution were the first line of defense. The preservation of state governments, popular elections of representatives, election of senators by states, the electoral college, local control of suffrage, the presidential veto, the power of the purse, and the impeachment powers are just a sample of the structural and procedural—rather than substantive—restraints on government powers. Moreover, the unamended Constitution, at least implicitly, limited the government of the United States to its delegated powers.

Some, however, were not satisfied with these elaborate structural protections alone. They wanted and demanded more. In urging a reluctant House to take up the question of a bill of rights, Madison observed:

> It cannot be a secret to the gentlemen in this House, that, notwithstanding the ratification of this system of Government by eleven of the thirteen United States, . . . yet still there is a great number of our constituents who are dissatisfied with it. . . . We ought not to disregard their inclination, but, on principles of amity and moderation, conform to their wishes, and expressly declare the great rights of mankind secured under this constitution.[75]

The critics wanted a safeguard. "I believe," Madison said, "that the great mass of the people who opposed [the Constitution], disliked

---

[74]This does not mean that constitutional rights would have been unprotected in the absence of enumeration. For, as noted above, if the Federalists' argument that a bill of rights was unnecessary is accepted as sincere, then, in the absence of any enumerated rights, judicial protection of the rights of the people would have been exclusively on the basis of unenumerated rights.

[75]Madison, *supra* note 9, at 449. This quotation also undermines the claim that the rights "retained by the people" are peculiarly English.

it because it did not contain effectual provisions against encroachments on particular rights."[76]

The Constitution as amended, therefore, was a product of conflicting, but ultimately reconcilable, intents. On the one hand, if the constitutional structure worked as its Framers hoped and intended, there would be little if any need to protect constitutional rights by judicial review. On the other hand, if government exceeded its proper boundaries and threatened the liberty and rights of the people, as its critics feared, then a declaration of constitutional rights might provide an invaluable second line of defense.

Accordingly, even if the designers of the original constitutional structure did not contemplate aggressive judicial protection of individual rights from legislative acts—even if they "would have rejected [it] out of hand"[77]—it does not follow that such judicial review is not a legitimate constitutional device from the perspective of the original scheme. For these Framers also did not contemplate that the structure they designed would fail to constrain the power of government as they hoped it would. If time has proved them wrong and their critics right on this count, then we must thank the critics for insisting on a fallback scheme of constitutional rights and James Madison for insisting that a reluctant House take up the issue.

Consider the following analogy. A group of ship designers devise a structure intended to ensure that the ship will stay afloat forever. Suppose they still add lifeboats and life preservers to the ship. As far as they are concerned, this is an entirely redundant exercise. They have absolutely no intention that passengers should ever use the lifeboats or life preservers. In fact, they fervently hope and believe that these devices will never be used. Years after the designers have died, as passengers board the ship, they too do not intend to use the lifeboats or life preservers. Without instruction by a knowledgeable crew, future generations may not even know that these devices are on board or how to use them. After a long enough period, however, even the crew may become complacent and forgetful.

---

[76]*Id.* at 450. Once again, the fact that Madison referred to the perceived threat to "particular rights" does not mean that the other rights retained by the people were to be left unprotected from encroachment. The Ninth Amendment was intended to negate this inference.

[77]Berger, *supra* note 5, at 2.

Suppose now that the unintended event occurs and the ship begins to sink. Would it make any sense to argue that passengers should refuse the lifeboats or life preservers because it was "never intended" that they use them? Would the "evidence" of this "lack of intent" provided by the designers' vigorous pre-voyage statements that the ship is seaworthy or even "unsinkable" support such an argument? Would such an argument be supported by the fact that the designers had spent virtually all of their time trying to perfect the ship's structure and hardly any time worrying about the lifeboats? Would it be supported by the fact that many or all of the ship's designers actually opposed having lifeboats and life preservers on board?

No, such an argument would be a non sequitur. Although the designers have spent little time fussing with the life preservers and never intended that passengers ever use them, although they provided the equipment "merely for greater caution" and continually insisted it was entirely unnecessary, and although the equipment might even have been an afterthought imposed upon the designers by an overly cautious shipowner to assuage the "unreasonable" fears of prospective passengers and induce their patronage, those who insisted that the equipment be on board certainly intended that the passengers use it if, God forbid, that became necessary.

In addition to the light it casts on arguments purporting to rest on the intent of the Framers, this analogy teaches a number of other lessons about the relationship of constitutional rights and the Ninth Amendment to the rest of the constitutional structure. First, it casts judicial review of legislation in the role of a "rights preserver." The fact that the Framers of the Constitution unquestionably preferred structural constraints to "paper barriers"[78] enforced by judges does not mean that they would have us ignore judicial review of such barriers if their structural constraints were found wanting in practice.

Second, this analogy puts into proper perspective the early disuse of the Ninth Amendment (and the other amendments as well[79]). Just as life preservers are not the preferred means of keeping pas-

---

[78]Madison, *supra* note 9, at 455. It is worth noting that the strategy of holding government to its enumerated powers also rests on paper barriers.

[79]It was, after all, 1965 before the Supreme Court first used the First Amendment to invalidate an act of Congress, in Lamont v. Postmaster General, 381 U.S. 301 (1965).

sengers afloat, judicial review was not the preferred means of protecting the liberties of the people. Both are fallback devices.

Third, just as lifeboats are preferred to life preservers, many have thought that it is safer to protect liberty by abstract interpretations of enumerated rights than by speculating about unenumerated rights. This technique, however, has its limits. Enumerated rights cannot always be interpreted to protect some very fundamental liberties without straining them beyond their reasonable capacity. But straining the text by pushing enumerated rights too far can undermine the perceived legitimacy of any judicial review based on textual analysis.

Fourth, after a long period in which the Ninth Amendment and other rights-preserving passages of the text were neither needed nor used, it is understandable why they would be almost forgotten. Yet this does not mean that the impetus for the Ninth Amendment was a momentary and passing sentiment. Seventy years after the adoption of the Ninth Amendment, the framers of another American constitution included virtually identical language: "The enumeration, in the Constitution, of certain rights, shall not be construed to deny or disparage others retained by the people of the several States."[80]

What Justifies Judicial Negation of Legislation?

The power-constraint conception described above suggests two developments that would justify reliance on judicial negation of legislation or executive acts on the basis of either enumerated or unenumerated rights: first, when the legislative or executive branch

---

[80]Const. of the Confederate States of America, art. VI, § 5 (1861). Section 6 of article VI reads: "The powers not delegated to the Confederate States by the Constitution, nor prohibited by it to the States, are reserved to the States, respectively, or to the people thereof." Const. of the Confederate States of America, art. VI, § 6 (1861), *reprinted in* 1 J. Davis, The Rise and Fall of the Confederate Government 672 (1958). Moreover, the Ninth Amendment came also to be widely copied in state constitutions drafted after its adoption. *See, e.g.,* Ala. Const. art. I, § 33; Ariz. Const. art. II, § 33; Ark. Const. art. II, § 29; Colo. Const. art. II, § 28; Fla. Const. art. I, § 1, par. XXVIII; Ill. Const. art. I, § 24; Iowa Const. art. I, § 25; Kan. Const. bill of rights, § 20; La. Const. art. I, § 24; Md. Const. declaration of rights, art. 45; Mich. Const. art. I, § 23; Miss. Const. art. 3, § 32; Neb. Const. art. I, § 26; Nev. Const. art. I, § 20; N.J. Const. art. I, par. 21; N.M. Const. art. I, § 23; Ohio Const. art. I, § 20; Okla. Const. art. II, § 33; Ore. Const. art. I, § 33; R.I. Const. art. I, § 23; Utah Const. art. I, § 25; and Wyo. Const. art. I, § 36.

abuses its delegated powers by using improper means that violate the rights of the people; and second, when the legislative or executive branch exceeds its rightful powers to pursue unconstitutional ends that violate the rights of the people.

These developments are likely to result from a gradual but persistent erosion of both structural constraints and the paper barriers of delegated powers. Over the past fifty years, for example, we have witnessed an enormous expansion in the scope of federal powers—especially the implied powers found in the Necessary and Proper Clause—and a corresponding inattention to structural constraints. This development, coupled with the failure to acknowledge an expanded scope to the implied rights referred to in the Ninth Amendment, has resulted in a constitutional structure that is ever more lopsided in the direction of increased government power.

Two different strategies may be used alone or together to restore some semblance of balance. Courts could cleave more rigorously than they have in recent decades to the original structural constraints of the Constitution—for example, they could more strictly enforce principles of separation of powers, federalism, and enumerated powers. This would reestablish a regime of limited government and greatly reduce (though not entirely eliminate) the need for judicial review based on constitutional rights—especially unenumerated rights.

On the other hand, if the expanded scope of government powers is maintained, courts must correspondingly expand the protection of both enumerated and unenumerated constitutional rights. This would entail, for example, a vigorous interpretation of the First Amendment, the Takings Clause, and the procedural rights established by the Fourth and Fifth Amendments. In the comparatively few remaining cases in which an honest interpretation of these provisions does not authorize serious scrutiny of government intrusion on individual liberties, the Ninth Amendment stands ready as a supplement.

Presumably, those who wrote the Constitution would consider the latter approach to be a second-best departure from the original structure. The structure they devised, however, has been permanently altered by such later developments as the Civil War Amendments, universal suffrage, the direct election of senators, and the creation of a national income tax. Even if those original structural restraints that have survived on paper were given new life, we cannot—and, in some significant respects, we would not want to—return to the original scheme. Moreover, the Constitution would not have been ratified without this second-best means of coping with expanded government powers because of those who withheld their consent until promised that rights-preserving amendments were forthcoming. And it was James Madison, the man who was converted to their cause, who kept that promise.

Interpreting Unenumerated Rights

Assuming that we wish to apply a power-constraint conception to the rights retained by the people, is there a practical way to do so? Below, I describe three possible methods of identifying unenumerated rights: the originalist method, the constructive method, and the presumptive method. These interpretive methods are not mutually exclusive. Although they may be used alone, they may also be used to complement each other. Before describing these methods, however, let me first turn to a philosophical concern that some may think impedes any effort to identify unenumerated rights.

What If the Ninth Amendment Was a Philosophical Mistake?

The Ninth Amendment refers to unspecified rights "*retained* by the people"—rights that the people had before forming a government.[81] One of the sources of intellectual resistance to a justiciable interpretation of the Ninth Amendment today is not constitutional, but philosophical. Until quite recently, many—if not most—modern

---

[81]In the balance of this introduction, I assume that the phrase "rights retained by the people" refers to rights that are antecedent to the formation of government and I do not consider the difficulties raised by such an interpretation. Although, in my view, this is the most plausible interpretation of this phrase, it is not the only possible one. Russell Caplan has argued that this phrase refers to rights created by state governments prior to the formation of the government of the United States. *See* Caplan, *supra* note 5.

One difficulty (among others) with a state law rights interpretation of the rights retained by the people is that, as Caplan acknowledges, these rights would fail to constrain the powers of either the federal or state governments. *See id.* at 261–62. According to this interpretation, Madison drafted, Congress approved, and the states ratified an essentially moot provision; consequently, this interpretation is subject to many of the same infirmities as a rights-powers conception of the Ninth Amendment. For other difficulties with this interpretation, *see* Sager, *You Can Raise the First, Hide Behind the Fourth, and Plead the Fifth. But What on Earth Can You Do with the Ninth Amendment?* 64 Chi.-Kent L. Rev. 239, 243–51 (1988).

philosophers insisted that there were no such things as natural rights; that in fact, government is the ultimate source of all rights.

Given a philosophical skepticism about rights, the reference in the Ninth Amendment to unspecified retained rights is no different from a constitutional prohibition of discrimination against ghosts. "Suppose," argues John Ely, "there were in the Constitution one or more provisions providing for the protection of ghosts. Can there be any doubt, now that we no longer believe there is any such thing, that we would be behaving properly in ignoring the provisions?"[82] For one who denies the existence of rights antecedent to government, a reference to unspecified retained rights is no different from "an amendment that says 'Congress shall make no' and then there is an inkblot, and you cannot read the rest of it, and that is the only copy you have."[83] This philosophical objection lurks behind many of the objections to judicial review of the rights retained by the people.[84]

According to this view, the Ninth Amendment is simply a mistake[85] and the nature of this mistake prevents any nonarbitrary interpretation of the rights retained by the people. If rights antecedent to government are mere illusions or ghosts, then judicial enforcement of these alleged "rights" can only be wholly subjective and arbitrary. Courts, in effect, would be "mak[ing] up what might be under

[82]J. Ely, *supra* note 16, at 39.

[83]Bork, *supra* note 2.

[84]*See* S. Macedo, The New Right v. the Constitution 39–48 (rev. ed. 1987) (contrasting the philosophical skepticism of some modern constitutional theorists with the philosophical views of the Framers).

[85]Ronald Dworkin has distinguished two kinds of mistakes:

[E]mbedded mistakes are those whose specific authority is fixed so that it survives their loss of gravitational force; corrigible mistakes are those whose specific authority depends on gravitational force in such a way that cannot survive this loss.

R. Dworkin, Taking Rights Seriously 121 (1977). Dworkin goes on to claim that according to a theory of legislative supremacy, statutory mistakes "will lose their gravitational force but not their specific authority." *Id.* Presumably, the doctrine of constitutional supremacy would lead to the same conclusion with regard to the Ninth Amendment. Thus, even if the Ninth Amendment is a mistake, it would not lose all of its authority. Perhaps the interpretations that deprive the Ninth Amendment of any effect while purporting to respect it can be viewed in Dworkin's theory as an effort to deprive this mistake of any gravitational force.

the inkblot."[86] Decisions that are unavoidably based on subjective preferences, the argument continues, ought to be made by the representative branch of government so as to reflect the preferences of the majority.

I reject the premises of this argument. Nevertheless, let us assume that the skeptics are correct and that rights independent of government are mere phantoms. Even so, because the Framers believed in the existence of "other" rights "retained by the people,"[87] the structure they created would take on an entirely different and unintended cast if the reality and acceptance of Ninth Amendment rights were not assumed. This fact should matter to those who allow a role for Framers' intent and to those who view the Constitution as a kind of contract entered into at the time of ratification—two views of the Constitution that are often hard to separate. Of course, many constitutional theorists take neither approach, but I would wager that those theorists who are also moral skeptics are disproportionately in one or both of these camps. Because they deny the possibility of discerning genuine rights independent of government, they require some other more palpable touchstone for finding constitutional values, be it original intent, some notion of consent, or both.

The relevance of the Framers' beliefs in natural rights to interpretations based on original intent is obvious. If the Framers intended that unenumerated rights be protected by the judiciary, then to honor that intent requires that we make some effort to discern and protect at least the kinds of rights the Framers had in mind when they ratified the Ninth Amendment. The obviousness of this position may explain the lengths to which some adherents to original intent have gone to defend the rights-powers theory.[88]

A similar analysis applies if one interprets the text of the Constitution as one would a contract. Determining the consensual terms or original meaning of any agreement requires that one take into account the background assumptions of the parties. Given the widespread belief in individual rights that prevailed at the time of

---

[86]Bork, *supra* note 2.

[87]*See, e.g.,* Corwin, *supra* note 33; Grey, *supra* note 33; Sherry, *supra* note 33; and Van Loan, *supra* note 5.

[88]*See, e.g.,* Berger, *supra* note 5; and Cooper, *supra* note 14. *See also* Office of Legal Policy, Department of Justice, Wrong Turns on the Road to Judicial Activism: The Ninth Amendment and the Privileges or Immunities Clause, Report to the Attorney General, 8–27.

the drafting of the Constitution, it is reasonable to assume that if those who vehemently insisted on a bill of rights to protect the liberties of the people had shared the philosophical skepticism of modern philosophy (or anticipated its coming), they would not have rested content with the abbreviated list of rights they received. They surely would have insisted on a greatly expanded list of enumerated rights. Only a handful of the many rights proposed by state ratification conventions were eventually incorporated in the Bill of Rights. The Ninth Amendment was offered precisely to "compensate" these critics for the absence of an extended list of rights. Putting this in contract terms, the Ninth Amendment "clause" served as the "consideration" for not insisting on a more elaborate statement of rights.[89]

The adoption of the Ninth Amendment forces those who reject the reality of such rights, but who seek to interpret the Constitution according to either original intent or original meaning, to hypothesize on the content of this expanded list. Without such an attempt, the scheme of delegated powers and reserved rights becomes fundamentally different from the one that the Framers promised and the people involved in the ratification process agreed on. Modern philosophical skepticism about rights is simply beside the point. Just as contract law seeks to enforce the "benefit of the bargain" as agreed to, enforcing the Constitution as enacted would seem to require protection of the retained rights and liberties of the people assumed by the Ninth Amendment in the same manner as we would if we believed these rights and liberties to be "real." From the perspective of either original intent or original meaning, ignoring the Ninth Amendment because it does not comport with modern moral philosophy is (to shift the metaphor) a form of constitutional bait and switch.

Three Methods of Interpreting Unenumerated Rights

Few will abandon the safe harbor of the rights-powers conception of the Ninth Amendment unless they are convinced that some practical method exists for determining the unenumerated rights retained by the people. In this section, I consider three methods for discerning the content of the unenumerated rights. One method

[89]Cf. Grey, The Uses of an Unwritten Constitution, 64 Chi.-Kent L. Rev. 211, 223–30 (1988) (analogizing differing approaches to the parol evidence rule to differing approaches to constitutional interpretation).

(suggested by the previous section) we may call the originalist method of interpreting unenumerated rights. A second method, which begins where the originalist method leaves off, is the constructive method. The third, and perhaps most practical, approach is the presumptive method. Although none of these methods is entirely without difficulty, any problems they pose are not unique to interpreting unenumerated rights. As Charles Black has observed:

> Maybe we ought to give up, and let the Ninth Amendment—and the priceless rights it refers to—keep gathering dust for a third century.
>
> But there is one thing to note about the very real troubles that face us when we turn to the search that the Ninth Amendment seems to command. *These are the troubles not of the Ninth Amendment itself, but of law.*[90]

The Originalist Method. If moral skeptics are correct and unenumerated rights are nonexistent, then it would seem that determining the content of such rights would be truly impossible. However, according to the methodology of those seeking either the original intent or the original meaning of the Ninth Amendment, they no more need to discern the content of actual or real rights than they need to discern searches that are "really" unreasonable or activity that is "really" commerce. Instead, they seek the Framers' understanding of the text. However difficult it may be, the task of interpreting the Ninth Amendment in this way is no different from the task of interpreting many other provisions of the Constitution.

Just as those concerned with original intent consult such materials as Madison's notes on the Constitutional Convention, we may also consult the lengthy lists of proposed amendments sent to Congress by several state ratification conventions.[91] Virginia, for example, proposed twenty provisions for "a declaration or bill of rights asserting, and securing from encroachment, the essential and unalienable

---

[90]Black, *supra* note 71, at 189.

[91]*See* 2 Debates in the Several State Conventions on the Adoption of the Federal Constitution 549 (J. Elliot ed. 2d. ed. 1836) [hereinafter J. Elliot] (amendments proposed by Maryland convention); 3 J. Elliot at 657 (amendments proposed by Virginia convention); and 4 J. Elliot at 242 (amendments proposed by North Carolina convention) (these and other proposed amendments are reprinted in Appendix B of this book).

rights of the people."[92]   Only a handful of the many proposed rights were incorporated into the Bill of Rights. In addition, the rights expressly stipulated by state constitutions at the time of the Constitution's ratification are potentially significant.[93] Some of these rights were conceived of as being retained by the people against state government. Certainly rights retained against state governments were not surrendered to the general government.[94]

These various lists are not, of course, definitive. After all, most of these rights were left out of the Bill of Rights, and it is nearly impossible to know why a decision was made to exclude a particular right. Nonetheless, the Ninth Amendment was intended to remove the need to enumerate every right retained by the people.[95] Thus, the mere fact that a right was excluded from the enumeration does not support a strong negative implication.

Moreover, just as those concerned with original intent consult such theoretical writings as *The Federalist* to interpret passages of the text, we may also consult the Framers' theoretical writings on natural rights that were contemporaneous with the Ninth Amendment, such as those of James Wilson quoted earlier.[96] Some of these writings are quite comprehensive and specific. Wilson, for example, summarized his analysis as follows:

> In his unrelated state, man has a natural right to his property, to his character, to liberty, and to safety. From his peculiar relations, as a husband, as a father, as a son, he is entitled to the enjoyment of peculiar rights, and obliged to the performance of peculiar duties. These will be specified in their due course. From his general relations, he is entitled to other rights, simple in their principle, but, in their operation, fruitful and extensive. . . . In these general relations, his rights are, to be free from injury, and to receive the fulfilment of the engagements, which are made to him;

[92]3 J. Elliot, *supra* note 90, at 657.

[93]*See, e.g.,* The Constitutions of the Several Independent States of America; The Declaration of Independence; The Articles of Confederation Between the Said States; The Treaties Between His Most Christian Majesty and the United States of America (1781).

[94]Russell Caplan and Calvin Massey agree on the relevance of state constitutional and common law rights to Ninth Amendment analysis but draw opposite conclusions on the implication of these rights for constitutional adjudication. *See* Caplan, *supra* note 5, at 254–56; and Massey, *supra* note 5, at 322.

[95]*See supra* notes 24–38 and accompanying text.

[96]*See supra* text accompanying notes 34–35.

his duties are, to do no injury, and to fulfil the engagements, which he has made. On these two pillars principally and respectively rest the criminal and the civil codes of the municipal law. These are the pillars of justice.[97]

Of course, some may argue that any discussion of rights based on this sort of historical inquiry would simply be too open-ended to provide judges with adequate guidance in interpreting the Ninth Amendment. However, adherents to original intent are hard-pressed to make such an argument. Their position requires that we engage in just such an enterprise to interpret the rest of the Constitution—including the open-ended Necessary and Proper Clause.

There is, then, no shortage of textual materials contemporaneous with ratification of the Ninth Amendment that would permit an elaboration of the rights retained by the people. These materials are comparable in every respect to those traditionally used to interpret the original intent of other provisions, and there is no inkblot that prevents us from reading them. Abandoning the originalist method only when considering the Ninth Amendment may lead to the desired result of greatly limiting the scope of constitutional rights—but only at the price of a consistent originalist methodology.

The Constructive Method. With the constructive method, we try to construct a coherent conception of rights from historical and hypothetical examples, as well as theoretical materials, and then apply this conception to the facts of an individual case to reach a legal result. For example, we may begin with the historical materials described in the previous section and use them to begin to construct a theory of the kinds of rights retained by the people. We may also take into account the examples of unenumerated rights that have been acknowledged by the courts over the past 200 years.[98] Many

---

[97]Wilson, *supra* note 34, at 308.

[98]One authority provides the following list of unenumerated rights that have already been recognized by the courts:

1. The right to retain American citizenship, despite even criminal activities, until explicitly and voluntarily renouncing it;
2. The right to receive equal protection not only from the states but also from the federal government;
3. The right to vote, subject only to reasonable restrictions to prevent fraud, and to cast a ballot equal in weight to those of other citizens;
4. The right to a presumption of innocence and to demand proof beyond a

of these—such as the right to travel within the United States and the right to the equal protection of the laws from the federal government—are now well accepted and provide paradigm examples or "easy cases" from which theories of unenumerated rights can be developed.[99] Whatever controversy still surrounds these acknowledged-but-unenumerated rights typically concerns not the rights themselves but either a particular application of these rights to new circumstances or, more generally, the legitimacy of judges protecting rights that are not written in the text.[100]

There are at least three reasons why our analysis of unenumerated rights may not be confined to historical examples but must also subject such examples to the theoretical scrutiny of the constructive method.

First, the rule of law requires that the enforcement of legal rights be as internally consistent and coherent as possible. This means that we cannot escape the task of rationalizing as best we can these received historical examples of rights. Legal theory is the principal means by which this is accomplished.

Second, as I have discussed elsewhere,[101] we must be concerned with the actual, as opposed to the apparent, legitimacy that constitutional processes impart to legislation. The mere fact that the individual cannot successfully resist the coercion of government does not explain why a citizen or government official is "bound in

---

reasonable doubt before being convicted of a crime;
5. The right to use the federal courts and other governmental institutions and to urge others to use these processes to protect their interests;
6. The right to associate with others;
7. The right to enjoy a zone of privacy;
8. The right to travel within the United States;
9. The right to marry or not to marry;
10. The right to make one's own choice about having children;
11. The right to educate one's children as long as one meets certain minimum standards set by the state;
12. The right to choose and follow a profession;
13. The right to attend and report on criminal trials.

See W. Murphy, J. Fleming, & W. Harris, American Constitutional Interpretation, 1083–84 (1986) (listing and providing citations for these unenumerated rights).

[99]See Schauer, Easy Cases, 58 S. Cal. L. Rev. 399 (1985) (describing and defending the use of easy cases in settling some constitutional issues).

[100]I discuss the use of paradigm or easy cases and the existence of hard cases of unenumerated rights in Barnett, *supra* note 10, at 57–64.

[101]Barnett, *supra* note 10 at 39–40.

conscience"[102] to obey legislation produced by constitutional processes. Might does not explain right; nor does the fact that a majority of some minority once cast a vote in favor of the Constitution.

If the Constitution imparts legitimacy to legislation such that legislation commands an ongoing moral obligation of obedience, it must be because the processes established by the Constitution produce results that are sufficiently consistent with a background set of individual rights that are both procedural and substantive in nature, corresponding to what Lon Fuller called the internal and external moralities of law.[103] If this view of constitutional legitimacy is correct, then the Ninth Amendment enhances the legitimacy of legislation by strengthening the link between enacted law that survives judicial review and the imperatives of justice based on individual rights. This objective can be accomplished only if received historical examples about unenumerated rights are subjected to rational analysis, such as that provided by moral theory.

Finally, whether or not we are bound to enforce written, rule-like constitutional strictures that our best legal or moral analysis reveals to be mistaken, we are not bound to adhere to the errors of our forebears in the realm of unenumerated rights. Unwritten mistakes are not embedded.[104] James Wilson's views of natural rights,[105] for example, are both sophisticated and illuminating. We are not, however, compelled to embrace any sexism that we may find in his words. As with the common law process, an attempt to construct a theory of the retained rights from historical examples requires the use of critical reason to eliminate mistakes—particularly when starting the analysis of unenumerated rights in midstream.

The Presumptive Method. Although I think a constructive method of interpretation has its place,[106] I know that many would question

---

[102]The phrase is taken from Thomas Aquinas. *See* T. Aquinas, Summa Theologica, in 20 Great Books of the Western World 233 (1980).

[103]*See* L. Fuller, The Morality of Law 96–97 (rev. ed. 1969).

[104]*See supra* note 85, for a discussion of different kinds of mistakes. I leave aside the issue of whether a precedent mistakenly granting protection to a purported right creates an embedded mistake that merits some degree of protection.

[105]*See supra* notes 34, 35, and 96 and accompanying text.

[106]As I briefly discuss below, the constructive method is particularly appropriate for construing unenumerated procedural rights. *See infra* notes 126–32 and accompanying text.

the competence of judges to engage in the interpretive enterprise that a constructive method would seem to require. Moreover, sharp theoretical disagreement seems inevitable. Although such disagreement does not undermine the actual legitimacy of unenumerated rights, it does serve to weaken the apparent legitimacy of their protection by judges.

There is good reason for doubting that one could specify in advance all of the rights retained by the people. In a classical liberal theory of rights, rights define a sphere of moral jurisdiction that persons have over certain resources in the world—including their bodies. This jurisdiction establishes boundaries within which persons are free to do what they wish. As long as people are acting within their respective jurisdictional spheres, their acts are deemed to be "rightful" (as distinguished from "good"), and others may not use force to interfere.[107] According to this approach, our specific rights are as numerous as the various acts we may perform within our respective jurisdictions. Although our actions must remain within proper jurisdictional bounds, within those bounds our rights are as varied as our imaginations. Given this conception of rights— a conception in keeping with that held at the time of the framing of the Ninth Amendment—it is simply impossible to specify in advance all the rights we have. As natural rights theorist James Wilson put it:

> [T]here are very few who understand the whole of these rights. All the political writers, from *Grotious* and *Puffendorf* down to *Vattel*, have treated on this subject; but in no one of those books, nor in the aggregate of them all, can you find a complete enumeration of rights appertaining to the people as men and as citizens. . . . Enumerate all the rights of men! I am sure, sirs, that no gentleman in the late Convention would have attempted such a thing.[108]

According to this conception of rights, then, it may be impossible to enumerate all the rights we have—and undesirable to try. It may also be unnecessary.

---

[107]There is, of course, much more to be said about this conception of rights. I have defended the reasonableness of this type of rights-based approach elsewhere. *See* Barnett, *Pursuing Justice in a Free Society: Part I—Power v. Liberty,* 4 Crim. Just. Ethics 50 (Summer/Fall, 1985).

[108]2 J. Elliot, *supra* note 91, at 454 (remarks of J. Wilson).

Instead of authorizing a search for particular rights, the Ninth Amendment can be viewed as establishing a general constitutional presumption in favor of individual liberty.[109] According to the presumptive approach, individuals are constitutionally privileged to engage in rightful behavior—acts that are within their sphere of moral jurisdiction—and such behavior is presumptively immune from government interference. Identifying rightful conduct by determining the proper contours of this moral jurisdiction is what distinguishes liberty from license. This kind of inquiry is exactly what common law courts have been doing for centuries with occasional assistance from legislatures. The freedom to act within the boundaries provided by one's common law rights may be viewed as a central background presumption of the Constitution—a presumption that is reflected in the Ninth Amendment.

This does not mean, however, that all legislative alterations of common law rights are constitutionally prohibited. Common law processes assume that legislation can occasionally be used to correct doctrinal errors perpetuated by a strong doctrine of precedent, to establish needed conventions, and to achieve uniformity among diverse legal systems. But legislation must be scrutinized by independent tribunals of justice to see whether, in the guise of performing these permissible functions, the legislature is seeking instead to invade individual rights. Legislation in pursuit of ends deemed by the Constitution to be appropriate—and defined at the federal level by the enumerated-powers provisions—may rebut the presumption in favor of rightful activity when such legislation passes the sort of meaningful scrutiny we associate with the infringement of other constitutional rights. As legislative activity becomes less extraordinary, however, increased skepticism of the purported justifications of legislation is warranted. Legislative inflation results in a diminution of legislative value.

According to the presumptive method, then, the unenumerated rights of the Ninth Amendment that protect individual liberty operate identically to enumerated rights. For example, courts have not

---

[109]Indeed, presumptions of this sort may be all that rules of law ever establish. *See* Epstein, *Pleadings and Presumptions,* 40 U. Chi. L. Rev. 556 (1973) (describing the operation of staged pleadings in legal analysis). *See also* Barnett, *A Consent Theory of Contract,* 86 Colum. L. Rev. 269, 309–19 (1986) (applying a presumptive methodology to contractual obligation). *Cf.* Fletcher, *The Right and the Reasonable,* 98 Harv. L. Rev. 949 (1985) (distinguishing between "flat" and "structured" legal thinking).

construed the First Amendment as literally barring any abridgment of "the freedom of speech." Such ancient common law principles as those governing fraud, copyright, and defamation provide boundaries (some of which are now codified in statutes) beyond which the rightful exercise of free speech may not go. Nonetheless, the First Amendment establishes a constitutional presumption in favor of speech that is within these common law boundaries. When legislation operates to restrict speech, such legislation is subjected to meaningful judicial scrutiny. The executive branch of government must justify to the judiciary any legislative or executive interference with such free speech. The bare fact that such legislation reflects a majority preference is insufficient to overcome the presumption established by the First Amendment. Moreover, the bare assertion that legislation abridging freedom of speech serves a legitimate legislative end is also insufficient. When the First Amendment is implicated, we maintain a healthy skepticism of legislative motivations.

In the same manner, the Ninth Amendment establishes a constitutional presumption in favor of other rightful activities. This presumption requires the executive branch of the government to justify to the judiciary any legislative or executive interference. The bare fact that such legislation reflects a majority preference is insufficient to overcome the presumption established by the Ninth Amendment. Moreover, the bare assertion that such legislation serves a legitimate end would also be insufficient. As with restrictions on speech, skepticism of legislative motivations is warranted when unenumerated rights are abridged.

In sum, the presumptive approach to the Ninth Amendment does not require an elaborate philosophical inquiry into the rights of mankind. It is critical, rather than constructive. It simply requires that government abridgment of personal or associational liberty be justified to a neutral third party. With such a constitutional presumption, freedom from unjustified government interference is not limited to speech or to the free exercise of religion but extends to all aspects of a citizen's life. As Steven Macedo has proposed, "[J]udges would critically examine the reasons and the evidence offered to support restrictions on liberty; they would infuse a measure of real 'critical bite' into their review of *all* governmental restrictions on constitutional liberty."[110]

---

[110]S. Macedo, *supra* note 84, at 60.

Charles Black has suggested a similar approach to the Ninth Amendment with his "proportionality principle":

> It seems to me that a serious *and thoroughly general* commitment to liberty is inconsistent with restrictions or deprivations grossly out of proportion, in their impact on persons, to the benefits that may reasonably be anticipated by the society that imposes them. . . . [T]here is likely to be no difficulty in identifying at least some instances in which most people would agree that the gross disproportion is visible—sometimes even grotesque.[111]

The main difference between Black's approach and mine is that the presumptive approach clearly places the burden of justification on the government. In any event, Black's concluding remarks apply equally to both proposals. "If we are committed to anything," he insists, "it is to the idea of 'liberty.' If that commitment doesn't really refer to anything except a good inner feeling, then we ought to shut up about it."[112]

As a practical matter, we must choose between two fundamentally different constructions of the Constitution, each resting on a different presumption. We either accept the presumption that in pursuing happiness persons may do whatever is not justly prohibited or we are left with a presumption that the government may do whatever is not expressly prohibited.[113] The presence of the Ninth Amendment in the Constitution strongly supports the first of these two presumptions. According to this interpretation of the Ninth Amendment, the Constitution established what Steven Macedo has called islands of governmental powers "surrounded by a sea of individual rights."[114] It did not establish "islands [of rights] surrounded by a sea of governmental powers."[115]

The Ninth Amendment is sometimes dismissed as a mere rule of construction. However, by eliminating the second of these two possible constructions of the Constitution and by supporting a presumption in favor of personal and associational liberty, the rule

[111]Black, *supra* note 71, at 193.

[112]*Id.* at 192.

[113]*See, e.g.*, Graglia, *Judicial Review on the Basis of "Regime Principles": A Prescription for Government by Judges*, 26 S. Tex. L.J. 435, 436 (1985) ("Very few occasions for . . . [judicial review] would arise, because the Constitution contains few limitations on self-government, and those limitations are almost never violated.").

[114]S. Macedo, *supra* note 84, at 32.

[115]*Id.*

of construction provided by the Ninth Amendment may be one of the most important provisions in the text.

Choosing Between the Constructive and Presumptive Methods. Given that there is more than one method available to interpret unenumerated rights, which one is the best? I have already given reasons that the originalist method is insufficient.[116] The choice between the constructive and presumptive methods of interpretation may reflect, at least in part, the dual function of constitutional rights. As discussed above,[117] constitutional rights constrain the powers of government in two ways: by reinforcing the limitations on the delegated powers or ends of government, and by placing additional restrictions on the means by which government may pursue its delegated ends.

The presumptive method is particularly effective at reinforcing and extending the limitations on delegated powers. By presuming the immunity of rightful conduct from government restriction, it forces the government to credibly articulate its purpose and to defend any exercise of government power as both necessary and proper. However, because restrictions on the means by which government may pursue its delegated ends often cannot be cast in terms of presumptive immunities from government action, the presumptive method is less helpful in establishing the proper manner or mode of government activity. Supplementing the enumerated procedural protections afforded by the Constitution requires that a theory of appropriate institutional or procedural rights be constructed from textual, historical, or other materials.

The choice between the constructive and presumptive methods will also be influenced by the need to prevent abuses of the judicial power to protect unenumerated rights. To appreciate this, we must consider the limits of the Ninth Amendment.

The Limits of the Ninth Amendment

Some may fear that openly protecting unenumerated rights will lead to abuses by the judiciary. Without minimizing the danger, I suggest that the worst way to address the problem of judicial abuse is to deny that courts may protect unenumerated rights. This would

---

[116]*See supra* notes 90–97 and accompanying text.

[117]*See supra* notes 37–47 and accompanying text.

amount to a preemptive surrender of these rights to the far greater threat of legislative or executive abuse. Instead, the problem of judicial abuse is best addressed at the level of general constitutional theory by strongly insisting on two formal constraints on judicial power and by using the structural constraints that are available to control judicial abuse. These traditionally recognized constraints concern the proper scope of all constitutional rights—whether enumerated or unenumerated.

Formal Constraints and the Choice of Interpretive Method. There are two formal constraints that concern the proper scope of both enumerated and unenumerated constitutional rights. Although I realize that these constraints are controversial, I shall not attempt a full elaboration or defense of them here. I do want to indicate, however, the ways in which these formal constraints are bolstered in practice by the choice between the constructive and presumptive methods of interpreting unenumerated rights.

First, substantive constitutional rights are, in the current vernacular, negative, not positive.[118] They do not generate affirmative claims against the government but legally protect rightful domains of discretionary conduct with which government may not interfere. These rights specify areas within which government ought not to act. As suggested above,[119] these kinds of constitutional rights reinforce and extend constitutional limits on government power. In contrast, procedural constitutional rights are both negative and positive, but they limit the manner by which government, not private citizens, may exercise its proper powers.[120] These rights specify areas within which government ought to act only in a particular mode.

Second, judges may exercise neither executive nor legislative powers—such as the power to tax or to appropriate funds—to enforce either enumerated or unenumerated rights. In Jefferson's

---

[118]*See* Currie, *Positive and Negative Constitutional Rights,* 53 U. Chi. L. Rev. 864 (1986). A more illuminating and neutral terminology would distinguish between liberty and welfare rights. *See* L. Lomasky, Persons, Rights, and the Moral Community 84 (1987).

[119]See *Supra* notes 46–47 and accompanying text.

[120]This is the much-belittled "public-private" distinction. *See* Barnett, *Foreword: Four Senses of the "Public-Private" Distinction,* 9 Harv. J. L. & Pub. Pol'y 267 (1986).

words, judges must be "kept strictly to their own department."[121] This means that, by and large, judges only have the power to strike down legislation or executive actions. Judges may only say "no"— and judicial negation is not legislation.[122]

The formal distinction between substantive and procedural constitutional rights is easier to maintain in practice if the constructive method is used to determine the unenumerated institutional or procedural rights that government must respect when exercising its powers, while only the presumptive method is used to protect the unenumerated background rights retained by the people from government infringement. By emphasizing the fact that judges are protecting immunities from government interference with rightful conduct, confining the enforcement of substantive rights to the presumptive method helps confine judges to exercising judicial negation.

To see how these constraints combine to effectively limit the scope of unenumerated rights, consider the tentative suggestion of Charles Black that the Ninth Amendment may authorize judges to protect the *"effective* pursuit of happiness"[123]—for example, to combat "physical and intellectual malnutrition in childhood."[124] Interpreted as a right of children against their parents, this claim does not require the Ninth Amendment for its foundation; it can be readily assimilated into the common law of guardianship. Interpreted as a consitutional right against the government, such a claim runs afoul of the constraints just discussed. Such a purported right is substantive, not procedural, but it is positive in nature; it requires the appropriation and expenditure of tax revenues, and it cannot be implemented by judicial negation. Further, such a claim cannot plausibly be cast as either a presumptive immunity from government interference with rightful conduct or as a restriction on the means by which government pursues a permissible end.

These formal limits on the use of the Ninth Amendment, bolstered by the appropriate use of the constructive and presumptive methods of interpretation, confine the judiciary to enforcing only those unenumerated rights that are comparable to the substantive and procedural rights that were enumerated. However, when leg-

---

[121]Letter from Thomas Jefferson to James Madison, *supra* note 61.

[122]I thank Leonard Liggio for suggesting to me this felicitous phase.

[123]Black, *supra* note 71, at 194.

[124]*Id.*

islatures decide to dispense benefits or provide government "services" through administrative agencies, assuming such schemes are otherwise permitted under the Constitution's enumerated powers, judges are not creating entitlements de novo when they insist that such schemes be administered in a manner consistent with such constitutional principles as due process of law and equal protection. Respect for such procedural constraints is the price of using public, as opposed to private, institutions to achieve social goals.

When necessary, the Ninth Amendment stands ready to supplement these and other expressed procedural rights. A good example of the importance of unenumerated procedural rights is provided by *Bolling v. Sharpe,* in which the Court held that a person has a right to the equal protection of the laws against both the federal government and state governments, notwithstanding the fact that the Equal Protection Clause of the Fourteenth Amendment applies only to the states.[125] Another example is *Richmond Newspapers Inc. v. Virginia,* in which the Ninth Amendment was used by a plurality of the Court to justify the protection of the right to attend and report on criminal trials.[126]

Structural Constraints. We are not limited to formal constraints to control judicial abuses. Constitutional amendment, judicial nomination by an elected president and confirmation by an elected Senate, and impeachment by an elected House (followed by a trial in the Senate) are some of the structural constraints on the judiciary. The rarity with which these and other structural constraints are used to alter judicial decisions does not necessarily mean that these constraints are ineffective. It could well mean that, for better or worse, judicial decisions have largely reflected the sentiments of the majority.

One structural limitation on the Ninth Amendment may now be considered archaic for most purposes. Like the rest of the Bill of Rights, the Ninth Amendment was most likely intended to apply only to the national government.[127] This did not mean that the people retained no rights against state governments. It meant only

---

[125]*See* Bolling v. Sharpe, 347 U.S. 497 (1954).

[126]*See* Richmond Newspapers Inc. v. Virginia, 448 U.S. 555, 579 n.15 (1980).

[127]This view is not, however, without its dissent. Some, such as Bennett Patterson, think the Ninth Amendment has always been directly applicable to the states. *See* B. Patterson, *supra* note 5, at 36–43.

that the federal government, including the federal judiciary, lacked jurisdiction in the original scheme to protect at least some of the rights retained by the people from infringements by the states.[128] With the passage of the Fourteenth Amendment, however, this jurisdictional limitation on the protection of the rights of the people was substantially altered.[129]

If the Privileges and Immunities Clause of the Fourteenth Amendment is viewed as establishing the same constitutional presumption in favor of individual and associational liberty against the states as the Ninth Amendment established against the federal government, then whether the unenumerated rights retained by the people are seen as protected by one provision or the other may be immaterial.[130] Nevertheless, the reconception of the Ninth Amendment urged here would undermine the argument that the Fourteenth Amendment should be limited to a very selective incorporation of the Bill of Rights. Given that the Fourteenth Amendment extends the protective mantle of constitutional rights to acts of state governments, the Ninth Amendment stands ready to respond to a crabbed construction that limits the scope of this protection to the enumerated rights (and even then to only certain of those rights).

Few would advocate preventing abuse of such expressed but abstract constitutional provisions as the Equal Protection or Due Process Clauses by ignoring them. Rather, we prevent judicial abuse of open-ended provisions by formal and structural constraints. The proper way to control abuses of the Ninth Amendment is no different. If constrained in these ways, the judicial protection of unenumerated rights need not constitute the exercise of illegitimate "legislative" power.

---

[128]Even the original scheme extended constitutional protection to some rights retained by the people against state governments—as, for example, with the Contracts Clause.

[129]*See* M. Curtis, No State Shall Abridge (1986).

[130]Sanford Levinson has suggested that the renewed interest in the Ninth Amendment has been spurred, in part, by the absence of Supreme Court precedent definitively inhibiting its use. In contrast, judicial scrutiny on the basis of the Privileges and Immunities Clause of the Fourteenth Amendment must confront the Slaughter-House Cases, 83 U.S. (16 Wall.) 36 (1873). *See* Levinson, *Constitutional Rhetoric and the Ninth Amendment*, 64 Chi.-Kent L. Rev. 131, 143–48 (1988).

Conclusion: Reconceiving the Ninth Amendment

The Ninth Amendment may be forgotten, but it is not gone. We can be grateful to James Madison for conceiving the Ninth Amendment. Without it, any claim that the people retain rights other than those specified in the Constitution would be dismissed today as the product of a fevered imagination. As it is, the Ninth Amendment has been all but imaginary in constitutional adjudication because the Supreme Court and most constitutional analysts have seriously misconceived it. Although the task of interpreting the Ninth Amendment and protecting unenumerated rights can never be complete, it must be commenced in earnest if balance is to be restored to our constitutional scheme.

The analyses presented in this book do not purport to answer all the questions that might be raised concerning the history and meaning of James Madison's Ninth Amendment.[131] Surely, however, Madison would interpret what follows as evidence that this particular effort of his to protect the rights and liberties of the people was not entirely in vain. Perhaps one day soon, James Madison's Ninth Amendment will be ours in practice as well.

---

[131]The articles reprinted or excerpted in this book appear as they were originally published, except that footnotes have been edited for consistency and obvious errors in the text have been corrected.

1. Speech to the House Explaining His Proposed Amendments and His Notes for the Amendment Speech

James Madison

. . . I will state my reasons why I think it proper to propose amendments, and state the amendments themselves, so far as I think they ought to be proposed. If I thought I could fulfil the duty which I owe to myself and my constituents, to let the subject pass over in silence, I most certainly should not trespass upon the indulgence of this House. But I cannot do this, and am therefore compelled to beg a patient hearing to what I have to lay before you. And I do most sincerely believe, that if Congress will devote but one day to this subject, so far as to satisfy the public that we do not disregard their wishes, it will have a salutary influence on the public councils, and prepare the way for a favorable reception of our future measures. It appears to me that this House is bound by every motive of prudence, not to let the first session pass over without proposing to the State Legislatures some things to be incorporated into the constitution, that will render it as acceptable to the whole people of the United States, as it has been found acceptable to a majority of them. I wish, among other reasons why something should be done, that those who have been friendly to the adoption of this constitution may have the opportunity of proving to those who were opposed to it that they were as sincerely devoted to liberty and a Republican Government, as those who charged them with wishing the adoption of this constitution in order to lay the foundation of an aristocracy or despotism. It will be a desirable thing to extinguish from the bosom of every member of the community, any apprehensions that there are those among his countrymen who wish to deprive them of the liberty for which they valiantly fought

Reprinted from 1 The Debates and Proceedings in the Congress of the United States 448 (J. Gales & W. Seaton ed. 1834).

and honorably bled. And if there are amendments desired of such a nature as will not injure the constitution, and they can be ingrafted so as to give satisfaction to the doubting part of our fellow-citizens, the friends of the Federal Government will evince that spirit of deference and concession for which they have hitherto been distinguished.

It cannot be a secret to the gentlemen in this House, that, notwithstanding the ratification of this system of Government by eleven of the thirteen United States, in some cases unanimously, in others by large majorities; yet still there is a great number of our constituents who are dissatisfied with it; among whom are many respectable for their talents and patriotism, and respectable for the jealousy they have for their liberty, which, though mistaken in its object, is laudable in its motive. There is a great body of the people falling under this description, who at present feel much inclined to join their support to the cause of Federalism, if they were satisfied on this one point. We ought not to disregard their inclination, but, on principles of amity and moderation, conform to their wishes, and expressly declare the great rights of mankind secured under this constitution. The acquiescence which our fellow-citizens show under the Government, calls upon us for a like return of moderation. But perhaps there is a stronger motive than this for our going into a consideration of the subject. It is to provide those securities for liberty which are required by a part of the community; I allude in a particular manner to those two States that have not thought fit to throw themselves into the bosom of the Confederacy. It is a desirable thing, on our part as well as theirs, that a re-union should take place as soon as possible. I have no doubt, if we proceed to take those steps which would be prudent and requisite at this juncture, that in a short time we should see that disposition prevailing in those States which have not come in, that we have seen prevailing in those States which have embraced the constitution.

But I will candidly acknowledge, that, over and above all these considerations, I do conceive that the constitution may be amended; that is to say, if all power is subject to abuse, that then it is possible the abuse of the powers of the General Government may be guarded against in a more secure manner than is now done, while no one advantage arising from the exercise of that power shall be damaged or endangered by it. We have in this way something to gain, and, if we proceed with caution, nothing to lose. And in this case it is necessary to proceed with caution; for while we feel all these inducements to go into a revisal of the constitution, we must feel for the constitution itself, and make that revisal a moderate one. I should be unwilling to see a door opened for a reconsideration of the whole structure of the Government—for a reconsideration of the principles and the substances of the powers given; because I doubt, if such a door were opened, we should be very likely to stop at that point which would be safe to the Government itself. But I do wish to see a door opened to consider, so far as to incorporate those provisions for the security of rights, against which I believe no serious objection has been made by any class of our constituents; such as would be likely to meet with the concurrence of two-thirds of both Houses, and the approbation of three-fourths of the State Legislatures. I will not propose a single alteration which I do not wish to see take place, as intrinsically proper in itself, or proper because it is wished for by a respectable number of my fellow-citizens; and therefore I shall not propose a single alteration but is likely to meet the concurrence required by the constitution. There have been objections of various kinds made against the constitution. Some were levelled against its structure because the President was without a council; because the Senate, which is a legislative body, had judicial powers in trials on impeachments; and because the powers of that body were compounded in other respects, in a manner that did not correspond with a particular theory; because it grants more power than is supposed to be necessary for every good purpose, and controls the ordinary powers of the State Governments. I know some respectable characters who opposed this Government on these grounds; but I believe that the great mass of the people who opposed it, disliked it because it did not contain effectual provisions against encroachments on particular rights, and those safeguards which they have been long accustomed to have interposed between them and the magistrate who exercises the sovereign power; nor ought we to consider them safe, while a great number of our fellow-citizens think these securities necessary.

It is a fortunate thing that the objection to the Government has been made on the ground I stated; because it will be practicable, on that ground, to obviate the objection, so far as to satisfy the public mind that their liberties will be perpetual, and this without endangering any part of the constitution, which is considered as essential to the existence of the Government by those who promoted its adoption.

The amendments which have occurred to me, proper to be recommended by Congress to the State Legislatures, are these:

First. That there be prefixed to the constitution a declaration, that all power is originally vested in, and consequently derived from, the people.

That Government is instituted and ought to be exercised for the benefit of the people; which consists in the enjoyment of life and liberty, with the right of acquiring and using property, and generally of pursuing and obtaining happiness and safety.

That the people have an indubitable, unalienable, and indefeasible right to reform or change their Government, whenever it be found adverse or inadequate to the purposes of its institution.

Secondly. That in article 1st, section 2, clause 3, these words be struck out, to-wit: "The number of Representatives shall not exceed one for every thirty thousand, but each State shall have at least one Representative, and until such enumeration shall be made;" and that in place thereof be inserted these words, to wit: "After the first actual enumeration, there shall be one Representative for every thirty thousand, until the number amounts to _____ , after which the proportion shall be so regulated by Congress, that the number shall never be less than _____ , nor more than _____ , but each State shall, after the first enumeration, have at least two Representatives; and prior thereto."

Thirdly. That in article 1st, section 6, clause 1, there be added to the end of the first sentence, these words, to-wit: "But no law varying the compensation last ascertained shall operate before the next ensuing election of Representatives."

Fourthly. That in article 1st, section 9, between clauses 3 and 4, be inserted these clauses, to wit: "The civil rights of none shall be abridged on account of religious belief or worship, nor shall any national religion be established, nor shall the full and equal rights of conscience be in any manner, or on any pretext, infringed.

"The people shall not be deprived or abridged of their right to speak, to write, or to publish their sentiments; and the freedom of the press, as one of the great bulwarks of liberty, shall be inviolable.

"The people shall not be restrained from peaceably assembling and consulting for their common good; nor from applying to the Legislature by petitions, or remonstrances, for redress of their grievances.

"The right of the people to keep and bear arms shall not be infringed; a well armed and well regulated militia being the best security of a free country: but no person religiously scrupulous of bearing arms shall be compelled to render military service in person.

"No soldier shall in time of peace be quartered in any house without the consent of the owner; nor at any time, but in a manner warranted by law.

"No person shall be subject, except in cases of impeachment, to more than one punishment or one trial for the same offense; nor shall be compelled to be a witness against himself; nor be deprived of life, liberty, or property, without due process of law; nor be obliged to relinquish his property, where it may be necessary for public use, without a just compensation.

"Excessive bail shall not be required, nor excessive fines imposed, nor cruel and unusual punishments inflicted.

"The rights of the people to be secured in their persons; their houses, their papers, and their other property, from all unreasonable searches and seizures, shall not be violated by warrants issued without probable cause, supported by oath or affirmation, or not particularly describing the places to be searched, or the persons or things to be seized.

"In all criminal prosecutions, the accused shall enjoy the right to a speedy and public trial, to be informed of the cause and nature of the accusation, to be confronted with his accusers, and the witnesses against him; to have a compulsory process for obtaining witnesses in his favor; and to have the assistance of counsel for his defense.

"The exceptions here or elsewhere in the constitution, made in favor of particular rights, shall not be so construed as to diminish the just importance of other rights retained by the people, or as to enlarge the powers delegated by the constitution; but either as actual limitations of such powers, or as inserted merely for greater caution."

Fifthly. That in article 1st, section 10, between clauses 1 and 2, be inserted this clause, to wit:

"No State shall violate the equal rights of conscience, or the freedom of the press, or the trial by jury in criminal cases."

Sixthly. That, in article 3d, section 2, be annexed to the end of clause 2d, these words, to-wit:

"But no appeal to such court shall be allowed where the value in controversy shall not amount to _____ dollars; nor shall any fact triable by jury, according to the course of common law, be otherwise re-examinable than may consist with the principles of common law."

Seventhly. That in article 3d, section 2, the third clause be struck out, and in its place be inserted the clauses following, to wit:

"The trial of all crimes (except in cases of impeachments, and cases arising in the land or naval forces, or the militia when on actual service, in time of war or public danger) shall be by an impartial jury of freeholders of the vicinage, with the requisite of unanimity for conviction, of the right of challenge, and other accustomed requisites; and in all crimes punishable with loss of life or member, presentment or indictment by a grand jury shall be an essential preliminary, provided that in cases of crimes committed within any county which may be in possession of an enemy, or in which a general insurrection may prevail, the trial may by law be authorized in some other county of the same State, as near as may be to the seat of the offense.

"In cases of crimes committed not within any county, the trial may by law be in such county as the laws shall have prescribed. In suits at common law, between man and man, the trial by jury, as one of the best securities to the rights of the people, ought to remain inviolate."

Eighthly. That immediately after article 6th, be inserted, as article 7th, the clauses following, to wit:

"The powers delegated by this constitution are appropriated to the departments to which they are respectively distributed: so that the legislative department shall never exercise the powers vested in the executive or judicial nor the executive exercise the powers vested in the legislative or judicial, nor the judicial exercise the powers vested in the legislative or executive departments.

"The powers not delegated by this constitution, nor prohibited by it to the States, are reserved to the States respectively."

Ninthly. That article 7th be numbered as article 8th.

The first of these amendments relates to what may be called a bill of rights. I will own that I never considered this provision so essential to the federal constitution, as to make it improper to ratify it, until such an amendment was added; at the same time, I always conceived, that in a certain form, and to a certain extent, such a provision was neither improper nor altogether useless. I am aware, that a great number of the most respectable friends to the Government, and champions for republican liberty, have thought such a provision, not only unnecessary, but even improper; nay, I believe some have gone so far as to think it even dangerous. Some policy has been made use of, perhaps, by gentlemen on both sides of the question: I acknowledge the ingenuity of those arguments which were drawn against the constitution, by a comparison with the policy of Great Britain, in establishing a declaration of rights; but there is too great a difference in the case to warrant the comparison: therefore, the arguments drawn from that source were in a great measure inapplicable. In the declaration of rights which that country has established, the truth is, they have gone no farther than to raise a barrier against the power of the Crown; the power of the Legislature is left altogether indefinite. Although I know whenever the great rights, the trial by jury, freedom of the press, or liberty of conscience, come in question in that body, the invasion of them is resisted by able advocates, yet their Magna Charta does not contain any one provision for the security of those rights, respecting which the people of America are most alarmed. The freedom of the press and rights of conscience, those choicest privileges of the people, are unguarded in the British constitution.

But although the case may be widely different, and it may not be thought necessary to provide limits for the legislative power in that country, yet a different opinion prevails in the United States. The people of many States have thought it necessary to raise barriers against power in all forms and departments of Government, and I am inclined to believe, if once bills of rights are established in all the States as well as the federal constitution, we shall find that although some of them are rather unimportant, yet, upon the whole, they will have a salutary tendency.

It may be said, in some instances, they do no more than state the perfect equality of mankind. This, to be sure, is an absolute truth, yet it is not absolutely necessary to be inserted at the head of a constitution.

In some instances they assert those rights which are exercised by the people in forming and establishing a plan of Government. In other instances, they specify those rights which are retained when particular powers are given up to be exercised by the Legislature. In other instances, they specify positive rights, which may seem to result from the nature of the compact. Trial by jury cannot be considered as a natural right, but a right resulting from a social compact which regulates the action of the community, but is as essential to secure the liberty of the people as any one of the pre-existent rights of nature. In other instances, they lay down dogmatic maxims with respect to the construction of the Government; declaring that the legislative, executive, and judicial branches shall be kept separate and distinct. Perhaps the best way of securing this in practice is, to provide such checks as will prevent the encroachment of the one upon the other.

But whatever may be the form which the several States have adopted in making declarations in favor of particular rights, the great object in view is to limit and qualify the powers of Government, by excepting out of the grant of power those cases in which the Government ought not to act, or to act only in a particular mode. They point these exceptions sometimes against the abuse of the executive power, sometimes against the legislative, and, in some cases, against the community itself; or, in other words, against the majority in favor of the minority.

In our Government it is, perhaps, less necessary to guard against the abuse in the executive department than any other; because it is not the stronger branch of the system, but the weaker. It therefore must be levelled against the legislative, for it is the most powerful, and most likely to be abused, because it is under the least control. Hence, so far as a declaration of rights can tend to prevent the exercise of undue power, it cannot be doubted but such declaration is proper. But I confess that I do conceive, that in a Government modified like this of the United States, the great danger lies rather in the abuse of the community than in the legislative body. The prescriptions in favor of liberty ought to be levelled against that quarter where the greatest danger lies, namely, that which possesses the highest prerogative of power. But this is not found in either the executive or legislative departments of Government, but in the body of the people, operating by the majority against the minority.

It may be thought that all paper barriers against the power of the community are too weak to be worthy of attention. I am sensible they are not so strong as to satisfy gentlemen of every description who have seen and examined thoroughly the texture of such a defense; yet, as they have a tendency to impress some degree of respect for them, to establish the public opinion in their favor, and rouse the attention of the whole community, it may be one means to control the majority from those acts to which they might be otherwise inclined.

It has been said, by way of objection to a bill of rights, by many respectable gentlemen out of doors, and I find opposition on the same principles likely to be made by gentlemen on this floor, that they are unnecessary articles of a Republican Government, upon the presumption that the people have those rights in their own hands, and that is the proper place for them to rest. It would be a sufficient answer to say, that this objection lies against such provisions under the State Governments, as well as under the General Government; and there are, I believe, but few gentlemen who are inclined to push their theory so far as to say that a declaration of rights in those cases is either ineffectual or improper. It has been said, that in the Federal Government they are unnecessary, because the powers are enumerated, and it follows, that all that are not granted by the constitution are retained; that the constitution is a bill of powers, the great residuum being the rights of the people; and, therefore, a bill of rights cannot be so necessary as if the residuum was thrown into the hands of the Government. I admit that these arguments are not entirely without foundation; but they are not conclusive to the extent which has been supposed. It is true, the powers of the General Government are circumscribed, they are directed to particular objects; but even if Government keeps within those limits, it has certain discretionary powers with respect to the means, which may admit of abuse to a certain extent, in the same manner as the powers of the State Governments under their constitutions may to an indefinite extent; because in the constitution of the United States, there is a clause granting to Congress the power to make all laws which shall be necessary and proper for carrying into execution all the powers vested in the Government of the United States, or in any department or officer thereof; this enables them to fulfil every purpose for which the Government was established. Now, may not laws be considered necessary and proper by Congress, for it is for them to judge of the necessity and propriety to accomplish those special purposes which they may have in contemplation, which laws in themselves are neither necessary nor proper; as well as improper laws could be enacted by the State Legislatures, for fulfilling the more extended objects of those Governments. I will state an instance, which I think in point, and proves that this might be the case. The General Government has a right to pass all laws which shall be necessary to collect its revenue; the means for enforcing the collection are within the direction of the Legislature; may not general warrants be considered necessary for this purpose, as well as for some purposes which it was supposed at the framing of their constitutions the State Governments had in view? If there was reason for restraining the State Governments from exercising this power, there is like reason for restraining the Federal Government.

It may be said, indeed it has been said, that a bill of rights is not necessary, because the establishment of this Government has not repealed those declarations of rights which are added to the several State constitutions; that those rights of the people, which had been established by the most solemn act, could not be annihilated by a subsequent act of that people, who meant, and declared at the head of the instrument, that they ordained and established a new system, for the express purpose of securing to themselves and posterity the liberties they had gained by an arduous conflict.

I admit the force of this observation, but I do not look upon it to be conclusive. In the first place, it is too uncertain ground to leave this provision upon, if a provision is at all necessary to secure rights so important as many of those I have mentioned are conceived to be, by the public in general, as well as those in particular who opposed the adoption of this constitution. Besides, some States have no bills of rights, there are others provided with very defective ones, and there are others whose bills of rights are not only defective, but absolutely improper; instead of securing some in the full extent which republican principles would require, they limit them too much to agree with the common ideas of liberty.

It has been objected also against a bill of rights, that, by enumerating particular exceptions to the grant of power, it would disparage those rights which were not placed in that enumeration; and it might follow, by implication, that those rights which were not singled out, were intended to be assigned into the hands of the General Government, and were consequently insecure. This is one of the most plausible arguments I have ever heard urged against the admission of a bill of rights into this system; but, I conceive, that it may be guarded against. I have attempted it, as gentlemen may see by turning to the last clause of the fourth resolution.

It has been said, that it is unnecessary to load the constitution with this provision, because it was not found effectual in the constitution of the particular States. It is true, there are a few particular States in which some of the most valuable articles have not, at one time or other, been violated; but it does not follow but they may have, to a certain degree, a salutary effect against the abuse of power. If they are incorporated into the constitution, independent tribunals of justice will consider themselves in a peculiar manner the guardians of those rights; they will be an impenetrable bulwark against every assumption of power in the legislative or executive; they will be naturally led to resist every encroachment upon rights expressly stipulated for in the constitution by the declaration of rights. Besides this security, there is a great probability that such a declaration in the federal system would be enforced; because the State Legislatures will jealously and closely watch the operations of this Government, and be able to resist with more effect every assumption of power, than any other power on earth can do; and the greatest opponents to a Federal Government admit the State Legislatures to be sure guardians of the people's liberty. I conclude, from this view of the subject, that it will be proper in itself, and highly politic, for the tranquillity of the public mind, and the stability of the Government, that we should offer something, in the form I have proposed, to be incorporated in the system of Government, as a declaration of the rights of the people.

In the next place, I wish to see that part of the constitution revised which declares that the number of Representatives shall not exceed the proportion of one for every thirty thousand persons, and allows one Representative to every State which rates below that proportion. If we attend to the discussion of this subject, which has taken place in the State conventions, and even in the opinion of the friends to the constitution, an alteration here is proper. It is the sense of the people of America, that the number of Representatives ought to be increased, but particularly that it should not be left in the discretion of the Government to diminish them, below that proportion which certainly is in the power of the Legislature as the constitution now stands; and they may, as the population of the country increases, increase the House of Representatives to a very unwieldy degree. I confess I always thought this part of the constitution defective, though not dangerous; and that it ought to be particularly attended to whenever Congress should go into the consideration of amendments.

There are several minor cases enumerated in my proposition, in which I wish also to see some alteration take place. That article which leaves it in the power of the Legislature to ascertain its own emolument, is one to which I allude. I do not believe this is a power which, in the ordinary course of Government, is likely to be abused. Perhaps of all the powers granted, it is least likely to abuse; but there is a seeming impropriety in leaving any set of men without control to put their hand into the public coffers, to take out money to put in their pockets; there is a seeming indecorum in such power, which leads me to propose a change. We have a guide to this alteration in several of the amendments which the different conventions have proposed. I have gone, therefore, so far as to fix it, that no law, varying the compensation, shall operate until there is a change in the Legislature; in which case it cannot be for the particular benefit of those who are concerned in determining the value of the service.

I wish also, in revising the constitution, we may throw into that section, which interdicts the abuse of certain powers in the State Legislatures, some other provisions of equal, if not greater importance than those already made. The words, "No State shall pass any bill of attainder, *ex post facto* law," etc. were wise and proper restrictions in the constitution. I think there is more danger of those powers being abused by the State Governments than by the Government of the United States. The same may be said of other powers which they possess, if not controlled by the general principle, that laws are unconstitutional which infringe the rights of the community. I should therefore wish to extend this interdiction, and add, as I have stated in the 5th resolution, that no State shall violate the equal right of conscience, freedom of the press, or trial by jury in criminal cases; because it is proper that every Government should be disarmed of powers which trench upon those particular rights. I know, in some of the State constitutions, the power of the Government is controlled by such a declaration; but others are not. I cannot see any reason against obtaining even a double security on those points; and nothing can give a more sincere proof of the attachment of those who oppose this constitution to these great and important rights, than to see them join in obtaining the security I have now proposed; because it must be admitted, on all hands, that the State Governments are as liable to attack these invaluable privileges as the General Government is, and therefore ought to be as cautiously guarded against.

I think it will be proper, with respect to the judiciary powers, to satisfy the public mind on those points which I have mentioned. Great inconvenience has been apprehended to suitors from the distance they would be dragged to obtain justice in the Supreme Court of the United States, upon an appeal on an action for a small debt. To remedy this, declare that no appeal shall be made unless the matter in controversy amounts to a particular sum; this, with the regulations respecting jury trials in criminal cases, and suits at common law, it is to be hoped, will quiet and reconcile the minds of the people to that part of the constitution.

I find, from looking into the amendments proposed by the State conventions, that several are particularly anxious that it should be declared in the constitution, that the powers not therein delegated should be reserved to the several States. Perhaps words which may define this more precisely than the whole of the instrument now does, may be considered as superfluous. I admit they may be deemed unnecessary; but there can be no harm in making such a declaration, if gentlemen will allow that the fact is as stated. I am sure I understand it so, and do therefore propose it.

These are the points on which I wish to see a revision of the constitution take place. How far they will accord with the sense of this body, I cannot take upon me absolutely to determine; but I believe every gentleman will readily admit that nothing is in contemplation, so far as I have mentioned, that can endanger the beauty of the Government in any one important feature, even in the eyes of its most sanguine admirers. I have proposed nothing that does not appear to me as proper in itself, or eligible as patronized by a respectable number of our fellow-citizens; and if we can make the constitution better in the opinion of those who are opposed to it, without weakening its frame, or abridging its usefulness, in the judgment of those who are attached to it, we act the part of wise and liberal men to make such alterations as shall produce that effect.

Having done what I conceived was my duty, in bringing before this House the subject of amendments, and also stated such as I wish for and approve, and offered the reasons which occurred to me in their support, I shall content myself, for the present, with moving "that a committee be appointed to consider of and report such amendments as ought to be proposed by Congress to the Legislatures of the States, to become, if ratified by three-fourths thereof, part of the constitution of the United States." By agreeing to this motion, the subject may be going on in the committee, while other important business is proceeding to a conclusion in the House. I should advocate greater despatch in the business of amendments, if I were not convinced of the absolute necessity there is of pursuing the organization of the Government; because I think we should obtain the confidence of our fellow-citizens, in proportion as we fortify the rights of the people against the encroachments of the Government.

Madison's Notes for Amendments Speech, 1789

Reasons for urging amendts.
  1. to prove fedts. friends to liberty.
  2. remove remaining inquietudes.
  3. bring in N. C. R. Island.
  4. to improve the Constitution.
Reasons for moderating the plan.
  1. No stop if door opened to theoretic amendts.
  2. as likely to make worse as better till tried.
  3. insure passage by 2/3 of Congs. & 3/4 of Sts:
Objectns. of 3 kinds vs. the Constn.
  1. vs. the theory of its structure.
  2. vs. substance of its powers—elections & [illegible].
  3. vs. omission of guards in favr. of rights & liberty.
The last most urged & easiest obviated.
Read the amendments—
They relate 1st. to private rights—
Bill of Rights—useful not essential—fallacy in both sides, aspects [?] as to English Decln. of Rts—
  1. mere act of parl:
  2. no freedom of press—Conscience Gl. Warrants—Habs. Corpus jury in civil causes—criml. attainders—arms to Protests.
frequent Parlts.—chief trust.
freedom of press & conscience unknown to Magna Cha—& Pet: Rts.
Contents of Bill of Rhts.
  1. assertion of primitive equality &c.
  2. do. of rights exerted in formg. of Govts.
  3. natural rights retained as speach [illegible].
  4. positive rights resultg. as trial by jury.
  5. Doctrinl. artics vs. Depts. distinct electn.
  6. moral precepts for the administrn. & natl. character—as justice—economy—&c.
Object of Bill Rhts.
  To limit & qualify powr. by exceptg. from grant cases in wch. it shall not be exercised or exd. in a particular manner.
to guard
  1. vs Executive & in Engl. &c—
  2. Legislative as in Sts—

3. Majority of people.
ought to point as greatest danger which in Rep: is Prerogative of majority—
Here proper, tho' less nessary than in small Repubs.
Objectns.—vs—Bill of Rhts.
1. in Elective Govts. all power in people hence unnecessary & improper—This vs Sts.
2. In fedl. Govt. all not given retained—Bill of powers—need no Bill of Rhts—
sweeping clause—Genl. Warrants &c.
3. St: Bills not repeald.
too uncertain
Some Sts have not bills—others defect:—others—injurious [illegible].
4. disparge other rights—or constructively enlarge—
The first goes vs. St: Bills—
both guarded vs. by amendts.
5. Not effectl.—vs Sts also—but some check.
Courts will aid—also Ex: also Sts Legisls: watch
Time sanctify—incorporate public Sentiment
Bill of Rts ergo proper.
II increase of Reps.—2 for each St.
III pay of Congs.
IV Interdict to Sts as to Conscience—press—& jury—
This more necsy. to Sts—ye. Congs.
V Check on appeals—comn law
VI partn. as to 3 Depts.—& do. as to Genl. & St Govts.

Reprinted from 2 B. Schwartz, The Bill of Rights; a Documentary History 1042 (1971).

2. The "Higher Law" Background of American Constitutional Law

Edward S. Corwin

Theory is the most important part of the dogma of the law, as the architect is the most important man who takes part in the building of a house.*

The Reformation superseded an infallible Pope with an infallible Bible; the American Revolution replaced the sway of a king with that of a document. That such would be the outcome was not unforeseen from the first. In the same number of *Common Sense* which contained his electrifying proposal that America should declare her independence from Great Britain, Paine urged also a "Continental Conference," whose task he described as follows:

> The conferring members being met, let their business be to frame a Continental Charter, or Charter of the United Colonies; (answering to what is called the Magna Charta of England) fixing the number and manner of choosing members of congress and members of assembly . . . and drawing the line of business and jurisdiction between them: (always remembering, that our strength is continental, not provincial) securing freedom and property to all men . . . with such other matter as it is necessary for a charter to contain. . . . But where, say some, is the King of America? Yet that we may not appear to be defective even in earthly honors, let a day be solemnly set apart for proclaiming the charter; let it be brought forth placed in the divine law, the word of God; let a crown be placed thereon, by which the world may know, that so far as we approve of monarchy, that in America the law is King.[1]

Editor's Note: In this excerpt, some footnotes have been edited and renumbered for consistency.

Excerpted, by permission, from 42 Harv. L. Rev. 149 (1928).

*Holmes, Collected Legal Papers 200 (1921).

[1] I Paine, Political Writings 45–46 (1837).

This suggestion, which was to eventuate more than a decade later in the Philadelphia Convention, is not less interesting for its retrospection than it is for its prophecy.

In the words of the younger Adams, "the Constitution itself had been extorted from the grinding necessity of a reluctant nation"[2]; yet hardly had it gone into operation than hostile criticism of its provisions not merely ceased but gave place to "an undiscriminating and almost blind worship of its principles"[3]—a worship which continued essentially unchallenged till the other day. Other creeds have waxed and waned, but "worship of the Constitution" has proceeded unabated.[4] It is true that the Abolitionists were accustomed to stigmatize the Constitution as "an agreement with Hell," but their shrill heresy only stirred the mass of Americans to renewed assertion of the national faith. Even Secession posed as loyalty to the *principles* of the Constitution and a protest against their violation, and in form at least the constitution of the Southern Confederacy was, with a few minor departures, a studied reproduction of the instrument of 1787. For by far the greater reach of its history, Bagehot's appraisal of the British monarchy is directly applicable to the Constitution: "The English Monarchy strengthens our government with the strength of religion."[5]

The fact that its adoption was followed by a wave of prosperity no doubt accounts for the initial launching of the Constitution upon the affections of the American people. Travelling through various parts of the United States at this time, Richard Bland Lee found "fields a few years ago waste and uncultivated filled with inhabitants and covered with harvests, new habitations reared, contentment in every face, plenty on every board. . . ." "To produce this effect," he continued, "was the intention of the Constitution, and it has succeeded." Indeed it is possible that rather too much praise was lavished upon the Constitution on this score. "It has been

[2]Adams, Jubilee Discourse on the Constitution 55 (1839).

[3]Woodrow, Wilson, Congressional Government 4 (13th ed. 1898).

[4]On the whole subject, see I Von Holst, Constitutional History ch. 2 (1877); Schechter, *Early History of the Tradition of the Constitution* 9 Am. Pol. Sci. Rev. 707 *et seq.* (1915).

[5]Bagehot, English Constitution 39 (2d ed. 1925). "The monarchy by its religious sanction now confirms all our political order. . . . It gives . . . a vast strength to the entire constitution, by enlisting on its behalf the credulous obedience of enormous masses." *Id.* 43–44.

usual with declamatory gentlemen," complained the astringent Maclay, "in their praises of the present government, by way of contrast, to paint the state of the country under the old (Continental) congress, as if neither wood grew nor water ran in America before the happy adoption of the new Constitution"; and a few years later, when the European turmoil at once assisted, and by contrast advertised, our own blissful state, Josiah Quincy voiced a fear that, "we have grown giddy with good fortune, attributing the greatness of our prosperity to our own wisdom, rather than to a course of events, and a guidance over which we had no influence."[6]

But while the belief that it drew prosperity in its wake may explain the beginning of the worship of the Constitution, it leaves a deeper question unanswered. It affords no explanation why this worship came to ascribe to the Constitution the precise virtues it did as an efficient cause of prosperity. To answer this question we must first of all project the Constitution against a background of doctrinal tradition which, widespread as European culture, was at the time of the founding of the English colonies especially strong in the mother country, though by the irony of history it had become a century and a half later the chief source of division between mother country and colonies.

It is customary nowadays to ascribe the *legality* as well as the *supremacy* of the Constitution—the one is, in truth, but the obverse of the other—exclusively to the fact that, in its own phraseology, it was "ordained" by "the people of the United States." Two ideas are thus brought into play. One is the so-called "positive" conception of law as a general expression merely for the particular commands of a human lawgiver, as a series of acts of human will[7]; the other is that the highest possible source of such commands, because the highest possible embodiment of human will, is "the people." The same two ideas occur in conjunction in the oft-quoted text of Justinian's *Institutes:* "Whatever has pleased the prince has the force of law, since the Roman people by the *lex regia* enacted concerning

[6]Schechter, *supra* note 4, at 720–21.

[7]Bentham, as quoted in Holland, Elements of Jurisprudence 14 (12th ed. 1916). For further definitions of "positive law," see *id.* 22–23; Willoughby, Fundamental Concepts of Public Law ch. 10 (1924).

his *imperium*, have yielded up to him all their power and authority."[8] The sole difference between the Constitution of the United States and the imperial legislation justified in this famous text is that the former is assumed to have proceeded immediately from the people, while the latter proceeded from a like source only mediately.

The attribution of supremacy to the Constitution on the ground solely of its rootage in popular will represents, however, a comparatively late outgrowth of American constitutional theory. Earlier the supremacy accorded to constitutions was ascribed less to their putative source than to their supposed content, to their embodiment of essential and unchanging justice. The theory of law thus invoked stands in direct contrast to the one just reviewed. *There are, it is predicated, certain principles of right and justice which are entitled to prevail of their own intrinsic excellence, altogether regardless of the attitude of those who wield the physical resources of the community. Such principles were made by no human hands; indeed, if they did not antedate deity itself, they will so express its nature as to bind and control it. They are external to all Will as such and interpenetrate all Reason as such. They are eternal and immutable. In relation to such principles, human laws are, when entitled to obedience save as to matters indifferent, merely a record or transcript, and their enactment an act not of will or power but one of discovery and declaration.*[9] The Ninth Amendment of the Constitution of the United States, in its stipulation that "the enumeration in the Constitution, of certain rights, shall not be construed to deny or disparage others retained by the people," illustrates this theory perfectly, except that the principles of transcendental justice have been here translated into terms of personal and private rights. The relation of such rights, nevertheless, to governmental power is the same as that of the principles from which they spring and

---

[8]Inst. I, 2, 6: "Quod principi placuit, legis habet vigorem, cum lege regia quae de ejus imperio lata est, populus ei et in eum, omne imperium suum et potestatem concessit."The source is Ulpian Dig I, 4, i. The Romans always regarded the people as the source of the legislative power. "Lex est, quod populus Romanus senatorie magistratu interrogante, veluti Consule, constituebat." Inst. I, 2, 4. During the Middle Ages the question was much debated whether the *lex regia* effected an absolute alienation (*translatio*) of the legislative power to the Emperor, or was a revocable delegation (*cessio*). The champions of popular sovereignty at the end of this period, like Marsiglio of Padua in his *Defensor Pacis*, took the latter view. *See* Gierke, Political Theories of the Middle Ages 150 n.158, n.159 (Maitland trans. 1922).

[9]For definitions of law incorporating this point of view, see Holland, *supra* note 7, at 19–20, 32–36. *Cf.* I W. Blackstone, Commentaries Intro.

which they reflect. They owe nothing to their recognition in the Constitution—such recognition was necessary if the Constitution was to be regarded as complete.

Thus the *legality* of the Constitution, its *supremacy*, and its claim to be worshipped, alike find common standing ground on the belief in a law superior to the will of human governors. . . .

The conveyance of natural law ideas into American constitutional theory was the work preëminently—though by no means exclusively—of John Locke's *Second Treatise on Civil Government,* which appeared in 1690 as an apology for the Glorious Revolution. The outstanding feature of Locke's treatment of natural law is the almost complete dissolution which this concept undergoes through his handling into the natural rights of the individual; or—to employ Locke's own phrase, borrowed from the debates between Stuart adherents and Parliamentarians—into the rights of "life, liberty, and estate."[10] The dissolving agency by which Locke brings this transformation about is the doctrine of the Social Compact, with its corollary notion of a State of Nature. . . .

The two features of the *Second Treatise* which have impressed themselves most definitely upon American constitutional law are the limitations which it lays down for legislative power and its emphasis on the property right. The legislature is the supreme organ of Locke's commonwealth, and it is upon this supremacy that he depends in the main for the safeguarding of the rights of the individual. But for this very reason legislative supremacy is supremacy within the law, not a power above the law. In fact, the word "sovereign" is never used by Locke in its descriptive sense except in reference to the "free, sovereign" individual in the state of nature. In detail, the limitations which Locke specifies to legislative power are the following[11]: First, it is not arbitrary power. Not even the majority which determines the form of the government can vest its agent with arbitrary power, for the reason that the

---

[10]2 Dunning, History of Political Theories 222, n.346 (1923). "Is it not a common principle that the law favoureth three things, life, liberty, and dower. . . . This because our law is grounded upon the law of nature. And these three things do flow from the law of nature. . . ." Bacon, *Argument in Calvin's Case* in 2 Bacon, Works 176. *See also* Hale, History of the Common Law § 13 (1779): "Of the Rights of the People or Subject," where it is said these are protected according to their "lives, their liberties, their estates."

[11]*Of the Extent of the Legislative Power,* in Locke, Second Treatise on Civil Government ch. 11, 183 et seq. (Everyman's Lib. ed. 1924).

majority right itself originates in a delegation by free sovereign individuals who had "in the state of nature no arbitrary power over the life, liberty, or possessions" of others, or even over their own. In this caveat against "arbitrary power," Locke definitely anticipates the modern latitudinarian concept of due process of law.

"Secondly, the legislative . . . cannot assume to itself a power to rule by extemporary, arbitrary decrees, but is bound to dispense justice and decide the rights of the subject by promulgated standing laws, and known authorised judges"; nor may it vary the law in particular cases, but there must be one rule for rich and poor, for favorite and the ploughman. In this pregnant passage, Locke foreshadows some of the most fundamental propositions of American constitutional law: *Law must be general; it must afford equal protection to all; it may not validly operate retroactively; it must be enforced through the courts—legislative power does not include judicial power.*

Thirdly, as also follows from its fiduciary character, the legislature "cannot transfer the power of making laws to any other hands: for it being but a delegated power from the people, they who have it cannot pass it over to others." More briefly, *legislative power cannot be delegated.*

Finally, *legislative power is not the ultimate power of the commonwealth,* for "the community perpetually retains a supreme power of saving themselves from the attempts and designs of anybody, even their legislators, whenever they shall be so foolish or so wicked as to lay and carry on designs against the liberties and properties of the subject." So while legislative supremacy is the normal sanction of the rights of men, it is not the final sanction. The identical power which was exerted against James II would in like case be equally available against Parliament itself.[12]

Locke's bias in favor of property is best shown in the fifth chapter of the *Treatise,* where he brings the labor theory of value to the defense of inequality of possessions, and endeavors to show that the latter is harmonious with the social compact. His course of reasoning is as follows: All value, or almost all, is due to labor; and as there were different degrees of industry, so there were apt to be different degrees of possession. Yet most property, in those early days, was highly perishable, whence arose a natural limit to the accumulation of wealth, to wit, that no man must hoard up more than he could make use of, since that would be to waste nature's

[12]Locke, *supra* note 11, at ch. 19, 224.

bounty. Nevertheless, "the exceeding of his just property" lay, Locke is careful to insist, not "in the largeness of his possession, but the perishing of anything uselessly in it." Accordingly, when mankind, by affixing value to gold, silver, and other imperishable but intrinsically valueless things for which perishable commodities might be traded, made exchanges possible, it thereby, as by deliberate consent, ratified unequal possessions; and the later social compact did not disturb this covenant.[13]

So, having transmuted the law of nature into the rights of men, Locke next converts these into the rights of ownership. The final result is to base his commonwealth upon the balanced and antithetical concepts of the rule of the majority and the security of property. Nor, thanks to the labor theory of value, is this the merely static conception that at first consideration it might seem to be. Taken up a century later by Adam Smith, the labor theory became the cornerstone of the doctrine of *laissez faire*.[14] It thus assisted to adapt a political theory conceived in the interest of a quiescent landed aristocracy to the uses of an aggressive industrial plutocracy. By the same token, it also assisted to adapt a theory conceived for a wealthy and civilized community to the exactly opposed conditions of life in a new and undeveloped country. In a frontier society engrossed in the conquest of nature and provided with but meagre stimulation to artistic and intellectual achievement, the inevitable index of success was accumulation, and accumulation did, in fact, represent social service. What is more, the singular affinity which Calvinistic New England early discovered for Lockian rationalism is in some measure explicable on like grounds. The central pillar of Calvinism was the doctrine of election. It goes without saying that all who believed this dogma also believed themselves among the elect; yet of this what better, what more objective

---

[13]*Id.*, "Of Property," at ch. 5, 129. Locke uses the term "property" with various degrees of precision. In Chapter 5 he is thinking of *things* with exchangeable value. In Chapter 7 he uses the word to cover "life, liberty, and estate." In *A Letter on Toleration* he says that the commonwealth exists to promote "civil interest," and "civil interest I call life, liberty, inviolability of Body, and the possession of such outward things as Money, Lands, Houses, Furniture, and the like." 2 Locke, Works 239 (1823), quoted by Laski, Grammar of Politics 181 (1925).

[14]Carey, Harmony of Interests, Agricultural, Manufacturing and Commercial (1872). Henry C. Carey attempts an application of Smith's theory to American conditions in favor of a protective tariff.

evidence than material success? Locke himself, it may be added, was a notable preacher of the gospel of industry and thrift.[15]

Two other features of Locke's thought deserve brief comment. The first is his insistence upon the "public good" as the object of legislation and of governmental action in general. It should not be supposed that this in any way contradicts the main trend of his thought. Rather he is laying down yet another limitation on legislative freedom of action.[16] That the public good might not always be compatible with the preservation of rights, and especially with the rights of property, never once occurs to him. A century later the possibility did occur to Adam Smith, and was waived aside by his "harmony of interests" theory. Also the dimensions which Locke assigns to executive prerogative are, in view both of the immediate occasion for which he wrote and of his "constitutionalism," not a little astonishing. On this matter he writes:

> Where the legislative and executive power are in distinct hands (as they are in all moderated monarchies and well-framed governments), there the good of the society requires, that several things should be left to the discretion of him that has the executive power: for the legislators not being able to foresee, and provide by laws, for all that may be useful to the community, the executor of the laws, having the power in his hands, has by the common law of nature a right to make use of it for the good of the society, in many cases, where the municipal law has given no direction, till the legislative can conveniently be assembled to provide for it;

[15]Foster, *International Calvinism Through John Locke and the Revolution of 1688* 32 Am. Hist. Rev. 475, 486 (1927). *See also* Robinson, Case of Louis the Eleventh and Other Essays (1928); Weber, *Protestantische Ethick u. der "Geist" des Kapitalismus*, 30 Archiv Für Sozial-wissenschaft u. Sozial Politik 1–54 (1904); 21 *id.* 1–110 (1905); Sombart, Quintessence of Capitalism 257–62 (1915); and Tawney, *Puritanism and Capitalism*, 46 New Republic 348 (1926). Puritanism has been not inaptly characterized as "a religious sublimation of the virtues of the middle class." Puritan abhorrence of beauty and amusement necessarily led to concentration on the business of money-getting; and the belief of the Puritans that they were "chosen people" worked to the same end, for it turned their attention to the Old Testament, where the idea that prosperity is proof of moral worth is repeatedly presented. Nor is the New Testament devoid of such ideas. Compare the parable of the Talents, *Matthew* 25:29; also *Romans* 12:11; and see especially the texts from Baxter, Christian Directory, quoted by Robinson, *supra*.

[16]"Their [the legislature's] power, in the utmost bounds of it, is limited to the public good of the society." Locke, *supra* note 11, at ch. 11, § 135; *cf.* §§ 89, 110, 134, 142, 158 with §§ 124, 131, 140.

Many things there are, which the law can by no means provide for; and those must necessarily be left to the discretion of him that has the executive power in his hands, to be ordered by him as the public good and advantage shall require: nay, it is fit that the laws themselves should in some cases give way to the executive power, or rather to the fundamental law of nature and government—viz., That as much as may be, all the members of the society are to be preserved."[17]

Extrication from the trammels of a too rigid constitutionalism through a broad view of executive power is a device by no means unknown to American constitutional law and theory.

Locke's contribution is best estimated in relation to Coke's. Locke's version of natural law not only rescues Coke's version of the English constitution from a localized *patois*, restating it in the universal tongue of the age, it also supplements it in important respects. Coke's endeavor was to put forward the historical procedure of the common law as a permanent restraint on power, and especially on the power of the English crown. Locke, in the limitations which he imposes on legislative power, is looking rather to the security of the substantive rights of the individual—those rights which are implied in the basic arrangements of society at all times and in all places. While Coke rescued the notion of fundamental law from what must sooner or later have proved a fatal nebulosity, yet he did so at the expense of archaism. Locke, on the other hand, in cutting loose in great measure from the historical method of reasoning, opened the way to the larger issues with which American constitutional law has been called upon to grapple in its latest maturity. Without the Lockian or some similar background, judicial review must have atrophied by 1890 in the very field in which it is today most active; nor is this to forget his emphasis on the property right. Locke's weakness is on the institutional side. While he contributed to the *doctrine* of judicial review, it was without intention; nor does he reveal any perception of the importance of giving imperative written form to the constitutional principles which he formulated. The hard-fisted Coke, writing with a civil war ahead of him instead of behind him, was more prescient.

---

[17]Locke, *supra* note 11, "Of Prerogative," at ch. 14, § 159.

* * *

The influence of higher law doctrine associated with the names of Coke and Locke was at its height in England during the period when the American colonies were being most actively settled, which means that Coke had, to begin with, the advantage since he was first on the ground. The presence of Coke's doctrines in the colonies during the latter two-thirds of the seventeenth century is widely evidenced by the repeated efforts of colonial legislatures to secure for their constituencies the benefits of *Magna Carta* and particularly of the twenty-ninth chapter thereof. Because of the menace they were thought to spell for the prerogative, the majority of such measures incurred the royal veto.[18] In point of fact, since the "law of the land" clause of chapter twenty-nine was interpretable as contemplating only law which was enacted by the colonial legislature, the menace went even further. Clothed with this construction, chapter twenty-nine afforded affirmation not only of rights of the individual, but also of local legislative autonomy.[19] The frequently provoked discussion of such matters, moreover, served to fix terminology for the future moulding of thought. *Magna Carta* became a generic term for all documents of constitutional significance, and thereby a symbol and reminder of principles binding on government.[20]

But more specific evidence of Coke's influence also occurs during this period. One such instance is furnished by the opinion of a Massachusetts magistrate in 1657 holding void a tax by the town of Ipswich for the purpose of presenting the local minister with a dwelling house. Such a tax, said the magistrate, "to take from Peter and give it to Paul," is against fundamental law. "If noe kinge or Parliament can justly enact or cause that one man's estate, in whole or in part, may be taken from him and given to another without his owne consent, then surely the major part of a towne or other inferior powers cannot doe it."[21] An opinion of the attorney general of the Barbados, rendered sometime during the reign of Anne, which held void a paper money act because it authorized summary process

---

[18]For details, see Hazeltine, Magna Carta Commemoration Essays 191–201 (1917). Mott, Due Process of Law chs. 1, 6 (1926), adds some further items.

[19]Hazeltine *supra* note 18, at 195.

[20]*Id.* at 199–200.

[21]2 Hutchinson, Papers 1–25 (Prince Soc. Pubs. 1865).

against debtors, is of like import. The entire argument is based on chapter twenty-nine of *Magna Carta* and "common right, or reason."[22] Evidence of the persistence of the dictum in *Bonham's Case*[23] also crops up outside New England now and then, even before its notable revival by Otis in his argument in the *Writs of Assistance Case*.[24] As late as 1759 we find a New York man referring quite incidentally to "a Judicial power of declaring them [laws] void."[25] The allusion is inexplicable unless it was to Coke's "dictum."

If the seventeenth century was Coke's, the early half of the eighteenth was Locke's, especially in New England. After the Glorious Revolution the migration to America of important English elements ceased. Immediate touch with political developments in the mother country was thus lost. The colonies were fain henceforth to be content for the most part with the stock of political ideas already on hand; and in fact these met their own necessities, which grew

[22]2 Chalmers, Opinions of Eminent Lawyers 27–38, especially at 30 (1814).

[23][Editor's Note: This footnote consists of a passage from a portion of the original text that has been omitted from this excerpt.] For students of the origins of American constitutional law and theory, however, no judicial utterance of Coke's—few indeed in language—can surpass in interest and importance his so-called dictum in *Dr. Bonham's Case*, which was decided by the Court of Common Pleas in 1610. [8 Co. 107a (1610), 2 Brownl. 255 (1610).] Holding that the London College of Physicians was not entitled, under the act of Parliament which it invoked in justification, to punish Bonham for practicing medicine in the city without its license, Coke said:

> And it appears in our books, that in many cases, the common law will controul acts of parliament, and sometimes adjudge them to be utterly void: for when an act of parliament is against common right and reason, or repugnant, or impossible to be performed, the common law will controul it and adjudge such act to be void.

[8 Co. 118a (1610). The best comment on the dictum is to be found in McIlwain, High Court of Parliament and its Supremacy ch. 4 (1910); and Plucknett, *Bonham's Case and Judicial Review*, 40 Harv. L. Rev. 30 *et seq.* (1926), Coxe, Judicial Power and Unconstitutional Legislation chs. 13–17 (1893) is of incidental value. Ellesmere's charge that Coke had the support of only one judge and that three others were against him seems to be refuted both by Coke's and by Brownlow's report of the case. Apparently only three judges participated, and all agreed with Coke's statement.]

In these words we have foreshadowed not merely the power which American courts today exercise in the disallowance of statutes on the ground of their conflict with the Constitution, but also that very test of "reasonableness" which is the ultimate flowering of this power.

[24]*See* Mott, *supra* note 18, at 91, n.19.

[25]2 New York Historical Society Collections 204 (1869).

chiefly out of the quarrels between the governors and the assemblies, extremely well. And along with this comparative isolation from new currents of thought in the mother country went the general intellectual poverty of frontier life itself. There were a few books, fewer newspapers, and little travel. But one source of intellectual stimulation for the adult there was, one point of contact with the world of ideas, and that was the sermon. Through their election sermons in particular and through controversial pamphlets, the New England clergy taught their flocks political theory, and almost always this was an elaboration upon the stock of ideas which had come from seventeenth century England. The subject has been so admirably treated in a recent volume that it is here necessary only to record some of the outstanding facts.[26]

After the Bible, Locke was the principal authority relied on by the preachers to bolster up their political teachings, although Coke, Puffendorf, Sydney, and later on some others were also cited. The substance of the doctrine of these discourses is, except at two points, that of the *Second Treatise*. Natural rights and the social compact, government bounded by law and incapable of imparting legality to measures contrary to law, and the right of resistance to illegal measures all fall into their proper place. One frequent point of deviation from the Lockian model is the retention of the idea of a compact between governed and governors; that notion fitted in too well with the effort to utilize the colonial charters as muniments of local liberty to be discarded.[27] The other point of deviation from Locke is more apparent than real, for all these concepts are backed up by religious sanction. Yet to the modern reader the difference between the Puritan God of the eighteenth century and Locke's natural law often seems little more than nominal. "The Voice of Nature is the Voice of God," asserts one preacher; "reason and the voice of God are one," is the language of another; "Christ confirms the law of nature," is the teaching of a third.[28] The point of view is thoroughly deistic; reason has usurped the place of revelation, and without affront to piety.

---

[26]Baldwin, The New England Clergy and the American Revolution (1928).

[27]The same fact may also account for John Wise's preference for Puffendorf over Locke, though this may be due to his having had a copy of the former and not of the latter.

[28]Baldwin, *supra* note 26, at n.29, 43, n.73.

Nor should it be imagined that all this teaching and preaching on political topics took place *in vacuo*—in deliberate preparation, as it were, for a great emergency as yet descried only by the most perspicacious. Much of it was evoked by warm and bitter controversy among the New England congregations themselves.[29] One such controversy was that which arose in the second decade of the eighteenth century over the question whether the congregations should submit themselves to the governance of a synod. Even more heated was the quarrel which was produced by the great awakening consequent on the preaching of George Whitefield in 1740. Whitefield's doctrine was distinctly and disturbingly equalitarian. A spirit of criticism of superiors by inferiors, of elders by juniors ensued from it; while, at the same time the intellectual superiority of the clergy was menaced by the sudden appearance of a great crop of popular exhorters. Men turned again to Locke, Sydney, and others, but this time in order to discover the sanctions of authority rather than its limitations. Still some years later the outbreak of the French and Indian Wars inspired a series of sermons extolling English liberty and contrasting the balanced constitution of England with French tyranny, sermons in which the name of Montesquieu was now joined with that of Locke.[30]

This kind of preaching was not confined to New England, nor even to dissenting clergymen. Patrick Henry from his eleventh to his twenty-second year listened to an Anglican preacher who taught that the British constitution was but the "voluntary compact of sovereign and subject." Henry's own words later were "government is a conditional compact between king and people . . . violation of the covenant by either party discharges the other from obligation"[31]; and more than half of the signers of the Declaration of Independence were members of the Church of England.[32] It is also an important circumstance that the famous Parson's Cause, in which Henry participated as the champion of local liberty, was

[29]*Id.* at chs. 5–6.

[30]*Id.* at 88–89.

[31]Van Tyne, *Influence of the Clergy on the American Revolution*, 14 Am. Hist. Rev. 49 (1913).

[32]Letter from G. MacLaren Brydon, N. Y. Times, May 30, 1927, citing Perry, The Faith of the Signers of the Declaration of Independence (1926). All the signers from the Southern Colonies except one from Maryland (a Catholic) and one from Georgia were Anglicans.

pending in Virginia from 1752 to 1758, helping to bring the people of Virginia during the period face to face with fundamental constitutional questions.[33] "On a small scale, the whole episode illustrates the clash of political theories which lay back of the American Revolution."[34] And meantime the first generation of the American bar was coming to maturity—students of Coke, and equipped to bring his doctrines to the support of Locke should the need arise.[35]

The opening gun of the controversy leading to the Revolution was Otis' argument in 1761 in the *Writs of Assistance Case*,[36] which, through Bacon's and Viner's *Abridgements*, goes straight back to *Bonham's Case*. Adams' summary of it reads: "As to acts of Parliament. An act against the Constitution is void: an Act against natural Equity is void; and if an Act of Parliament should be made, in the very few words of the petition, it would be void. The Executive Courts must pass such Acts into disuse.—8 Rep. 118, from Viner."[37] "Then and there," exclaims Adams, "the child Independence was born."[38] Today he must have added that then and there American constitutional law was born, for Otis' contention goes far beyond Coke's: an ordinary court may traverse the specifically enacted will of Parliament, and its condemnation is final.

The suggestion that the local courts might be thus pitted against an usurping Parliament in defense of "British rights," served to bring the idea of judicial review to the very threshold of the first American constitutions, albeit it was destined to wait there unattended for some years. Adams himself in a plea before the Governor and Council of Massachusetts, turned Otis' argument against the Stamp Act,[39] while a Virginia county court actually declared that

[33]Scott, *The Constitutional Aspects of the "Parson's Cause,"* 31 Pol. Sci. Q. 558 *et seq.* (1916). The controversy evoked much talk of "void laws," though from the clerical party and with reference to acts of the Virginia Assembly.

[34]*Id.* at 577.

[35]Warren, History of the American Bar chs. 2–8 (1911); Lecky, American Revolution 15–16 (Woodburn ed. 1922).

[36]Quincy 51–57, and appendices, 395–552, of which 469–85 are especially relevant (Mass. 1761); also 2 Adams, Life and Works 521–25 (C.F. Adams ed. 1850); 10 *id.* at 232–362 *passim.*

[37]Quincy 474 (Mass. 1761).

[38]10 Adams, *supra* note 36, at 248.

[39]2 *id.* at 158–59; Memorial of Boston, Quincy 200–02 (Mass. 1765). Otis also spoke to the same effect. *Id.* at 205. Adams reiterated his argument in *Letters of Clarendon* in 3 Adams, *supra* note 36, at 469. An argument greatly stressed against the Stamp

measure void. "The judges were unanimously of the opinion," a report of the case reads, "that the law did not bind, affect, or concern the inhabitants of Virginia 'inasmuch as they conceived the said act to be unconstitutional.' "[40] As late as 1776, Chief Justice William Cushing of Massachusetts, who was later one of Washington's first appointees to the Supreme Court of the United States, was congratulated by Adams for telling a jury of the nullity of acts of Parliament.[41]

Nor did the controversy with Great Britain long rest purely on Coke's doctrines. Otis himself, declares Adams,

> was also a great master of the law of nature and nations. He had read Puffendorf, Grotius, Barbeyrac, Burlamaqui, Vattel, Heineccius. . . . It was a maxim which he inculcated in his pupils . . . that a lawyer ought never to be without a volume of natural or public law, or moral philosophy, on his table or in his pocket.[42]

Otis' own pamphlet, *The Rights of the British Colonies Asserted and Proved*, none the less was almost altogether of Lockian provenience. The colonists were entitled to "as ample rights, liberties, and privileges as the subjects of the mother country are and in some respects to more. . . . Should the charter privileges of the Colonists be disregarded or revoked, there are natural, inherent, and inseparable rights as men and citizens that would remain."[43] And Adams argues

---

Act was its tendency to abolish trial by jury contrary to Magna Charta, through its extension of the jurisdiction of the admiralty courts, over penalties incurred under the act. *Id.* at 470. Governor Hutchinson wrote at this period: "The prevailing reason at this time is, that the Act of Parliament is against Magna Charta, and the natural Rights of Englishmen, and therefore, according to Lord Coke, null and void." Appendix, Quincy n.527 (Mass. 1769); and to same effect, *id.* at 441, 445.

[40]5 McMaster, History of the American People 394 (1920).

[41]9 Adams, *supra* note 36, at 390. Meanwhile, the dictum, with a strong Lockian infusion, had been invoked against domestic legislation. See George Mason's argument in Robin V. Hardaway, Jefferson 109–23 (Va. 1772), in which an act of the Virginia Assembly, passed in 1682, was declared void. Mason relied mainly on Coke and Hobart.

[42]10 Adams, *supra* note 36, at 275.

[43]The date of the pamphlet is 1764. A summary of it in 10 Adams, *supra* note 36, at 293, is a summary of Locke's eleventh chapter. In Otis, Vindication of the House of Representatives (1762), Locke is characterized as "one of the most wise . . . most honest . . . most impartial men that ever lived . . . as great an ornament . . . the Church of England ever had to boast of."

the year following in his dissertation on *The Canon and the Feudal Law* for

> Rights antecedent to all earthy government—Rights that cannot be repealed or restrained by human laws—Rights derived from the great legislator of the universe. . . . British liberties are not the grants of princes or parliaments, but original rights, conditions of original contracts . . . coeval with government. . . . Many of our rights are inherent and essential, agreed on as maxims, and established as preliminaries, even before a parliament existed.[44]

But it is the Massachusetts Circular Letter of 1768 that perfects the blend of Coke and Locke, while it also reformulates in striking terms, borrowed perhaps from Vattel, the medieval notion of authority as intrinsically conditioned. The outstanding paragraph of the letter is the following:

> The House have humbly represented to the ministry, their own sentiments, that his Majesty's high court of Parliament is the supreme legislative power over the whole empire; that in all free states the constitution is fixed, and as the supreme legislative derives its power and authority from the constitution, it cannot overleap the bounds of it, without destroying its own foundation; that the constitution ascertains and limits both sovereignty and allegiance, and, therefore, his Majesty's American subjects, who acknowledge themselves bound by the ties of allegiance, have an equitable claim to the full enjoyment of the fundamental rules of the British Constitution; that it is an essential, unalterable right, in nature, engrafted into the British constitution, as a fundamental law, and ever held sacred and irrevocable by the subjects within the realm, that what a man has honestly acquired is absolutely his own, which he may freely give, but cannot be taken from him without his consent; that the American subjects may, therefore, exclusive of any consideration of charter rights, with a decent firmness, adopted to the character of free men and subjects, assert this natural and constitutional right.[45]

Notwithstanding all this, as late as the first Continental Congress there were still those who opposed any reliance whatsoever on

---

[44]3 Adams, *supra* note 36, at 448–64, especially at 449, 463.

[45]MacDonald, Documentary Source book 146–50 (1768). *Cf.* Vattel, Law of Nations bk. i. ch. 3, § 34 (London trans. 1797). The subordination of the legislative authority and that of the Prince to the constitution is the gospel of this and the succeeding chapter. The work first appeared in 1758.

natural rights. One of "the two points which we laboured most" John Adams records in his *Diary* was "whether we should recur to the law of nature, as well as to the British constitution, and our American charters and grants. Mr. Galloway and Mr. Duane were for excluding the law of nature. I was strenuous for retaining and insisting on it, as a recourse to which we might be driven by Parliament much sooner than we were aware."[46] The "Declaration and Resolves" of the Congress proves that Adams carried the day. The opening resolution asserts "that the inhabitants of the American colonies in North America," by the immutable laws of nature, the principles of the British constitution, and the several charters or compacts "are entitled to life, liberty, and property."[47]

Nor did the corollary notion of a single community claiming common rights on the score of a common humanity, escape American spokesmen. It was in this same first Continental Congress that Patrick Henry made his famous deliverance: "Government is dissolved. . . . Where are your landmarks, your boundaries of Colonies? We are in a state of nature, sir. . . . The distinctions between Virginians, Pennsylvanians, New Yorkers, and New Englanders, are no more. I am not a Virginian, but an American."[48] And the less casual evidence of everyday speech is to like effect: "the people of these United Colonies," "your whole people," "the people of America," "the liberties of Americans," "the rights of Americans," "American rights," "Americans."[49] The constant recurrence of such phrases in contemporary documents bespeaks the conscious identity of Americans everywhere in possession of the rights of men. Natural rights were already on the way to become national rights.

At the same time it is necessary to recognize that the American Revolution was also a contest for local autonomy as well as one for individual liberty. The two motives were in fact less competitive than complementary. The logical deduction from the course of political history in the colonies, especially in the later decades of it, was that the best protection of the rights of the individual was to

[46]2 Adams, *supra* note 36, at 374.

[47]MacDonald, *supra* note 44, at 162–66.

[48]2 Adams, *supra* note 36, at 366–67.

[49]Baldwin, View of the Origin and Nature of the Constitution of the United States 15–16 (1837); Dillon, Laws and Jurisprudence of England and America 46–48 (1895). *See also* Niles, Principles and Acts 134–35, 148 (1876).

be found in the maintenance of the hard-won prerogatives of the colonial legislatures against the royal governors; in other words, of what they locally termed their "Constitutions."[50] The final form of the American argument against British pretentions was, therefore, by no means a happy idea suggested by the stress of contention, but was soundly based on autochthonous institutional developments. As stated by Jefferson in his *Summary View*, published in 1774, it comprised the thesis that Parliament had no power whatsoever to legislate for the colonies, whether in harmony with the rights of men or no; that the colonies were mutually independent communities, equal partners in the British Empire with England herself; that each part had its own parliament which was the supreme law making power within its territorial limits; that each was connected with the Empire only through the person of a common monarch, who was "no more than the chief officer of the people, appointed by the laws . . . to assist in working the great machine of government erected for their use."[51] The Declaration of Independence, two years later from the same hand, proceeds on the same theory. It is addressed not to Parliament but to the king, since it was with the king alone that the bond about to be severed had subsisted; in it the American doctrine of the relation of government to individual rights finds its classic expression; these rights are vindicated by the assertion of the independence of the thirteen states.[52]

[50]For this use of the term "Constitution," sometimes referring to the colonial charter, sometimes referring to the established mode of government of the colony, see 2 Journals of the House of Representatives of Massachusetts 370 (1720); 8 *id.* at 279, 302, 318 (1728). In New Jersey, which had no charter after 1702, the term "constitution" referred altogether to the mode of government that had developed on the basis of the royal governor's instructions, but may have been suggested by the Fundamental Constitutions of 1683 of East Jersey. C. R. Erdman, The New Jersey Constitution of 1776 (to be printed).

[51]11 Jefferson, Writings 258; The Jeffersonian Cyclopedia 963–68 (Foley ed. 1900). Jefferson characteristically claimed his to be the first formulation of this position. 9 Jefferson, Writings 258 (Mem. ed. 1903). But in this he was seriously in error. Richard Bland, Stephen Hopkins, John Adams, James Wilson, Benjamin Franklin, Roger Sherman, James Iredell, and others all preceded him, Hopkins and Franklin by nearly ten years. Indeed, advocates had developed a similar doctrine in Ireland's behalf in the seventeenth century. On the whole subject, *see* Adams, Political Ideas of the American Revolution chs. 3, 5 (1922); Becker, The Declaration of Independence (1922), at ch. 3; McIlwain, The American Revolution (1923).

[52]Jefferson's indebtedness to the Virginia Declaration of Rights of 1776 appears

From the destructive phase of the Revolution we turn to its constructive phase. This time it was Virginia who led the way. The Virginia constitution of 1776 is preceded by a "Declaration of rights made by the representatives of the good people of Virginia . . . which rights do appertain to them and their posterity, as the basis and foundation of government."[53] In this document, antedating the Declaration of Independence by a month, are enumerated at length those rights which Americans, having laid claim to them first as British subjects and later as men, now intended as citizens to secure through governments of their own erection. For the first time in the history of the world the principles of revolution are made the basis of settled political institutions.

What was the nature of these governments? Again the Virginia constitution of 1776 may serve as a model.[54] Here the horn of the legislative department is mightily exalted, that of the executive correspondingly depressed. The early Virginia governors were chosen by the legislature annually and were assisted by a council of state also chosen by the legislature, and if that body so desired, from the legislature. The governor was without the veto power, or any other participation in the work of law-making, and his salary was entirely at the mercy of the assembly. The judges were in somewhat better case, holding their offices "during good behavior," yet they too were the legislature's appointees, and judicial review is nowhere hinted. Finally, both judges and governors were subject to impeachment, which as still defined by English precedents, amounted to a practically unrestricted inquest of office. The underlying assumption of the instrument, gatherable from its various provisions, is that the rights of the individual have nothing to fear from majority rule exercised through legislative assemblies

---

more striking when the Declaration of Independence is compared with the former as it came from the hands of George Mason. Niles, Principles and Acts 301–03. The phrase "pursuit of happiness" was probably suggested by Blackstone's statement that the law of nature boils down to "one paternal precept, 'that man should pursue his own true and substantial happiness' " I W. Blackstone, Commentaries 41. Burlamaqui, Principles of Natural and Political Law (1859), an English translation of which appeared in 1763 (the work was first published in 1747), teaches the same doctrine at length. See, e.g., id. at 18. The phrase "a long train of abuses," is Jefferson's recollection of Locke, Second Treatise on Civil Government § 225, ch. 19.

[53] 7 Thorpe, Federal and State Constitutions, Colonial Charters and Other Organic Laws 3812–14 (1909).

[54] Id. at 3814–19.

chosen for brief terms by a restricted, though on the whole democratic, electorate. In short, as in both Coke and Locke, the maintenance of higher law is intrusted to legislative supremacy, though qualified by annual elections. Fortunately or unfortunately, in 1776 the influence of Coke and Locke was no longer the predominant one that it had been. In the very process of controversy with the British Parliament, a new point of view had been brought to American attention, the ultimate consequences of which were as yet unforeseeable.[55]

Lord Acton has described the American Revolution as a contest between two ideas of legislative power. Even as late as the debate on the Declaratory Act of 1766, the American invocation of a constitution setting metes and bounds to Parliament did not fail of a certain response among the English themselves. Burke, it is true, brushed aside all questions of prescriptive rights and based his advocacy of the American cause on expediency only; but Camden, who possessed the greatest legal reputation of the age, quoted both Coke and Locke in support of the proposition that Parliament's power was not an unlimited one; while Chatham, taking halfway ground, pretended to discover a fundamental distinction between the power of taxation and that of legislation, qualifying the former by the necessity of representation.[56] Camden and Chatham were, none the less, illustrious exceptions. The direction which the great weight of professional opinion was now taking was shown when Mansfield, who a few years earlier had as solicitor general quoted the dictum in *Bonham's Case* with approval, arose in the House of Lords to support the Declaratory Act.[57] The passage of that measure by an overwhelming majority committed Parliament substantially

---

[55]On the Revolutionary state constitutions, see generally Nevins, The American States During and After the Revolution (1924); Morey, *First State Constitutions*, 4 Ann. Am. Acad. Pol. and Soc. Sci. 201–32 (1893); Webster, *Comparative Study of the State Constitutions of the American Revolution*, 9 *id.* at 380–420 (1897).

[56]*See* the debate on the Declaratory Bill, 16 Hansard, Parliamentary History 163–81, 193–206 *passim* (1813). Camden was especially vehement: The bill is "illegal, absolutely illegal, contrary to the fundamental laws of nature, contrary to the fundamental laws of this constitution." *Id.* 178. On the other hand, it was denied that *Magna Carta* was any proof "of our Constitution as it now is. The Constitution of this country has been always in a moving state, either gaining or losing something." *Id.* at 197.

[57]*Id.* at 172–75.

to Milton's conclusion of a century earlier that "Parliament was above all positive law, whether civil or common."[58]

The vehicle of the new doctrine to America was Blackstone's *Commentaries*, of which, before the Revolution, nearly 2,500 copies had been sold on this side of the Atlantic,[59] while the spread of his influence in the later days of the pre-Revolutionary controversy is testified to by Jefferson in his reference to that "young brood of lawyers" who, seduced by the "honeyed Mansfieldism of Blackstone, . . . began to slide into Toryism."[60] Nor is Blackstone's appeal to men of all parties difficult to understand. Eloquent, suave, undismayed in the presence of the palpable contradictions in his pages, adept in insinuating new points of view without unnecessarily disturbing old ones, he is the very exemplar and model of legalistic and judicial obscurantism.

While still a student, Blackstone had published an essay on *The Absolute Rights of British Subjects,* and chapter one of book one of his greater work bears a like caption. Here he appears at first glance to underwrite the whole of Locke's philosophy, but a closer examination discloses important divergences. "Natural liberty" he defines as "the power of acting as one thinks fit, without any restraint or control, unless by the law of nature." It is "inherent in us by birth," and is that gift of God which corresponds with "the faculty of free will." Yet every man, he continues, "when he enters into society, gives up a part of his natural liberty as the price of so valuable a purchase," receiving in return "civil liberty," which is natural liberty "so far restrained by human laws (and no farther) as is neces-

---

[58]McIlwain, High Court of Parliament 94. On the rise of the notion of Parliamentary sovereignty, see Holdsworth, Some Lessons from Our Legal History 112–41 (1928). The first to assert the supremacy of the King in Parliament over the King out of Parliament was James Whitlocke, in the debate on Impositions, in 1610. *Id.* at 124. A division on the subject is shown in the debate on the Septennial Act of 1716. *Id.* at 129; 7 Hansard, Parliamentary History 317, 334, 339, 348–49. The doctrine of the Declaratory Act evoked numerous protests outside of Parliament. Mott, Due Process of Law n.63. For a belated expression of the doctrine of limited Parliamentary power, see *id.* at n.67, citing various works of Toulmin Smith. Smith, however, was no advocate of judicial review, but warned his people against such an institution as the Supreme Court of the United States. *Id.* at n.68.

[59]The first volume appeared in 1765, the fourth in 1769. An American edition appeared in Philadelphia in 1771–72, of the full work, 1,400 copies having been ordered in advance. Warren, History of the American Bar 178.

[60]II Jefferson, *supra* note 51, at iv. Jefferson had no high opinion of "Blackstone lawyers." He termed them "ephemeral insects of the law."

sary and expedient for the general advantage of the public."[61] The divergence which this phraseology marks from the strictly Lockian position is two-fold. Locke also, as we saw above, suggests public utility as one requirement of allowable restraints upon liberty, but by no means the sole requirement; nor is the law-making power with him, as with Blackstone, the final arbiter of the issue.

The divergence becomes even more evident when the latter turns to consider the positive basis of British liberties in *Magna Carta* and "the corroborating statutes." His language in this connection is peculiarly complacent. The rights declared in these documents, he asserts, comprise nothing less than

> either that residuum of natural liberty, which is not required by the laws of society to be sacrificed to public convenience, or else those civil privileges, which society hath engaged to provide in lieu of the natural liberties so given up by individuals. These, therefore, were formerly, either by inheritance or purchase, the rights of all mankind; but, in most other countries of the world, being now more or less debased and destroyed, they at present may be said to remain, in a peculiar and emphatical manner, the rights of the people of England.[62]

Yet when he comes to trace the limits of the "rights and liberties" so grandiloquently characterized, his invariable reference is simply to the state of the law in his own day—never to any more exalted standard.

And so by phraseology drawn from Locke and Coke themselves, he paves the way to the entirely opposed position of Hobbes and Mansfield. In elaboration of this position he lays down the following propositions: First, "there is and must be in all of them [states] a supreme, irresistible, absolute, uncontrolled authority . . ."; secondly, this authority is the "natural, inherent right that belongs to the sovereignty of the state . . . of making and enforcing laws"; thirdly, to the law-making power "all other powers of the state" must conform "in the execution of their several functions or else the Constitution is at an end"; and, finally, the law-making power in Great Britain is Parliament, in which, therefore, the sovereignty resides.[63] It follows, of course, that neither judicial disallowance of

[61]I Blackstone, Commentaries 125–26.
[62]*Id.* at 127–29.
[63]*Id.* at 49–51.

acts of Parliament nor yet the right of revolution has either legal or constitutional basis. To be sure, "Acts of Parliament that are impossible to be performed are of no validity"; yet this is so only in a truistic sense, for "there is no court that has power to defeat the intent of the legislature, when couched in . . . evident and express words."[64] As to the right of revolution—"So long . . . as the English Constitution lasts, we may venture to affirm that the power of Parliament is absolute and without control."[65]

Nor does Blackstone at the end, despite his previous equivocations, flinch from the conclusion that the whole legal fabric of the realm was, by his view, at Parliament's disposal. Thus he writes:

> It hath sovereign and uncontrollable authority in the making, confirming, enlarging, restraining, abrogating, repealing, reviving, and expounding of laws . . . this being the place where that absolute, despotic power which must in all governments reside somewhere, is entrusted by the Constitution of these kingdoms. All mischiefs and grievances, operations and remedies that transcend the ordinary course of the laws, are within the reach of this extraordinary tribunal. . . . It can, in short, do everything that is not naturally impossible, and therefore some have not scrupled to call its power by a figure rather too bold, the omnipotence of Parliament. True it is, that what the Parliament doth no authority upon earth can undo.[66]

This absolute doctrine was summed up by De Lolme a little later in the oft-quoted aphorism that "Parliament can do anything except make a man a woman or a woman a man."

Thus, was the notion of legislative sovereignty added to the stock of American political ideas.[67] Its essential contradiction of the elements of theory which had been contributed by earlier thinkers is manifest. What Coke and Locke give us is, for the most part, cautions and safeguards against power; in Blackstone, on the other hand, as in Hobbes, we find the claims of power exalted. This occurred, moreover, at a moment when, as it happened, not merely the actual structure of government in the United States, but this

---

[64]*Id.* at 91.

[65]*Id.* at 161–62.

[66]*Id.* at 160–61.

[67]Blackstone, however, was not the first to introduce the notion in the Colonies. See some earlier pulpit utterances recorded in Baldwin, *supra* note 26, at n.42: "The Legislature is Accountable to none. There is no Authority above them."

strong trend of thought among the American people afforded the thesis of legislative sovereignty every promise of easy lodgement.

The formula laid down by the Declaration of Independence regarding the right of revolution is a most conservative one. The right is not to be exercised for "light and transient causes," but only to arrest a settled and deliberate course of tyranny. Yet within a twelve month of the Declaration we find one Benjamin Hichborn of Boston proclaiming the following doctrine:

> I define civil liberty to be not a "government by laws," made agreeable to charters, bills of rights or compacts, but a power existing in the people at large, at any time, for any cause, or for no cause, but their own sovereign pleasure, to alter or annihilate both the mode and essence of any former government, and adopt a new one in its stead.[68]

Ultimately the doctrine of popular sovereignty thus voiced was to be turned against both legislative sovereignty and at a critical moment against state particularism. But at the outset it aided both these ideas, because the state was conceived to stand nearer to the people than the Continental Congress, and because, within the state, the legislature was conceived to stand nearer to the people than the other departments.[69] Thus legislative sovereignty, a derivative from the notion of popular sovereignty in the famous text from Justinian which was quoted at the outset of this study, was recruited afresh from the parent stream, with the result that all the varied rights of man were threatened with submergence in a single right, that of belonging to a popular majority, or more accurately, of being represented by a legislative majority.[70]

---

[68]Niles, Principles and Acts 47.

[69]On the growth of particularism, as shown by the proceedings in the Continental Congress, especially regarding the Articles of Confederation, see Adams, Jubilee Discourse on the Constitution 13 et seq. (1839).

[70]"The Law of nature is not, as the English utilitarians in their ignorance of its history supposed, a synonym for arbitrary individual preferences, but on the contrary it is a living embodiment of the collective reason of civilized mankind. . . . But it has its limits. . . . Natural justice has no means . . . of choosing one practical solution out of two or more which are in themselves equally plausible. Positive law, whether enacted or customary, must come to our aid in such matters." Pollock, Expansion of the Common Law 128 (1904). The arguments of the analytical school against higher law notions must be conceded to this extent: it is better to confine the term "law" to rules enforced by the state. But that fact does not prove that the term should be applied to all such rules. In urging that it should be, the analytical

Why, then, did not legislative sovereignty finally establish itself in our constitutional system? To answer at this point solely in terms of institutions, the reason is twofold. In the first place, in the American *written Constitution*, higher law at last attained a form which made possible the attribution to it of an entirely new sort of validity, the validity of a *statute emanating from the sovereign people*. Once the binding force of higher law was transferred to this new basis, the notion of sovereignty of the ordinary legislative organ disappeared automatically, since that cannot be a *sovereign* law-making body which is subordinate to another law-making body. But in the second place, even statutory form could hardly have saved the higher law as *a recourse for individuals* had it not been backed up by *judicial review*. Invested with statutory form and implemented by judicial review, higher law, as with renewed youth, entered upon one of the great periods of its history, and juristically the most fruitful one since the days of Justinian.

---

thinkers endeavor to steal something—they try to transfer to unworthy rules supported by the state the prestige attaching to the word "law" conceived of as the embodiment of justice. The trouble with the analysts, in other words, is not that they define "law" too narrowly, but too broadly.

3. The Ninth Amendment of the Federal Constitution

Knowlton H. Kelsey

Certain editorial comment on the death of California's "Little A. A. A." at the hands of the California Supreme Court, following closely upon the invalidation of the A. A. A. at the hands of the "Nine Old Men," led to the suggestion that a discussion of the Ninth Amendment would be of interest to this bar.[1]

The comment was to the effect that the power of regulation must reside somewhere and the implication was that all power must reside in either the Federal or State governments. The comment ignored the fact that powers are reserved to the people as well as to the states, and, further, that rights, which preclude power, are also reserved to the people.

To suggest that the power to regulate agriculture, industry, business or any other particular activity, must, of necessity, be in either the Federal or the State governments is to deny the whole philosophy of limited government created by and of individual rights recognized by the Constitution of the United States and under the constitutions of the several states.

The subject here considered has to do with only a small part of the implications contained in the editorial comment above mentioned. We are here to consider only a small part of the limitations on the government of the United States—that limitation or prohibition contained in the Ninth Amendment: *"The enumeration in the Constitution, of certain rights, shall not be construed to deny or disparage others retained by the people."*

That provision is a companion to and in a measure the complement of the Tenth Amendment: "The powers not delegated to the

---

Reprinted, by permission, from 11 Ind. L.J. 309 (1936).
[1]Gen. Hugh E. Johnson: "the Nine Old Men in their black kimonos."

United States by the Constitution, nor prohibited by it to the States, are reserved to the States respectively, *or to the people.*"

Together, these articles of amendment express the fundamental theory of American government, National and State—the theory of reserved rights and of delegated powers. The former article specifies *rights,* the latter specifies *powers.* When the two provisions are laid beside each other, it becomes evident that there was some distinction in the minds of the framers of those amendments between *declarations of right* and *limitations on* or *prohibitions of power.* If no distinction had been in mind, the Ninth Amendment would have been unnecessary. The Tenth Amendment, reserving powers to states and people, would have been enough, when taken with certain limitations or on reservations of power and with certain reservations of rights in the body of the Constitution or in other amendments.

In a consideration of the Ninth Amendment and an inquiry into the nature of the rights mentioned or suggested therein, we are concerned, not with rights at sufferance, not rights enjoyed by the failure to exercise powers granted, but with relatively absolute rights, if any right may be said to be absolute in any society, with natural, or inherent, or inalienable rights—whatever natural, inherent or inalienable rights may be. And particularly, our question here is as to what rights, if any, not enumerated, are retained by the people. A thorough consideration of the subject would involve a process of determination and of elimination—determination as to what the rights of the people are or were, as considered by the framers of the Constitution and of the several amendments, and elimination of those rights or portions of right which are referred to as being enumerated.

Rights may arise or rather appear by reason of limitations placed upon or by the limits of granted powers, as: the right to uniformity or to apportionment of taxation.[2] Such rights may be pointed out by a prohibition against the exercise of power or by a specification of rights, as in Article I, Sec. 9, and by the several amendments among the first ten, and which may be difficult to classify as prohibitions of power or as enumerations of right. Rights may also exist in having the granted powers exercised, or in having them exercised in the manner and for the purpose for which granted,

---

[2]Art. I, sec. 8, sub. 1; art I, sec. 9, subs. 4 & 5.

e.g.: Article IV, Sec. 4, the guarantee of a republican form of government.

Rights, whether asserted, indicated, or set out as prohibitions of or as limitations on power, may be assumed to be enumerated. Thus the limitations on taxation,[3] on suspension of the writ of habeas corpus,[4] on trial of crimes[5] and conviction of treason,[6] and the prohibitions against bills of attainder,[7] ex post facto laws,[8] corruption of blood[9] or forfeiture,[10] are probably among those referred to in the Ninth Amendment as being enumerated. Those which with more certainty can be classed as being enumerated are set out by the other amendments and include: freedom of speech,[11] religion,[12] press,[13] assemblage,[14] petition,[15] to keep and bear arms,[16] on quartering troops,[17] from search and seizure,[18] of presentment and indictment,[19] against double jeopardy, against self incrimination,[20] against deprivation of life, liberty or property,[21] against taking of property,[22] for fair and speedy trials in criminal matters,[23] for jury trials in civil suits at common law,[24] against excessive bail,[25] and

[3]See note 2, sub.1; art. I, sec. 9, subs. 4 & 5.
[4]Art I, sec. 9, sub. 2.
[5]Art. III, sec. 2, sub. 3.
[6]Art. III, sec. 3.
[7]Art. I, sec. 9, sub. 3; art. III, sec. 3, sub. 2.
[8]Art. I, sec. 9, sub. 3.
[9]Art. III, sec. 3, sub. 2.
[10]*Id.*
[11]Amend. I.
[12]*Id.*
[13]*Id.*
[14]*Id.*
[15]*Id.*
[16]Amend. II.
[17]Amend. III.
[18]Amend. IV.
[19]Amend. V.
[20]*Id.*
[21]*Id.*
[22]*Id.*
[23]Amend. VI.
[24]Amend. VII.
[25]Amend. VIII.

against cruel and unusual punishments.[26] As against the states, individual rights specified in the Constitution, but not necessarily included in the scope of the Ninth Amendment, include: freedom from bills of attainder,[27] ex post facto laws,[28] laws impairing the obligation of contract,[29] abridgement of privileges and immunities,[30] deprivation of life, liberty or property,[31] for equal protection of law,[32] and against denial of suffrage.[33]

The list seems imposing. A recital of the rights in this manner enumerated or pointed out seems like a catalogue of human rights. But do the rights, surrendered by the grant of power, express or implied, or expressly reserved by enumeration, prohibition or limitation, exhaust the list of human rights? Are no other rights retained by the people? Is the Ninth Amendment, and is the closing phrase of the Tenth Amendment as well, merely like the words of a sale bill specifying "other articles too numerous to mention" on the improbable chance that something worth while may have been forgotten?

It has been held that in interpreting the Constitution, every word must have its due force and meaning; that no word was unnecessarily used or needlessly added; that no word can be rejected as superfluous and unmeaning.[34]

With this rule in mind we must therefore assume that in the minds of the framers of this amendment, other rights than those "enumerated" did, and supposedly do now, exist.

Natural rights, such as are declared to be inalienable and which, as such, are personal to every individual as a citizen of a free community, include: the right to personal liberty, to personal security, to acquire and enjoy property, to religious liberty, to freedom

---

[26]*Id.*

[27]Art. I, sec. 10, sub. 1.

[28]*Id.*

[29]*Id.*

[30]Amend. XIV.

[31]*Id.*

[32]*Id.*

[33]Amends. XV & XIX.

[34]Ogden v. Saunders, 12 Wheat. 213, 6 L. ed. 606. Knowlton v. Moore, 178 U.S. 41, 44 L. ed. 969. Holmes v. Jennison, 14 Pet. 540, 10 L. ed. 579. Blake v. McClung, 172 U.S. 239, 43 L. ed. 432. Cohens v. Virginia, 6 Wheat. 264, 5 L. ed. 257. Myers v. U.S., 272 U.S. 52, 71 L. ed. 160.

of conscience, to freedom of contract, to freedom of press, speech, assemblage, petition, to freedom to engage in profession, trade, business, or calling, and the right of privacy.[35] Natural rights have been defined as: (1) Such rights as appertain originally and essentially to man, such as are inherent in his nature, and which he enjoys as a man, independent of any particular act on his side; also (2) Those which grow out of the nature of man and depend upon personality as distinguished from those created by law; also (3) Those rights which are innate, and which come from the very laws of nature, such as life, liberty, pursuit of happiness, and self preservation.[36] Natural rights, arising, if they do arise, from the nature of man or from the laws of nature, may be as indefinite as the law of nature which Bentham says is but a phrase to justify some individuals in their personal classification of what is right and what is wrong.[37] But Bentham's philosophy of utility, of pain and pleasure, had little if any influence upon the American thought which framed the Constitution and the first ten amendments. The Colonists had argued, petitioned and contended, and finally waged war, not for philosophic perfection of any utilitarian doctrine of rights, but for the rights of Englishmen. These rights were best expressed by and most familiar to the colonists in Blackstone's Commentaries, whether the work of that writer was a reliable guide to philosophic or historical jurisprudence or not.

According to Edmund Burke (Conciliation Speech, Mar. 22, 1776), nearly as many of Blackstone's Commentaries were sold in America as in England. It would not seem improbable that the natural and inherent rights of Englishmen listed by Blackstone and fought for in the War of Independence, are more exact statements of the rights set out in the Constitution and referred to under the Ninth Amendment, than any theoretical or philosophic classification by Bentham, Austin or any other critic, on whose opposition to the teaching of Blackstone the more modern school of jurisprudence seems based.[38] It has been held that:

> The first ten amendments were not meant to lay down any novel principles of government, but simply to embody certain guaran-

[35]12 C. J. Constitutional Law.

[36]45 C. J. 394, n.96.

[37]Bentham, Principles of Morals and Legislation, ch. II, sec. XV, n.6. *See* Bentham, Principles of Legislation 82 & 84.

[38]Hicks, Men and Books Famous in the Law 129.

tees and immunities, which we had inherited from our English ancestors, and which had been from time immemorial subject to well recognized exceptions.[38a]

Further it has been held that:

As the object of the first eight amendments to the Constitution was to incorporate into the fundamental law of the land certain principles of natural justice which had become permanently fixed in the jurisprudence of the mother country, the construction given to those principles by the English courts is cogent evidence of what they were designed to secure and the limitations that should be put upon them.[38b]

Blackstone[39] classifies the fundamental rights of Englishmen under three heads: (i) Personal Security, (ii) Personal Liberty, (iii) Private Property, with numerous subdivisions and refinements of and limitations of each classification and with certain subordinate rights. To these, Chancellor Kent adds, as a specific and characteristic contribution of American law, (iv) Religious Freedom.

By certain of the States the Constitution, like the Covenant of the League of Nations, was ratified with certain reservations, certain "impressions," certain suggestions.

With specified "impressions" Virginia ratified.[40] These "impressions" may be summarized as follows: that the powers granted under the Constitution, being derived from the people, may be resumed by them whenever perverted to their injury; that every power not therein granted remains in the people at their will; that no right of any denomination can be cancelled, abridged, restrained or modified except in the instances and for the purposes for which power is given; and that among other essentials, liberty of the press and of conscience cannot be abridged. And to the ratification by Virginia was added: "That there be a Declaration or Bill of Rights asserting and securing from encroachment the essential and unalienable rights of the people." This addition suggested that: "there are certain natural rights of which men, when they form a social compact cannot deprive or divest their posterity, among which are the enjoyment of life and liberty, with the means of acquiring,

---

[38a]Robertson v. Baldwin, 165 U.S. 281.

[38b]Brown v. Walker, 161 U.S. 600, 40 L. ed. 819.

[39]Blackstone's Commentaries, bk. 1, pp. 129–45.

[40]Formation of the Union 1027.

possessing and protecting property, and pursuing and obtaining happiness and safety," and further: "that the doctrine of non-resistance to arbitrary authority is absurd," and to these were added: no hereditary offices, separation of powers of government, free and frequent elections by general suffrage, no suspension of laws, jury trials with unanimous verdict, due process, jury trials in cases involving property or character, free complete and speedy justice, reasonable bail and punishment, freedom from unreasonable search and seizure, freedom of assembly, petition, press, religion, conscience, and to bear arms, and subjection of the military. The document reads like an excerpt from or summary of Blackstone on the subject of rights, or like a list of concessions demanded from a tyrant sovereign.

New York[41] ratified under similar reservations or "impressions," adding double jeopardy and habeas corpus to the list. The Bill of Rights suggested by South Carolina[42] followed closely that of Virginia as did also that of Rhode Island.[43] (See Formation of the Union.)

By this brief review of the reservations, if so they may be called, of these four states to their ratifications of the Constitution, it is not implied that their enumerations of rights have or had any binding force. They are reviewed solely to get some possible suggestion as to what the authors of the Ninth Amendment may have had in mind when the amendment was proposed, and what the people who ratified that amendment thought, and what the words, as a part of our basic law, now mean, if they now mean anything.

The proponents of the Constitution, as drawn up and submitted by the Convention, argued as against the objection of the lack of any Bill of Rights: (i) that all essential rights were already safeguarded by specific enumeration of many essential rights,[44] (ii) that the government created was one of enumerated powers only,[45] (iii) that a positive declaration of some essential rights could not be obtained with the requisite latitude,[46] (iv) that the jealousy of the

---

[41]*Id.* 1034.

[42]*Id.* 1044.

[43]*Id.* 1052.

[44]Federalist No. 84 (A. Hamilton); 3 Jefferson, Works 4, 13, & 101; 2 *id.* 329, 358.

[45]3 Jefferson, Works 4, 13, & 101; 2 *id.* 329, 358.

[46]*Id.*

states against encroachment of their own powers was a safeguard,[47] and (v) that the teachings of experience proved the inefficacy of a bill of rights.[48]

Hamilton,[49] in answering the advocates of a bill of rights, maintained that the Constitution did contain a number of provisions in favor of particular rights and privileges, but that

> a minute detail of particular rights is certainly far less applicable to a constitution like that under consideration, which is merely intended to regulate the general political interests of the nation, than to a constitution which has the regulation of every species of personal and private concerns.[50]

His contention was, further, that a bill of rights would be dangerous because, containing various exceptions to powers not granted, the exceptions would afford a colorable pretext to claim more powers than were granted.[51]

Jefferson[52] maintained that a constitutive act, which leaves some precious articles unnoticed, and raises implications against others, makes necessary a bill of rights by way of supplement; that if a sufficiently comprehensive declaration could not be formulated to secure all rights, nevertheless such as possible should be secured; that if the jealousy of states is to be a safeguard against encroachments of Federal power, a declaration of rights was needed upon which states could found their opposition; that the inconveniences, attending the limitations on government by bills of right which may cramp the government in its useful exertions, are short lived and reparable, while those inconveniences, resulting from the want of such a declaration of rights, are permanent and irreparable, moving from bad to worse. He adds:

> The executive, in our government, is not the sole, it is scarcely the principal, object of my jealousy. The tyranny of legislatures is

---

[47]Id.

[48]Federalist No. 84 (A. Hamilton); 3 Jefferson, Works 4, 13 & 101; 2 id. 329, 358.

[49]Federalist No. 84 (A. Hamilton).

[50]See Kohl v. U.S., 91 U.S., p. 372. Power of eminent domain held implied by the prohibition in the Fifth Amendment against taking private property for public use without compensation, although no express power of condemnation was granted under the Constitution. (The power was afterwards asserted as a necessary attribute of sovereignty.)

[51]Id.

[52]3 Jefferson Works 4, 13 & 101; 2 id. 329, 358.

the most formidable dread at present, and will be for many years. That of the executive will come in its turn; but it will be at some remote period.

Justice Joseph Story says that the real point for argument is "not whether a bill of rights is necessary, but what such a bill of rights should contain"; that a "bill of rights is important, and is often indispensable, whenever it operates as a qualification upon powers actually granted by the people to the government"; that a bill of rights may be important even when it goes beyond powers supposed to be granted because "it is not always possible to foresee the extent of the actual reach of certain powers which are given in general terms"; which "may be construed (and perhaps fairly) to certain classes of cases which did not at first appear to be within them." In such a case a "bill of rights, then, operates as a guard upon any extravagant or undue extension of such powers."[53]

> It requires more than ordinary hardihood and audacity of character to trample down principles which our ancestors have consecrated with reverence; which we have imbibed in our early education; which recommend themselves to the world by their truth and simplicity; and which are constantly placed before the eyes of the people, accompanied with the imposing force of constitutional sanction.[54]

Kent observes:

> The necessity of declaratory codes of rights has been frequently questioned, in as much as the government * * * is the creature of the people * * * and made responsible for maladministration. It may be observed, on the one hand, that no gross violation of those absolute rights which are clearly understood and settled by the common reason of mankind is to be apprehended in the ordinary course of public affairs; and as to extraordinary instances of faction and turbulence, and the corruption and violence which they necessarily engender, no parchment checks can be relied on as affording, under such circumstances, any effectual protection to public liberty. When the spirit of liberty has fled, and truth and justice are disregarded private rights can easily be sacrificed under the forms of law."[55]

[53] 2 Story on the Constitution 623–27.

[54] Id.

[55] 2 Kent's Commentaries (12 Ed.) 8. (Followed by unacknowledged excerpts from Story.)

Opposition to the adoption of the Constitution on the ground of the lack of a bill of rights was so general and so determined, that the advocates of adoption were forced to the argument that the means and method of amendment were readily available, and it was only by the assurance of the speedy adoption of amendments embodying a declaration of all essential rights, that the assent of the requisite number of states was obtained. It may reasonably be said that the adoption of the first ten amendments was a condition on the ratification of the Constitution.[56]

And the preamble to the joint resolution of Congress, submitting twelve amendments (including the first ten) to the states for ratification, recited:

> The conventions of a number of States having at the time of their adopting the Constitution expressed a desire, in order to prevent misconstruction or abuse of its powers, that further declaratory and restrictive clauses should be added. And as extending the ground of public confidences in the Government will best insure the beneficent ends of its institution. [1 Stat. L. 97.]

The advocates of a Bill of Rights prevailed, and the first ten amendments were adopted. The Ninth and Tenth Amendments seem to be designed to meet the Hamiltonian argument and to deny specifically any unmentioned grant of power or any unnamed surrender of rights[57]; and also to meet the objection mentioned by Jefferson[58] and to quiet the fear that a sufficiently broad and positive declaration could not be formulated to cover all essential rights.

Of the Ninth Amendment, Story[59] says:

> This clause was manifestly introduced to prevent any perverse or ingenious misapplication of the well known maxim, that an affirmation in particular cases implies a negation in all others; and, *e converso*, that a negation in particular cases implies an affirmation in all others [citing the Federalist No. 83]. The maxim, rightly understood, is perfectly sound and safe; but it has often been strangely forced from its natural meaning into the support of the most dangerous political heresies. The amendment was undoubt-

---

[56]O'Neil v. Vermont, 144 U.S. 370. 6 Am. & Eng. Enc. of Law 960.

[57]Formation of the Union 1052.

[58]3 Jefferson, Works 4, 13, & 101; 2 *id*. 329, 358.

[59]2 Story on the Constitution 623–27.

edly suggested by the reasoning of the Federalist on the subject of a general bill of rights [citing the Federalist No. 84].

Story further says:

> In regard to another suggestion, that the affirmance of certain rights might disparage others, or might lead to argumentative implications in favor of other powers, it might be sufficient to say that such a course of reasoning could never be sustained upon any solid basis; and it could never furnish any just ground of objection that ingenuity might pervert or usurpation overleap the true sense. That objection will equally lie against all powers, whether large or limited, whether national or state, whether in a bill of rights or in a frame of government. But a conclusive answer is, that such an attempt may be interdicted (as it has been) by a positive declaration in such a bill of rights, that the enumeration of certain rights shall not be construed to deny or disparage others retained by the people.[60]

There seems to be no case that decides the scope of the Ninth Amendment even in part. In decisions where it is mentioned, it is either grouped with the Tenth Amendment in decisions based upon or involving the latter, and hence concerning reservation or denial of power, or it is merely classified as one of the first ten which are held to be limitations on national and not on state power. No case has been found that uses the Ninth Amendment as the basis for the assertion or vindication of a right.

Yet the Ninth Amendment concerns rights and every word in the Constitution has meaning.

The paucity of judicial decision on the meaning and effect of the provision here considered may result from a number of causes. (1) All essential human rights may have been covered by the express declarations of right in the original Constitution or in the other amendments. (2) All essential human rights, not enumerated, may be covered by the limits of or limitations upon the express and implied grant of powers. (3) Any additional rights thought to have been protected thereby may have been covered by judicial construction and extension of expressly enumerated rights, especially those under the Fifth Amendment, to cover not only the general classifications of rights catalogued by the great commentators, but also all proper subdivisions and refinements thereof. (4) Other rights

[60]2 Story on the Constitution 626, sec. 1867.

may exist which have not heretofore been invaded, or which have not heretofore been vindicated by the ingenuity of the legal profession or the discernment of the courts. (5) Rights not expressly enumerated may have been extinguished by long acquiescence of the people in legislative extension of Federal power or by judicial decisions on the extent of power.

A survey of decided cases concerning the specifically enumerated rights leads to the conclusion that most general rights, if not each variation or refinement thereof, listed by English and American commentators, as well as rights discussed in connection with the adoption of the Constitution and amendments, have been considered by the courts and, in a proper case, vindicated. Judicial decisions on the limits of or the limitations on granted powers have resulted in the vindication of rights. Decisions on due process have resulted in the words life, liberty and property being expanded to such a degree, especially as to property, that they seem to include much, if not all of that, which is included under the usual general classifications of rights.

The general, undefined, and illusive right "to the pursuit of happiness," the elemental right of self preservation, and the general statement in the Virginian "reservations" as to the right to the "means of acquiring, possessing and protecting property and obtaining happiness and safety," insofar as they are rights, and insofar as they contain elements not embraced within the enumerated rights, may be protected by the Ninth Amendment. The right of privacy may contain essentials beyond the prohibitions of the Fourth Amendment against unreasonable search and seizure, and as to such essentials may come within the category of unenumerated rights. In other words, there may be a right to freedom from persecution and annoyance by those temporarily intrusted with power, when no fraud, concealment or wrong doing is shown, as was recently held by the Circuit Court of the Third Circuit, which ruled that a second investigation into the business transactions of individuals, after the lapse of three years, for no other apparent cause than the order of superior officers, constituted not only a violation of the prohibition against unlawful search and seizure, but was also "a violation of the natural law of privacy in one's own affairs which exists in liberty loving people and nations, no right being more vital to 'liberty and pursuit of happiness' than the protection of a citizen's private affairs, their right to be let alone."

Property is directly mentioned three times in the Constitution—twice in the Fifth and once in the Fourteenth Amendment. Most of the other provisions which declare rights or set limitations on power are concerned with personal rights as distinguished from property rights. This fact should be remembered when criticism is made that the Constitution exalts property above human rights. The document was drawn by men of substance, and both it and its amendments ratified by conventions or by legislatures elected for the most part by limited suffrage, and yet the fundamental declaration of law has little of property in it. Can it be that rights in property, its use, enjoyment, ownership—all the attributes of private ownership—were expected as being so fundamental as to need no safeguard beyond the limits of or limitations on power, or beyond the Fifth Amendment? Or was the Ninth Amendment designed to cover axiomatic rights to property as well as any unmentioned but axiomatic personal rights?

Rights, more or less abstract rights, may exist in having the government discharge its governmental function and also in having the government refrain from undertakings outside of the sphere of governmental authority. Such rights may be abstract rights because of the limits on the judicial function, which depends on the proper presentation of a justiciable issue, and the assertion of right by one having a substantial or ascertainable interest therein. Thus the right to challenge a questionable appropriation has been denied to a State as the representatives of its citizens and to one who could show no specific interest in the fund appropriated,[61] but has been granted where a specific and direct interest could be shown.[62]

The Ninth Amendment (as well as the Tenth) was invoked by the petitioners in the recent T.V.A. case, and the Court there held that the "Ninth Amendment, insuring the rights retained by the people, does not withdraw the *rights* which are expressly granted to the federal government." Under this case, as defined and limited by the Court, the exercise of governmental powers (to the extent) considered by the decision, did not violate any unenumerated right. The right of the government to use its almost limitless power to tax, and its constitutional right to spend, to compete with its citizens has not been settled. The power to tax and destroy has been long established. The power to spend and destroy has not.

[61]Massachusetts v. Mellon, 262 U.S. 447.
[62]United States v. Butler, 80 L. ed. 287.

The Fifth Amendment enumerates rights to which each great substantive power of Congress is subject.[63] Is this true, in a proper case, of each enumerated right? And are unenumerated rights weaker because unnamed? A right that yields to the exercise of authorized power, express or implied, is no right.

The legislative and the executive, throughout our history, have been, in the main, as zealous as the courts in their respect and regard of individual rights, and, as a consequence, courts, passing only on litigated matters of right, and binding themselves to resolve every reasonable intendment in favor of the constitutionality of the acts of a co-ordinate branch of government—have seldom been under the necessity of exercising the power of judgment to vindicate reserved rights, and have, doubtless, hesitated to raise up out of the past and to define any unenumerated right.

Yet the Ninth Amendment is not meaningless or superfluous. Surely it is more than a mere negative on implied grants of power that might otherwise be asserted because of the express enumeration of rights in respect of matters where no power was granted. It must be more than a mere net to catch fish in supposedly fishless water. It is certainly more than a mere emphasis on the doctrine of delegated and enumerated powers. It must be a positive declaration of existing, though unnamed rights, which may be vindicated under the authority of the amendment whenever and if ever any governmental authority shall aspire to ungranted power in contravention of "unenumerated rights."

---

[63]Louisville Joint Stock Land Bank v. Radford, 295 U.S. 587, 589. 79 L. ed. 1593, 1604.

4. The Forgotten Ninth Amendment

Bennett B. Patterson

Obvious Meaning of the Ninth Amendment

There should really be little or no doubt with respect to the intended meaning of the Ninth Amendment, because from its language, its purpose and intent are obvious.

The Ninth Amendment to the Constitution is a basic statement of the inherent natural rights of the individual. On its face this amendment states that there are certain unenumerated rights that are retained by the people. It is a mere assertion that while certain enumerated rights have been expressly protected by the Constitution, the reservation in the Constitution should not be taken to deny or disparage any unenumerated right which was not so apparently protected. Nothing could be clearer than this statement. It is a declaration and recognition of individualism and inherent right, and such a declaration is nowhere else to be found in the Constitution. Its absence elsewhere in the Constitution accounts for its very presence in this amendment.

The concept of individual sovereignty and supremacy in the realm of natural and inherent rights and liberties was not a creature of the Constitution of the United States. This basic concept of individual liberty was absolute in the theory of American Government from the very beginning of American Government. This theory was carried over from the English Constitution, and as we have remarked before, the framers of the Constitution and the signers of the Declaration of Independence were Englishmen by blood, tradition, and citizenship until the signing of the Declaration of Independence. Therefore, the framers of the Constitution and the Bill of Rights carried with them into their work the English concept of individual liberties, as being inherent in the individual

Excerpted from *The Forgotten Ninth Amendment* (Indianapolis: Bobbs-Merrill, 1955), pp. 19–26, 36–44, 51–56.

irrespective of the form of government. The last thought in their minds was that the Constitution would ever be construed as a grant to the individual of inherent rights and liberties. Their theory of the Constitution was that it was only a body of powers which were granted to the government, and nothing more than that.

It might be said that the theory of individual inherent rights is a part of our unwritten Constitution, in the same manner in which portions of the unwritten English Constitution are recognized and enforced. But we feel that it is much more than the unwritten Constitution; the individual inherent rights and liberties antedate and are above constitutions and may be called pre-constitutional rights.

This idea has been aptly expressed in 16 C. J. S. page 578, paragraph 199, as follows:

> The Constitutions are not the sources of our personal rights. Our theory of government is that the people, in full possession of inherent, inalienable rights, have formed the government in order to protect these rights, and have incorporated them into the organic law as a shield against unwarrantable interference by any department of governments.

John Adams, the second great President of the United States, assured the people as follows: "You have rights antecedent to all earthly governments: rights that cannot be repealed or restrained by human laws; rights derived from the Great Legislator of the Universe."

. . .

As great as is our reverence, gratitude, and respect for the Constitution of the United States, the undoubted and fundamental belief of the people of the United States in the security of their individual liberties existed long before the Constitution of the United States was ever thought of. The doctrine of individual liberty was championed in the great liberty documents which preceded the Constitution by many years. The Virginia Resolutions, the various declarations adopted by the other colonies, and the addresses and orations of patriots like Patrick Henry proved without doubt their pre-constitutional belief in individual rights.

This philosophy of government was summarized in the preamble to the Declaration of Independence:

> When, in the course of human events, it becomes necessary for one people to dissolve the political bonds which have connected

them with another, and to assume among the powers of the earth the separate and equal station *to which the laws of nature and of nature's God entitle them*, a decent respect to the opinions of mankind requires that they should declare the causes which impel them to the separation.

> We hold these truths to be self-evident: That all men are created equal; that they are endowed by their Creator with certain unalienable rights; that *among these* are life, liberty, and the pursuit of happiness [emphasis added].

This statement closely followed the Virginia Bill of Rights adopted by the convention of delegates on June 12, 1776. Article 1 of that document states:

> That all Men are by Nature equally free and independent, and have certain inherent Rights, of which, when they enter into a State of Society, they cannot, by any Compact, deprive or divest their Posterity; namely, the Enjoyment of Life and Liberty, with the Means of acquiring and possessing Property, and pursuing and obtaining Happiness and Safety.

We particularly note that the Declaration of Independence was careful to state that liberties and human rights were not man made. The source of human liberty was not government. The source of individual liberty as stated by the Declaration of Independence is the "Creator" of men. The Declaration of Independence is not only a philosophic document but it is also a legal document. May the day soon come when our courts, in the vindication of individual liberties, will cite the Declaration of Independence as legal authority for the doctrine that individual liberty is natural and inherent, instead of attempting to show that these rights stem from the Constitution of the United States, which was never intended to be anything other than the protector of these rights, and not the creator of them.

The Declaration of Independence was a forerunner of the Ninth Amendment. Note how carefully the words "among these" are used in the enumeration of any human rights.

The only published treatise or legal discussion relating to the Ninth Amendment is found in a brilliant article by the Honorable Knowlton H. Kelsey in Volume 11, No. 4, page 309, of the Indiana Law Journal (1936), in which he states that the colonists waged war, "not for philosophic perfection of any utilitarian doctrine of rights, but for the rights of Englishmen."

Then we see that the Ninth Amendment is nothing new in principle, but is merely a restatement of the old.

Basically a right as referred to in the Ninth Amendment is not a right at all unless it is recognized any time, any place, and anywhere.

The real meaning and substance of the Ninth Amendment to the Constitution of the United States has been lost through an erroneous classification of this amendment in the earlier decisions by the Supreme Court of the United States, as a limitation upon the powers of the Federal Government, and not upon the States.

Typical of these decisions is Fox vs. State of Ohio, 12 L. Ed. 213, 5 How. 410, in which the Court stated the following:

> The prohibition alluded to as contained in the amendments to the Constitution, as well as others with which it is associated in those articles, were not designed as limits upon the State governments in reference to their own citizens. They are exclusively restrictions upon federal power, intended to prevent interference with the rights of the States, and of their citizens. Such has been the interpretation given to those amendments by this court, in the case of Barron v. The Mayor and City Council of Baltimore [7 Peters 243].

In sweeping declarations of this type, our Courts have failed to recognize a distinction between the first eight amendments included in the Bill of Rights, and the Ninth Amendment. It is quite true that the first eight amendments to the Constitution were intended as restrictions upon the powers of the Federal Government, arising out of a distrust of the several States of a strong centralized and Federal Government. A careful analysis of the Ninth Amendment will reveal that the Ninth Amendment cannot be classified as a restrictive clause at all, because it is on the contrary a great declaration of the rights of natural endowment.

Irrespective of such decisions as Fox vs. Ohio, *supra*, and the general language contained therein with respect to a general grouping of the first ten amendments to the Constitution as restrictive inhibitions upon the National Government, there has been no specific decision by any Court in the United States that forecloses the utility of further research and study as to the real intent and meaning of this amendment. The rule of stare decisis has not closed the door to the results of research, or to the proper construction of this amendment.

It is not strange that it has never been used as the basis for the vindication of any basic human liberty, because under the cloud of its classification as a restrictive clause, it can have no reasonable meaning whatsoever. Under such construction, this amendment could only mean that "the Federal Government is restricted from denying or disparaging any unenumerated human rights, but the power to deny and disparage such rights is reserved to the States." It is no criticism of the Supreme Court of the United States that the Ninth Amendment has not been construed. The question has simply never been presented to that Court for review. As we shall later see, the Supreme Court of the United States has in its decisions recognized a difference between the first eight amendments and the Ninth.

The failure to discover the real meaning of the Ninth Amendment is probably due to a mechanical error or misstatement in the early case of Lessee of Livingston vs. Moore et al., 7 Peters 469, 8 L. Ed. 751 (781). In that case, the Constitutional question that was before the Court was the right of trial by jury. In the decision of this case, the Court stated that the legislative acts under consideration were charged with being contrary to the Ninth Article of the amendments of the Constitution of the United States. The Supreme Court over-ruled this contention, holding that it was then settled law "that those amendments do not extend to the States." A careful study of this decision reveals that the Ninth Amendment to the Constitution was not discussed either by counsel or by the Court. The question involved was solely the right of trial by jury, covered by the Seventh Amendment.

This view is best stated in Constitution of the United States of America revised and annotated (1938), page 711, which is the compilation and revision which was authorized by Senate Concurrent Resolution No. 35, adopted May 14, 1936. The volume was compiled in the Legislative Reference Service of the Library of Congress and published by the United States Printing Office. We quote the only annotation of this amendment contained in this volume as follows:

> This amendment is in terms referred to as a ground of the argu-ment in Livingston v. Moore, 7 Pet. 469, 551 (1833), and the Court meets the argument with a general statement that "the amend-ments of the Constitution" do not extend to the States. But the context shows clearly that the reference intended was the Seventh Amendment. The whole sentence involved is as follows: "They (certain laws of Pennsylvania) are charged with being contrary to

the ninth article of the amendments of the Constitution of the United States, and the sixth section of the Pennsylvania bill of rights, securing the trial by jury." The argument of Mr. Ingersoll (p. 482) specifically makes the point to "* * * the Seventh Amendment of the Constitution of the United States." The discrepancy is doubtless to be explained by the fact that numbers 1 and 2 of the 12 amendments proposed for adoption in 1789 were never ratified, and consequently number 9 became number 7 of the amendments adopted. A similar example of reference to an amendment by its number among the proposed amendments rather than among those adopted, may be seen in Re Burford, 3 Cr. 448, 451 (1806), where counsel referred to the "Sixth Article" relating to issue of warrants, i.e., Amendment 4.

It might further be stated that there is no provision in the Constitution which sets a definite date for ratification of amendments which are submitted to the several States. There was no such practice at that time as now prevails of fixing a limit of seven years, or some other definite period in which the States shall ratify a proposed constitutional amendment. Therefore, when the case of Livingston vs. Moore was decided, the first and second proposed amendments were technically still pending for ratification by the States, since there was no deadline for ratification. The amendments at that time were therefore referred to only as "amendments," and had not at that time been by accepted usage called the "Bill of Rights." This explains why the Court was in all probability referring to the Seventh Amendment to the Constitution, numbered in accordance with their adoption by the States, while referring to it in their opinion as the ninth article of amendment, or ninth proposal. This matter has been detailed in order that it may definitely be established that the case of Livingston vs. Moore is not to be considered or construed as a decision by the Supreme Court of the United States definitely and finally classifying the Ninth Amendment solely as a restriction upon the Federal Government similar to the classification of the first eight amendments to the Constitution. However, this decision has been sufficient to create doubt and confusion. Just how much influence this decision has had upon the subsequent decisions of the Supreme Court in grouping all of the ten amendments together in this respect is not known. However, it is certain that when broad statements with respect to the restrictive nature of the first ten amendments appear in the decisions of the Supreme Court of the United States, the case of Livingston vs. Moore has been usually cited as authority.

We hope that some day our courts, when called upon to do so, in the vindication of one of the unenumerated rights, will find or rediscover the Ninth Amendment with the full force of its meaning. It is now covered with the "dust of antique time," but it is hoped that the dust may be swept away and the cloud removed, and that the "mountainous error" has not been piled so high that "truth cannot o'er peer it."

We will ultimately find that this amendment is a succinct expression of the inherent dignity and liberty of the individual and a recognition of the soul of mankind, a belief in his spiritual nature, and an humble acknowledgement of the infinity of our Creator and our nature.

We do not find an expression of this philosophy in any portion of the Constitution. "We, the people" is not an expression of individual rights as much as it is an expression of the collective sovereignty of the people in matters of government.

It is not found in the due process clauses, because the rights protected under due process are not protected because such rights are natural rights, but because they are expressly protected by the Constitution.

How unfortunate it is that with this fundamental expression in our Constitution and in the Declaration of Independence, no occasion has ever been found for any court in the United States to ever utilize the Ninth Amendment or the Declaration of Independence as the basis for the vindication of natural and inherent liberty. Is there such a thing, or do our rights arise out of the Constitution? . . .

The Ninth Amendment Is Applicable to State Governments

From a legal and from a historic viewpoint we must not confuse the underlying meaning and intent of the Ninth Amendment with the reason for its inclusion in the Bill of Rights.

We have seen that long before its inclusion in the Constitution, it was a basic and underlying philosophy of life.

It is true that this amendment was among the first that were added to the Constitution, and the reason for its inclusion was because of the fear of the people of a strong national government. But, it is fallacious and illogical to insist that by expressly protecting our liberties from the force of the Federal Government, the same liberties would not be protected from the force of State governments. Irrespective of whether this provision was included in the original Constitution, in the amendments, or whether it was omitted entirely, its great principle has always existed, and always will exist as long as there is human life. We must not discount or limit its meaning because of the circumstances which made it a part of the Constitution.

We have a choice of the theory of liberty and rights by natural endowment as announced in the Declaration of Independence, and again in the Ninth Amendment, and in the other liberty documents, or we have the choice of the theory that all of our inherent and fundamental rights were surrendered to State governments and that the governments of the States are the creators of our rights and liberties. We are forced to the position that the States, and the States alone, with forty-eight possible divergent views, have the power and the sole power to define and protect our native human liberties and rights. We believe that no such idea was ever intended. It is impossible to believe that human rights and individual liberties were wrung from tyrants and despots through suffering, sacrifice and death, and announced in the Declaration of Independence and in other liberty documents, only to be surrendered up to State governments where they could be destroyed by the sovereign people acting en masse, or by a tyranny acting in the name of the people of the several States. The power to destroy or define negatives the idea of natural human rights.

However, the following reasons definitely established that the Ninth Amendment was not intended solely as a restrictive inhibition against the National Government, but as a great declaration of the liberty of mankind:

(1) Opinions of the Supreme Court of the United States beginning with Eilenbecker vs. District Court of Plymouth County, Iowa, 134 U.S. 131, 33 L. Ed. 801, definitely show that only the first eight amendments to the Constitution were intended to be narrowly construed as inhibitions upon the National Government. Since the decision of this case in 1890, the Supreme Court of the United States has abandoned the dust-covered dictum that the first ten amendments to the Constitution were intended as restrictions upon the National Government, and now holds that only the first eight amendments were so intended. Since the decision of the Eilenbecker case, there has been no decision of the Supreme Court of the United States and no dictum which has adhered to the old text. The mechanical error in the case of Livingston vs. Moore definitely

establishes that it is no precedent or authority for the narrow construction of the Ninth Amendment.

Therefore, the Ninth Amendment is unshackled from its early erroneous classification and the cloud has been removed, and it is now ready for use any time our courts or our people may discover an unenumerated human right.

(2) Our constitutions are not the sources of our liberties. In Calder vs. Bull, 3 Dallas 386, 1 L. Ed. 648, and in Savings and Loan Association vs. Topeka, 87 U.S. 686, 22 L. Ed. 455, cited also in the next succeeding chapter, the Supreme Court of the United States has recognized the doctrine of inherent human rights which are entitled to protection against the legislative acts of the several States, even though such rights may be unenumerated in the Constitution of the United States. These cases proceed upon the theory that there are rights in every free government which are beyond the control of State governments. These cases recognized the doctrine of the implied reservation of individual rights. This is the doctrine of the Ninth Amendment. Although the decision of Calder vs. Bull has been questioned, these cases have been cited many times with approval, and we do not find any decision which has overruled or distinguished the holding in these cases.

These decisions can be construed in no other way except to establish that inherent rights, whether enumerated in the Constitution of the United States or not, are entitled to protection, not only against the Federal Government, but also as against the governments of the several States.

(3) The debates in the Constitutional Convention, and in the First Congress which drew the amendments for submission, and the entire historic background established that the rights of natural endowment were intended to be universal and entitled to protection against all governments, either State or National.

There is nothing in the historic background of the Bill of Rights that even remotely suggests that these liberties were to be protected from abuse by the Federal Government only, but that such rights would be surrendered to the governments of the several States without protection. The entire historic background definitely establishes that our forefathers were merely, through an abundance of caution, protecting their rights against the powers of a strong National Government. There is no suggestion anywhere in any historical document that we have been able to find, that could constitute the slightest indication of the abandonment of their liberties to the control of State governments. On the other hand, they felt that their individual liberties were safe at the hands of a State government, whether expressly enumerated in State constitutions or not. This thought is forcibly emphasized in a statement made by Mr. Jackson, the Representative from Georgia, in a debate on the floor of Congress on June 8, 1789, in which he opposed the addition of the Bill of Rights as being "dangerous, improper and unnecessary," and in this debate he made the following statement:

> But do gentlemen suppose bills of rights necessary to secure liberty? If they do, let them look at New York, New Jersey, Virginia, South Carolina and Georgia. Those States have no bills of rights, and is the liberty of the citizens less safe in those States, than in the other of the United States? I believe it is not.

Mr. Jackson made the same argument that was made by Alexander Hamilton in The Federalist. They both feared that by enumerating our present liberties, there would be a disparagement of those liberties not enumerated. Their fears will certainly have been duly justified if the enumeration of certain inherent rights should be construed not only as a disparagement of other enumerated rights, but also construed in such a manner as to strip the individual of inherent rights in so far as State governments are concerned.

If this erroneous construction should prevail, the necessary result is that inherent rights are recognized by neither our National or our State governments unless they are expressly enumerated and spelled out in both the Federal and State Constitutions. This means, then, that men have no inherent rights and that all of our rights are granted to us by the State. This, of course, was never intended. We might add at this point that our country is the strong advocate of human dignity and human liberty in the family of nations throughout the earth. Can it be possible that we advocate such natural liberty for others, yet enjoy no such natural liberties ourselves?

(4) The Ninth Amendment as a part of the Constitution must be given some meaning. This construction is the only logical construction that could be given it. Any other construction as an inhibition against the National Government would only lead to an untenable conclusion. Such a construction would mean that the several States reserve to themselves the right to deny and disparage natural rights. This, of course, could not have been the intention of the First Congress.

The meaning which we urge is the only reasonable construction that could be given to this amendment. (5) The very language of the amendment negatives such a narrow construction. The words "the enumeration *in the Constitution*" definitely show that the language was language of general import, as applied generally to the Constitution, instead of special import and restricted only to the first ten amendments. If a narrower construction had been intended, the amendment would have read "the enumeration *in these amendments*."

We bear in mind the fact that the body of the Constitution spelled out and protected a number of other basic individual rights. It would therefore be unreasonable to hold that this amendment related only to the rights enumerated in amendments one to eight in the Bill of Rights and did not relate to the other individual rights protected in the body of the Constitution. If it is contended that the Ninth Amendment was required as a safeguard against the infringement of the rights enumerated in the first eight amendments only, it would seem strange that no such safeguard should be thrown around the enumeration of other individual rights protected in the body of the Constitution.

Therefore, its provisions can only be construed as a broad declaration relating to the Constitution as a whole, and it certainly cannot be construed as a narrow limitation to be considered only in connection with the first ten amendments to the Constitution.

(6) The historic legislative background of the amendment shows definitely that Madison, who was the father of both the Constitution and the Bill of Rights, and the particular author of the Ninth Amendment, never intended that it should ever be so narrowly restricted. Without repetition of its historic background, the fact that his original draft included the language "here or elsewhere in the Constitution," coupled with the fact that Madison never intended that the amendments to the Constitution would appear as an appendage thereto, definitely proves that this amendment was always intended to be a broad declaration relating to the Constitution as a whole without any narrow or restricted construction.

(7) The preamble to the twelve proposed articles of amendment which states that "further declaratory and restrictive clauses should be added," definitely shows that of the twelve amendments submitted for ratification, some were considered by the Congress of the United States and particularly the Senate, as being broad declarations rather than restrictive inhibitions. The first and second

proposed amendments relating to per capita representation and salaries of government officers, certainly could not be classified under this language as "declaratory" clauses. Undoubtedly the Senate and the House of Representatives realized the distinction between the first eight amendments to the Constitution, and Amendments Nine and Ten as ultimately adopted. This introductory clause, which seldom if ever appears on the conventional printing of the Bill of Rights, but which does appear upon the original in the archives of the Library of Congress, is very convincing.

(8) However, we do not need the preamble to immediately recognize the difference between the first eight amendments and the Ninth and Tenth Amendments. The first eight amendments are negative in their statements and of course can be classified no other way than with a restrictive intent.

No stretch of the imagination could ever convert a broad declaration of human liberty into any kind of a restriction. It can only be classed as a declaration.

(9) The broad and historic concept of human rights and human liberty establishes such unenumerated rights as pre-constitutional rights, and such rights were not abridged by the Constitution of the United States, or any State constitution, or any power, Government or person whomsoever.

We either believe in inherent human rights, or we do not believe in them; if we believe in such inherent rights, then such rights must be protected against the unwarranted power of either the National or the State Governments, otherwise they fail and cannot be classed as an inherent right at all.

We would like to suggest as a basis for further study that the chief difficulty surrounding the subject of this chapter arises out of the fact that in the colonial days, and under State governments as they existed prior to the adoption of the Constitution, each State had its own method of jury trial and criminal procedure. Each State regarded jury trial, particularly in criminal cases, as an inherent right. As was pointed out in the letter from Washington to Lafayette heretofore quoted,[1] the framers of the Federal Constitution thought

---

[1]"For example: there was not a member of the convention, I believe, who had the least objection to what is contended for by the Advocates of a Bill of Rights and Tryal by Jury. The first, where the people evidently retained everything which they did not in express terms give up, was considered nugatory as you will find to have been more fully explained by Mr. Wilson and others:—And as to the second, it was

of jury trial as a consideration separate and apart from a Bill of Rights. They desired to leave to the several States their respective methods of jury trial and criminal procedure. There was no thought in their minds that by closing the draft of the Constitution without including a provision guaranteeing jury trial, the several States would be justified in refusing jury trial. It would have been difficult, however, to have included any provision with respect to the manner in which jury trial should be conducted, because the procedure in each of the States was different.

These circumstances may throw some light upon which of the rights enumerated in the first eight amendments to the Constitution shall be classified as fundamental rights and which shall not be so classified.

There is another consideration which is worthy of careful thought. There is no provision in the Constitution which shall prevent the Government of the United States from protecting inherent rights. There is only a restraint upon their impairment or denial by the Federal Government. We believe that there could be no constitutional objection to any national legislation enacted for the purpose of the protection of natural rights.

We feel that American liberties are no less safe in the hands of those who administer the Federal Government than those who administer State Government.

There is no danger in the destruction of our individual liberties through either State or Federal Government, except the danger that exists in the quality of statesmanship of the men who administer both. However, whatever may be the complaints against the administration of a strong centralized national government, the historical fact stands that since 1789 the Federal Government, and in particular the Supreme Court of the United States, has been the greatest champion of individual liberties. We shudder to think what might have been the result if our human liberties had been left to final determination by the courts of forty-eight states. The undisputed truth is that in practically all important instances where human rights have been denied, it has been at the hands of the government of a State or its inferior subdivisions. It is to be expected that more

---

only the difficulty of establishing a mode which should not interfere with the fixed modes of any of the States, that induced the Convention to leave it, as a matter of future adjustment."—ED.

cases would arise out of State action because there are forty-eight more chances for this to occur. However, there have been very few incidents in which it could even be claimed that the Supreme Court of the United States has imposed upon the fundamental liberties of individuals. There is no logical reason why State governments and those who administer State governments are superior either in mentality or integrity to those who administer our National Government. If we have poor administrators in either branch of our government, the fault does not lie so much in the men whom we have chosen to administer, but in ourselves, and in our lack of morale and patriotism.

We believe that in the one hundred and sixty and more years of the history of our Federal Government, the quality of statesmanship of Federal officers has been on the whole of a higher character than those who administer State governments.

However, there is nothing in the Constitution of the United States that gives the Federal Government the right or power to destroy human liberties. There is nothing and should be nothing in any power reserved to the States that gives the States the right to destroy such liberties, and such power was never intended.

What Are the Unenumerated Rights?

In order that this entire treatise may not be purely academic, and in order that it may have present practical value and purpose, it must be shown that there are unenumerated inherent rights. Since we are without definite legal precedent as a guide, and since rights appear only gradually in the evolution of the human race, and are incapable of classification under any fixed or steadfast rule, the task of presenting the existence of the unenumerated rights is the most difficult chapter to write.

Before beginning the discussion, however, it is believed that if recognition is given to the Ninth Amendment, and it is recognized as announcing a living and vital philosophy, a use will be found for this amendment, and that hereafter it will be given the opportunity to function under the guidance of stable but spiritual intellect as the course of history shall unfold.

Needless to say, it is our belief that the unenumerated rights permit of no exact definition. To attempt to define these rights would be contrary to the obvious intent and meaning of the amendment.

. . .

But we shall try to illustrate the unenumerated rights with some supposed examples. The governors of two States in recent years have threatened that they intended to procure the enactment of statutes controlling newspaper publicity and criticism of executive officers. Such statutes would be construed to be in violation of the Fourteenth Amendment by the incorporation of the First Amendment therein. But such a statute would also be void under the Ninth Amendment. This is true because it is an inherent human right and is one of the basic requirements for the existence of a free people. Such a right is a part of the British Constitution, and is an inherent right of the English people, although such a right is unenumerated in any portion of the British Constitution, and there is not one written word which protects the freedom of the press. Freedom of the press has been recognized as an inherent right protected under the Fourteenth Amendment by the Supreme Court of the United States, but it is also such an inherent right as should be protected under the Ninth Amendment.

Suppose, for instance, that a State should pass an act abolishing jury trial in criminal cases. We believe that such a statute would be void under the Ninth Amendment as destroying an inherent human right. While no effort has been made on the part of the Federal Government to determine the method of jury trial and criminal procedure to be employed by the several States, because the framers of the Constitution preferred to leave the States to the various modes which they had used at the time of the adoption of the Constitution, nevertheless there is no decision which can be construed to uphold the abolition of jury trial in criminal cases.

Suppose a legislature of a State should pass an act fixing punishment of certain crimes by death, and declaring that the means of execution should be inhuman and torturous, such as gradual mutilation of the body, burial alive, or some other form of cruel punishment. Do we have any doubt but that the Supreme Court of the United States would declare such a statute to be void?

Suppose that some of the States should enact statutes providing for imprisonment for ordinary debt and reestablish the old debtor's prison. There is no guarantee in the Constitution which prohibits imprisonment for debt. In fact, at the time of the adoption of the Constitution this practice prevailed under the statutes of several of the States. To the great shame of the American people, Robert Morris, who was the principal donor of money to finance the American Revolution, and who was a member of the Constitutional

Convention, died in a debtor's prison. We believe that this form of punishment is no longer a part of the American concept of morality or justice, and that our Supreme Court would quickly declare unconstitutional any statute enacted by either the Federal or a State Government which provided for imprisonment for ordinary debt at this time.

At the time of the adoption of the Constitution it was common practice in several of the States that a person convicted of crime should be branded with a branding iron as an outward proof of his iniquity. No court would tolerate such a practice at this time, even though it was not considered cruel and unusual punishment at the time of the adoption of the Constitution.

At the time of the founding of this Government, there was still wide-spread belief in witchcraft, and statutes of some of the States punished its practice. After a hundred and sixty-five years of enlightment, would we now tolerate the punishment of any individual for witchcraft?

These examples are hypothetical. However, the Supreme Court of the United States in Calder vs. Bull and in Savings and Loan Association vs. Topeka have given some other examples of what the unenumerated rights may be.

We believe that the Ninth Amendment was intended to protect the unenumerated rights, not only as they have now appeared, but also as such rights may appear as history and the future shall unfold. As the race becomes more evolved, and as the respect for the dignity of human life increases; as we become more intelligent and spiritual human beings, then we shall learn more of the fundamental truths about human nature.

In my research I have discovered only one treatise on the subject of the Ninth Amendment to the Federal Constitution. This is a learned and scholarly discussion by Honorable Knowlton H. Kelsey published in the Indiana Law Journal in April 1936, entitled "The Ninth Amendment to the Federal Constitution." This author points out that while the human liberties enumerated in the Constitution are imposing, nevertheless they do not exhaust the list of human rights. He urges that the Ninth Amendment was never intended as a mere Mother Hubbard clause which is usually contained in a bill of sale specifying "all articles too numerous to mention on the improbable chance that something worthwhile may have been forgotten." He further urges that no word can be unnecessarily rejected as superfluous and meaningless, and that the Ninth Amendment does have some meaning.

Mr. Kelsey further aptly points out that the American Revolution was not a doctrinary war, or a war for "philosophic perfection of any utilitarian doctrine of rights, but for the rights of Englishmen." He points out that these rights were best expressed in Blackstone's Commentaries, and carefully analyzes the natural rights of men as set out in Blackstone's Commentaries and recommends this authority as a study for their definition.

However, it is our belief that the philosophy of the Ninth Amendment is a living and growing philosophy. It was intended to be so in the same manner that the Magna Charta was intended and has been interpreted as part of a living and growing Constitution. The Magna Charta has not been restricted by English law to the rights of Englishmen as they existed in 1215 on the field at Runnymede. In the same manner the natural rights of Americans should not be static and fixed as of the date of the adoption of the Constitution and the Bill of Rights. To interpret the Ninth Amendment in this manner would take it out of its clearly intended meaning. Such an interpretation would mean that there was a cutoff date at the time of the adoption of the Bill of Rights; that prior to that date rights of natural endowment were recognized, but after said date only such rights as were enumerated or known to exist would be protected. This interpretation destroys the distinction between "enumerated" and "unenumerated," and restricts its meaning to be read as "such enumerated rights as are now known to exist."

We can only see from the stream of history that human rights are the product of the growth of civilization. It was never intended that civilization in other phases of life should progress, but that human liberty and rights of natural endowment can only be defined as they existed almost two centuries ago, and that however apparent such a right may become in the light of current history, such a natural right could never be recognized except by a statute or constitutional amendment. We do not believe that it was ever intended that the science of the law should become so fixed and archaic, while all other sciences may go forward in the discovery of truth and may utilize it wherever it is found. We should not attempt to harness our rights to a civilization as it existed one hundred and sixty-five years ago, and it was not the intention of the framers of the Bill of Rights that we should do so.

The law is necessarily built upon retrospect and is founded upon tradition. It is difficult for such a science to keep abreast and maintain progress with other business and professions. We have been, more or less, unjustly compared to the crab who never looks where he is going but only wants to see where he has been. There are those who urge that this is a weakness of the system of the English common law, and that in an expanding world of business and commerce in the machine age, we must ultimately come to a system of codification or a system of justice which is more visibly defined and executed.

With this view we do not agree, but we believe that although the demands of a fast moving, business commercial world require a large degree of codification and visible certainty, and the laws relating to property must in a great manner be fixed and static, the rule should be different in the field of human relationships.

As we become more civilized, we learn more about the natural forces of the world, such as the use and properties of our elementary minerals, steam, electricity, and other natural forces. We also increase in spiritual and intellectual growth and are capable of understanding natural rights and liberties that have always existed, but which have been beyond our limited intellect to comprehend.

We believe that the great and underlying truths of human nature are yet to be discovered, in the same manner that we are from year to year expanding our knowledge of the natural and physical forces of the universe. The framers of our Constitution and the signers of the Declaration of Independence actually understood, defended and vindicated human rights to the greatest extent that they had ever been recognized up to that time. However, they had little or no conception of human rights as we understand them today. We ourselves cannot possibly have any conception of what natural and human rights of the future may be, in the light of the progress and development of the race, after a century or two centuries of civilization and intellectual and spiritual growth. We cannot doubt this when we remember that less than a century ago we permitted slavery and human bondage and the majority of our people did not consider slavery as being morally or spiritually wrong; and when we further remember that only a little more than a quarter of a century ago we liberated women from political disfranchisement and gave them the right to participate in the government. These examples illustrate the changes in our moral philosophies that have taken place in the short era of a century.

Our thesis is that human rights which are not enumerated in the Constitution will be revealed and become apparent in the future, and it is within the spirit of the Constitution, and the letter of the Ninth Amendment, that these rights should be recognized and protected.

Some of the rights may now be making their appearance. The right of privacy may be such a right. If there is such a right, it is difficult to classify it under any right that is enumerated in the Constitution. This is a right which is of comparatively recent recognition. Some courts call it a fundamental right. While the courts seem to feel that it should exist, there is a great timidity and lack of forthrightness in the protection of this right, because its existence is not to be found in the written and enumerated law.

There are many questions surrounding our labor problems that might appropriately come under the classification of rights of natural endowment. Do men have a natural or inherent right to strike? Does an employer have the right or privilege to choose those whom he desires as employees, or can such employer be forced to employ against his will? Is there a fundamental right to work?

Such rights are not discussed in any clause of the Constitution, but if such rights exist, shall they be denied simply because they are not enumerated?

Another possible inherent right is the right to participate in government. This includes the right to have votes counted. The clause insuring to the States a republican form of government has not been effectively interpreted so as to save our States or the various subdivisions and municipalities in our States from virtual dictatorships in matters of franchise and elections, and even the operation and management of government on a few occasions. It may be possible that the Ninth Amendment is a means of insuring the voters in any subdivision of government against the virtual destruction of his franchise and right to participate in government, through fraudulent elections and the usurpation of dictatorial powers by the executive branch of the government.

There are, no doubt, many other rights of natural endowment that have already become apparent to those who possess a richer experience than the writer. We are content if we have established the Ninth Amendment as embodying a living philosophy, and helped the law of human rights to be given an opportunity to grow as other sciences have grown.

We believe that the law should grow, and our Constitution should be interpreted in the light of current history, as was stated by one of the eminent courts of last resort of one of the States: "The law should be construed in reference to the habits of business prevalent in the country at the time it was enacted. The law was not made to create or shape the habits of business, but to regulate them, as then known to exist."

There must be some unenumerated rights. The amendment must be given some meaning. Its value and meaning should not be lost through disuse. This amendment can only be saved by our courts.

5. Are There "Certain Rights . . . Retained by the People"?

Norman Redlich

The overriding constitutional issue of our time has been the split between those who view the Bill of Rights as a firm judicial mandate empowering the Supreme Court to invalidate procedures and statutes which violate its specific prohibitions and those who consider the Bill of Rights more as a general expression of our nation's tenets to be balanced on the judicial scales along with such factors as the legislative needs and the judge's understanding of basic standards of decency and justice.

As a result of constant restatements of strongly held positions, the libertarian justices have conveyed the impression that individual liberties can best be protected by a vigorous enforcement of the first eight amendments and by the application of these amendments to the states either in whole or in major part. While this is an understandable position in terms of the great constitutional controversies of the past twenty years, we may be approaching an era where human dignity and liberty will require the protection of rights other than those contained in the first eight amendments. It is the purpose of this discussion to consider whether a libertarian judicial philosophy can stand firmly for a strict interpretation of the Bill of Rights and be sufficiently flexible to meet new and formidable challenges to individual liberty.

. . .

The well-publicized case concerning the constitutionality of Connecticut's birth control laws may provide the opportunity for a reconsideration of basic judicial attitudes toward the individual's rights in a free society. When the well thought out formulae of the past fail to provide the answer to a case which raises issues of such

Excerpted, by permission, from 37 N.Y.U. L. Rev. 787 (1962).
Editor's Note: In this excerpt, some footnotes have been edited for consistency.

fundamental importance, perhaps it is time to pause and look for fresh concepts.

The Birth Control Case

Under Connecticut law any person "who uses any drug, medicinal article or instrument for the purpose of preventing conception shall be fined not less than fifty dollars or imprisoned not less than sixty days nor more than one year or be both fined and imprisoned."[1] In addition, the "accessories" provision of Connecticut's laws permits the punishment "as if he were the principal offender" of any person "who assists, abets, counsels, causes, hires or commands another to commit any offense."[2]

In 1940 the state, in what has been described as a test case, prosecuted two doctors and a nurse as "accessories," charging them with disseminating contraceptive information. The Supreme Court of Errors and Appeals of Connecticut sustained the constitutionality of the act and the state promptly moved to dismiss the information.[3] Three years later the United States Supreme Court held that a doctor, who sought a declaration of unconstitutionality on grounds that the act endangered the health of his patients, did not have "standing to assert" the constitutional question.[4]

In 1961 the Supreme Court in *Poe v. Ullman*[5] again refused to decide the constitutionality of the act even though the action for a declaratory judgment was brought by married individuals who claimed that the enforcement of the statute would imperil their health and life. An additional action was brought by the doctor asserting that the statute, by preventing him from giving advice to one of the patients mentioned in the other action, deprived him of liberty and property without due process of law. The Court held that the failure of the state to enforce the statutes "deprives these controversies of the immediacy which is an indispensable condition of constitutional adjudication."[6] Justice Frankfurter's opinion, in which three other Justices joined, said that the patients themselves

---

[1]Conn. Gen. Stat. Rev. § 53–32 (1958).
[2]Conn. Gen. Stat. Rev. § 54–196 (1958).
[3]State v. Nelson, 126 Conn. 412, 11 A.2d 856 (1940).
[4]Tileston v. Ullman, 318 U.S. 44 (1943).
[5]367 U.S. 497 (1961).
[6]*Id.* at 508.

had no legitimate fear of prosecution and that the doctor's fear of prosecution was too "chimerical" to form the basis of a justiciable controversy either with regard to the doctor or his patients.

Justice Brennan concurred in a brief opinion stating that the proper time to consider the constitutional question is when individuals are prosecuted for the opening of birth control clinics or when "the State makes a definite and concrete threat to enforce these laws against individual married couples."[7] Justices Black and Stewart dissented on the issue of justiciability and Justices Harlan and Douglas, in separate opinions, argued that the case should have been heard and that the statute was unconstitutional. Since the state has subsequently prosecuted individuals for operating a birth control clinic and for giving information about the use of contraceptives,[8] it is almost certain that the case will come back to the Court in a form which will compel adjudication.

If one views the Connecticut statute simply as a state regulation of health and morals, there would be little difficulty in sustaining its validity in terms reminiscent of the ringing dissents in the cases where the Court sanctified such concepts as freedom of contract. One could easily transpose the words of the first Justice Harlan, dissenting in Lochner v. New York:

> Our duty, I submit, is to sustain the statute as not being in conflict with the Federal Constitution, for the reason—and such is an all-sufficient reason—it is not shown to be plainly and palpably inconsistent with that instrument. Let the state alone in the management of its purely domestic affairs, so long as it does not appear beyond all question that it has violated the Federal Constitution. This view necessarily results from the principle that the health and safety of the people of a state are primarily for the state to guard and protect.[9]

At one time or another the leading exponents of the varying judicial philosophies on the Court have expressed themselves in similar terms when dealing with matters which could reasonably be said to affect the safety, health, morals, or general welfare of the

---

[7]*Id.* at 509.

[8]Connecticut v. Griswold and Connecticut v. Buxton, CR6-5653 and CR6-5654, Conn. Cir. Ct., Jan. 2, 1962, *appeal docketed*, App. Div., Jan. 12, 1962.

[9]198 U.S. 45, 73 (1905).

state.[10] And it is not difficult to portray the Connecticut statute in those terms. Could not reasonable men believe that the use of contraceptives will encourage adultery and other types of nonmarital sexual relations because the fear of pregnancy is substantially reduced? If the state permits contraceptives to be available for some purposes, it increases the likelihood that they will be available for the purposes which the state has a right to prohibit.[11] Therefore, it is argued, a law which forbids the use of contraceptives and the dissemination of information concerning their use is a reasonable means toward the attainment of a legitimate state objective. The Sunday closing law cases recently demonstrated that even Justices most closely associated with protection of individual rights may vote to sustain legislation if no specific constitutional guarantee appears to bar it and if the legislation can be designated as within such traditional areas of the police power as safety, health, welfare, and morals.[12]

But for one who feels that the marriage relationship should be beyond the reach of a state law forbidding the use of contraceptives, the birth control case poses a troublesome and challenging problem of constitutional interpretation. He may find himself saying, "The law is unconstitutional—but why?" There are two possible paths to travel in finding the answer. One is to revert to a frankly flexible due process concept even on matters that do not involve specific constitutional prohibitions. The other is to attempt to evolve a new constitutional framework within which to meet this and similar problems which are likely to arise.

Flexible Due Process

It is not surprising that Justice Harlan, who has consistently resisted the linking of due process with any specific provision in the Bill of Rights,[13] would have little difficulty invalidating the

[10]McGowan v. Maryland, 366 U.S. 420, 425–26 (1961) (opinion of Chief Justice Warren); Day-Brite Lighting, Inc. v. Missouri, 342 U.S. 421, 423 (1952) (opinion of Justice Douglas); Lincoln Federal Labor Union v. Northwestern Iron & Metal Co., 335 U.S. 525, 536–37 (1949) (opinion of Justice Black); West Virginia State Bd. of Educ. v. Barnette, 319 U.S. 624, 666 (1943) (dissenting opinion of Justice Frankfurter).

[11]See discussion in Comment, 70 Yale L.J. 322, 331 (1960).

[12]See Braunfield v. Brown, 366 U.S. 599 (1961) (opinion of Chief Justice Warren); McGowan v. Maryland, 366 U.S. 420 (1961) (opinion of Chief Justice Warren).

[13]Mapp v. Ohio, 367 U.S. 643, 679 (dissenting opinion); Lanza v. New York, 370 U.S. 139 (1962) (concurring opinion).

Connecticut law in a manner quite consistent with his judicial philosophy. His words express the familiar philosophy of *Twining*, *Adamson*, and *Betts v. Brady:*

> Due process has not been reduced to any formula; its content cannot be determined by reference to any code. The best that can be said is that through the course of this Court's decisions it has represented the balance which our Nation, built upon postulates of respect for the liberty of the individual, has struck between that liberty and the demands of organized society.[14]

Unlike the earlier due process cases, however, in *Poe v. Ullman* this approach leads Justice Harlan to invalidate the Connecticut law because it intrudes "the whole machinery of the criminal law into the very heart of marital privacy."[15] Although re-emphasizing that the Fourteenth Amendment does not incorporate any particular amendment or right found in the first eight amendments, Justice Harlan concludes that the Fourth Amendment's concept of "privacy," which has previously been regarded as a fundamental right, includes the privacy of a married couple's sexual relations. When such a right is threatened, it is not enough that the statute is "rationally related to the effectuation of a proper state purpose."[16] The state must demonstrate a compelling justification, which Connecticut failed to do.

Civil libertarians may find this approach more satisfying when it is used to uphold individual rights rather than to deny them, but in either event it is subject to the criticism that it leaves judges without any fixed textual standard in determining which rights are fundamental. By refusing to acknowledge the incorporation of any of the specific provisions of the Bill of Rights, relying instead only on "fundamental" rights, Justice Harlan's philosophy creates the grave danger that Justices may fail to regard as fundamental the more important provisions of the Bill of Rights. It would be difficult for a believer in a strict interpretation of the Bill of Rights to accept Justice Harlan's route to invalidation of the birth control laws.[17]

[14]*Poe v. Ullman*, 367 U.S. 497, 542 (dissenting opinion).

[15]*Id.* at 553.

[16]*Id.* at 554.

[17]It is interesting to note that although Justice Harlan relied on the right of privacy which he derived from the Fourth Amendment, he dissented vigorously in *Mapp v. Ohio* and argued against extending to the states the full measure of the constitutional protection of the Fourth Amendment, which, for purpose of the dissent, Justice

As Justice Douglas demonstrated in his dissent in *Poe v. Ullman*,[18] however, it is possible to interpret the due process clause of the Fourteenth Amendment to include rights in addition to those specified in the first eight amendments. Justice Murphy expressed this position in his brief dissent in the *Adamson* case, where he said:

> I agree that the specific guarantees of the Bill of Rights should be carried over intact into the first section of the Fourteenth Amendment. But I am not prepared to say that the latter is entirely and necessarily limited by the Bill of Rights. Occasions may arise where a proceeding falls so far short of conforming to fundamental standards of procedure as to warrant constitutional condemnation in terms of a lack of due process despite the absence of a specific provision in the Bill of Rights.[19]

Although Justice Douglas had not joined in Justice Murphy's *Adamson* dissent,[20] he clearly adopted this position in *Poe v. Ullman* and rejected the idea that the only limits on the exercise of state power were the explicit guarantees of the Constitution.

The substantive right which Justice Douglas sought to protect was the same as that defended by Justice Harlan—the privacy of the marital relationship:

> But when the State makes "use" a crime and applies the criminal sanction to man and wife, the State has entered the innermost sanctum of the home. If it can make this law, it can enforce it. And proof of its violation necessarily involves an inquiry into the relations between man and wife.
>
> That is an invasion of the privacy that is implicit in a free society.[21]

We have seen that basic to the "incorporation" theory of Justice Black or the "absorption" approach of Justice Brennan is the

---

Harlan assumed to include the exclusionary rule. Mapp v. Ohio, 367 U.S. 643, 678–79 (1961). Thus, in one opinion a right to the privacy of the marital relationship, which has never been specifically included in the Fourth Amendment, is deemed to be protected against the state infringement, while in another case a right which is assumed to be included in the Fourth Amendment is denied application at the state level.

[18]367 U.S. 497, 509 (1961).

[19]332 U.S. 46, 124 (1947). Justice Rutledge joined in this dissent.

[20]In *Adamson*, Justice Douglas joined with Justice Black. *Poe v. Ullman* appears to mark his first public adoption of the *Murphy-Rutledge* dissent in *Adamson*.

[21]367 U.S. at 520–21.

assumption that the Fourteenth Amendment, either by original intention in 1868 or by subsequent interpretation, includes certain rights which, prior to 1868, were available to Americans only as a protection against intrusion by the federal government. One would be hard pressed, however, to find anything in the first eight amendments which would have barred the United States from adopting for the District of Columbia a law similar to the Connecticut statute. In fact, neither Justice Douglas nor Justice Harlan relied explicitly on any constitutional amendment in reaching the conclusion that the Connecticut law deprives the married couple of liberty without due process of law. Arguably, the due process clause of the Fifth Amendment could serve this purpose, but the narrow scope of the Fifth Amendment's due process clause in substantive areas[22] may have inhibited Justice Douglas from taking this route.

If Justice Douglas has thus accepted the view that the Fourteenth Amendment is not confined, either by original intention or subsequent interpretation, to the federal rights set forth in the first eight amendments, is he not open to the same criticism which Justice Black (originally supported by Justice Douglas) leveled at the *Adamson* majority, namely, that a departure from the text of the Bill of Rights will make it easier for other Justices either to limit the application of those rights or roam freely across the judicial terrain substituting their own standard of reasonableness for that of the legislature? Justice Douglas attempts to answer these criticisms directly.

He retreats not one inch from his previously expressed view that the Fourteenth Amendment includes the first eight amendments. These rights, he argues, were "indispensable to a free society" in 1791 and the "constitutional conception of 'due process' must, in my view, include them all until and unless there are amendments that remove them."[23] Perhaps there is implicit in the willingness of Justice Douglas to broaden the concept of due process an awareness of the fact that, as we have shown, the major provisions of the Bill of Rights have either been applied to the states or are likely to be so applied in the near future. The danger felt by Justice Black is thus much less real than it was in 1947.

But if the Connecticut statute is invalidated under a concept of due process which speaks of rights "implicit in a free society," does

---

[22]*See infra* notes 29 & 30.

[23]367 U.S. at 516.

this not invite a repetition of the pre–New Deal experience? The reply by Justice Douglas is that

> The error of the old Court . . . was not in entertaining inquiries concerning the constitutionality of social legislation but in applying the standards that it did. . . . Social legislation dealing with business and economic matters . . . has a wide scope for application. . . . The regime of a free society needs room for vast experimentation. . . . Yet to say that a legislature may do anything not within a specific guarantee of the Constitution may be as crippling to a free society as to allow it to override specific guarantees so long as what it does fails to shock the sensibilities of a majority of the Court.[24]

Then, as if to answer the charge from Justice Black that this is nothing more than personal jurisprudence, Justice Douglas says, "This notion of privacy is not drawn from the blue. It emanates from the totality of the constitutional scheme under which we live."[25]

There is unquestionably a difference between this concept of flexible due process and that advocated by Justice Harlan. As applied by Justice Douglas it establishes the Bill of Rights as a minimum protection and it leaves the legislature free to deal with economic and social regulation so long as certain ill-defined rights, not mentioned in the Bill of Rights, are protected. And Justice Douglas correctly points to instances where the Court has seemingly recognized such rights.[26] As a practical matter this approach may

[24]*Id.* at 517–18.

[25]*Id.* at 521.

[26]In *Poe v. Ullman* Justice Douglas cited Meyer v. Nebraska, 262 U.S. 390 (1923), for the proposition that the Court has recognized the right to " 'establish a home and bring up children.' " 367 U.S. at 517. The danger of using the due process clause of the Fourteenth Amendment to reach this result, without relying on any provision of the Bill of Rights, is apparent from the very case which Justice Douglas cites, because the paragraph of the *Meyer* opinion which upholds the right to "establish a home and bring up children" also speaks of "the right of the individual to contract," which few today would defend as being an essential component of liberty. 262 U.S. at 399. Justice Douglas might also have referred to his own opinion in Skinner v. Oklahoma, 316 U.S. 535, 536 (1942), in which he referred to the "right to have offspring" as "basic to the perpetuation of a race," although deciding the case on the basis of the equal protection clause of the Fourteenth Amendment. See concurring opinion of Justice Stone who stated that the statute, which provided for compulsory sterilization, did not afford an opportunity for a hearing "to discover whether . . . [petitioner's] criminal tendencies are of an inheritable type." 316 U.S. 535, 544

enable the Court to allow flexibility to the states in areas where flexibility is called for, while at the same time preventing the states from tampering with such concepts as the right to determine the size of one's family.

An Expanded Bill of Rights—Amendments Nine and Ten

Whatever may be its practical appeal, Justice Douglas' forceful reaffirmation of Justice Murphy's *Adamson* dissent is, nevertheless, hardly likely to fit the intellectual pattern of those Justices who have looked to the Federal Bill of Rights as the source of judicial restrictions on state and federal power. And this is not simply a matter of conceptual neatness. Recent developments in the field of heredity control suggest that governmental intrusions into basic personal relationships may take forms which have hitherto been relegated to the domain of science-fiction.[27] "Selective breeding" may well be within the extended reach of man, in which event federal and state regulation may become a necessity.[28]

(1942). Moreover, in the area of procedural due process we have many instances in which the Court invalidates state trials based on conceptions of "fairness" rather than on a specific guarantee in the first eight amendments. *See* Alcorta v. Texas, 355 U.S. 28 (1957). *See In re* Oliver, 333 U.S. 257, 273 (1948), in which Justice Black states that the "right to reasonable notice" and the "right to examine the witnesses against him, to offer testimony" are "basic in our system of jurisprudence." See also Lambert v. California, 355 U.S. 225 (1957), in which Justice Douglas, speaking for the Court, held unconstitutional a statute which required persons who had been convicted of a felony to register within five days of their arrival in Los Angeles. The opinion seems to be based on procedural due process because of a lack of notice of the duty to register. There is a serious question, however, whether procedural due process calls for this type of notice, which appears to be merely the existence of the statute, or whether the opinion is really based on substantive due process concepts of fairness.

[27]*See* Lasagna, *Heredity Control: Dream or Nightmare?* N.Y. Times Magazine, Aug. 5, 1962, p. 7. The author states, "It would seem that while drastic changes in the manipulation of human heredity are not yet here, they are not so remote as one would have thought even a decade ago. . . . Scientists cannot be expected to act in any other way but to accelerate our now limited abilities along the lines of genetic control." *Id.* at 59, col. 3. *See also* Engel, *The Race to Create Life*, Harper's, Oct. 1962, p. 40: "Before long we will have to decide whether we want chemical control of human heredity . . . and if so, how it should be exercised. And we will all have to take part in the decision as citizens. There are problems that are much too important to be left to scientists alone. This is one of them."

[28]If science does develop the means to control eugenic factors or to determine the sex of offspring, few would question the interest of both the states and federal

The Fourteenth Amendment has frequently been used as a barrier against state action which a majority of the Court finds shocking. But the first eight amendments contain specific restrictions, and except for an interlude when the due process clause of the Fifth Amendment was used to invalidate laws involving economic regulation,[29] the Bill of Rights has not been viewed as a device for substantive review of federal legislation passed pursuant to the enumerated or implied powers.[30] Even the much-criticized opinions

---

government to regulate the private use of these techniques. How, then, do we limit governmental activity in this area? Dr. Lasagna, *supra* note 27, at 59, quotes Sir Charles Darwin, speaking on the centennial of his grandfather's Origin of Species, as follows: " 'There can be little doubt that if any country should carry out a eugenic policing for even a few generations, that country should dominate all its neighbors by the sheer increase in the ability of its people. . . .' The accuracy of this prediction is unimportant; if large numbers of people believe it to be true, the possibilities are indeed frightening." *See* Engel, *supra* note 27.

[29]*See* Adkins v. Children's Hosp., 261 U.S. 525 (1923), *overruled*, West Coast Hotel Co. v. Parrish, 300 U.S. 379 (1937). *See also* Railroad Retirement Bd. v. Alton R.R., 295 U.S. 330 (1935). Justice Douglas in Kent v. Dulles, 357 U.S. 116 (1958), states the proposition that "freedom to travel" is part of the liberty protected by the due process clause of the Fifth Amendment. That case held that Congress had not delegated to the Secretary of State the power to deny a passport because of Communist Party membership. If Congress had actually authorized the Secretary of State to withhold passports for this reason, then presumably the constitutional question raised would have been in terms of the political rights of the First Amendment rather than the due process clause of the Fifth.

[30]In Bolling v. Sharpe, 347 U.S. 497 (1954), the due process clause of the Fifth Amendment was broadened to include the concept of equal protection in matters of racial discrimination. It is unlikely, however, that this decision, which involved the constitutionality of racially segregated public schools in the District of Columbia, could be said to justify the use of the Fifth Amendment as a basis for substantive review of federal legislation. The Court in *Bolling v. Sharpe* considered equal protection to be "a more explicit safeguard of prohibited unfairness" than due process and held that some forms of invidious discrimination would violate due process. In essence the Court was incorporating into the Fifth Amendment a specific provision whose meaning had been developed through the interpretation of the identical clause in the Fourteenth Amendment. Although litigants have frequently invoked the due process clause of the Fifth Amendment in attacking federal legislation as unreasonable, we find very few instances where the Court has given substantive content to the provision other than in procedural terms. *See* Dumbauld, The Bill of Rights 93–98 (1957). In those few instances where such claims have been sustained, the Court has spoken of the legislation as being without reasonable basis. *See* Railroad Retirement Bd. v. Alton R.R., 295 U.S. 330, 361 (1935); Chicago R.I. & P. Ry. v. United States, 284 U.S. 80, 97 (1931); Adkins v. Children's Hosp., 261 U.S. 525, 554–55 (1923), *overruled*, West Coast Hotel Co. v. Parrish, 300 U.S. 379 (1937). The difficulty with the birth control law or laws which might attempt "selective breeding"

of the mid-1930's, striking down key New Deal legislation, were based primarily on a narrow interpretation of certain federal powers rather than on the application of the Bill of Rights.[31]

If we are unable to draw upon any portion of the Bill of Rights to meet problems such as those raised by the Connecticut birth control law,[32] and other possible similar statutes, limitations on federal action in this area appear quite uncertain, and flexible due process would loom as the best immediate answer to the problem at the state level.

---

is that they will have a reasonable relationship to objectives which society has a right to effectuate through legislation.

[31]*See, e.g.,* Carter v. Carter Coal Co., 298 U.S. 238 (1936); United States v. Butler, 297 U.S. 1 (1936); Schechter Poultry Corp. v. United States, 295 U.S. 495 (1935); Railroad Retirement Bd. v. Alton R.R., 295 U.S. 330 (1935). Although the *Butler* case was based in part on the Tenth Amendment, this was because of a conclusion that Congress had no power to regulate agricultural production. Therefore, an expenditure to regulate agricultural production invaded the powers reserved to the states.

[32]Justice Douglas argued, in his dissenting opinion in *Poe v. Ullman,* that the Connecticut statute violated the First and Fourteenth Amendments because "of course a physician can talk freely and fully with his patient without threat of retaliation by the State." 367 U.S. at 514. It would be extremely unfortunate if those who argue most strenuously for the "absolute" interpretation of First Amendment rights attempt to place within the protection of the First Amendment words which are inseparably linked with conduct which the state has a right to regulate. Surely the state has a right to regulate the practice of medicine. The state may, for example, make it a crime for a physician to give injections of vaccines other than those approved by a state board. May not the state also make it a crime for a physician to advise the patient where these illegal injections may be obtained. Illegal medical practices may take the form of words spoken by a doctor to a patient and the inclusion of such activity within the area of protected free speech would materially weaken the position of those who have correctly, in my view, argued for an absolute prohibition against laws abridging freedom of speech. A similar problem was created in the area of peaceful picketing. *See* Giboney v. Empire Storage & Ice Co., 336 U.S. 490 (1949); Thornhill v. Alabama, 310 U.S. 88 (1940). In Justice Harlan's dissenting opinion in *Poe v. Ullman,* the view was expressed that the Connecticut law violates the Fourth Amendment's concept of privacy. Justice Harlan is able to apply the right of privacy in this manner because he does not feel compelled to base a Fourteenth Amendment decision on a particular provision of the Bill of Rights. He can, thus, speak in terms of concepts which underlie a provision of the Bill of Rights without feeling concerned that the particular provision in the Bill of Rights might not be so interpreted if it were brought into play in a case involving the federal government. It is doubtful whether Justices who base their Fourteenth Amendment decisions on specific provisions in the Bill of Rights would follow Justice Harlan's reasoning in *Poe v. Ullman.*

But the Bill of Rights contains two additional amendments—the Ninth and Tenth, whose history suggests that they might be peculiarly suited to meet the unique and important problems suggested by the Connecticut birth control law case.

The Ninth Amendment provides: "The Enumeration in the Constitution of certain rights, shall not be construed to deny or disparage others retained by the people." The Tenth Amendment, better-known because it has been invoked more often in litigation, provides: "The powers not delegated to the United States by the Constitution, nor prohibited by it to the States, are reserved to the States respectively, or to the people."

These two amendments have frequently been linked together and, particularly in recent years, written off as redundancies adding "nothing to the rest of the Constitution."[33] A careful reading of the words and history of the two amendments, however, indicates that they were intended to play a role in our constitutional scheme and ought not to be so lightly dismissed.

The Ninth Amendment was drafted by Madison to cope with the problem created by the enumeration of specific rights in a Bill of Rights. Fearing that the enumeration of these rights would imperil others not enumerated, Madison said:

> It has been objected also against a bill of rights, that, by enumerating particular exceptions to the grant of power, it would disparage those rights which were not placed in that enumeration; and it might follow, by implication, that those rights which were not singled out, were intended to be assigned into the hands of the General Government, and were consequently insecure. This is one of the most plausible arguments I have ever heard urged against the admission of a bill of rights unto this system; but, I conceive, that it may be guarded against. I have attempted it, as gentlemen may see by turning to the last clause of the fourth resolution.[34]

Earlier, in The Federalist No. 37, Madison expressed the closely allied idea that words were incapable of expressing complex ideas

[33]Dumbauld, *supra* note 30, at 65.

[34]I Annals of Cong. 456 (1834). The clause referred to contains the present Ninth Amendment.

with complete accuracy.[35] The fear that certain rights may have been omitted, and that the vagaries of language might adversely affect other rights intended to be included, led Madison to the Ninth Amendment.

Although the claim has been made that this amendment was intended to restrict the states as well as the federal government, the sketchy legislative history would seem to support the holding in *Barron v. Baltimore*[36] that it was intended to restrict only the federal government. The adoption of the Fourteenth Amendment in 1868, however, provided the framework for applying these restrictions against the states, even though they may have been originally intended to apply only against the United States.

The Tenth Amendment, it will be recalled, speaks not of "rights retained by the people" but of "powers" which are "reserved to the States respectively, or to the people." Were it not for the last four words, the Tenth Amendment could easily be dismissed as a redundancy in a constitution establishing a government of limited powers. These four words—"or to the people"—were not included

---

[35]The use of words is to express ideas. Perspicuity therefore requires not only that the ideas should be distinctly formed, but that they should be expressed by words distinctly and exclusively appropriated to them. But no language is so copious as to supply words and phrases for every complex idea, or so correct as not to include many equivocally denoting different ideas. Hence, it must happen, that however accurately objects may be discriminated in themselves, and however accurately the discrimination may be considered, the definition of them may be rendered inaccurate by the inaccuracy of the terms in which it is delivered.

The Federalist No. 37, at 256 (Cooke ed. 1961).

[36]32 U.S. (7 Pet.) 242 (1833). In his book on the Ninth Amendment, Mr. Bennett B. Patterson argues that the amendment was intended from the start as a restriction upon the states. Patterson, The Forgotten Ninth Amendment 13 (1955). There is strong contrary evidence, however. When Madison intended an amendment to restrict the states in his proposal to prevent the states from abridging free speech or press, he was quite specific. *See infra* note 40 and accompanying text. Moreover, under Madison's original proposal the Ninth Amendment would have appeared as part of article I, section 9, which deals with specific restrictions against the Federal Government. I Annals, *supra* note 34, at 451–52. It is unlikely that Madison would have inserted at this point a provision designed to restrict the states. Madison's phrasing of the amendment is different from the final version: "The exceptions here or elsewhere in the constitution, made in favor of particular rights, shall not be so construed as to diminish the just importance of other rights retained by the people, or as to enlarge the powers delegated by the constitution; but either as actual limitations of such powers, or as inserted merely for greater caution." *Id.* at 452.

in Madison's original draft, which may account for the fact that when Madison introduced his proposed amendments, he said that the words of the Tenth Amendment "may be considered superfluous. I admit they may be deemed unnecessary; but there can be no harm in making such a declaration, if gentlemen will allow that the fact is as stated."[37]

The Senate added the words "or to the people," but we have no record of the Senate debates and this addition did not occasion any further debate in the House, which ultimately accepted the Senate version.[38]

One might argue that the addition of the last four words was intended to place certain powers beyond the reach of the states, but it is extremely unlikely that a decision of such importance would have slipped through the First Congress with no debate.[39] Moreover, the Senate had rejected another of Madison's proposed amendments which would have prevented the states from infringing the rights of trial by jury, free speech, free press, and the "rights of conscience."[40] It would be unrealistic to attribute to the Senate an intent to impose ill-defined legally enforceable restraints on the states in light of this rejection.

The principal reason why the Tenth Amendment is currently thought of as a redundancy is that it has been invoked by litigants who have claimed that certain federal laws were unconstitutional because they invaded powers "reserved to the states." As between the federal government and the states the Tenth Amendment *is* a redundancy. Although the Court has on occasion appeared to give substantive content to the Tenth Amendment,[41] these cases can

---

[37]*Supra* note 34, at 459.

[38]Debate on the Tenth Amendment centered primarily around various attempts to limit the powers of the federal government by providing that all powers not "expressly" delegated are reserved to the states. *See* I Annals, *supra* note 34, at 790, 797. *See* Dumbauld, *supra* note 30, at 42, n.32.

[39]Article I, section 10, imposes certain restrictions on the states, such as the enactment of bills of attainder or ex post facto laws. It is unlikely, however, that the reserved powers referred to these restrictions, because the second clause in the Tenth Amendment makes it clear that the amendment is dealing with those powers *not* prohibited by the Constitution to the states.

[40]I Annals, *supra* note 34, at 452, 458. Madison is quoted in the Annals as considering "this to be the most valuable amendment in the whole list." *Id.* at 784.

[41]*See* The Constitution of the United States, Analysis and Interpretation 915–21 (Corwin ed.), S. Doc. No. 170, 82 Cong. 2d Sess. (1953).

more appropriately be viewed as having been based on a restrictive view of the delegated federal powers. Reliance on the Tenth Amendment in cases like *Hammer v. Dagenhart*[42] and *United States v. Butler*[43] resulted from a preliminary decision that the asserted federal power was not within the purview of the commerce clause or the taxing power. When the Court overruled *Hammer v. Dagenhart*, it stated, "Our conclusion is unaffected by the Tenth Amendment which . . . states but a truism that all is retained which has not been surrendered."[44]

But the Tenth Amendment becomes a "truism" only if it is viewed as defining the division of powers between the federal government and the states. This was all the amendment contained when Madison described it as "superfluous." The amendment would not be a truism, however, if the last four words are viewed as delineating powers possessed by neither the federal government nor the states. Since, as we have indicated, the amendment was not intended to restrict the states, the last four words have meaning only if they were intended to impose additional restrictions on the federal government. The pieces start to fall into place when the Tenth Amendment is considered in conjunction with the Ninth Amendment.

Once "certain rights . . . retained by the people" had been removed from the scope of federal power, it would have been inconsistent to provide that all powers resided either in the federal government or the states. The last four words of the Tenth Amendment must have been added to conform its meaning to the Ninth Amendment and to carry out the intent of both—that as to the federal government there were rights, not enumerated in the Constitution, which were "retained . . . by the people," and that because the people possessed such rights there were *powers* which neither the federal government nor the states possessed.

In an age where men looked to the states as the chief guardians of individual rights, it was not surprising that the barrier of the Ninth and Tenth Amendments was erected against only the federal government. The adoption of the Fourteenth Amendment in 1868

---

[42]247 U.S. 251 (1918).

[43]297 U.S. 1 (1936).

[44]United States v. Darby, 312 U.S. 100, 124 (1941). *See* Case v. Bowles, 327 U.S. 92, 102 (1946); Northwestern Elec. Co. v. Federal Power Comm'n, 321 U.S. 119 (1944).

provides the constitutional basis for judicial enforcement of both amendments against the states.

Thus far, neither amendment has been specifically invoked by a Supreme Court majority for the protection of individual rights not specified in the Constitution, even though they would appear to have been designed for this purpose. The Ninth Amendment has been mentioned in several cases but no decision has ever been based on it.[45] And while several decisions appear to have been based on the Tenth Amendment, it has not been because of rights reserved "to the people" but because, in the Court's view, the federal government was exercising powers which were not delegated or implied and which were, therefore, reserved to the states.[46]

If the Court decided to approach the Connecticut birth control law through the Ninth and Tenth Amendments, it could start with the strong historical argument that they were intended to apply in a situation where the asserted right appears to the Court as fundamental to a free society but is, nevertheless, not specified in the Bill of Rights.[47] Those Justices who consider the Fourteenth Amendment as having embodied either or all the major portions of the Bill of Rights could appropriately consider the Ninth and Tenth Amendments as "incorporated" or "absorbed" into the first paragraph of the Fourteenth Amendment. Certainly those Justices who have viewed the Fourteenth Amendment as limited only to "fundamental" rights unrelated to the specific provisions of the Bill of Rights should have no difficulty in adopting a Constitutional provision which appears to have been almost custom-made for this approach. The Ninth and Tenth Amendments, moreover, provide a formula for protecting the individual against both the federal and state governments in the enjoyment of these rights, something which the approach of Justice Murphy in *Adamson* and Justice Douglas in *Poe v. Ullman* failed to offer.

---

[45]It has been discussed in several cases. *See, e.g.,* United Public Workers v. Mitchell, 330 U.S. 75, 94–96, 99 (1947). For a summary of the judicial interpretation of the Ninth Amendment, see Patterson, supra note 36, at 27–35.

[46]*See supra* notes 41–44.

[47]In addition to the Madison statement, *supra* note 35, Madison had written to Jefferson in October 1788 explaining his grounds for the omission of a Bill of Rights from the original Constitution. He said, "My own opinion has always been in favor of a bill of rights; provided it be so framed as not to imply powers not meant to be included in the enumeration." Letter from Madison to Jefferson, Oct. 17, 1788, in 5 Writings of James Madison 269–75, at 271 (Hunt ed. 1906).

The Connecticut statute would provide a particularly appropriate vehicle for giving life to these dormant constitutional provisions. A birth control law is totally unlike the regulatory laws of the 1920's and 1930's whose invalidation spurred an entire generation of Justices to keep hands off legislative experimentation in this area. The birth control law invades the privacy of the marital relationship by preventing a married couple from limiting the size of its family. Whether the decision not to have children is based on economic factors, health, simple personal preference, or a multitude of other possible reasons, no government in this country should force a husband and wife to choose between abandoning this most basic of human choices and either breaking the law or abstaining from sexual relations.[48] In Justice Harlan's words, "In sum, the statute allows the State to enquire into, prove and punish married people for the private use of their marital intimacy."[49]

The Court could hold that the Ninth and Tenth Amendments reserve to a married couple the right to maintain the intimacy of the marital relationship without government interference. This would include the right of a married couple to use medically acceptable contraceptive techniques in order to limit the size of their family.

When we move into the question of the right to have children, we run into the compulsory sterilization laws and Justice Holmes' famous quip in *Buck v. Bell:* "Three generations of imbeciles is enough."[50] The Court has specified that the person to be sterilized must be afforded a fair hearing to determine whether he falls within the state-designated category.[51] Moreover, the state must justify its designation of a particular group in terms which are more stringent than usually required for state regulatory legislation.[52] But the constitutional validity of compulsory sterilization laws creates a disturbing precedent for future governmental control of eugenic devel-

---

[48]See Comment, 70 Yale L.J. 322, 328–29 (1960).

[49]Poe v. Ullman, 367 U.S. 497, 548 (1961).

[50]Buck v. Bell, 274 U.S. 200, 207 (1927).

[51]*Id.* at 206–07.

[52]*See* Skinner v. Oklahoma, 316 U.S. 535 (1942). In this case a compulsory sterilization law for "habitual criminals" was held to violate the equal protection clause. The customary deference which would be accorded to state classifications would not be followed in the case of "legislation which involves one of the basic civil rights of man." In a concurring opinion, Justice Stone stated that the state must afford the individual an opportunity to demonstrate that he does not have the inheritable qualities which the state has assumed are possessed by the entire group.

opment.[53] How easily might a judge say, "Three generations of subnormal I.Q.'s is enough."

The Ninth and Tenth Amendments could well form the basis for limiting *Buck v. Bell* to a situation where the evidence clearly demonstrates that the undesirable traits are not only likely to be inherited but are of the nature which, if possessed by an individual, will cause either criminal behavior or a mental state which could justify commitment. This would preclude a legislative majority or an administrator from using the technique of sterilization or selective application of drugs to develop certain physical characteristics in the population or to eradicate others. Rights retained by the people need not necessarily be absolute, just as not all the rights in the Bill of Rights are expressed in absolute terms. The right to have children would be a preferred right which the state could restrict only under the type of strictly circumscribed standards indicated here.[54]

Judicial Criteria

What criteria are judges to apply when faced with a claim that the Government is infringing a right reserved to the people and which is not enumerated in the Constitution? Is there any textual standard or have we merely substituted one constitutional formula for another by which judges are to apply their own notions of fundamental justice and fairness?

When the question of standards is posed within the context of the Ninth and Tenth Amendments, rather than in terms of due process, a definite pattern starts to emerge. To comply with the purposes of these amendments, the textual standard should be the entire Constitution. The original Constitution and its amendments project through the ages the image of a free and open society. The Ninth and Tenth Amendments recognized—at the very outset of our national experience—that it was impossible to fill in every detail

---

[53]It should be added that the rapid developments in medical treatment of the mentally ill might completely preclude the state from making the irrevocable decision of sterilization. A trait which one legislature believes to be inheritable might actually be limitable or curable. In that event *Buck v. Bell* might well be overruled.

While one could conceive of conditions where the state might limit the free choice of adult men and women to marry, the same factors which lead to the limiting or possible overruling of *Buck v. Bell* would apply with regard to marriage.

[54]For possible attempts to decide the birth control case under other provisions, see discussion *supra,* text accompanying notes 12–28.

of this image. For that reason certain rights were reserved to the people. The language and history of the two amendments indicate that the rights reserved were to be of a nature comparable to the rights enumerated. They were "retained . . . by the people" not because they were different from the rights specifically mentioned in the Constitution, but because words were considered inadequate to define all of the rights which man should possess in a free society and because it was believed that the enumeration might imply that other rights did not exist.

Let us consider a few examples. The right of employees to contract with employers concerning hours of work, which was the right upheld in *Lochner v. New York*,[55] hardly fits into the scheme of rights set forth in our Constitution. But the right of a married couple to maintain the intimacy of their marital relationship free from the criminal sanction of the state does fit into the pattern of a society which set forth in its national charter that men should be free from unreasonable searches and seizures.[56] Similarly, the state might sterilize an individual upon clear and convincing proof that this particular individual possesses inheritable characteristics likely to produce criminal conduct or insanity. But if the Government were to enforce a policy of selective breeding, designed to produce a genetically superior race, the individual could claim that among the rights reserved to the people is the right freely to choose a spouse and to produce children. Only through the most obnoxious invasion of personal privacy could such a program be enforced. Moreover, a Constitution which specifically provides that a person guilty of treason could not be deprived of the right to transmit property[57] would hardly countenance taking from law-abiding citizens the right to transmit life.

Taking an example from an earlier period, *Crandall v. Nevada*[58] held that a state tax on every person leaving the state was uncon-

---

[55]198 U.S. 45 (1905).

[56]It is interesting that Justices Harlan and Douglas both relied on a specific provision in the Bill of Rights to invalidate the birth control law, although they did so within a context of flexible due process. Instead of altering the contours of the Fourth and First Amendments, it would have been possible to rely on the Ninth and Tenth Amendments, as incorporated in the Fourteenth Amendment, using other amendments to substantiate the claim that the right was of the nature of those reserved to the people.

[57]U.S. Const. art. III, § 3.

[58]73 U.S. (6 Wall.) 35 (1867).

stitutional. Instead of relying on a specific provision, the Court said that the Constitution established a national government whose existence requires that the people have access to the seat of government, its courts, and its offices wherever they may be located in the several states. It might have added that since the states are forbidden to tax imports or exports, it would be inconsistent to permit a state to prevent, through taxation or regulation, an individual from reaching a seaport to carry on the business of importing or exporting. Both of these reasons could have justified the result under the Ninth and Tenth Amendments because they are related to the general pattern of government established by our Constitution.[59]

The Ninth and Tenth Amendments, unlike other portions of the Bill of Rights, should be viewed as dealing not with absolute rights but generally with preferred rights, where the balancing of interests is appropriate. We are concerned here with areas where there would normally be a presumption of constitutionality and a willingness to uphold the statute if it appears reasonably related to a valid legislative end. When the individual asserts rights recognized under the Ninth and Tenth Amendments, however, the Court should sound a different note:

> These are rights which a free society reserves to the people. You may not "deny or disparage" them by a mere showing of reasonableness. In areas of general economic and social policy we defer to your judgment and your constitutional power. But when you extend this power to regulate rights which we consider an essential ingredient of the free society established by our Constitution, we require overwhelming proof of necessity and the absence of other and less burdensome means to achieve your objectives.

In this realm, as in others, there exists no purely objective set of criteria. That the criteria are loose, however, does not mean that they do not exist. Our Constitution provides the basic text for the delineation of rights retained by the people with respect to which state and federal governments have been denied the power to act. Accordingly, the Ninth and Tenth Amendments should be used to

[59]A similar approach could have been used in Edwards v. California, 314 U.S. 160 (1941), which held invalid a statute making it a crime for a person to bring an indigent person into California. The *Edwards* case might also have been decided on the basis of the privileges and immunities clause of the Fourteenth Amendment, which was not available at the time of Crandall v. Nevada, *supra* note 58.

define rights adjacent to, or analogous to, the pattern of rights which we find in the Constitution. They should not be used as a substitute for a vigorous application of those rights which are specified in the Constitution or for the adoption of rights which bear no connection to our constitutional scheme. To define the rights "retained by the people," judges must, of course, make personal judgments. What has been suggested here is a judicial approach for making these judgments which is at least consistent with our constitutional theory and history.

6. Natural Rights and the Ninth Amendment

Eugene M. Van Loan III

[A] lawyer friend asked me in a friendly way what I thought the Ninth Amendment to the Constitution meant. I vainly tried to recall what it was. . . . What are those other rights retained by the people? To what law shall we look for their source and definition? . . . [T]he Ninth Amendment rights which are not to be disturbed by the Federal Government are still a mystery to me.[1]

This reaction of even a Supreme Court Justice undoubtedly reflects a characteristic response to any mention of the ninth amendment to the Constitution.[2] Prior to 1965, the ninth amendment had never been used in a Supreme Court opinion as a basis for a decision.[3] A

Excerpted, by permission, from B.U.L. Rev. (1968).

Editor's Note: In this excerpt, some footnotes have been edited for consistency.

[1]Jackson, The Supreme Court and the American System of Government 74–75 (1955).

[2]"The enumeration in the Constitution, of certain rights, shall not be construed to deny or disparage others retained by the people." U.S. Const. amend. IX.

[3]The amendment had, however, been raised by the parties and discussed by the Court in several pre-1965 opinions. In the few cases where anything more than a cursory reference to the ninth appeared, it was lumped with the tenth, as an innocuous rule of construction limiting the federal government to its delegated powers. Roth v. United States, 354 U.S. 476, 492–93 (1957); United Pub. Workers of America v. Mitchell, 330 U.S. 75, 94–96 (1947); Ashwander v. TVA, 297 U.S. 288, 330–31 (1935); Hoke v. United States, 227 U.S. 308, 311, 320 (1913); see Bute v. Illinois, 333 U.S. 640, 650–51 (1948). On the other hand, in the dicta of Woods v. Cloyd W. Miller Co., 333 U.S. 138, 144 (1948) and Dred Scott v. Sandford, 60 U.S. (19 How.) 393, 511 (1857) (Campbell, J. concurring) faint implications arose that the ninth amendment, although still bound to the tenth, could impose substantive limitations on federal power. See also Tennessee Power Co. v. TVA, 306 U.S. 118, 122, 143–44 (1939). In the other cases where the ninth was raised, either the constitutional issues were not reached, United States v. C.I.O., 335 U.S. 106 (1948); McCurdy v. United States, 246 U.S. 263 (1918); Roosevelt v. Mever, 68 U.S. (1 Wall.) 512 (1863), or a decision on the merits was rendered without any independent discussion of the ninth amendment, Singer v. United States, 380 U.S. 24 (1965); Katzenbach v. McClung,

limited number of articles specifically devoted to the ninth amendment had been written in the previous decade,[4] and passing reference to it had been made in several notable treatises on the Constitution[5] and in several works on the Bill of Rights.[6] Nevertheless, its existence and potential application was essentially ignored by constitutional scholars and practicing lawyers.

But the decision of the Supreme Court in *Griswold v. Connecticut*[7] has radically altered this situation and stimulated a new interest in the ninth amendment. The majority opinion by Justice Douglas used the ninth amendment as a support for the existence of a "penumbra" of privacy surrounding certain specific rights in the first eight amendments.[8] Because it infringed this right of privacy, the use provision of the Connecticut birth control statute was declared unconstitutional by the Court. Justice Goldberg wrote a concurring opinion in which he elaborated upon the history and application of the ninth amendment, concluding that it was a rule of construction which reinforced the development of unenumerated rights in the

---

379 U.S. 294 (1964); United States v. Barnett, 376 U.S. 681 (1964); Slagle v. Ohio, 366 U.S. 259 (1961); NLRB v. Friedman–Harry Marks Clothing Co., 301 U.S. 58 (1937).

[4]Most of this material was devoted primarily to meticulous historical research and analysis. Patterson, The Forgotten Ninth Amendment (1955), reviewed, Forage, 60 Dick. L. Rev. 288 (1956), Pollit, 27 Miss. L.J. 161 (1956), Parry, 31 Notre Dame Law. 329 (1956); Call, *Federalism and the Ninth Amendment*, 64 Dick. L. Rev. 121 (1960); Dunbar, *James Madison and the Ninth Amendment*, 42 Va. L. Rev. 627 (1956); Rogge, *Unenumerated Rights*, 47 Calif. L. Rev. 787 (1959). The remainder were oriented more toward explicating the contemporary content and application of the ninth. Franklin, *The Relation of the Fifth, Ninth and Fourteenth Amendments to the Third Constitution*, 4 How. L.J. 170, 174–77 (1958); Kelsey, *The Ninth Amendment of the Federal Constitution*, 11 Ind. L.J. 309 (1936); Price, *The Ninth Amendment*, 48 Women Lawyer's J. 19 (Winter, 1962); Redlich, *Are There "Certain Rights . . . Retained by the People"?* 37 N.Y.U. L. Rev. 787 (1962). *See also* Corwin, *The "Higher Law" Background of American Constitutional Law*, 42 Harv. L. Rev. 149, 152–53 (1928), 365 (1928–29).

[5]Corwin, The Constitution and What It Means Today 113 (1930); Cooley, General Principles of Constitutional Law 36–37 (3d ed. 1898); 1 Hockett, Constitutional History of the United States 226 (1939); Miller, Lectures on the Constitution 650 (1891); 2 Story, Commentaries on the Constitution of the United States 626–27, 651 (5th ed. 1891).

[6]Black, The Bill of Rights, 35 N.Y.U. L. Rev. 865, 871 (1960); Dumbauld, The Bill of Rights and What It Means Today 63–64 (1957); Hamlin, *The Bill of Rights or the First Ten Amendments to the United States Constitution*, 68 Com. L.J. 233, 236–37 (1963).

[7]381 U.S. 479 (1965).

[8]*Id.* at 484.

due process clauses of the fifth and fourteenth amendments.[9] The result of this explicit reliance upon the ninth amendment in *Griswold* has been to rejuvenate that provision of the Constitution[10] and to stimulate a flurry of academic commentary and speculation concerning its future role in constitutional adjudication.[11]

As the Court struggles in the future with the problems created by the impact of an increasingly complex and populous society upon the individual, it may discover that some substantial interests are inadequately protected by the Constitution from governmental encroachment. If so, the *Griswold* opinion may provide a precedent for reliance upon the ninth amendment as a textual basis for the establishment of new constitutional rights. Support for such a process is found in the words of Chief Justice Marshall in *Marbury v. Madison:* "It cannot be presumed that any clause of the constitution is intended to be without effect."[12] The development of a new constitutional text, however, should not be initiated by the Court

---

[9]*Id.* at 492 (Brennan, J. and Warren, C.J. joining).

[10]Since the *Griswold* case, it has been mentioned in Osborn v. United States, 385 U.S. 323, 341, 352–53 (1966) (Douglas, J. dissenting) and Rosenblatt v. Baer, 383 U.S. 75, 92 (1966) (Stewart, J. concurring).

[11]Although the decision was announced on June 7, 1965, numerous articles on the ninth have already been published. Abrams, *What are the Rights Guaranteed by the Ninth Amendment?* 53 A.B.A. J. 1033 (1967); Franklin, *The Ninth Amendment as Civil Law Method,* 40 Tul. L. Rev. 487 (1966); Kelley, *The Uncertain Renaissance of the Ninth Amendment,* 33 U. Chi. L. Rev. 814 (1966); Comment, The Ninth Amendment, 30 Albany L. Rev. 89 (1966); Note, *Griswold v. Connecticut: Peripheral Rights and Rights Retained by the People Under the Ninth Amendment,* 40 Conn. B.J. 704 (1966); Note, The Ninth Amendment, 11 S.D.L. Rev. 172 (1966); *The Ninth Amendment Guidepost to Fundamental Rights,* 8 Wm. & Mary L. Rev. 101 (1966). *See also* Symposium, *Comments on the Griswold Case,* 64 Mich. L. Rev. 197–288 (1965); Katin, *"Griswold v. Connecticut": The Justices and Connecticut's "Uncommonly Silly Law,"* 42 Notre Dame Law. 680 (1967); Kelly, *Clio and the Court: An Illicit Love Affair,* 1965 Sup. Ct. Rev. 119, 149; Pollack, *Natural Rights: Conflict and Consequence,* 27 Ohio St. L.J. 559 (1966). For student comments and case notes on Griswold, see 32 Brooklyn L. Rev. 172 (1965); 69 Dick. L. Rev. 417 (1965); 79 Harv. L. Rev. 162 (1965); 37 Miss. L.J. 304 (1966); 17 Syracuse L. Rev. 553 (1965); 35 U. Cin. L. Rev. 134 (1966); 38 U. Colo. L. Rev. 267 (1966); 34 U. Mo. Kansas City L. Rev. 95 (1965); 18 Vand. L. Rev. 2037 (1965); 5 Washburn L.J. 286 (1966); 12 Wayne L. Rev. 479 (1966); 17 W. Res. L. Rev. 601 (1966).

[12]5 U.S. (1 Cranch) 137, 174 (1803). *And see* Griswold v. Connecticut, 381 U.S. 479, 491 (1965) ("The Ninth Amendment to the Constitution may be regarded by some as a recent discovery and may be forgotten by others, but since 1791 it has been a basic part of the Constitution which we are sworn to uphold."); Myers v. United States, 272 U.S. 52, 151 (1926); Knowlton v. Moore, 178 U.S. 41, 87 (1900); Blake v. McClung, 172 U.S. 239, 260–61 (1898).

without a thorough comprehension of its historical origin and an examination into its contemporary jurisprudential potentialities and disabilities. It is the function of this article to undertake such an analysis of the ninth amendment.

The utility of history in the explication provision is limited. Its value is restricted by the source material available, the inherent inadequacy of words to express accurately what the Framers "meant" or "intended," and the passage of nearly two centuries of social change since the drafting of the Constitution.[13] History is more often than not ambiguous; therefore, it should seldom be determinative. Such conclusiveness not only imposes unwarranted restrictions upon the Court's flexibility, but also subjects the Court to unnecessary and destructive academic criticism.[14] Rather, history should serve as one analytical weapon in the Court's interpretative arsenal. Because we deal with a written constitution, history is no doubt essential, but its proper function is to illuminate the permissible alternatives open to the Court and to provide an insight into the wisdom and experience of the past.[15] It is with these goals in mind that the following history of the ninth amendment is reviewed and interpreted.

On May 14, 1787, the Constitutional Convention met in Philadelphia. Its mandate was the revision of the Articles of Confederation so as to "render the federal constitution adequate to the

[13]See generally Wofford, The Blinding Light: The Uses of History in Constitutional Interpretation, 31 U. Chi. L. Rev. 502 (1964).

[14]E.g., Justice Black's grounding of his theory of incorporation in the history of the fourteenth amendment [Adamson v. California, 332 U.S. 46, 92 (1947) (appendix)] provoked a substantial controversy over the validity of his historical conclusions. Fairman, Does the Fourteenth Amendment Incorporate the Bill of Rights? 2 Stan. L. Rev. 5 (1949); Crosskey, Charles Fairman: "Legislative History" and the Constitutional Limitations on State Authority, 22 U. Chi. L. Rev. 1 (1954); Fairman, A Reply to Professor Crosskey, 22 U. Chi. L. Rev. 144 (1954); Kelly, The Fourteenth Amendment Reconsidered, 54 Mich. L. Rev. 1049 (1956); see Brant, The Bill of Rights: Its Origin and Meaning, 1966 Wis. L. Rev. 1201; cf. Comment, The Adamson Case, A Study in Constitutional Technique, 58 Yale L.J. 268 (1949). For a general attack on the Court's historical expertise, see Kelly, supra note 11; Howe, Split Decisions, N.Y. Review of Books 14, 16 (July 1, 1965). But see Daly, The Use of History in the Decisions of the Supreme Court: 1900–1930 (1954).

[15]Wofford, supra note 13, at 529–32; Wyzandki, History and Law, 26 U. Chi. L. Rev. 237, 242 (1959); see Freund, Storm Over the American Supreme Court, 21 Modern L. Rev. 345, 350 (1958).

exigencies of Government & the preservation of the Union."[16] The deficiencies and weaknesses of the Confederation were infamous[17]; the primary task of the delegates was to remedy these weaknesses and establish a strong, viable national government. The Revolutionary War was less than a decade old, and the members of the Convention had no intention of creating a government with the power to infringe their hard-won liberties.[18] Several important provisions protecting these liberties against potential abuse were indeed adopted,[19] but no serious consideration was given to a comprehensive bill of rights.

Commenting on the delegates' failure to include a bill of rights, James Wilson said in the Pennsylvania ratification convention, "I believe the truth is, that such an idea never entered the mind of many of them. I do not recollect to have heard the subject mentioned till within about three days of the time of our rising; and even then, there was no direct motion offered for any thing of the kind."[20] Wilson's memory was not perfect, but it was essentially correct. A motion had been made on September 12, 1787, by Elbridge Gerry of Massachusetts and seconded by George Mason of Virginia to establish a committee to study a bill of rights, but it was unani-

[16]Resolution of Congress, February 21, 1787, 3 Farrand, Records of the Federal Convention of 1787, 14 (rev. ed. 1937) [hereinafter cited as Farrand].

[17]*See* Rossiter, 1787: The Grand Convention 41–57 (1966); Letter to George Washington (March 15, 1784), 3 Writings of Thomas Jefferson 420 (Hunt ed. 1892–99) [hereinafter cited as Jefferson]; The Federalist Nos. 15–21 (Hamilton and Madison) (Mod. Lib. ed.) [hereinafter cited as The Federalist].

[18]Letter from Washington to La Fayette (April 28, 1788), 3 Farrand 297.

[19]The writ of habeas corpus may not be suspended except in emergency, U.S. Const. art. I, § 9; neither the federal nor state governments may pass a bill of attainder or ex post facto law, U.S. Const. art. I, §§ 9 & 10; the states may not impair the obligation of contracts, U.S. Const. art. I, § 10; trial by jury for all crimes but impeachment is guaranteed, U.S. Const. art. III, § 2; a treason conviction must be based on the testimony of two witnesses and it shall work no corruption of the blood or forfeiture except during the offender's life, U.S. Const. art. III, § 3; the citizens of each state are entitled to the privileges and immunities of the citizens of the several states, U.S. Const. art. IV, § 2; each state is guaranteed a republican form of government, U.S. Const. art. IV, § 4; and no religious test may be required as a qualification for a federal position, U.S. Const. art. VI.

[20]2 Elliot, Debates of the State Conventions on the Federal Constitution 435–36 (2d ed. 1836, 1901 printing) [hereinafter cited as Elliot, Debates].

mously defeated.[21] On the final day of deliberations in the Convention, September 15, Edmund Randolph of Virginia moved to permit the states to propose amendments to the Constitution and then to call a new convention to reconsider the whole matter; he was seconded by Mason and Gerry, but the motion was rejected and the Constitution adopted by all the state delegations.[22] When the engrossed draft was presented to the delegates for signing on September 17, all signed but Randolph, Mason and Gerry,[23] and each of them gave as one reason for his refusal the absence of a bill of rights.[24] Nevertheless, the new Constitution had been accepted. The Convention was thereupon adjourned and the Constitution rapidly dispatched to conventions in the thirteen states to face the ordeal of ratification.

The failure to include a bill of rights, however, soon proved to be one of the most objectionable features of the Constitution. Thomas Jefferson, writing to James Madison in 1787, said about the new Constitution,

> I will now add what I do not like. First the omission of a bill of rights providing clearly, for freedom of religion, freedom of the press, protection against standing armies, restriction of monopolies. . . . Let me add that a bill of rights is what the people are entitled to against every government on earth, general or particular; and what no just government should refuse, or rest on inference.[25]

Another prominent Revolutionary War figure, Patrick Henry, spoke vehemently against the Constitution in the Virginia convention; no other aspect of that document was more repugnant to him than its lack of a bill of rights:

> I trust that gentlemen, on this occasion, will see the great objects of religion, liberty of the press, trial by jury, interdiction of cruel

---

[21]2 Ferrand 588. A motion had also been made two days later by Charles Pinckney of South Carolina and Gerry to insert a provision on the inviolability of the press, but that was also rejected. 2 Ferrand 617–18.

[22]2 Ferrand 631–33.

[23]2 Ferrand 648–49.

[24]Mason's objections to this Constitution of Government began, "There is no Declaration of Rights, and the laws of the general government being paramount to the laws and constitution of the several States, the Declaration of Rights in the separate States are no security." 2 Ferrand 633.

[25]Letter to James Madison (Dec. 20, 1787), 4 Jefferson 473, 476–77.

punishments, and every other sacred right, secured, before they agree to that paper. . . . My mind will not be quited till I see something substantial come forth in the shape of a bill of rights.[26]

Such criticisms were repeated in all the state conventions and in the public debate that was carried on throughout the country in newspapers and pamphlets.[27] Moreover, it was apparently the bill of rights issue which primarily attracted the attention of and distressed the great mass of common folk in each of the states.

Although the Federalists[28] were perhaps surprised by the furor over a bill of rights, they did marshall a substantial number of arguments against the necessity of such an addition to the Constitution. First, they pointed out that several of the states themselves had no bill of rights and yet apparently no one considered the people's liberties in those states to be in jeopardy.[29] Furthermore, the Constitution had indeed already made provision for several important rights such as habeas corpus and a jury trial in criminal cases[30]; in fact, the Constitution itself served as a bill of rights by specifically defining the powers, structure and procedures of the federal government.[31]

But the most frequent and perhaps the most persuasive of the Federalists' arguments concerned the nature of a limited government. The speech of James Wilson in the Pennsylvania convention best expressed that argument:

> But in a government consisting of enumerated powers, such as is proposed for the United States, a bill of rights would not only be unnecessary, but, in my humble judgment, highly imprudent. In

---

[26]3 Elliot, Debates 462.

[27]For criticisms outside the state conventions, see generally Pamphlets on the Constitution (Ford ed. 1888).

[28]The terms "Federalists" and "Antifederalists" are commonly used to denote the supporters and opponents of the Constitution, respectively. *E.g.*, Rutland, The Ordeal of the Constitution (1966).

[29]The Federalist No. 84, at 555 (Hamilton); 2 Elliot, Debates 436 (James Wilson). The states not having a bill of rights at the time of the Constitution's ratification were Connecticut, Georgia, New Hampshire, New Jersey, New York and South Carolina. Wright, American Interpretations of Natural Law 112–14 (1931) [hereinafter cited as Wright, Natural Law].

[30]The Federalist No. 84, at 556 (Hamilton). *See generally* provisions cited at *supra* note 19.

[31]The Federalist No. 84, at 561 (Hamilton).

all societies, there are many powers and rights which cannot be particularly enumerated. A bill of rights annexed to a constitution, is an *enumeration of the powers* reserved. If we attempt an enumeration, every thing that is not enumerated, is presumed to be given. The consequence is, that an imperfect enumeration would throw all implied power into the scale of the government, and the rights of the people would be rendered incomplete.[32]

There are two complementary aspects to Wilson's thesis: First, since this is a government of delegated powers and since it has been granted no power to impair fundamental liberties, a bill of rights is unnecessary[33]; second, the very addition of a bill of rights might imply the delegation of additional powers over rights not specifically excepted out.[34] Alexander Hamilton used the second half of Wilson's argument in *The Federalist*, but in a narrower form than Wilson. He argued that, for example, the reservation of freedom of the press might imply that a power to regulate the press had been conferred upon the government.[35] In other words, Hamilton felt that the enumeration of certain rights might imply a power to act upon *those rights*, presumably to the extent that their reservation had been incomplete.[36] Wilson, however, had argued that an imperfect enumeration might imply power over *other rights*, not enumerated.

Wilson's argument was phrased in terms of implied powers. An alternative, but substantially equivalent, form of his argument was stated in terms of reserved rights. This argument took the form of a suggestion that an enumeration of certain rights might imply that

---

[32]2 Elliot, Debates 436.

[33]*And see* The Federalist No. 84, at 558 (Hamilton); 3 Elliot, Debates 620 (Madison); 4 Elliot, Debates 315–16 (Pinckney); 3 Elliot, Debates 466–69 (Randolph—who had refused to sign the Constitution, but became one of its more forceful advocates in the Virginia convention. See 3 Elliot, Debates 24–26).

[34]*And see* 3 Elliot, Debates 620 (Madison); 4 Elliot, Debates 315–16 (Pinckney).

[35]The Federalist No. 84, at 559.

[36]In The Federalist No. 37, at 227–30, Madison refers to the general problem created by the inadequacy of words to convey the precise meaning of a complex idea. This is probably what Hamilton had in mind when he spoke of the dangers involved in a reservation of "liberty of the press." A similar notion is expressed by Dumbauld in The Bill of Rights and What It Means Today 63, n.9 (1957): "An example of the type of interpretation which Madison intended to preclude is the argument that the president may abridge freedom of speech since the First Amendment only prohibits Congress from doing so."

no other rights existed or had been reserved by the people.[37] This concern over imperfect enumeration took one final form in a personal concern of James Madison, which he expressed in a letter to Jefferson,

> [T]here is great reason to fear that a positive declaration of some of the most essential rights could not be obtained in the requisite latitude. I am sure that the rights of conscience in particular, if submitted to public definition would be narrowed much more than they are likely ever to be by an assumed power. . . .[38]

Nevertheless, however expressed, the fear was the same. All argued that a bill of rights could never be comprehensive enough and that its addition to the Constitution, while protecting certain rights, would result in the sacrifice of all unenumerated rights.

These arguments and assurances of the Federalists, however, fell on deaf ears. The proponents of a bill of rights were not placated by academic arguments about delegated and implied powers; they wanted explicit guarantees of substance written into the Constitution. Patrick Henry well expressed the distrust felt by many over the fervor of the Federalist arguments: "When we see men of such talents and learning compelled to use their utmost abilities to convince themselves that there is no danger, is it not sufficient to make us tremble?"[39] Some Antifederalists even proposed the calling of a new convention to redraft the Constitution, or at least that ratification by the states be made conditional upon the annexation of a bill of rights.[40] These divisive measures were strongly resisted by Madison, Hamilton and the other Federalists because they knew that postponement of universal ratification would only permit the dissidents to gather their forces and mount a full-scale attack upon the proposed union.

By February, 1788, the Federalists had succeeded in obtaining ratification in Connecticut, Delaware, Georgia, New Jersey and

---

[37]*E.g.*, 3 Elliot, Debates 620 (Madison).

[38]Letter to Thomas Jefferson (Oct. 17, 1788), 5 Writings of James Madison 271–72 (Hunt ed. 1901–10) [hereinafter cited as Madison].

[39]3 Elliot, Debates 317.

[40]Even Jefferson once suggested that four of the thirteen states withhold ratification in order to pressure the other nine into adopting a bill of rights. Letter to James Madison (Feb. 6, 1788), 5 Jefferson 5.

Pennsylvania.[41] But opposition to the Constitution was increasing in some of the other states and the conventions of two of the most important states, New York and Virginia, had not even commenced. The solution to the deadlock over a bill of rights was finally provided by Massachusetts. Nine proposed amendments were appended to its act of ratification with an expression of "opinion" that they would "remove the fears and quiet the apprehensions of many of the good people of the commonwealth."[42] Thereafter, Maryland was the only other state to ratify without proposing any amendments; South Carolina, New Hampshire, Virginia and New York all followed the example of Massachusetts and attached numerous proposed amendments to their acts of ratification.[43] It seems quite clear that this compromise over amendments was of fundamental significance in defeating the Antifederalists and assuring the ratification of the Constitution.[44] On the other hand, the Federalists, in effect, had made a binding pledge to secure the addition of a bill of rights in the first Congress[45]; if this moral obligation had been ignored, the acceptability of the new federal government would have been severely impaired.

The first Congress of the United States met in New York on March 4, 1789. On June 8, Madison introduced into the House of Representatives a set of amendments to the Constitution which he had culled from the various proposals of the states. From his suggestions Congress eventually selected twelve amendments which were then submitted to the states for ratification. With the ratification of Virginia on December 15, 1791, the last ten of these became our Bill of Rights.

The Bill of Rights was essentially the product of James Madison; he was its architect and mentor. Therefore, it is important to under-

[41]Rossiter, *supra* note 17, at 285–87.

[42]2 Elliot, Debates 177.

[43]Rossiter, *supra* note 17, at 288–94. North Carolina and Rhode Island also proposed amendments, but their suggestions were moot because neither of them ratified until after the first Congress had already met and adopted twelve amendments to the Constitution. *Id.* at 303.

[44]*Id.* at 303–04; Rutland, *supra* note 28, at 33–34.

[45]In Madison's campaign for a seat in the first Congress, support for a bill of rights was a major plank in his election platform. Letter to George Eve (Jan. 2, 1789), 5 Madison 319, n.1; Rutland, *supra* note 28, at 297; *see* 1 The Debates and Proceedings in the Congress of the United States 775 (Gales and Seaton eds. 1834) [hereinafter cited as Congressional Proceedings].

stand his thinking about it. His views admittedly cannot be historically conclusive; before it became part of the Constitution, the Bill of Rights had to pass both houses of Congress and the legislatures of eleven states, all of whose members thereupon became "Framers."[46] On the other hand, at least with the ninth amendment, the paucity of debate over its meaning compels us to turn to the views of its author for historical guidance.

Madison was never overly optimistic about the efficacy of a bill of rights as a curb on governmental power. As he stated in his October 17, 1788, letter to Jefferson: "Repeated violations of these parchment barriers have been committed by overbearing majorities in every state."[47] His private view was that the primary value of a bill of rights was its capacity to instill the precepts of a free society in the community at large and the possibility that it would act as a moral check upon those in authority.[48] When he introduced his proposed amendments in the House of Representatives, he gave as an additional reason for Congressional adoption the fact that a bill of rights was necessary to "extinguish from the bosom of every member of the community, any apprehensions that there are those among his countrymen who wish to deprive them of the liberty for which they valiantly fought and honorably bled."[49] Moreover, he was well aware of the continuing efforts of the Antifederalists to call a new convention for the wholesale revision of the Constitution; no doubt concern over such a possibility gave him a further motivation for his proposal of a bill of rights.[50]

This is not to say that Madison considered the annexation of a bill of rights as a mere political maneuver or as a superfluous addition to the Constitution. He had always been a strong advocate of the necessary and proper clause[51] as an essential adjunct to the enumerated powers of government. In *The Federalist* he had argued that, "without the *substance* of this power, the whole Constitution

---

[46]*See* Wofford, *supra* note 13, at 508–09. *See generally* Brant, *The Madison Heritage,* 35 N.Y.U. L. Rev. 882 (1960).

[47]5 Madison 269, 272.

[48]*Id.* at 274; 1 Congressional Proceedings 455–57.

[49]1 Congressional Proceedings 449.

[50]*See generally* Rutland, *supra* note 28, at ch. XV.

[51]U.S. Const. art. I, § 8.

would be a dead letter."[52] Therefore, although he did agree that the federal government was essentially one of delegated powers, he realized that some incidental powers might be implied.[53] As against such implied powers a reservation of rights would be necessary. In the introduction to his proposals, Madison gave an example of where an amendment might be required to restrain the government in the exercise of a power which it conceivably possessed under the necessary and proper clause: "The General Government has a right to pass all laws which shall be necessary to collect its revenue; the means for enforcing the collection are within the discretion of the Legislature: may not general warrants be considered necessary for this purpose. . . ?"[54] At a prior point in his introduction he had distinguished the various types of rights which his amendments were designed to protect. He noted that some, like trial by jury, were "positive rights" that "cannot be considered as a natural right, but a right resulting from a social compact which regulates the action of the community, but is as essential to secure the liberty of the people as any one of the pre-existent rights of nature."[55] It thus emerges that Madison accepted certain procedural limitations upon government such as trial by jury and the prohibition against general warrants which might not otherwise be implied in the Constitution and consequently might be infringed by a broad construction of governmental power through the necessary and proper clause. To this extent, therefore, a bill of rights would actually serve to restrict the powers of government and thereby would be an addition of substance to the Constitution.

On the other hand, Madison believed that there were other fundamental rights over which the federal government had been

---

[52]No. 44, at 292. Later his draft of what became the tenth amendment came under fire in Congress, and several attempts were made to insert the word "expressly" before the word "delegated." 1 Congressional Proceedings 790, 797. Madison, however, "objected to this amendment, because it was impossible to confine a Government to the exercise of express powers; there must necessarily be admitted powers by implication, unless the constitution descended to recount every minutia." 1 Congressional Proceedings 790.

[53]In his letter to Jefferson about a bill of rights, *supra* note 38, at 271, Madison stated as one reason for his opposition, "I conceive that in a certain degree, though not in the extent argued by Mr. Wilson, the rights in question are reserved by the manner in which the federal powers are delegated."

[54]1 Congressional Proceedings 456.

[55]1 Congressional Proceedings 454.

delegated no power and over which none could be implied. On several occasions he argued against the implication of a power in the area of certain fundamental rights:

> There is not a shadow of right in the general government to intermeddle with religion. Its least interference with it would be a most flagrant usurpation.[56]

> [I]t would seem scarcely possible to doubt that no power whatever over the press was supposed to be delegated by the Constitution. . . .[57]

The preamble to the Congressional resolution adopting Madison's amendments spoke of them as being "declaratory or restrictive clauses."[58] For Madison the enumeration of fundamental rights such as freedom of speech and religion was merely "declaratory" and added nothing to the Constitution that had not already existed. Although he recognized that others believed that, in the absence of a bill of rights, the federal government might have power to infringe these rights,[59] he himself never accepted that such rights had in any way been surrendered.

But there was another reason that the federal government did not possess any power over fundamental rights. Madison and the other men who were involved in the framing of the Constitution and the Bill of Rights were guided by a philosophical tradition dictating that power over certain rights *could not* be delegated to *any* government.

> The largest part of the intellectual baggage of the Framers, whether of stars like Madison, Mason and Wilson or of bit-players like Richard Dobbs Spaight, Jared Ingersoll, and William Pierce, was a tempered version of the oldest and most famous liberty-oriented political philosophies: the school of natural law and natural rights.[60]

[56]3 Elliot, Debates 330. *And see* 2 Elliot, Debates 455 (Wilson); 3 Elliot, Debates 469 (Randolph).

[57]Madison's Report on the Virginia Resolutions (1800), 4 Elliot, Debates 546, 572. *And see* 3 Elliot, Debates 469 (Randolph).

[58]1 Elliot, Debates 338.

[59]Report on the Virginia Resolutions (1800), 4 Elliot, Debates 546, 571–73; 1 Congressional Proceedings 758.

[60]Rossiter, *supra* note 17, at 59. *See generally* Adams, Political Ideas of the American Revolution (1922); Mullett, Fundamental Law and the American Revolution (1933); Wright, Natural Law; Corwin, *supra* note 3, at 365.

The theory of natural rights taught that certain rights were unalienable; they were beyond the powers of government and could not be surrendered to it, despite even a written constitution to the contrary. Such thinking was epitomized by the second paragraph of the Declaration of Independence: "We hold these truths to be self-evident, That all men are created equal, that they are endowed by their creator with certain unalienable rights; that among these are life, liberty and the pursuit of happiness."[61] Admittedly, these were the words of an advocate of rebellion and therefore were phrased in the most virulent terms. However, the same natural rights philosophy also infused almost every argument made in favor of a bill of rights.[62] Madison himself spoke of the "pre-existent rights of nature" in the introduction of his amendments in Congress.[63]

The source of these unalienable, natural rights was to be found in the law of nature. The secular natural law theorists of England, especially Locke, Coke and Blackstone, were thoroughly familiar to the educated populace of eighteenth century America.[64] This heritage was enriched by the religious natural law doctrines promulgated by the colonial churches.[65] In accordance with this hybrid philosophy, the colonials believed that "the laws of nature are those which are expressive of the will of God, the true nature of man, the constitution of the universe. And they doubted not their ability to discover those laws."[66] Added to the pure natural law theory were the "rights of Englishmen" that the colonists had inherited from the mother country, or at least to which they looked for precedent.[67] This conglomeration produced a philosophy which had many variations, some of them internally inconsistent, and few of them adequately articulated. Nevertheless, the existence of natural law and

[61]Becker, The Declaration of Independence 8 (1942) and see surrounding text. *And see* Wright, Natural Law 93. *See also* Virginia Declaration of Rights (1776) in 7 Thorpe, The Federal and State Constitutions 3812–13 (1909).

[62]Wright, Natural Law 125–48; Haines, *The Law of Nature in State and Federal Judicial Decisions,* 25 Yale L.J. 617, 624–25 (1916); *see* John Quincy Adams, The Jubilee of the Constitution 40–41 (1839). *See generally* Pamphlets on the Constitution (Ford ed. 1888).

[63]1 Congressional Proceedings 454.

[64]Wright, Natural Law 8–11; Mullett, *supra* note 60, at ch. II; Corwin, *supra* note 3, at 394–99.

[65]Wright, Natural Law 327–28.

[66]*Id.* at 12.

[67]*See id.* at 92; Becker, *supra* note 61, at ch. 111.

natural rights and the latter's immunity from governmental regulation were accepted by almost all. Natural rights, therefore, were those which required no constitutional protection, and the addition of amendments covering them would only be "declaratory" of their inviolability.

The original of the ninth amendment must be considered in the light of the preceding general history of the Bill of Rights and Madison's thinking about those rights, in particular. For it was the debate over a bill of rights that inspired the ninth amendment, and it was Madison's views about the nature of rights and powers which colored the form the amendment took.

Madison's original draft of the ninth amendment (the last clause of his fourth resolution) was phrased alternatively, as either a reservation of unenumerated rights or a rule of strict construction of powers:

> The exceptions here or elsewhere in the Constitution, made in favor of particular rights, shall not be so construed as to *diminish the just importance of other rights retained by the people*, or as to *enlarge the powers delegated by the Constitution*; but either as actual limitations of such powers, or as inserted merely for greater caution.[68]

Madison's explanation of this amendment in his introductory speech in the House contains a similar ambiguity:

> It has been objected also against a bill of rights, that, by enumerating particular exceptions to the grant of power, it would *disparage those rights which were not placed in that enumeration*; and it might follow, by implication, that those rights which were not singled out, were intended to be *assigned into the hands of the General Government*, and were consequently insecure. This is one of the

---

[68] 1 Congressional Proceedings 452 (emphasis added). The ninth amendment was based upon ratification proposals of Virginia and New York, except that those proposals referred only to a strict construction of government power: Virginia No. 17: "That those clauses which declare that Congress shall not exercise certain powers, be not interpreted, in any manner whatsoever, to extend the powers of Congress; but that they be construed either as making exceptions to the specified powers where this shall be the case, or otherwise, as inserted merely for greater caution." 3 Elliot, Debates 661 (same as North Carolina No. 18., 4 Elliot, Debates 246). New York para. 4: "[T]hose clause in the said Constitution, which declare, that Congress shall not have or exercise certain Powers, do not imply that Congress is entitled to any Powers not given by the said Constitution; but such Clauses are to be construed either as exceptions to certain specified Powers, or as inserted merely for greater Caution." 1 Elliot, Debates 327 (same as Rhode Island art. III., 1 Elliot, Debates 334).

most plausible arguments I have ever heard urged against the admission of a bill of rights into this system; but, I conceive, that it may be guarded against. I have attempted it, as gentlemen may see by turning to the last clause of the fourth resolution.[69]

It is my belief that this alternative phraseology indicates that Madison utilized the ninth amendment to protect unenumerated *substantive* rights similar to freedom of speech and religion because, like the ninth amendment rights, freedom of speech and religion were not delegated to the federal government and were also retained by the people through a constitutional amendment. As explained previously, Madison believed that procedural rights could already be infringed under the necessary and proper clause of the Constitution as it stood, without a bill of rights.[70] The addition of a bill of rights would, therefore, probably add little additional threat to unenumerated procedural rights. But even if they were considered more in jeopardy than before and a protective amendment were deemed appropriate, Madison would have phrased it only in terms of unenumerated retained rights; a limitation to delegated powers would have been ineffectual. Unenumerated substantive rights, however, could be endangered by the addition of a bill of rights. To the extent that they were fundamental or natural rights, the government would have been delegated no power over them in the absence of a bill of rights; but an imperfect enumeration in a bill of rights might imply such a power. The ninth amendment was phrased in the alternative to guard against either the implication of a power or the implication of the nonexistence of a right; the only rights which were subject to both dangers were fundamental *substantive* rights.[71]

The final form of the ninth amendment referred only to the disparagement of unenumerated rights. It had been submitted, along with Madison's other proposals, to a Select Committee, to be

---

[69]1 Congressional Proceedings 456 (emphasis added).

[70]*See supra* notes 52–55 and accompanying text.

[71]Madison's biographer, Irving Brant, apparently agrees that the ninth amendment protected substantive rights: "Other rights—substantive—are protected by the guarantees of the First Amendment—freedom of religion, speech, press, assembly, petition, association. Closely related are voting rights. To this list should be added, either as elements of these privileges and immunities or under the Ninth Amendment, the right of silence and the right of travel." Brant, The Bill of Rights 77 (1965). *See* Abrams, *supra* note 11. *But see* Dunbar, *supra* note 3, at 641; Kelly, *supra* note 11, at 154.

further studied and reported back to the full House.[72] The Committee reported the ninth out as: "The enumeration in this Constitution of certain rights shall not be construed to deny or disparage others retained by the people."[73] There is no record in the House debates of the change from "this Constitution" to "the Constitution" and the addition of commas before and after the phrase "of certain rights"; these are the only things distinguishing the Committee's version from the final form of the amendment. The only recorded debate about the content of the amendment relates to an unsuccessful motion to substitute "impair" for "disparage."[74] The debates of the Senate were still secret; consequently, there is no indication of how that house interpreted the amendment.[75]

After the amendments had been circulated among the states for ratification, it came to Madison's attention that Edmund Randolph objected to the final form of the ninth amendment on the grounds that it should have been stated "rather as a provision against extending the powers of Congress by their own authority, than a protection to rights reducible to no definite certainty."[76] Madison's response to this objection in a letter to Washington further supports the interpretation of the ninth as protecting substantive rights:

> [T]he distinction be, as it appears to me, altogether fanciful. If a line can be drawn between the powers granted and the rights retained, it would seem to be the same thing, whether the latter to be secured by declaring that they shall not be abridged, or that the former shall not be extended.[77]

Since Madison indicates that the two forms of expression are equivalent, he could not have been concerned with unenumerated *procedural* rights; a statement that government shall be limited to its delegated powers would not have protected procedural rights against infringement under the necessary and proper clause. Only unenumerated fundamental *substantive* rights would have been pro-

---

[72]1 Congressional Proceedings 690–91.

[73]*Id.* at 783.

[74]*Id.*

[75]1 Congressional Proceedings 15–16. The Proceedings do record some Senate debate on the proposed amendments, but the record is mostly in summary form. *E.g.*, 1 Congressional Proceedings 77, 80, 85–86, & 90.

[76]Letter to George Washington (Dec. 5, 1789), 5 Madison 431.

[77]*Id.* at 432.

tected by such a restriction of government's powers.[78] The letter also eliminates the possibility that the first part of the original draft was meant to protect procedural rights and the second part to protect substantive rights. Madison's acceptance of the two clauses as alternatives indicates that they were both intended to guard against the same danger, and only substantive rights would be protected by either clause.

Suggestions have been made that Madison, as a member of the Select Committee, altered his original form of the ninth amendment because he had no intention of limiting the powers of the federal government and wanted to avoid the possibility that the ninth would be given such a construction.[79] This amounts to saying that he had made a mistake in his original alternative phraseology. If such an analysis were correct, my previous conclusion that the ninth amendment does include a strict construction of the delegated powers and, for that reason, protects only substantive rights might very well be questioned. But Madison's arguments against the constitutionality of Hamilton's national bank bill apparently refute this suggestion. Madison argued in Congress that passage of the bank bill would be the exercise of a power not delegated to the federal government. As evidence that the federal government was restricted to delegated powers and that even the necessary and proper clause was not unlimited, he pointed to, among other things, the ninth amendment.[80] Furthermore, Madison's letter to Washing-

---

[78]For the result of not recognizing that Madison's failure to distinguish between reserving rights and limiting powers makes perfect sense in the context of fundamental substantive rights, see the treatment which Madison's statement in his letter to Washington receives in Dunbar, *supra* note 3, at 633 ("This might seem a meaningless distinction, and so at one time Madison permitted himself to rationalize."), and in Kelley, *supra* note 11, at 822 n.36 ("This analysis can hardly be accepted.")

[79]Kelley, *supra* note 11, at 821–22; Call, *supra* note 3, at 126; see Rogge, *supra* note 3, at 793–96. Madison had said that he wanted to "make the revisal [of the Constitution] a moderate one" and that he did not want the adoption of amendments to open the door "for a reconsideration of the whole structure of the government." 1 Congressional Proceedings 450.

[80]2 Congressional Proceedings 1901: "He [Madison] read several of the articles proposed [in the first Congress as amendments to the Constitution], remarking particularly on the 11th [Ninth Amendment] and 12th [Tenth Amendment], the former, as guarding against a latitude of interpretation; the latter, as excluding every source of power not within the Constitution itself." *And see* 2 Congressional Proceedings 1902. Madison was using the ninth amendment here only to buttress his general argument that the federal government was limited to delegated powers.

ton, answering Randolph's suggestion that the ninth amendment would have been more appropriately phrased as a limit on implied powers, definitely indicates that he thought that the final form of the amendment was equivalent to a restriction on powers. In fact, the most likely explanation of the Select Committee's revision was that it was done to eliminate what was considered to be a redundancy. The Committee merely pruned the amendment so that it would be stated in a more concise, simplified form.

Another conceivable interpretation of the Committee's revisions is that the eliminated portion of the amendment was absorbed by the tenth amendment's broad restriction on implied federal power.[81] Some support is lent to this by Madison's use of the tenth amendment instead of the ninth to establish that the federal government had been delegated no power to pass the Alien and Sedition Acts.[82] One would think that the ninth amendment would have been a more appropriate text upon which to base an argument that the federal government had no power to legislate over a fundamental right, here free speech. Furthermore, the unexplained addition of "or to the people" to the tenth amendment[83] suggests the possibility that it was meant to supplement the rephrased form of the ninth amendment; thus the ninth stated that the people retained unenumerated rights and the tenth that they reserved undelegated powers.[84]

Such an interpretation of the ninth and tenth amendments cannot be accepted. To do so would be to render Madison's response to Randolph's objections meaningless. Certainly he would have pointed to the tenth amendment as satisfying Randolph's objection to the final form of the ninth if the former had been meant to supersede the ninth as a limitation upon the federal government to delegated powers in the area of fundamental liberties. On the contrary, Madison's argument that the national bank bill offended both the ninth

---

Nowhere does he point to any right explicitly protected by the ninth amendment, but one of his arguments against the bank was that, "It involves a monopoly, which affects the equal rights of every citizen." 2 Congressional Proceedings 1900.

[81]*Cf.* Griswold v. Connecticut, 381 U.S. 479, 489 n.4 (1965) (concurring opinion).

[82]The Virginia Resolutions (1798), 4 Elliot, Debates 528 (Madison). *And see* The Kentucky Resolutions (1798–99), 4 Elliot, Debates 540 (Jefferson).

[83]1 Congressional Proceedings 790. The tenth amendment now reads: "The powers not delegated to the United States by the Constitution, nor prohibited by it to the States, are reserved to the States respectively, or to the people."

[84]Redlich, *supra* note 3, at 806–07 (1962).

and tenth amendments because it exceeded the delegated powers of the federal government[85] indicates that he viewed them both as power-limiting provisions. The tenth amendment was viewed essentially as a limit on federal power vis-à-vis the states and the ninth as a limit on federal power vis-à-vis the rights of the people. The annexation of "or to the people" to the tenth was merely designed to recognize that some powers were delegated to neither the federal nor the state governments[86]; if this had not been added, the tenth amendment itself could have been construed as a delegation to the states of all powers not granted to the federal government. Finally, it should be noted that even if this interpretation of the ninth and tenth amendments were correct, it would not substantially affect the conclusion that the ninth amendment was designed to protect substantive rather than procedural rights; it would only mean that the tenth amendment was the lone constitutional provision intended expressly to limit the powers of the federal government.

One final interpretation of the ninth amendment deserves brief mention. It is that the ninth was Madison's answer to his own fear that political obstacles might result in an insufficiently comprehensive definition of some rights.[87] This concern was apparently peculiar to Madison, and it is somewhat implausible that the ninth amendment was solely responsive to his fears in this regard. Both Virginia and New York had proposed prototypes to his amendment in their acts of ratification,[88] and there is no evidence whatsoever that those conventions shared Madison's personal concern. Madison's introductory remarks in Congress indicated that he himself was dealing with the more general problem of the implication of unenumerated powers.[89] The only right which Madison had mentioned as the object of his concern, freedom of religion, was incorporated into the first amendment essentially as he proposed it,[90] and yet he still supported the need for the ninth amendment. Madison's purpose in advocating the ninth amendment was

---

[85]*See supra* note 80.

[86]2 Story, Commentaries on the Constitution of the United States 652 (5th ed. 1891); Redlich, *supra* note 3, at 807.

[87]Kelly, *supra* note 11, at 153. *See also supra* note 38 and accompanying text.

[88]*See supra* note 69.

[89]*See supra* note 69 and accompanying text.

[90]Kelley, *supra* note 11, at 824–25.

undoubtedly broader than this interpretation suggests; it was to protect those fundamental substantive rights which, for one reason or another, were omitted from the enumeration in the Bill of Rights. Madison's conception of these unenumerated substantive rights retained by the ninth amendment poses an interesting contrast to the method of constitutional adjudication developed by the Supreme Court. Madison would not have anticipated the confrontation of a legitimate federal power, express or implied, and an unenumerated substantive right. As has been suggested by others, he believed that such rights are in the area of "no-power."[91] If a federal governmental act were challenged as encroaching upon an unenumerated right,[92] it would be irrelevant whether the Court declared the act unconstitutional because it had encroached upon the alleged right or because it had extended beyond the limits of permissible power. American constitutional history, however, reveals little sympathy with a power-limiting approach. Although the Supreme Court has given ready recognition to substantive rights, both enumerated and unenumerated, the main stream of its interpretative methodology, especially in recent years, has been to reject a construction of the Constitution which places a limit on the power, as such, of government.

State governments are endowed with a broad panoply of powers compendiously referred to as the "police power." This has been defined as the power to "prescribe regulations to promote the health, peace, morals, education, and good order of the people, and to legislate so as to increase the industries of the State, develop its resources, and add to its wealth and prosperity."[93] No doubt some of the early twentieth century cases concerning state economic and social regulations contained language to the effect that the police power is not unlimited and may not be exerted in an "arbitrary or oppressive manner."[94] But these same cases also spoke

[91]*Id.* at 822–23; Dunbar, *supra* note 3, at 641.

[92]"Unenumerated rights" will hereafter refer to unenumerated substantive rights.

[93]Barbier v. Connolly, 113 U.S. 27, 31 (1885). And see Jacobson v. Massachusetts, 197 U.S. 11, 25 (1905); Holden v. Hardy, 169 U.S. 366, 392 (1898).

[94]McLean v. Arkansas, 211 U.S. 539, 547 (1909). *See, e.g.*, Adams v. Tanner, 244 U.S. 590, 595–96 (1917); Coppage v. Kansas, 236 U.S. 1, 16–18 (1915); Lochner v. New York, 198 U.S. 45, 58 (1905).

about the "liberty of contract"[95] or the "rights of property"[96] which were being unconstitutionally infringed. Moreover this whole line of cases has been explicitly repudiated by the Supreme Court in a number of its decisions during and after the New Deal.[97] Situations in which a state law is held substantively unconstitutional on the ground that state power is lacking normally occur only where the Constitution explicitly withdraws the power[98] or where the state law conflicts with a proper federal law made paramount by the supremacy clause.[99] Otherwise, a state law is held substantively unconstitutional only if it conflicts with a protected individual right.[100]

The construction of federal powers is governed by different considerations, but the result here has been essentially the same. Although the powers of the federal government are restricted to those delegated and those implied under the necessary and proper clause, the Supreme Court's construction of those powers has been very broad. Chief Justice Marshall's historic rendering of the necessary and proper clause to permit any means which are "appropriate"[101] has made Congress virtually the final arbiter of the

[95]E.g., Adams v. Tanner, 244 U.S. 590 (1917); Lochner v. New York, 198 U.S. 45, 61 (1905).

[96]E.g., Tyson & Brother v. Banton, 273 U.S. 418, 429 (1927); Coppage v. Kansas, 236 U.S. 1, 18 (1915).

[97]E.g., Ferguson v. Skrupa, 372 U.S. 726, 730 (1963); Olsen v. Nebraska ex rel. Western Reverence & Bond Ass'n, 313 U.S. 236 (1941); West Coast Hotel Co. v. Parrish, 300 U.S. 379 (1937). But see Griswold v. Connecticut, 381 U.S. 479, 502 (1965) (White, J. concurring); Ferguson v. Skrupa, 372 U.S. 726 (1963) (Harlan, J. concurring). See generally Pound, Liberty of Contract, 18 Yale L.J. 454 (1909); Haines, Revival of Natural Law Concepts (1930).

[98]E.g., Brown v. Maryland, 25 U.S. (12 Wheat.) 419 (1827) (duty on imports); Trustees of Dartmouth College v. Woodward, 17 U.S. (4 Wheat.) 518 (1819) (impairment of the obligation of contract); see McCollum v. Board of Education, 333 U.S. 203 (1948) (establishment of religion).

[99]E.g., Pennsylvania v. Nelson, 350 U.S. 497 (1956) (protection against violent overthrow); Hood & Sons, Inc. v. Du Mond, 336 U.S. 525 (1949) (commerce clause); Southern Pacific Co. v. Jensen, 244 U.S. 205 (1917) (maritime power).

[100]E.g., Griswold v. Connecticut, 381 U.S. 479 (1965) (right of privacy); New York Times Co. v. Sullivan, 376 U.S. 254 (1964) (freedom of speech and the press); Cantwell v. Connecticut, 310 U.S. 296 (1940) (freedom of speech and religion); see Reynolds v. Sims, 377 U.S. 533 (1964) (right to vote); Brown v. Board of Educ., 347 U.S. 483 (1954) (right to education); Skinner v. Oklahoma, 316 U.S. 535 (1942) (right of procreation).

[101]McCulloch v. Maryland, 17 U.S. (4 Wheat.) 159, 207 (1819). For Madison's adverse reaction to this opinion, see Letter to Spencer Roane (Sept. 2, 1819), 8 Madison 447.

means it may use to effectuate a delegated end. Those delegated ends over which Congress may exercise power have also been quite liberally interpreted. Under the commerce clause, the federal government has apparently been granted something akin to the police power,[102] insofar as it regulates interstate commerce.[103] And by virtue of the taxing and spending power,[104] the power to coin and regulate the value of money,[105] the war power[106] and the enforcement provisions of the fourteenth amendment,[107] federal power is substantial enough to comprehend the regulation of almost anything which cannot be reached by the commerce clause.

Even the tenth amendment has been of little consequence in halting this expansion of federal powers, except for a few cases in the New Deal and pre–New Deal period.[108] Although phrased as a limitation on the powers of the national government, the tenth amendment has been rendered superfluous by construction: "The

[102]Heart of Atlanta Motel v. United States, 379 U.S. 241, 257 (1964) ("That Congress was legislating against moral wrongs in many of these areas rendered its enactments no less valid."). *But see* Prigg v. Pennsylvania, 41 U.S. (16 Pet.) 539, 625 (1842). *See also, e.g.,* United States v. Darby, 312 U.S. 100 (1941) (wages and hours); NLRB v. Jones & Laughlin Steel Corp., 301 U.S. 1 (1937) (union organization); Champion v. Ames, 188 U.S. 321 (1903) (gambling). *See generally* Jacobson, *Federalism and Property Rights,* 15 N.Y.U.L.Q. Rev. 319 (1938); Stern, *The Commerce Clause and the National Economy, 1933–1946* (parts 1 & 2), 59 Harv. L. Rev. 645, 883 (1946).

[103]"Interstate commerce" has also been so broadly defined that most local enterprises can be reached by Congressional power. *E.g.,* Katzenbach v. McClung, 379 U.S. 294 (1964); United States v. Sullivan, 332 U.S. 689 (1948); Wickard v. Filburn, 317 U.S. 111 (1942). For the power of the executive in interstate commerce, see Youngstown Sheet & Tube Co. v. Sawyer, 343 U.S. 579 (1952); *In re* Debs, 158 U.S. 564 (1895).

[104]United States v. Sanchez, 340 U.S. 42 (1950); Steward Machine Co. v. Davis, 301 U.S. 548 (1937); Helvering v. Davis, 301 U.S. 619 (1937); *see* United States v. Butler, 297 U.S. 1, 64–67 (1936).

[105]*E.g.,* Norman v. Baltimore & Ohio R.R., 294 U.S. 240 (1935); Legal Tender Cases, 79 U.S. (12 Wall.) 457 (1871).

[106]*E.g.,* Woods v. Miller, 333 U.S. 138 (1948); Korematsu v. United States, 323 U.S. 214 (1944); Steward v. Kahn, 78 U.S. (11 Wall.) 493 (1870).

[107]Katzenbach v. Morgan, 384 U.S. 641 (1966); United States v. Guest, 383 U.S. 745, 777 (1966) (separate opinion of Brennan, J.); *Ex parte* Virginia, 100 U.S. 339 (1880); *see* South Carolina v. Katzenbach, 383 U.S. 301 (1966) (fifteenth amendment).

[108]United States v. Butler, 297 U.S. 1 (1936); Hopkins Fed. Sav. & Loan Ass'n. v. Cleary, 296 U.S. 315 (1935); Bailey v. Drexel Furniture Co., 259 U.S. 20 (1922); Hammer v. Dagenhart, 247 U.S. 251 (1918); *see* Collector v. Day, 78 U.S. (11 Wall.) 113, 124 (1871). *See generally* Block, *The "Silent" Amendments,* 27 Texas B.J. 155 (1964).

amendment states but a truism that all is retained which has not been surrendered. There is nothing in the history of its adoption to suggest that it was more than declaratory of the relationship between the national and state governments. . . ."[109] If any basis for the exercise of federal power is found, the inquiry under the tenth amendment is terminated.[110] As in the state cases, when a federal act is struck down on substantive grounds, it is usually because the Constitution expressly withholds a power from the federal government[111] or because the exercise of the power results in the infringement of a protected right.[112]

The Supreme Court therefore has been reluctant to follow Madison's conception that there are areas where, even in the absence of express limitations, government has no power.[113] This hesitation to indulge in a power-limiting analysis stems from a belief in the doctrine of separation of powers. If the judiciary is to pass upon the ends of government without reliance upon an express constitutional text, it is left without a standard by which to make its judgments. Necessarily, it must indulge in the same determinations

---

[109]United States v. Darby, 312 U.S. 100, 124 (1941). *And see* New York v. United States, 326 U.S. 572 (1946) (opinion of Frankfurter, J.).

[110]United Pub. Workers of America v. Mitchell, 330 U.S. 75, 95–96 (1947).

[111]Pollack v. Farmers' Loan & Trust Co., 158 U.S. 601 (1895) (direct tax). For quasi-substantive limits on federal power, see the cases of what might be called "legislative due process" (2 Freund, Suterland, Howe & Brown, Constitutional Law 1062 (1961)). *Ex parte* Garland, 71 U.S. (4 Wall.) 333 (1867) (ex post facto law); United States v. Brown, 381 U.S. 437 (1965) (bill of attainder); United States v. Cardiff, 344 U.S. 174 (1952) (vagueness and contradictory commands). See generally on this topic, Fuller, The Morality of Law ch. 2 (1964). See also the separation of powers cases, Schecter Poultry Corp. v. United States, 295 U.S. 495 (1935); Humphrey's Ex'r v. United States, 295 U.S. 602 (1935); Youngstown Sheet & Tube Co. v. Sawyer, 343 U.S. 579 (1952).

[112]*E.g.*, Lamont v. Postmaster Gen., 380 U.S. 301 (1965) (right to receive mail); Aptheker v. Secretary of State, 378 U.S. 500 (1964) (right of travel); Schneider v. Rusk, 377 U.S. 163 (1964) (citizenship). *And see* Afroyim v. Rusk, 387 U.S. 253 (1967); Trop. v. Dulles, 356 U.S. 86, 105 (1958) (Brennan, J. concurring).

[113]The Court has even been cautious in its construction of express substantive limitations. Home Bldg. & Loan Ass'n v. Blaisdell, 290 U.S. 398 (1934) (impairment of the obligation of contracts); Stanton v. Baltic Mining Co., 240 U.S. 103, 114 (1916) (direct tax). Note that counsel for the State of Connecticut in Griswold v. Connecticut, 381 U.S. 479, 505 (1965) (concurring opinion), avoided forcing the Court to pass on the legitimacy of a state's exercise of power justified only as an enactment of moral law. *See generally* Emerson, *Nine Justices in Search of a Doctrine*, 64 Mich. L. Rev. 219, 225–27 (1965).

about the propriety, adequacy, and effectiveness of a law that a legislature does. These are judgments which a court is ill-equipped to make, and which, in a democracy, are more properly lodged in a representative body.[114] Since the New Deal period, the Court has stated many times that it does not sit as a "superlegislature" to judge the wisdom or reasonableness of laws.[115] As has been discussed above, even in the construction of the delegated powers of the federal government, the Court has shown a great deference to legislative determinations about the nature and extent of governmental power.[116]

The protection of individual liberties, however, has traditionally been a judicial function. The Court has often been characterized as *the* institutional bulwark against the oppression of minorities.[117] In advocating the adoption of the Bill of Rights in the first Congress, Madison himself said,

> If they [his proposed amendments] are incorporated into the constitution, independent tribunals of justice will consider themselves in a peculiar manner the guardians of those rights; they will be an impenetrable bulwark against every assumption of power in the legislative or executive; they will be naturally led to resist every encroachment upon rights expressly stipulated for in the constitution by the declaration of rights.[118]

[114]*But see* Strure, *The Less-Restrictive-Alternative Principle and Economic Due Process,* 80 Harv. L. Rev. 1463 (1967).

[115]Griswold v. Connecticut, 381 U.S. 479, 482 (1965); Day-Brite Lighting, Inc. v. Missouri, 342 U.S. 421, 423 (1952); Jay Burns Baking Co. v., Bryan, 264 U.S. 504, 534 (1924) (Brandeis, J. dissenting).

[116]Harisiades v. Shaughnessy, 342 U.S. 580 (1952). *But see* Trop v. Dulles, 356 U.S. 86, 105 (1958) (Brennan, J. concurring). Compare *In re* Rahrer, 140 U.S. 545 (1891) with Leisy v. Hardin, 135 U.S. 100 (1890). The closest the Court comes to a strict construction of delegated federal powers is its practice of construing Congressional acts so as to avoid a constitutional issue. *See* Kent v. Dulles, 357 U.S. 116 (1958); International Ass'n of Machinists v. Street, 367 U.S. 740 (1961). Even under the first amendment speech clause, the Court has viewed its function as the protection of freedom of speech rather than an interpretation of the phrase, "Congress shall make no law." *See* Dennis v. United States, 341 U.S. 494 (1951). *But see Justice Black and First Amendment "Absolutes": A Public Interview,* 37 N.Y.U. L. Rev. 549 (1962); Meiklejohn, *The First Amendment is an Absolute,* 1961 Sup. Ct. Rev. 245.

[117]*E.g.,* Sutherland, *Privacy in Connecticut,* 64 Mich. L. Rev. 283, 284 (1965); Brennan, *Constitutional Adjudication,* 40 Notre Dame Law. 559, 567 (1965).

[118]1 Congressional Proceedings 457. *See also* Letter to James Madison (March 15, 1789), 5 Jefferson 80. In The Federalist No. 51, Madison had expressed a fear of his

The Court's institutional isolation from political pressure gives it a unique capacity to temper the will of the majority and guarantee a minimum of protection to the overwhelmed individual. This is also a function which the Court is peculiarly competent to perform. The confrontation of an individual's fundamental liberties and the power of government provides a more focused issue for the Court than the wide-ranging investigations which are required in judging the necessity or adequacy of a positive law. To use Professor Fuller's phrase, the problems are not as "polycentric"[119] as those involved in a determination of the proper ends of government. It is therefore suggested that the Court's instinct in rejecting a power-limiting analysis and relying upon the development of substantive rights has proved, and will prove, to be the most appropriate way to limit the unjustified exercise of governmental power.[120]

The fact that the ninth amendment was in part designed as a rule of construction to limit governmental power and the fact that the Supreme Court has repudiated such an approach, should not, for those reasons alone, result in a relegation of the ninth amendment to the limbo now occupied by the tenth amendment.[121] The amendment as phrased, and as in part originally intended, speaks in terms of unenumerated rights; this language should be respected. Furthermore, the very fact that Madison never anticipated the broad construction of delegated powers which the Court has adopted[122]

that an unrestrained majority would trample the rights of an out-voted minority. *And see* 1 Congressional Proceedings 454–55 (Madison); de Toqueville, *Unlimited Power of the Majority,* in 1 Democracy in America ch. XV (Vintage ed. 1954).

[119]Fuller, *Collective Bargaining and the Arbitrator,* 1963 Wis. L. Rev. 3, 32–34. *See* Baker v. Carr, 369 U.S. 186, 266 (1962) (Frankfurter, J. dissenting); Fordham, *Judicial Policy-Making at Legislative Expense,* 34 Geo. Wash. L. Rev. 829 (1966); *cf.* Brown v. Bd. of Educ., 349 U.S. 294 (1955). This is not to suggest, however, that the issues involved are any less subtle or less perplexing. *See generally* Freund, *Constitutional Dilemmas,* 45 B.U.L. Rev. 13 (1965).

[120]An extended essay into the nature of judicial review is beyond the scope of this paper; for such works, see Bickel, The Least Dangerous Branch (1962); Black, The People and the Court (1960); Supreme Court and Supreme Law (Cahn ed. 1954); Freund, On Understanding the Supreme Court (1949); Hand, The Bill of Rights (1958).

[121]This is what Justice Black would have the Court do. Griswold v. Connecticut, 381 U.S. 479, 520 (1965) (dissenting opinion). *And see* Rogge, *supra* note 3, at 790 & 805–06. *Contra* Kelley, *supra* note 11, at 827; Dunbar, *supra* note 3, at 643.

[122]Letter to Spencer Roane, *supra* note 101, at 450. For a review of Madison's recantation of his faith in the necessary and proper clause, see Rogge, *supra* note 3, at 794–96.

militates in favor of a revival of the ninth amendment as a counter-weight to expansive governmental power.[123] As Chief Justice Marshall once said, "[W]e must never forget that it is a *constitution* we are expounding."[124] Both the history of the ninth amendment itself and the development of the Court as the guardian of individual liberties indicate the propriety of construing that amendment as a textual guarantee of unenumerated rights.

But if history alone were relevant, it would be clear that the ninth amendment could only be utilized against the federal government. Madison's fourth resolution, of which the ninth amendment was the last clause, contained most of the eight amendments which became the Bill of Rights. This whole resolution had originally been intended to be inserted in Article I, section 9 between the ex post facto clause and the direct tax clause.[125] In other words, it was to be placed in that part of the Constitution which was devoted solely to limitations on the federal government. Furthermore, Madison's fifth resolution, which safeguarded certain rights against state impairment, contained no reference to unenumerated rights,[126] nor did Madison's introduction of his fifth resolution mention the existence of unenumerated rights vis-à-vis the states.[127] The fact that the original draft of the ninth amendment said that "the exceptions *here or elsewhere* in the Constitution, made in favor of particular rights, shall not be construed as to diminish the importance of other rights retained by the people"[128] can hardly be deemed sufficient grounds to infer that it was referring to the rights enumerated in the fifth resolution,[129] for that would be to disregard the context in which this language appears. The sentence continues, "or as to enlarge the *powers delegated* by the constitution."[130] The Constitution was essentially a delegation of powers only to the federal government, and therefore the ninth amendment was directed against the

---

[123]*See* Risjord, *The Bill of Rights: Comments on Its Historical Development,* 1966 Wis. L. Rev. 1201.

[124]McCulloch v. Maryland, 17 U.S. (4 Wheat.) 316, 407 (1819). *And see* United States v. Weems, 217 U.S. 349, 373 (1910).

[125]1 Congressional Proceedings 451.

[126]*Id.* at 452.

[127]*Id.* at 458.

[128]*Id.* at 452 (emphasis added).

[129]*Contra* Patterson, *supra* note 3, at ch. 6.

[130]1 Congressional Proceedings 452 (emphasis added).

implication of federal powers and, in that context only, the derogation of individual rights.

This historical background, however, should not provide a great obstacle to application of the ninth amendment to the states. None of the first eight amendments were originally intended to restrict the state governments and, at first, the Court refused to so construe them.[131] Initially, the passage of the fourteenth amendment did little to change this situation.[132] But through the process of what has come to be known as "selective absorption," the Court has gradually drawn the rights in the first eight amendments into the due process clause of the fourteenth.[133] There is no reason why the ninth amendment rights should not be subject to the same process of absorption. Those rights which have been absorbed into the

---

[131]*E.g.*, Barron v. Baltimore, 32 U.S. (7 Pet.) 243 (1833).

[132]*See* United States v. Cruikshank, 92 U.S. 542, 552 (1876) (first amendment, assembly); Prudential Ins. Co. of America v. Cheek, 259 U.S. 530, 543 (1922) (first amendment, speech); Presser v. Illinois, 116 U.S. 252, 265 (1886) (second amendment); Weeks v. United States, 232 U.S. 383, 398 (1914) (fourth amendment); Hurtado v. California, 110 U.S. 516, 538 (1884) (fifth amendment, grand jury indictment); Palko v. Connecticut, 302 U.S. 319, 328 (1937) (fifth amendment, double jeopardy); Twining v. New Jersey, 211 U.S. 78, 113 (1908) (fifth amendment, self-incrimination); Maxwell v. Dow, 176 U.S. 581, 595 (1900) (sixth amendment, jury trial in criminal case); West v. Louisiana, 194 U.S. 258, 262 (1904) (sixth amendment, confrontation); Betts v. Brady, 316 U.S. 455 (1942) (sixth amendment, counsel); Walker v. Sauvinet, 92 U.S. 90, 92 (seventh amendment, civil jury trial); In re Kemmler, 136 U.S. 436 (1890) (eighth amendment, cruel and unusual punishment).

[133]Gitlow v. New York, 268 U.S. 652 (1925) (first amendment, speech); Near v. Minnesota, 283 U.S. 697 (1931) (first amendment, press); DeJonge v. Oregon, 299 U.S. 353 (1937) (first amendment, assembly); N.A.A.C.P. v. Alabama, 357 U.S. 449 (1958) (first amendment, association); Cantwell v. Connecticut, 310 U.S. 296 (1940) (first amendment, freedom of religion); Everson v. Board of Education, 330 U.S. 1 (1947) (first amendment, establishment clause); Elkins v. United States, 364 U.S. 206 (1960) (fourth amendment); Chicago B. & Q.R. Co. v. Chicago, 166 U.S. 226 (1897) (fifth amendment, compensation for private property); Malloy v. Hogan, 378 U.S. 1 (1964) (fifth amendment, self-incrimination); Gideon v. Wainwright, 372 U.S. 335, 344–45 (1963) (sixth amendment, counsel); Pointer v. Texas, 380 U.S. 400 (1965) (sixth amendment, confrontation); In re Oliver, 333 U.S. 257 (1948) (sixth amendment, notice of charge) (by implication); Klopfer v. North Carolina, 386 U.S. 213 (1967) (sixth amendment, speedy trial); Washington v. Texas, 388 U.S. 14 (1967) (sixth amendment, compulsory process); Robinson v. California, 370 U.S. 660, 666 (1962) (eighth amendment, cruel and unusual punishment). The Court has also held that once a right in the first eight amendments has been absorbed, it applies against the states with the same force as it does against the federal government. Malloy v. Hogan, *supra* at 10; Ker v. California, 374 U.S. 23 (1963).

fourteenth amendment are only those which are "fundamental personal rights."[134] If the rights encompassed by the ninth amendment are the natural rights of man, analogous to speech and religion, surely they must be ranked as "fundamental." Even as a practical matter, it is highly unlikely that the Supreme Court would develop any unenumerated right under the ninth amendment which it would not classify as "fundamental."[135] Therefore, it is almost axiomatic that if an unenumerated right is good against the federal government by virtue of the ninth amendment, it is good against the state governments by virtue of the fourteenth amendment.

Hopefully, the preceding discussion has established three things: first, that historically the ninth amendment was intended to safeguard unenumerated fundamental substantive rights, both by giving constitutional stature to the rights themselves and by narrowly limiting the federal government to the powers then believed to have been delegated to it; second, the fact that the Supreme Court has not accepted the latter approach in its constitutional interpretations should not preclude a utilization of the ninth amendment for that reason alone; and third, that if the ninth amendment were used by the Court, it could easily be made effective against the states through the fourteenth amendment.

. . .

---

[134]Griswold v. Connecticut, 381 U.S. 479, 488 (1965) (Goldberg, J. concurring); Palko v. Connecticut, 302 U.S. 319, 325 (1937); Snyder v. Massachusetts, 291 U.S. 97, 105 (1934); Herbert v. Louisiana, 272 U.S. 312, 316 (1926). *See generally* Cushman, *Incorporation: Due Process and the Bill of Rights*, 51 Cornell L.Q. 467 (1966); Frankfurter, *Memorandum on "Incorporation,"* 78 Harv. L. Rev. 746 (1965); Lacey, *The Bill of Rights and the Fourteenth Amendment*, 23 Wash. & Lee L. Rev. 37 (1966); Loewy, *The Supreme Court Revisits "Palko v. Connecticut,"* 40 Conn. B.J. 408 (1966); Rudman, *"Incorporation" Under the Fourteenth Amendment—The Other Side of the Coin*, 3 Law in Trans. Q. 141 (1966).

[135]*See* Griswold v. Connecticut, 381 U.S. 479, 492 (1965) (concurring opinion).

7. The Ninth Amendment

John Hart Ely

The Ninth Amendment, which applies to the federal government, provides that "[t]he enumeration in the Constitution, of certain rights, shall not be construed to deny or disparage others retained by the people." Occasionally a commentator will express a willingness to read it for what it seems to say, but this has been, and remains, a distinctly minority impulse. In sophisticated legal circles mentioning the Ninth Amendment is a surefire way to get a laugh. ("What are you planning to rely on to support that argument, Lester, the Ninth Amendment?") The joke is somewhat elusive. It's true that read for what it says the Ninth Amendment seems open-textured enough to support almost anything one might wish to argue, and that thought can get pretty scary. But this is equally true of the "substantive due process" concept, which *is* generally accepted, albeit with some misgivings, in the selfsame sophisticated circles. That puts the world exactly upside down, however, for whereas the Due Process Clause speaks of process, the Ninth Amendment refers to unenumerated rights.

The received account of the Ninth Amendment, which Justice Black once went so far as to say "every student of history knows,"[1] goes like this. There was fear that the inclusion of a bill of rights in the Constitution would be taken to imply that federal power was not in fact limited to the authorities enumerated in Article I, Section 8, that instead it extended all the way up to the edge of the rights stated in the first eight amendments. (As in "Obviously the federal

Reprinted, by permission, from *Democracy and Distrust* (Cambridge: Harvard University Press, 1980), pp. 34–41. © 1980 by the President and Fellows of Harvard College.

Editor's Note: In this excerpt, the footnotes have been renumbered and edited for consistency.

[1]Griswold v. Connecticut, 381 U.S. 479, 520 (1965) (Black, J., dissenting). *See also, e.g.,* R. Berger, Government by Judiciary 390 (1977); E. Dumbauld, The Bill of Rights 63–65 (1957).

government has authority to do everything *except* abridge freedom of speech and so forth.") The Ninth Amendment, the received version goes, was attached to the Bill of Rights simply to negate that inference, to reiterate that ours was a government of "few and defined powers."

Every student of history does not know this. It is true that there was fear, no matter how strained it may seem to a contemporary observer, that the addition of a bill of rights might be taken to imply the existence of congressional powers beyond those stated in the body of the Constitution. It is also true that the alleviation of this fear was one reason Madison gave for adding the Ninth Amendment to the Bill of Rights. The conclusion that that was the *only* reason for its inclusion does not follow, however, and in fact it seems wrong. The Tenth Amendment, submitted and ratified at the same time, completely fulfills the function that is here being proffered as all the Ninth Amendment was about. That amendment provides that "[t]he powers not delegated to the United States by the Constitution, nor prohibited by it to the States, are reserved to the States respectively, or to the people." This says—in language as clearly to the point as the language of the Ninth Amendment is not—that the addition of the Bill of Rights is not to be taken to have changed the fact that powers not delegated are not delegated. It does seem that a similar thought was part of what animated the Ninth Amendment, but if that were *all* that amendment had been calculated to say, it would have been redundant.

There isn't much legislative history bearing on the Ninth Amendment, but what there is unsurprisingly confirms that one of the thoughts behind it was the thought that its terms convey. A letter Madison wrote to Jefferson in October 1788 gave the reasons why the writer, though in favor of a Bill of Rights, had not yet pressed for the inclusion of one:

> My own opinion has always been in favor of a bill of rights; provided it be so framed as not to imply powers not meant to be included in the enumeration. . . . I have not viewed it in an important light—1. because I conceive that in a certain degree . . . the rights in question are reserved by the manner in which the federal powers are granted. 2. because there is great reason to fear that a positive declaration of some of the most essential rights could not be obtained in the requisite latitude. I am sure that the rights of conscience in particular, if submitted to public definition

would be narrowed much more than they are likely ever to be by an assumed power.[2]

When it came to Madison's explanation of the Ninth Amendment on the floor of Congress the following June, however, the clarity of the letter to Jefferson—separating the question of unenumerated powers from the question of unenumerated rights—gave way to some confusion:

> It has been objected also against a bill of rights, that, by enumerating particular exceptions to the grant of power, it would disparage those rights which were not placed in that enumeration; and it might follow by implication, that those rights that were not placed in that enumeration, that those rights which were not singled out, were intended to be assigned into the hands of the General Government, and were consequently insecure. This is one of the most plausible arguments I have ever heard urged against the admission of a bill of rights into this system; but, I conceive, that it may be guarded against. I have attempted it, as gentlemen may see by turning to the last clause of the fourth resolution.[3]

Here the points are telescoped, and the possibility that unenumerated rights will be disparaged is seemingly made to do service as an intermediate premise in an argument that unenumerated powers will be implied (though at the very end of the first sentence it seems to flip again and the possibility that unenumerated powers will be inferred now seems threatening because of what that would mean to unenumerated rights). The confusion is understandable in context: a good deal of the debate over a bill of rights was marked by what we would today regard as a category mistake, a failure to recognize that rights and powers are not simply the absence of one

---

[2] 5 Writings of James Madison 271–72 (Hunt ed. 1904).

[3] 1 Annals of Cong. 439 (1789). *See also* 3 J. Story, Commentaries on the Constitution of the United States § 1861 (1833); 1 *Annals of Cong.* 435 (1789) (version originally submitted by Madison): "The exceptions here or elsewhere in the Constitution, made in favor of particular rights, shall not be so construed as to diminish the just importance of other rights retained by the people, or as to enlarge the powers delegated by the Constitution; but either as actual limitations of such powers, or as inserted merely for greater caution."

another but that rights can cut across or "trump" powers.[4] (As in "A law prohibiting the interstate shipment of books may be a regulation of commerce, but it violates the First Amendment and thus must fall.") What is important is that even here Madison, though he may have linked them in a way that seems unnatural today, made both the points he had made more clearly earlier— that he wished to forestall *both* the implication of unexpressed powers *and* the disparagement of unenumerated rights. What is more important is that just as the Tenth Amendment clearly expresses the former point, the Ninth Amendment clearly expresses the latter. And it is, of course, that language on which the Congress and the state legislatures were asked to vote. Thus the Ninth Amendment speaks clearly of unenumerated rights and in addition there is evidence, though I'd argue it's unnecessary, that its author understood what he had written.[5]

---

[4]*E.g.,* 5 Writings of James Madison 431–32 (Hunt ed. 1904). This is not to say that the proper relation between the two concepts was never apprehended *See, e.g.,* The Federalist no. 84, at 535 n.* (B. Wright ed. 1961) (Hamilton): "To show that there is a power in the Constitution by which the liberty of the press may be affected, recourse has been had to the power of taxation." Hamilton went on to argue that the example is faulty because taxes on newspapers cannot violate freedom of the press—*but see* Grosjean v. American Press Co., 297 U.S. 233 (1936)—but the structure of the discussion nonetheless demonstrates that the possibility of a governmental act's being supported by one of the enumerated powers and at the same time violating one of the enumerated rights is one our forebears were capable of contemplating. That is also demonstrated by the inclusion in the body of the original Constitution of the prohibitions against federal bills of attainder and ex post facto laws despite the fact that no affirmative power to pass such offending laws had anywhere been granted in terms.

[5]All this encounters an argument first made by Alfred Kelly, that "if the Ninth Amendment were concerned primarily with safeguarding individual liberties, one might expect to find similar provisions in some of the bills of rights of contemporary state constitutions; but the Ninth Amendment is unique." P. Brest, Processes of Constitutional Decisionmaking 708 (1975), relying on Kelly, *Clio and the Court: An Illicit Love Affair,* 1965 Sup. Ct. Rev. 119, 154. The word "contemporary" makes the claim technically accurate: no such provision appears in any eighteenth-century state bill of rights. But that interpretation, which is the only one that can preserve the claim's accuracy, makes the entire argument somewhat misleading, since there weren't many state bills of rights of any sort—or for that matter many states—back then. And when one reviews the period when most state bills of rights in fact were drafted, the nineteenth century, one discovers that no fewer than twenty-six of them contained provisions indicating that the enumeration of certain rights was not to be taken to disparage others retained by the people, and indeed several of them were quite clear about distinguishing this caveat from another we have seen, namely that

That doesn't mean we're home free, though. For once the received "federalism" account has been discarded, a further choice comes into focus. It still might be the case that the Ninth Amendment was intended to indicate not that there were other federal constitutional rights, but rather that the enumeration of certain rights in the first eight amendments was not to be taken to deny or disparage the existence of *other sorts of rights*—rights that do not rise to the constitutional, at least not to the federal constitutional, level. That is, it might have been intended to make clear that despite the Bill of Rights Congress could create further rights, or that state legislatures (or common law courts) could do so, or that a state could do so in its own constitution.

This is a possibility that seems more plausible than the received "federalism" construction, since it is vastly more consistent with the amendment's language. It seems pretty clear, however, that it too must be rejected. One thing we know to a certainty from the

---

unenumerated powers are not to be inferred. (Alabama 1819; Arkansas 1836; California 1849; Colorado 1876; Florida 1885; Georgia 1865; Iowa 1846; Kansas 1855; Louisiana 1868; Maine 1819; Maryland 1851; Minnesota 1857; Mississippi 1868; Missouri 1875; Montana 1889; Nebraska 1866–67; Nevada 1864; New Jersey 1844; North Carolina 1868; Ohio 1851; Oregon 1857; Rhode Island 1842; South Carolina 1868; Virginia 1870; Washington 1889; Wyoming 1889. All will be found in the seven volumes of The Federal and State Constitutions (F. Thorpe ed. 1909). Those distinguishing the two caveats include the Kansas, Nebraska, North Carolina, Ohio, and South Carolina constitutions mentioned.) Indeed, the presence of such "little Ninth Amendments" in state constitutions was so common that in 1911 Professor Corwin referred to "*the usual caveat* that enumeration of certain rights should not be construed to disparage other rights not so enumerated." Corwin, *The Doctrine of Due Process of Law Before the Civil War*, 24 Harv. L. Rev. 366, 384 (1911) (emphasis added). I haven't the slightest doubt that many of the provisions, though there are a number of minor variations in language, were inspired by the Ninth Amendment: a good deal of imitation is evident throughout the state constitutions. But that doesn't reduce their relevance a whit. The framers of the various state constitutions did not, for reasons that are entirely obvious, copy or paraphrase Article I, Section 8 or other provisions of the federal Constitution that related to the bounds of federal power. They *did* copy or paraphrase the Ninth Amendment.

It is therefore true that no eighteenth-century state bill of rights included a provision analogous to the Ninth Amendment, and that fact merits mention. But the nineteenth-century provisions do as well, in a way that tends not simply to neutralize Kelly's argument, but indeed to turn it around. The fact that the constitution-makers in, say, Maine and Alabama in 1819 saw fit to include in their bills of rights provisions that were essentially identical to the Ninth Amendment is virtually conclusive evidence that they understood it to mean what it said and not simply to relate to the limits of federal power.

historical context is that the Ninth Amendment was not designed to grant Congress authority to create additional rights, to amend Article I, Section 8 by adding a general power to protect rights. That power did not come, if it ever did, until Section 5 of the Fourteenth Amendment was ratified seventy-seven years later. (Nor is "others retained by the people" an apt way of saying "others Congress may create.") Thus unless the reference was to other, unstated federal constitutional rights, it must have been to other rights protected by state law—statutory, common, or constitutional. That interpretation seems to make just as little sense, however. It is quite clear that the original framers and ratifying conventions intended the Bill of Rights to control only the actions of the federal government. It is just as clear, and was then too, that state law, even state constitutional law, is incompetent to do so and must therefore content itself with controlling the actions of the state government. We thus run up against an inference that seems so silly it would not have needed rebutting. What felt need could there have been to rebut the inference that the Bill of Rights, controlling only federal action, had somehow preempted the efforts of the people of various states to control the actions of their state government?[6]

Apropos of the incorporation debate, Dean Wellington has argued that "[c]ontemporary technology, a population moving frequently across state lines, and the expanding role of the federal government in law enforcement have made America too much one country for considerations of federalism to sustain at a constitutional level" the idea that the states are subject to significantly less stringent restrictions than those the Bill of Rights imposes on the federal government.[7] Maybe that's right, but the argument is at least as strong the other way around: in terms of respect for the judgments of federal courts and the success of enforcement efforts it seems important that the states not be bound by a set of textually unstated constitutional rights that do not restrain the actions of the federal government. Of course this is essentially the argument that prevailed in *Bolling v. Sharpe*, but with one critical difference: the Ninth Amendment, unlike the Due Process Clause on which the Court

---

[6]The "need" to rebut the inference that the Bill of Rights meant that state legislatures and courts could no longer order relations among their citizens by the creation of *non*constitutional "rights" would have been, if anything, still more attenuated.

[7]Wellington, *Common Law Rules and Constitutional Double Standards: Some Notes on Adjudication*, 83 Yale L.J. 221, 274 (1973).

attempted to balance its *Bolling* result, will bear the meaning tendered. In fact, the conclusion that the Ninth Amendment was intended to signal the existence of federal constitutional rights beyond those specifically enumerated in the Constitution is the only conclusion its language seems comfortably able to support.

Justice Black's response to the Ninth Amendment was essentially to ignore it.[8] Usually more than willing to return to the original understanding when intervening precedent stood in his way, he displayed a curious contentment with the crabbed interpretations of his predecessors on this point. Of course it really isn't curious at all—he didn't like the jurisprudential implications of such an open-ended provision: "I discuss the due process and Ninth Amendment arguments together because on analysis they turn out to be the same thing—merely using different words to claim for this Court and the federal judiciary power to invalidate any legislative act which the judges find irrational, unreasonable or offensive."[9] But Black most of all shouldn't behave this way. He urged us, correctly, to behave like lawyers rather than dictators or philosopher kings and thus to heed the directions of the various constitutional clauses. On candid analysis, though, the Constitution turns out to contain provisions instructing us to look beyond their four corners. That instruction troubled him, but he was a man who spent his life railing against people who ignored the language and purpose of constitutional clauses because they didn't like where they led. There is a difference between ignoring a provision, such as the First Amendment, because you don't like its specific substantive implications and ignoring a provision, such as the Ninth Amendment, because you don't like its institutional implications. But it's hard to make it a difference that should count.

An interpretivist like Black has two possible answers left. The first, which I've never heard, would go something like this. Suppose there were in the Constitution one or more provisions providing for the protection of ghosts. Can there be any doubt, now that we

---

[8]It appears that he went along with the Court's active use of the Equal Protection Clause up until the point at which it became impossible not to recognize that the power to review classifications is an authority as broad and powerful as straight-out can-they-do-it substantive review. *Compare, e.g.,* Griffin v. Illinois, 351 U.S. 12 (1956) (Black, J., for the plurality), *with* Harper v. Virginia Board of Elections, 383 U.S. 663, 670 (1966) (Black, J., dissenting).

[9]Griswold v. Connecticut, 381 U.S. 479, 511 (1965) (Black, J., dissenting).

no longer believe there is any such thing, that we would be behaving properly in ignoring the provisions? The "ghost" here is natural law, and the argument would be that because natural law is the source from which the open-ended clauses of the Ninth and Fourteenth Amendments were expected to derive their content, we are justified, now that our society no longer believes in natural law, in ignoring the clauses altogether.

This argument is too slick. Although there were during both relevant eras people who expected the Constitution to be informed by natural law, this theme was far from universally accepted and probably was not even the majority view among those "framers" we would be likely to think of first.

> Some of the intellectual stalwarts of rebellion, like James Otis, actually came to associate principles of natural law and natural equity with positive law—to assert that what is right is therefore law. But those giants who managed the awesome transition from revolutionaries to "constitutionaries"—men like Adams and Jefferson; Dickinson and Wilson; Jay, Madison, Hamilton, and, in a sense, Mason and Henry—were seldom, if ever, guilty of confusing law with natural right. These men, before 1776, used nature to take the measure of law and to judge their own obligations of obedience, but not as a source for rules of decision.[10]

These people—needless to say they have their Reconstruction counterparts—certainly didn't have natural law in mind when the Constitution's various open-ended delegations to the future were inserted and approved, which undoubtedly is one reason the Constitution at no point refers to natural law. If it did, *then* we'd have our ghosts case.

The second answer is that even granting that clauses like those under consideration established constitutional rights, they do not readily lend themselves to principled *judicial* enforcement and should therefore be treated as if they were directed exclusively to the political branches. (This suggestion I *have* seen—from the pen, surprisingly, of Felix Frankfurter, who indicated in correspondence in the late 1950s that he wished the Due Process Clause, his idea of an open-ended provision, had been so treated.[11]) It would be a cheap shot to note that there is no legislative history specifically

---

[10]R. Cover, Justice Accused 27 (1975).

[11]See Purcell, *Alexander M. Bickel and the Post-Realist Constitution*, 11 Harv. C.R.—C.L. L. Rev. 521, 533 (1976).

indicating an intention that the Ninth Amendment was to receive judicial enforcement. There was at the time of the original Constitution little legislative history indicating that *any* particular provision was to receive judicial enforcement: the Ninth Amendment was not singled out one way or the other. What is mildly instructive, and it cuts the other way, is that the precursor decisions typically cited as "proof" that judicial review was intended—though they are too few and unclear really to amount to that—were often "noninterpretivist" decisions, drawing their mandates not from any documentary prohibition but rather from some principle derived externally.[12] As far as the Fourteenth Amendment is concerned, it is true that the (misplaced) anticipation seems to have been that it would receive its most meaningful enforcement by Congress, acting under Section 5, rather than by the courts. It is also true that at the time of its ratification only three Acts of Congress had been declared unconstitutional by the Supreme Court. That doesn't mean the authority went unnoticed, however. *Dred Scott* drew heavy fire, and even prior to that time,

> [W]e may draw two conclusions concerning the criticism of the Supreme Court: first, the court was criticized quite as much for not declaring congressional acts unconstitutional as for doing so; second, it seems clear that both Federalist and Republican criticism during these years was directed not so much at the possession of the power of the court to pass on the validity of acts of Congress as at the effect of its exercise in supporting or invalidating some particular party measure.[13]

It is also relevant that a number of *state* statutes had been struck down in the first half of the nineteenth century. The Reconstruction Amendments were, after all, primarily directed at the states. The Republican criticism of *Dred Scott*, and of *Barron v. Baltimore*[14] as

[12]*E.g.*, Dr. Bonham's Case, 8 Coke Rep. 107, 118a (1610).

[13]Monroe, *The Supreme Court and the Constitution*, 18 Am. Pol. Sci. Rev. 737, 740 (1924).

[14]7 Pet. 243 (1833). Fairman argued that even clear statements that "the bill of rights" was to be incorporated wouldn't have meant in the mid-nineteenth century what they would mean today, since the term "bill of rights" was then sometimes used, specifically by Congressman Bingham, to signal not the first eight or nine amendments but rather only the Due Process Clause of the Fifth Amendment and Article IV's Privileges and Immunities Clause. Fairman, *Does the Fourteenth Amendment Incorporate the Bill of Rights? The Original Understanding*, 2 Stan. L. Rev. 5, 26 (1949). This does appear to have been the usage sometimes, though I think not most

well, continued throughout the drafting and ratification processes. Naturally this sometimes spilled over into a general distrust of the institution of judicial review,[15] but in general the institution was assumed and the attack was limited to the specific offending instances. Surely there was nothing remotely resembling a consensus that judicial authority to review was generally to be curtailed: if anything, the consensus ran the other way.[16] More important for present purposes, there was no indication that the Fourteenth Amendment was to be treated any differently in this respect from other provisions.[17]

---

often. See, e.g., Cong. Globe, 39th Cong., 1st Sess. 1089–90 (1866) (remarks of Congressman Bingham, referring to "the bill of rights under the articles of amendment to the Constitution" in the course of a criticism of Barron v. Baltimore, 7 Pet. 243 (1833), which had refused to apply what we would call the Bill of Rights to the states). You will also have noticed that Howard's statement is clear to the same effect.

Assume for the sake of argument, however, that Fairman was right that "bill of rights" often meant only the Fifth Amendment's Due Process Clause and the Privileges and Immunities Clause. But now factor in the additional datum that it was at least a sometime part of the rhetoric of abolitionism that the Fifth Amendment's Due Process Clause already incorporated most of the rest of what we would call the Bill of Rights. Recent scholarship tends to downplay the influence of such seemingly eccentric pre-War constitutional views. This particular view, however, had been adopted by the Supreme Court in 1855. . . . One who held it, of course, need only have thought he was incorporating the Fifth Amendment's Due Process Clause to believe that most of what we would call the Bill of Rights was being incorporated. And we shall see that assumptions concerning the sweeping coverage of Article IV's Privileges and Immunities Clause were even more widespread.

It was also part of antislavery rhetoric that Barron v. Baltimore had been wrongly decided and was therefore a nullity. See sources cited in Fairman, supra, at 26–36, 118–20. Again we must be careful not to attribute too much influence to such views, but it is at least worthy of note that this one appears to have been held by Bingham himself. See Cong. Globe, 39th Cong., 1st Sess. 2542–44 (1866). In terms of the original understanding, Barron was almost certainly decided correctly. But if you were committed to the proposition that the Bill of Rights already applied to the States, your silence on the subject of whether the Fourteenth Amendment would apply the Bill of Rights to the states wouldn't mean much, would it?

[15]Cf. H. Graham, Everyman's Constitution 447–48 (1968).

[16]See also Strong, Bicentennial Benchmark: Two Centuries of Evolution of Constitutional Processes, 55 N.C.L. Rev. 1, 42–43 (1976).

[17]One taking the view under discussion would also have to face the question of which phrases are on which side of the line. As we have seen, the Constitution is not divided into two sets of provisions, precise and open-ended. What, for example, would the view in question make of the Cruel and Unusual Punishment and Just Compensation Clauses? Would they be judicially enforceable? One has to assume

This, however, is a question on which history cannot have the last word, at least not the last affirmative word. If a principled approach to judicial enforcement of the Constitution's open-ended provisions cannot be developed, one that is not hopelessly inconsistent with our nation's commitment to representative democracy, responsible commentators must consider seriously the possibility that courts simply should stay away from them. Given the transparent failure of the dominant mode of "noninterpretivist" review, Justice Black's instinct to decline the delegation was healthy. But the dominant mode can be improved upon.

---

so. But although the compass of each is limited, each surely requires the injection of content not to be found in the document.

8. The Ninth Amendment

Raoul Berger

The Forgotten Ninth Amendment Bennett Patterson entitled his little book in 1955,[1] hardly anticipating that the amendment would be invoked in more than a thousand cases[2] after Justice Goldberg rescued it from obscurity[3] in his concurring opinion in *Griswold v. Connecticut,*[4] the 1965 contraceptive case. Justice Goldberg was not alone, being joined by Chief Justice Warren and Justice Brennan[5]; in the opinion of the Court, Justice Douglas included the ninth amendment among the provisions in the Bill of Rights that have "penumbras formed by emanations from [those] guarantees."[6] Thus

Reprinted, by permission, from 66 Cornell L. Rev. 1 (1980).

[1]B. Patterson, The Forgotten Ninth Amendment (1955). One hundred thirty-two pages are devoted to appendices and a reprint of the legislative history. Most of the 85-page discussion is a hymn to "individual inherent rights," that are unenumerated and independent of constitutional grant.

[2]A Lexis computer search in September, 1980, located 1,296 cases after 1965 from the "General Federal" and "States" libraries. Lexis is a registered trademark of Mead Data Central, Inc.

[3]Prior to Griswold v. Connecticut, 381 U.S. 479 (1965), the Court had few occasions to probe the meaning of the ninth amendment. In United Public Workers v. Mitchell, 330 U.S. 75, 95 (1947), a case challenging the Hatch Act prohibition against political activities by federal employees, the Court fleetingly referred to "the freedom of the civil servant under the First, Ninth and Tenth Amendments," but held that they interposed no obstacle to federal regulation where constitutional power is granted. Earlier, the Court had rejected an appeal to the ninth amendment as a restraint on government action because it "does not withdraw the rights which are expressly granted to the Federal Government." Ashwander v. TVA, 297 U.S. 288, 330–31 (1936).

[4]381 U.S. 479, 486 (1965).

[5]Justices Harlan and White separately concurred in the judgment. Id. at 499, 502. Justices Black and Stewart dissented. Id. at 507, 527.

[6]381 U.S. at 484. Justice Douglas did not win a plurality for his interpretation. And he has since wavered. In Olff v. East Side Union High School Dist., 404 U.S. 1042, 1044 (1972), he dissented from a denial of certiorari in a case involving regulation of schoolboy hairstyle, saying "[t]he word 'liberty' [in the fourteenth amendment] . . .

inspired, litigants have invoked the ninth to assert the inherent rights of schoolboys to wear long hair,[7] challenge school textbooks,[8] prevent imprisonment in a maximum security section,[9] protect against conscription,[10] immunize the transportation of lewd materials in interstate commerce,[11] and claim a right to a healthful environment.[12] Justice Goldberg declared that

> [t]he language and history of the Ninth Amendment reveal that the Framers of the Constitution believed that there are additional fundamental rights, *protected* from governmental infringement, which exist alongside those fundamental rights specifically mentioned in the first eight constitutional amendments.[13]

Who is to protect undescribed rights? Justice Goldberg would transform the ninth amendment into a bottomless well in which the judiciary can dip for the formation of undreamed of "rights" in their limitless discretion, a possibility the Founders would have rejected out of hand.[14] And, as Professor Robert Bork points out, an imputed authorization judicially "to develop new individual rights . . . correspondingly create[s] new disabilities for democratic government"[15]; it disables the states from governing in those areas. Whatever the meaning of the ninth amendment, one thing it clearly did not contemplate—encroachment on state control of local matters except as the constitution otherwise authorized. It is undisputed that such a claim had not been made by the Court in the more than 150 years since the adoption of the Bill of Rights.[16] Justice

---

includes at least the fundamental rights 'retained by the people' under the Ninth Amendment." On the other hand, concurring in Doe v. Bolton, 410 U.S. 179, 210 (1973), in which the Court found Georgia's abortion law unconstitutional, he declared that "[t]he Ninth Amendment obviously does not create federally enforceable rights."

[7]Freeman v. Flake, 405 U.S. 1032 (1972) (denial of certiorari) (although four circuits upheld and four struck down regulations of schoolboy hair style).

[8]Williams v. Board of Educ., 388 F. Supp. 93 (S.D.W. Va. 1975).

[9]Burns v. Swenson, 430 F.2d 771 (8th Cir. 1970).

[10]United States v. Uhl, 436 F.2d 773 (9th Cir. 1970).

[11]United States v. Orito, 413 U.S. 139 (1973).

[12]Tanner v. Armco Steel Corp., 340 F. Supp. 532 (S.D. Tex. 1972).

[13]381 U.S. at 488 (emphasis added).

[14]*See infra* text accompanying notes 122 & 125.

[15]Bork, *The Impossibility of Finding Welfare Rights in the Constitution*, 1979 Wash. U.L.Q. 695, 697.

[16]Griswold v. Connecticut, 381 U.S. at 491 n.6 (Goldberg, J., concurring); *id.* at 520 (Black, J., dissenting); *id.* at 529–30 (Stewart, J., dissenting).

Stewart remarked in his dissent that "to say that the Ninth Amendment has anything to do with this case is to turn somersaults with history."[17]

The ninth amendment provides that "[t]he enumeration in the Constitution, of certain rights, shall not be construed to deny or disparage others retained by the people."[18] Paired with it is the tenth: "The powers not delegated to the United States by the Constitution, nor prohibited by it to the States, are reserved to the States respectively, or to the people."[19] The two are complementary: the ninth deals with *rights* "retained by the people," the tenth with *powers* "reserved" to the states or the people. As Madison perceived, they are two sides of the same coin. During the debates on ratification of the Bill of Rights in Virginia, he wrote to Washington:

> If a line can be drawn between the powers granted and the rights retained, it would seem to be the same thing, whether the latter be secured by declaring that they shall not be abridged, or that the former shall not be extended. If no such line can be drawn, a declaration in either form would amount to nothing.[20]

Understanding of the ninth amendment is aided by appreciation of the background from which it emerged. The Founders were deeply attached to their local governments: these were the tried and true whereby they had resisted the impositions of royal governors and judges.[21] That attachment constituted a formidable obstacle

---

[17]*Id.* at 529.

[18]U.S. Const. amend. IX.

[19]U.S. Const. amend. X.

[20]Letter from James Madison to George Washington (Dec. 5, 1789), *reprinted in* 5 The Writings of James Madison 432 (G. Hunt ed. 1904).

[21]In his 1791 Philadelphia lectures, Justice James Wilson, who had been a leading architect of the Constitution, explained that before the Revolution

> the executive and the judicial powers of government . . . were derived from . . . a foreign source . . . [and] were directed to foreign purposes. Need we be surprised, that they were objects of aversion and distrust? . . . On the other hand, our assemblies were chosen by ourselves: they were the guardians of our rights, the objects of our confidence, and the anchor of our political hopes. . . .
>
> Even at this time [1791], people can scarcely devest themselves of those opposite prepossessions. . . .
>
> But it is high time that we should chastise our prejudices.

J. Wilson, *Of Government,* in 1 Works of James Wilson 292–93 (R. McCloskey ed. 1967).

to the adoption of the Constitution[22]; there was widespread distrust of the remote newcomer, a federal government removed by vast distances from the governed, wherein large states might outvote the small, and in which there would be clashing sectional interests.[23] The measure of that distrust may be gathered from the fact that after providing for "inferior" federal courts, the First Congress committed the initial enforcement of constitutional issues to the state courts,[24] where it remained for the next seventy-seven to eighty-six years.[25] Allied to this was insistence on a government of limited powers arising from a pervasive fear of "despotic government"[26]; hence the outcries against unlimited power. As Jefferson said, "[i]t is jealousy and not confidence which prescribes limited constitutions to bind down those whom we are obliged to trust with power."[27]

[22]Madison acknowledged this "habitual attachment of the people." 1 M. Farrand, The Records of the Federal Convention of 1787 at 284 (1911). It was condemned by Gouverneur Morris: "State attachments, and State importance have been the bane of this Country," *id.* at 530, but the current ran strongly the other way. *See* R. Berger, Congress v. The Supreme Court 260–64 (1969). It was to "state Governments," Oliver Ellsworth said at the Convention, that he "turned his eyes . . . for the preservation of his rights." 1 M. Farrand, *supra*, at 492. There, Elbridge Gerry asked, "[w]ill any man say that liberty will be as safe in the hands of eighty or a hundred men taken from the whole continent, as in the hands of two or three hundred taken from a single State?" 2 *id.* at 386. James Wilson told the Pennsylvania Ratification Convention that "the framers of [the Constitution] were particularly anxious . . . to preserve the state governments unimpaired." 3 *id.* at 144. Madison assured the Ratifiers that the jurisdiction of the proposed government "extends to certain enumerated objects only, and leaves to the several States a residuary and inviolable sovereignty over all other objects." The Federalist No. 39, at 249 (J. Madison) (Mod. Lib. ed. 1937).

[23]R. Berger, *supra* note 22, at 31–33.

[24]*Id.* at 263 & 273.

[25]C. Wright, Handbook of the Law of Federal Courts 3–4 (3d ed. 1976). Appeals to the Supreme Court were not defended on the ground that the Court must be enabled to rewrite state legislation, but because, in Hamilton's words, "Thirteen independent courts of final jurisdiction over the same causes, arising upon the same laws, is a hydra in government from which nothing but contradiction and confusion can proceed." The Federalist No. 80, at 516 (A. Hamilton) (Mod. Lib. ed. 1937). The password was "uniformity." R. Berger, *supra* note 22, at 272. Even so, there were those like Gerry who feared that "the judicial department will be oppressive." 3 M. Farrand, *supra* note 22, at 128.

[26]H. Adams, John Randolph 38 (1882).

[27]C. Warren, Congress, The Constitution, and the Supreme Court 153 (1925). *See* R. Berger, *supra* note 22, at 13. *See also* H. Adams, *supra* note 26, at 8–14.

The drive for the Bill of Rights was fed by such distrust. At the outset of the deliberations in the First Congress, Madison, who drafted the proposed Bill of Rights, averred that "the abuse of the powers of the General Government may be guarded against in a more secure manner than is now done."[28] Elbridge Gerry alluded to the "great body of our constituents opposed to the Constitution as it now stands, who are apprehensive of the enormous powers of Government," and added, "[t]he ratification of the Constitution in several States would never have taken place, had they not been assured that the objections would have been duly attended to by Congress."[29] Madison recalled to the House that the proposed amendments were "most strenuously required by the opponents to the constitution" in the state ratification conventions.[30] A number of states accompanied their ratifications with proposed amendments.[31] Toward the close of the First Congress Gerry said, "This declaration of rights, I take it, is intended to secure the people against the mal-administration of the [federal] Government."[32]

Even stronger evidence that the Bill of Rights was to have no application to the states is furnished by the fate of the first sentence of Madison's fifth resolution: "*No State* shall violate the equal rights of conscience, or the freedom of the press, or the trial by jury in criminal cases."[33] Madison explained that "every Government should be disarmed of powers which trench upon *those particular rights.* . . . [T]he State Governments are as liable to attack *these* invaluable privileges as the General Government is, and therefore ought to be as cautiously guarded against."[34] When the clause came before the Committee of the Whole, Madison urged that this provision was "the most valuable amendment in the whole list," and that it was "equally necessary" that "*these* essential rights" should be "secured

---

[28]1 Annals of Cong. 432 (Gales & Seaton eds. 1836) (printing bearing running title "History of Congress").

[29]*Id.* at 446–47.

[30]*Id.* at 746. *See also id.* at 661 (remarks of Rep. Page).

[31]*See, e.g.,* 3 J. Elliot, Debates in the Several State Conventions on the Adoption of the Federal Constitution 657–63 (2d ed. 1876) (Virginia); *cf.* 2 *id.* at 542–46 (Pennsylvania); 2 *id.* at 177 (Massachusetts); 2 *id.* at 413–14 (New York).

[32]1 Annals of Cong., *supra* note 28, at 749.

[33]*Id.* at 435 (emphasis added).

[34]*Id.* at 441 (emphasis added).

against the State Governments."[35] As Professor Norman Redlich observed, "When Madison intended an amendment to restrict the states in his proposal to prevent the states from abridging free speech or press, he was quite specific."[36] The clause was adopted by the House but rejected by the Senate,[37] underscoring that the Founders well knew how to limit state authority, as is again evidenced by their reference in the tenth amendment to power not "prohibited by [the Constitution] to the States."

The words "rights retained by the people" in the ninth amendment expressed a political postulate explained by Jefferson: "the purposes of society do not require a surrender of all our rights to our ordinary governors," and it followed that there remained reserved to the people an area of unsurrendered rights.[38] Opponents of a Bill of Rights had urged that it was unnecessary because, as Washington wrote Lafayette, "the people evidently retained every thing which they did not in express terms give up."[39] In the words of

[35]*Id.* at 755 (emphasis added).

[36]Redlich, *Are There "Certain Rights"* . . . . *Retained by the People?* 37 N.Y.U. L. Rev. 787, 805 n.87 (1962).

[37]*See* Warren, *The New "Liberty" Under the Fourteenth Amendment,* 39 Harv. L. Rev. 431, 433–35 (1926). Redlich concluded, "It would be unrealistic to attribute to the Senate an intent to impose ill-defined legally enforceable restraints on the states in light of this rejection." Redlich, *supra* note 36, at 806. Thus, the records of the First Congress confirm Chief Justice Marshall's holding in Barron v. Mayor of Baltimore, 32 U.S. (7 Pet.) 243 (1833), that the Bill of Rights did not apply to the states.

[38]E. Dumbauld, The Bill of Rights 145 (1957). *See also* G. Wood, The Creation of the American Republic 1776–1787 at 293–94 (1969). For Thomas Cooley, the ninth amendment affirmed "the principle that constitutions are not made to create rights in the people, but in recognition of, and in order to preserve them." T. Cooley, The General Principles of Constitutional Law in the United States of America 31–35 (2d ed. 1891). The ninth amendment "was an affirmation of the principle that, as rights in the United States are not created by government, so they are not to be diminished by government, unless by the appropriate exercise of an express power." Dunbar, *James Madison and the Ninth Amendment,* 42 Va. L. Rev. 627, 638 (1956).

[39]29 The Writings of George Washington 478 (Fitzpatrick ed. 1939). In his letter to Lafayette, Washington referred to James Wilson's assurance to the Pennsylvania Ratification Convention that by the Constitution the citizens dispense "a part of their original power in what manner and what proportion they think fit. They never part with the whole; and they retain the right of recalling what they part with. . . . To every suggestion concerning a bill of rights, the citizens of the United States may always say, We reserve the right to do what we please." 2 J. Elliot, *supra* note 31, at 437.

C. C. Pinckney told the South Carolina House of Representatives that "by dele-

Hamilton, quoted by Justice Goldberg, "why declare that things shall not be done which there is no power to do?" instancing "no power is given by which restrictions [on "liberty of the press"] may be imposed."[40] Madison admitted that the amendments "may be deemed unnecessary; but there can be no harm in making such a declaration."[41] Thus viewed, the Bill of Rights added nothing,[42] but was merely declaratory.

Others, however, were deeply concerned by the effect of the maxim *expressio unius est exclusio alterius:* what is expressed excludes what is not.[43] They feared that an enumeration of some rights might deliver those not enumerated into the hands of the federal govern-

---

gating express powers, we certainly reserve to ourselves every power and right not mentioned." 3 M. Farrand, *supra* note 22, at 256. In the First Congress, Rep. Hartley observed that "it had been asserted in the convention of Pennsylvania, by the friends of the Constitution, that all the rights and power that were not given to the Government were retained by the States and the people thereof. This was also his own opinion." 1 Annals of Cong., *supra* note 28, at 732.

[40]381 U.S. at 489 n.4 (quoting The Federalist No. 84, at 558–59 (A. Hamilton) (Mod. Lib. ed. 1937)).

[41]1 Annals of Cong., *supra* note 28, at 441.

[42]Dumbauld justly sums up: "The Ninth Amendment was not intended to add anything to the meaning of the remaining articles in the Constitution. . . . [It] was designed to obviate the possibility of applying the maxim *expressio unius exclusio alterius* in interpreting the Constitution. It was adopted in order to eliminate the grant of powers by implication." E. Dumbauld, *supra* note 38, at 63. Earlier, Justice Story wrote that the ninth amendment "was manifestly introduced to prevent any perverse or ingenious misapplication of the well-known maxim, that an affirmation in particular cases implies a negation in all others." J. Story, Commentaries on the Constitution of the United States § 1905 (5th ed. 1891). *See also infra* note 43.

Parenthetically, this confutes those who argue that the rules of statutory construction should not apply to interpretation of the Constitution, and those like Professor Dean Alfange, who ridicule the application of a canon of construction as an authoritative guide to constitutional interpretation. *See* Alfange, *On Judicial Policymaking and Constitutional Change: Another Look at the "Original Intent" Theory of Constitutional Interpretation,* 5 Hastings Const. L.Q. 603, 618–19 (1978). *See also* Berger, *"Government by Judiciary": Judge Gibbons Argument Ad Hominem,* 59 B.U. L. Rev. 783, 805 (1977).

[43]James Wilson assured the Pennsylvania Convention that "everything not expressly mentioned will be presumed to be purposely omitted." 3 M. Farrand, *supra* note 22, at 144. Chief Justice Thomas McKean also assured that Convention that congressional power, being enumerated in the Constitution "and *positively* granted, can be no other than what this positive grant conveys." 2 J. Elliot, *supra* note 31, at 540. For a similar expression in South Carolina by C. C. Pinckney, see 3 M. Farrand, *supra* note 22, at 256. Rep. Jackson of Georgia alluded to the maxim in the First Congress. 1 Annals of Cong., *supra* note 28, at 442.

ment. Madison's response to such fears is quoted by Justice Goldberg:

> It has been objected also against a bill of rights, that, by enumerating particular exceptions to the grant of power, it would disparage those rights which were not placed in that enumeration; and it might follow by implication, that those rights which were not singled out, were intended *to be assigned* into the hands of the General Government, and were consequently insecure. This is one of the most plausible arguments I have ever heard urged against the admission of a bill of rights into this system; but, I conceive, that *it may be guarded against*. I have attempted it, as gentlemen may see by turning to the last clause of the fourth resolution [the ninth amendment].[44]

As Justice Black pointed out,

> th[is] very material . . . shows that the Ninth Amendment was intended to protect against the idea that "by enumerating particular exceptions to the grant of power" to the Federal Government, "those rights which were not singled out, were intended to be assigned into the hands of the General Government."[45]

Madison, in short, meant to bar the implication that unenumerated rights were "assigned" to the federal government, for enforcement or otherwise, returning to the theme he had sounded at the outset: "[T]he great object in view is to limit and qualify the powers of Government, by excepting out of the grant of power those cases in which the *Government ought not to act*, or to act only in a particular mode."[46]

Justice Goldberg neglected to turn "to the last clause of the fourth resolution" in order to learn how Madison proposed that the unde-

---

[44]381 U.S. at 489–90 (quoting 1 Annals of Cong., *supra* note 28, at 439 (emphasis added)).

[45]*Id.* at 519 (Black, J., dissenting). *See supra* note 42.

[46]1 Annals of Cong., *supra* note 28, at 437 (emphasis added). Leslie Dunbar observes that Madison "seems to have thought of rights under two main headings. One, as stipulating agreed upon methods by which in particular cases the government shall exercise its powers. . . . Secondly, he thought of another class of rights as declarations of areas *totally outside the province of government*." Dunbar, *supra* note 38, at 635 (emphasis added). Madison's intention was "to define those fields into which *powers do not extend at all*." *Id.* at 636 (emphasis added). Even prior to *Griswold*, Justice Black concluded that the ninth amendment merely "emphasize[d] the limited nature of the Federal Government." Black, *The Bill of Rights*, 35 N.Y.U. L. Rev. 865, 871 (1960).

sirable implication "may be guarded against." That last clause, the progenitor of the ninth amendment, provided:

> The exceptions here or elsewhere in the constitution, made in favor of particular rights, shall *not* be so construed as to diminish the just importance of other rights retained by the people, or as *to enlarge the powers* delegated by the constitution; but either as *actual limitations* of such powers, or as inserted merely for greater caution.[47]

Madison's disclaimer of intention " to enlarge the powers delegated by the constitution" by non-enumeration of "other rights" and his emphasis upon enumeration as "actual limitations" on such powers bars a construction which would endow the federal government with the very powers that were denied. It is incongruous, moreover, to read the text of the ninth amendment as expanding *federal* powers at the very moment that the tenth was reserving to the states or the people all "powers not delegated."[48] Then too, because the federal government may not "*deny*" unenumerated rights, it does not follow that it may *enforce* them against the states.

In fact, enforcement was to be confined to expressly "stipulated rights." "[T]he great mass of the people who opposed [the Constitution]," said Madison, "disliked it because it did not contain effectual provisions against encroachments *on particular rights*."[49] Hence, Madison explained, if the Bill of Rights were

> incorporated into the Constitution, independent tribunals of justice will consider themselves in a peculiar manner the guardians of *those rights;* they will be an impenetrable bulwark against every assumption of power in the legislative or executive [not the states]; they will be naturally led to resist every encroachment upon rights

[47]1 Annals of Cong., *supra* note 28, at 435 (emphasis added). On October 17, 1788, Madison wrote to Jefferson that he favored a Bill of Rights "provided it be so formed *as not to imply powers not* to be included *in the enumeration*." 5 The Writings of James Madison, *supra* note 20, at 271.

[48]As the Court held in Holmes v. Jennison, 39 U.S. (14 Pet.) 540, 587 (1840): "[S]o far from the states which insisted upon these amendments contemplating any restraint or limitation by them on their own powers; the very cause which gave rise to them, was a strong jealousy on their part of the power which they had granted in the Constitution."

[49]1 Annals of Cong., *supra* note 28, at 433 (emphasis added).

expressly stipulated for in the constitution by the declaration of rights.[50]

For present purposes, the relevant provision of article III, section two, clause one, which enumerates the various categories of federal court jurisdiction, is "all cases . . . arising under this Constitution."[51] A right "retained" by the people is not embodied in the Constitution, and a suit brought on such a right does not "arise" thereunder, as Madison made plain in stressing judicial protection for "particular" rights "expressly stipulated." It does violence to the historical record to construe the ninth amendment to give the courts a roving commission to enforce a catalog of unenumerated rights against the will of the states.[52] What the Constitution expressed was the will of the people to reserve unto themselves all powers not delegated and all unenumerated rights,[53] a will likewise articulated in the article V provision for amendment. With Leslie Dunbar, I would hold that the ninth amendment "is an affirmation that rights exist independently of government, that they constitute an area of no-power."[54]

How does Justice Goldberg meet these materials? On the one hand he states,

> I do not mean to imply that the Ninth Amendment is applied against the States by the Fourteenth. Nor do I mean to state that the Ninth Amendment constitutes an independent source of rights protected from infringement by either the States or the Federal Government.[55]

[50]*Id.* at 440 (emphasis added). Leslie Dunbar comments, "[T]he practical effect of enumeration is the enlistment of the protection of positive law, spoken through the courts, for rights which otherwise could be defended only through political action." Dunbar, *supra* note 38, at 643.

[51]U.S. Const. art. III, sec. 2.

[52]"Had Congress engaged in the extraordinary occupation of improving the constitutions of the several states by affording the people additional protection from the exercise of power by their own governments in matters which concerned themselves alone, they would have declared this purpose in plain and intelligible language." Barron v. Mayor of Baltimore, 32 U.S. (7 Pet.) 243, 250 (1833). *See infra* text accompanying notes 117–18.

[53]*See supra* note 39.

[54]*See* Dunbar, *supra* note 38, at 641. *See also* Redlich, *supra* note 36, at 807 (quoted at *infra* text accompanying note 103); *supra* note 46.

[55]381 U.S. at 492 (concurring opinion).

On the other hand, he argues that

the Ninth Amendment is relevant in a case dealing with a *State's* infringement of a fundamental right. While the Ninth Amendment—and indeed the entire Bill of Rights—originally concerned restrictions upon *federal* power, the subsequently enacted Fourteenth Amendment prohibits the States as well from infringing fundamental personal liberties.[56]

Justice Goldberg goes on to explain that

the Ninth Amendment, in indicating that not all such liberties are specifically mentioned in the first eight amendments, is surely relevant in showing the *existence* of other fundamental personal rights, now *protected* from state, as well as federal, infringement. In sum, the Ninth Amendment simply lends strong support to the view that the "liberty" protected by the Fifth and Fourteenth Amendments from infringement by the Federal Government or the States is not restricted to rights specifically mentioned in the first eight amendments.[57]

Justice Goldberg leaps too lightly from the "existence of rights" retained by the people to a federal power to *protect* them. That no such power was conferred is disclosed by Madison's disavowal of any implication that the enumerated rights were "assigned into the hands of the General Government," least of all for diminution of States' rights, his affirmation that there was no intention to enlarge but rather to limit the delegated powers, and his demarcation of "cases in which the Government ought not to act."[58]

Goldberg's appeal to the "liberty" of the fifth amendment's due process clause for authority to "protect" the unspecified rights retained by the people under the ninth amendment implies that what the ninth plainly withheld was conferred under the rose by the fifth. But why should the Founders take pains to exclude federal power with regard to the unenumerated right of the ninth if they were simultaneously conferring it *sub silentio* by the fifth? That is inexplicable. In fact, the Founders fenced off "cases in which the Government ought not to act," and it requires evidence that those fences were torn down by the fifth. Then too, the "liberty" of the fifth amendment on which Goldberg relies referred to freedom from

[56]*Id.* at 493.
[57]*Id.* (emphasis added).
[58]*See supra* text accompanying notes 44, 46, & 47.

imprisonment and freedom of locomotion,[59] which with fine casuistry the Court, overturning a maximum hours law in *Lochner v. New York*,[60] perverted into "liberty of contract"—the "liberty" of a bakery worker to contract for sixty hours of labor a week. Notwithstanding his caustic dissent in *Lochner*, Justice Holmes later drew on this "liberty" for a better cause: free speech "must be taken to be included in the Fourteenth Amendment, *in view of* the scope that has been given to the word 'liberty.'"[61] Thus "liberty" has been expanded in our own time from a shrivelled root. Then too, the due process clause of the fifth amendment was meant only to protect against deprivation of "liberty" without judicial proceedings, not to endow the courts with visitorial powers over legislation.[62] Not a glimmer of intention exists in the history of the fourteenth amendment to alter that meaning and deliver the last word on state legislation to federal judges.[63] James Wilson, chairman of the House Judiciary Committee during the fourteenth amendment debates, indicated that the due process clause furnished a "remedy" to secure the "fundamental rights" enumerated in the Civil Rights Act of 1866[64]—a law considered by the framers to be "exactly" like

[59]*See* Shattuck, *The True Meaning of the Term "Liberty" in those Clauses in the Federal and State Constitutions Which Protect "Life, Liberty, and Property,"* 4 Harv. L. Rev. 365 (1891); Warren, *The New "Liberty" Under the Fourteenth Amendment*, 39 Harv. L. Rev. 431, 442–45 (1926). *See generally* R. Berger, Government by Judiciary: The Transformation of the Fourteenth Amendment 270 (1977).

Blackstone defined "the personal liberty of individuals" as consisting "in the power of locomotion . . . or moving one's person to whatsoever place one's own inclination may direct, without imprisonment of restraint, unless by due course of law." 2 W. Blackstone, Commentaries *134. During the debates about the fourteenth amendment, James Wilson read Blackstone to the House. Cong. Globe, 39th Cong., 1st Sess. 1118 (1866).

[60]198 U.S. 45 (1905).

[61]Gitlow v. New York, 268 U.S. 652, 672 (1925) (Holmes, J., dissenting) (emphasis added).

[62]On the eve of the Federal Convention, Hamilton stated in the New York assembly: "The words '*due process*' have a precise technical import, and are only applicable to the process and proceedings of the courts of justice; they can never be referred to an act of legislature." 4 Papers of Alexander Hamilton 35 (Syrett & Cooke eds. 1962). He summarized 400 years of history. *See* Berger, "*Law of the Land*" *Reconsidered*, 74 Nw. U.L. Rev. 1 (1979).

[63]*See* Berger, *supra* note 59, at 201–06. *See also* Ely, *Constitutional Interpretivism: Its Allure and Impossibility*, 53 Ind. L.J. 399, 416 (1978).

[64]Cong. Globe, 39th Cong., 1st Sess. 1294–95 (1866).

the fourteenth amendment.[65] Those "fundamental rights" are far removed from Goldberg's ambitious catalog. In the words of the draftsman of the Act, Senator Lyman Trumbull, chairman of the Senate Judiciary Committee, they were "the right to acquire property, the rights to go and come at pleasure [freedom of locomotion], the right to enforce rights in the courts, [and] to make contracts. . . ."[66] It took the wonder-working Warren Court to transform the fourteenth amendment into a cornucopia of "rights" *excluded* by the framers.[67]

Possibly I do not appreciate the subtle differentiation between "incorporation" of the ninth amendment in the fourteenth and enforcement of the unspecified rights "retained" under the ninth by resort to the "liberty" of the fourteenth, but to my mind the distinction is purely semantic. Let me therefore reiterate that the argument that the Bill of Rights was incorporated in the fourteenth amendment is without historical warrant, as Charles Fairman demonstrated, and as is widely acknowledged.[68] Since it must draw

---

[65]*See* R. Berger, *supra* note 59, at 22–23. Justice Bradley declared: "[T]he civil rights bill was enacted at the same session, and but shortly before the presentation of the fourteenth amendment; . . . [it] was in pari materia; and was probably intended to reach the same object. . . . [T]he first section of the bill covers the same ground as the fourteenth amendment." Live-Stock Dealers' & Butchers Ass'n v. Crescent City Live-stock Landing & Slaughterhouse Co., 15 F. Cas. 649, 655 (C.C. La. 1870) (No. 8,408).

[66]Cong. Globe, 39th Cong., 1st Sess. 475 (1866). This was a paraphrase of the terms of the Civil Rights Bill. *See* R. Berger, *supra* note 59, at 24.

[67]*See* R. Berger, *supra* note 59, at 52–68 & 117–33. *See also* Berger, *supra* note 42, at 793–94. Senator William Fessenden, Chairman of the Joint Committee on Reconstruction of both Houses, stated, "We cannot put into the Constitution, owing to existing prejudices and existing institutions, an entire exclusion of all class distinctions. . . ." Cong. Globe, 39th Cong., 1st Sess. 705 (1866). Time and again attempts to ban *all* discriminations were defeated. *See* R. Berger, *supra* note 59, at 163–64.

[68]*See* Fairman, *Does the Fourteenth Amendment Incorporate the Bill of Rights?* 2 Stan. L. Rev. 5 (1949); Morrison, *Does the Fourteenth Amendment Incorporate the Bill of Rights?* 2 Stan. L. Rev. 140 (1949). *See also* R. Berger, *supra* note 59, at 137; A. Bickel, The Least Dangerous Branch 102 (1962).

Professor Dean Alfange, an activist, wrote, "[I]t is all but certain that the Fourteenth Amendment was not intended to incorporate the Bill of Rights and thus to revolutionize the administration of criminal justice in the states." Alfange, *supra* note 42, at 607. Professor Charles E. Merriam noted that the Founders believed government must be limited in many ways:

[I]t must be checked at every possible point; it must be at all times under suspicion. . . . Too much emphasis cannot well be laid upon the fear which

upon the due process clause,[69] and since "due process" in the fifth and fourteenth amendments is identical, the argument makes nonsense of the Bill of Rights. For incorporation of the "first eight" amendments into the "due process" of the fifth renders all the rest superfluous. The framers' attachment to state sovereignty[70] led the 39th Congress to limit federal intrusion to the ban on discrimination with respect to the "fundamental rights" enumerated by Trumbull.[71] In particular, Chairman Wilson emphasized, "[w]e are not making a general criminal code for the States."[72] The last thing the framers had in mind was to vest the distrusted judiciary[73] with the power of controlling state administration of local matters. Thus, the Court's long journey from the fifth amendment through the fourteenth to the ninth amendment exemplifies the unremitting expansion of judicial usurpation, from what is first disputed to what

---

the "Fathers" had of government. To them the great lesson of history was, that government always tends to become oppressive, and it was the greatest foe of individual liberty.

C. Merriam, A History of American Political Theories 76–77 (1903). Let one bit of contemporary evidence suffice. The Kentucky Resolutions of 1798, drafted by Jefferson, stated that "limited constitutions [are designed] to bind down those whom we are obliged to trust with power," to bind them "down from mischief by the chains of the Constitution." 4 J. Elliot, *supra* note 31, at 543.

Professor Philip Kurland wrote of the Court's decisions that the due process clause of the fourteenth amendment made the religion clauses of the first amendment applicable to the states:

Of course, nothing in the history of the fourteenth amendment suggests that this was among its purposes or goals. The transmogrification occurred solely at the whim of the Court. An attempt to pass a constitutional amendment providing for the application of the religion clauses to the states, the Blaine amendment, failed in 1876, eight years after effectuation of the fourteenth amendment.

Kurland, *The Irrelevance of the Constitution: The Religion Clauses of the First Amendment and the Supreme Court*, 24 Vill. L. Rev. 3, 9–10 (1978) (citations omitted).

[69]R. Berger, *supra* note 59, at 139–41.

[70]*See* Cong. Globe, 39th Cong., 1st Sess. 358 (1866) (remarks of Rep. Conkling); *id.* at 1292–93 (remarks of Rep. Bingham). *See generally* R. Berger, *supra,* note 59, at 60–64.

[71]*See supra* note 66 and accompanying text.

[72]Cong. Globe, 39th Cong., 1st Sess. 1120 (1866).

[73]*See* R. Berger, *supra* note 59, at 222–23; Berger, *The Fourteenth Amendment: Light From the Fifteenth*, 74 Nw. U.L. Rev. 311, 350–51 (1979).

becomes Holy Writ and is then further dilated.[74] In a crowning irony, Justice Black, who fathered the "incorporation" doctrine, at last cried "halt":

> [F]or a period of a century and a half no serious suggestion was ever made that the Ninth Amendment, enacted to protect state powers against federal invasion, could be used as a weapon of federal power to prevent state legislatures from passing laws they consider appropriate to govern local affairs. Use of any such broad, unbounded judicial authority would make of this Court's members a day-to-day constitutional convention.[75]

This is not, as Justice Goldberg argued, "to give . . . [the ninth amendment] no effect whatsoever."[76] Ample effect, overlooked by Goldberg, was commonsensically furnished by Dean Roscoe Pound: "Those [rights] not expressly set forth are not forever excluded but are, if the Ninth Amendment is read with the Tenth, left to be secured by the states or by the people of the whole land by constitutional change, as was done, for example, by the Fourteenth Amendment."[77] In "retaining" the unenumerated rights, the people reserved to themselves power to add to or subtract from the rights enumerated in the Constitution by the process of amendment exclusively confided to them by article V. If this be deemed supererogatory, be it remembered that according to Madison the ninth amendment itself was "inserted merely for greater caution."

Bennett Patterson

It is tempting to dismiss Patterson's *The Forgotten Ninth Amendment* out of hand.[78] But the fact that it has Roscoe Pound's

---

[74]Thus the Court has fulfilled the colonists' fear of power's "endlessly propulsive tendency to expand itself beyond legitimate boundaries." B. Bailyn, The Ideological Origins of the American Revolution 56 (1967).

[75]381 U.S. at 520 (Black, J., dissenting). *See also supra* note 52.

[76]381 U.S. at 491 (Goldberg, J., concurring). In this error Goldberg had been anticipated by Patterson. *See* B. Patterson, *supra* note 1, at 24.

[77]Pound, foreword to B. Patterson, *supra* note 1, at iv. Pound reiterated: "[T]hese reserved rights may be defined and enforcement of them may be provided by the states, except as may be precluded by the Fourteenth Amendment, or may be defined and acquire secured enforcement by the people of the United States by constitutional amendment." *Id.* at vi.

[78]Patterson's unreliability may be quickly illustrated. He states:

> We believe that the law should grow and our Constitution should be inter-

encomium[79]—although his own conclusions were diametrically opposed to those of Patterson—and that it has been cited by others[80] calls for more considered judgment.[81] Although more than half of Patterson's 217 pages are devoted to a reprint of the debates in the First Congress on the Bill of Rights, he gleans little therefrom. He mentions Gerry's unsuccessful proposal to change the word "disparage" in the ninth to "impair"[82]; and sets out the "last clause of Madison's fourth resolution,"

> The exceptions here or elsewhere in the Constitution, made in favor of particular rights, shall not be so construed as to diminish the just importance of other rights retained by the people, or as to enlarge the powers delegated by the Constitution; but either as actual limitations of such power, or as inserted merely for greater caution.[83]

Instead of noticing this disclaimer of intention "to enlarge," but rather to impose "actual limitations" on the powers "delegated by the Constitution," Patterson seizes on the words "the exceptions *here or elsewhere* in the Constitution."[84] From this he concludes that the language "definitely demonstrates that the clause was intended as a *general* declaration of human rights . . . a general clause relating to the entire Constitution, and not a specific clause relating only to the proposed amendments."[85] Without doubt it "related to any

---

preted in the light of current history, as was stated by one of the eminent courts of last resort of one of the States, [quoting] "The law should be construed in reference to the habits of business prevalent in the country *at the time it was enacted*. The law . . . *as then known* to exist."

Id. at 56 (emphasis added). Patently, the case expresses exactly the opposite of Patterson's proposition that "the law should grow."

[79]Pound, foreword to B. Patterson, *supra* note 1, at vi–vii.

[80]*See, e.g.*, 381 U.S. at 409 n.9 (Goldberg, J., concurring); E. Dumbauld, *supra* note 38, at 138; Redlich, *supra* note 36, at 805 n.87.

[81]"The flaccid acceptance of shoddy work ha[s] long been a scandal of scholarly and literary journals." O. Handlin, Truth in History 149 (1973).

[82]B. Patterson, *supra* note 1, at 16.

[83]*See supra* text accompanying note 47.

[84]B. Patterson, *supra* note 1, at 13. He also set forth Madison's response to the "assignment" objection to a Bill of Rights, *see supra* text accompanying note 44, without comment on its significance.

[85]B. Patterson, *supra* note 1, at 13 (emphasis added).

other rights *enumerated* . . . in the Constitution,"[86] but it is a non sequitur to conclude that these words constitute "a general declaration of human rights." The specific is not the "general."

Patterson also construes a proposed Senate preamble to the Bill of Rights recognizing state desires to "prevent misconstruction or abuse of [the granted] powers" by adding "further *declaratory* and restrictive clauses"[87] to mean that the ninth and tenth amendments are a "declaration of principles" rather than "restrictive clauses."[88] The word "declaratory" means to declare the law or rights as they stand, rather than a "declaration" of new law or rights.[89] Thus, the framers regarded the proposed amendments as merely declaring what was implicit: unenumerated powers are not granted.[90]

True it is that the Constitution is not to "be construed as a *grant* to the individual of inherent rights or liberties"[91]; rather, as Hamilton said of a "declaration of rights," it is a "limitation . . . of the power of the government itself."[92] But it was the federal government, not the states, that was so limited.[93] Patterson finds it "impossible to believe that human rights and individual liberties" had been

---

[86]*Id.* (emphasis added).

[87]*Id.* at 17.

[88]*Id.* at 18.

[89]So far as the amendments were not "actual limitations," said Madison, they were "inserted merely for greater caution." *See supra* text accompanying note 47. *See also supra* text accompanying note 41.

[90]*See supra* notes 42 & 43. Justice Stone stated that the tenth "amendment states but a truism that all is retained which has not been surrendered." It was merely "declaratory" of the existing relationship between state and federal governments; its purpose was to "allay fears that the new federal government might seek to exercise powers not granted, and that the states might not be able to exercise fully their reserved powers." United States v. Darby, 312 U.S. 100, 124 (1941).

[91]B. Patterson, *supra* note 1, at 19 (emphasis added).

[92]The Federalist No. 84, at 558 (A. Hamilton) (Mod. Lib. ed. 1937).

[93]It needs constantly to be remembered that

the sovereign powers vested in the State governments, by their respective constitutions, remained unaltered and unimpaired, except so far as they were granted to the government of the United States.

. . .

The government, then, of the United States, can claim no powers which are not granted to it by the constitution, and the powers actually granted, must be such as are expressly given, or given by necessary implication.

Martin v. Hunter's Lessee, 14 U.S. (1 Wheat.) 304, 325–26 (1816) (Story, J.).

fought for "only to be surrendered up to State governments where they could be destroyed by the sovereign people acting en masse."[94] He forgets that the Bill of Rights issued out of state distrust of the powers of the general government. "In an age where men looked to the states as the chief guardians of individual rights," Professor Redlich observed, "it was not surprising that the barrier of the Ninth and Tenth Amendments was erected against only the federal government."[95] Patterson would fetter the "sovereign people" themselves, although the ninth amendment provides that unenumerated rights are "retained by the people," not by some superior body that will protect against them.

The bulk of Patterson's discussion is beside the point—a sustained panegyric to "inherent natural rights of the individual."[96] Be they as wide as all outdoors,[97] he assumes rather than proves that the enforcement of unenumerated rights "retained by the people"

---

[94]B. Patterson, *supra* note 1, at 36–37.

[95]Redlich, *supra* note 36, at 808. *See supra* note 22. Patterson infers from the statement in Eilenbecker v. District Court of Plymouth County, 134 U.S. 31, 34 (1890), that "the first eight articles of the amendments to the Constitution have reference to powers *exercised* by the government of the United States and not to those of the States," that the ninth amendment did not contain such limitation. B. Patterson, *supra* note 1, at 28 (emphasis added). *Eilenbecker* considered challenges under the fifth, sixth, and eighth amendments, and the Court had no occasion to wander beyond the first eight. In addition, it was the "exercise," not the "reservation" of rights or powers that was at issue. It would take more than *Eilenbecker* to translate the ninth's *retention* of rights by the states or the people into *limits* upon the states, let alone that history precludes the Patterson differentiation.

[96]B. Patterson, *supra* note 1, at 19. Throughout he exalts the status of the individual over the collective. But to the Revolutionists of 1776, "individual rights, even the basic civil liberties that we consider so crucial, possessed little of their modern theoretical relevance when set against the will of the people." G. Wood, *supra* note 38, at 63.

The individual with whom Patterson, a member of a Houston law firm, B. Patterson, *supra* note 1, at 99, was concerned is the capitalist, who must be shielded from the "sentimental over-generosity and assistance that will in short time weaken our people by doing for them the things which they should be able and willing to do for themselves, and thus stifle genius and destroy their stamina."

"[S]ome of us," he counsels, "will have greater material wealth than others and none of our people can permit themselves to rankle and become bitter, because it is a part of our system to believe in private ownership of property." *Id.* at 84.

[97]The sovereign people's power to create "rights" knows no bounds: "The other rights 'retained by the people' may be, of course, justified by derivation from natural law theory; but they could just as well be ascribed . . . to the consensus of the American people." Dunbar, *supra* note 38, at 640.

was handed over to the General Government by the ninth amendment. His insistence that "[t]here is no provision in the Constitution which shall prevent the Government of the United States from protecting inherent rights"[98] overlooks the elementary fact that the federal government has only such powers as are granted.[99] His is the error in rejecting the proposition that "in order to protect a native human or inherent right, we must find the source of its protection in the Constitution."[100]

Professor Norman Redlich

More sophisticated than Patterson, Professor Redlich appreciates the import of the legislative history: "[T]he sketchy legislative history would seem to support the holding in *Barron v. Baltimore* that it was intended to restrict only the federal government."[101] He considers that "[i]t would be unrealistic to attribute to the Senate," which had added to the tenth amendment the words "or to the people," an "intent to impose ill-defined legally enforceable restraints on the states."[102] Those

> last four words of the Tenth Amendment must have been added to conform its meaning to the Ninth Amendment and to carry out the intent of both—that as to the federal government there were rights, not enumerated in the Constitution, which were "retained . . . by the people," and that because the people possessed such rights were *powers* which *neither* the federal government nor the States *possessed*.[103]

[98]B. Patterson, *supra* note 1, at 42.

[99]*See supra* notes 43 & 93.

[100]B. Patterson, *supra* note 1, at 45. Like Patterson, Knowlton Kelsey jumps to his conclusion without prior demonstration that it is compelled by text or history: "[The ninth] must be a positive declaration of existing, though unnamed rights, which may be vindicated under the authority of the Amendment whenever and if ever any governmental authority shall aspire to ungranted power in contravention of 'unenumerated rights.' " Kelsey, *The Ninth Amendment of the Federal Constitution*, 11 Ind. L.J. 309, 323 (1936).

[101]Redlich, *supra* note 36, at 805–06 (footnote omitted).

[102]*Id.* at 806.

[103]*Id.* at 807 (emphasis added). For present purposes there is no need to inquire whether the reservation of powers not delegated to the federal government also operates against the states. The Founders feared federal, not state power, as Redlich himself recognizes. *See supra* text accompanying note 95.

These remarks, plus his observation that the Founders "looked to the states as the chief guardians of individual rights" and consequently that the "barrier of the Ninth and Tenth Amendments was erected against only the federal government,"[104] require the conclusion that the ninth amendment has no application to the states. It is therefore puzzling to read that the ninth and tenth amendments "might be peculiarly suited to meet the unique and important problems suggested by the Connecticut birth control law case."[105]

The starting point for Redlich is a "strong historical argument" that the ninth and tenth amendments "were intended to apply in a situation where the asserted right appears to the Court as fundamental to a free society but is, nevertheless, not specified in the Bill of Rights."[106] Apparently Redlich assumes that the Court is to be the enforcer of these "not specified" rights.[107] That role apparently is premised in his statement that the ninth and tenth amendments "appear to have been designed" for "the protection of individual rights not specified in the Constitution."[108] But it is incompatible with his statement that "because the people possessed such [retained] rights, there were *powers* which *neither* the federal government nor the States *possessed*."[109] Among such "no-powers" is the "protection" of those retained rights.

Anticipating Justice Goldberg, Redlich attempts to bridge this chasm by invoking the fourteenth amendment to provide "the framework for applying these restrictions against the states, even though they may have been originally intended to apply only against the United States."[110] First, he suggests that those Justices "who consider the Fourteenth Amendment as having embodied either or all the major portions of the Bill of Rights could appropriately consider the Ninth and Tenth Amendment as 'incorporated' or 'absorbed' into the first paragraph of the Fourteenth Amendment."[111] Thus the discredited "incorporation" doctrine is to serve

---

[104]Redlich, *supra* note 36, at 808.

[105]*Id.* at 804.

[106]*Id.* at 808.

[107]It is not only such judicially recognized "fundamental" rights, but *all* unenumerated rights which are "retained by the people."

[108]Redlich, *supra* note 36, at 808.

[109]*Id.* at 807 (emphasis added).

[110]*Id.* at 806.

[111]*Id.* at 808.

as the vehicle of yet another arrogation, a result on which even the apostle of "incorporation," Justice Black, gagged. Redlich would have the tenth amendment, which reserves powers not delegated, and against which all "general" delegations are to be read, swallowed up by the fourteenth![112] Next, Redlich turns to "those Justices, who have viewed the Fourteenth Amendment as limited only to 'fundamental' rights unrelated to the specific provisions of the Bill of Rights [who] should have no difficulty in adopting a Constitutional provision which appears to have been almost custom-made for this approach."[113] This collides with his conclusion that the retention of rights was accompanied by the withholding of correlative power.

John Hart Ely

Stamping Chief Justice Warren's holding in *Bolling v. Sharpe* "that the Due Process Clause of the Fifth Amendment incorporates the Equal Protection Clause of the Fourteenth Amendment" as "gibberish both syntactically and historically,"[114] Professor John Hart Ely turns to the ninth amendment, asserting that "such an open-ended provision is appropriately read to include an 'equal protection' component."[115] Indeed, he considers that "the conclusion that the Ninth Amendment was intended to signal the existence of federal constitutional rights beyond those specifically enumerated in the Constitution is the only conclusion its language seems comfortably able to support."[116]

If I do not mistake his meaning, Ely confines his invocation of the ninth amendment to the federal domain. We are agreed that "[i]t is quite clear that the original framers and ratifying conventions

---

[112]Senator Frederick Frelinghuysen, a framer who construed the fourteenth amendment broadly, said in 1871 that "the Fourteenth Amendment must . . . not be used to make the General Government imperial. It must be read . . . together with the Tenth Amendment." Cong. Globe, 42nd Cong., 1st Sess. 501 (1871). In a more innocent decade (1957), Professor Dumbauld wrote, "The Ninth and Tenth Amendments, being reservations for the benefit of the states, of course give no occasion for raising the question whether they are made applicable against the states by the Fourteenth Amendment." E. Dumbauld, *supra* note 38, at 138.

[113]Redlich, *supra* note 36, at 808.

[114]J. Ely, Democracy and Distrust 32 (1980).

[115]*Id.* at 33.

[116]*Id.* at 38.

intended the Bill of Rights to control only the actions of the federal government."[117] It therefore bears emphasis that Ely's "federal constitutional rights" can be asserted only against the federal government and not the states, for he does not here call on incorporation into the fourteenth amendment.

Ely's reference to the "existence of federal constitutional rights" requires explication. Both the rights expressed in the Bill of Rights and the unspecified rights retained by the people "exist," but only the former are "constitutional rights." To my mind, a right "retained" by the people and not described has not been embodied in the Constitution. Madison made clear that the retained rights were not "assigned" to the federal government: to the contrary, he emphasized that they constitute an area in which the "Government ought not to act." This means, in my judgment, that the courts have not been empowered to enforce the retained rights against either the federal government or the states.

Ely himself observes, "One thing we know to a certainty from the historical context is that the Ninth Amendment was not designed to grant Congress authority *to create* additional rights, to amend Article I, Section 8 by *adding a general power* to protect rights."[118] Without protection, a "right" is empty. And he justly points out that the phrase " 'others retained by the people' [is not] an apt way of saying 'others Congress may create.' "[119] That power of creation equally was withheld from the courts; the Founders did not regard the courts as "creators," or lawmakers, but as discoverers of law.[120] For them, the separation of powers, as Madison said in the First Congress, was a "sacred principle"[121] reinforced by a "profound fear" of judicial discretion.[122] It does not, therefore, advance the case for judicial enforcement of the ninth amendment that "[t]here

---

[117]*Id.* at 37.

[118]*Id.*

[119]*Id.*

[120]"[J]udges conceived of their role as merely that of discovering and applying preexisting legal rules." Horwitz, *The Emergence of an Instrumental Conception of American Law 1780–1820,* in 5 Perspectives in American History 287, 297 (1971).

[121]1 Annals of Cong., *supra* note 28, at 596–97 (Gerry referring to Madison's argument).

[122]G. Wood, *supra* note 38, at 298. In 1769 Chief Justice Hutchinson of Massachusetts declared: "[T]he judge should never be the *Legislator:* Because, then the will of the Judge would be the Law: and this tends to a State of Slavery." Horwitz, *supra* note 120, at 292.

was at the time of the original Constitution little legislative history indicating that *any* particular provision was to receive judicial enforcement: the Ninth Amendment was not singled out one way or the other."[123] All the presuppositions the Founders brought to the task militate against a blank check to that branch which Hamilton assured them "was next to nothing."[124] Ely himself remarks that "read for what it says the Ninth Amendment seems open-textured enough to support almost anything one might wish to argue, and that thought can get pretty scary."[125] "[T]hat thought," I venture, would have scared the Founders out of their wits. It runs against Madison's explanation that the Bill of Rights would impel the judiciary "to resist encroachments upon rights expressly stipulated for . . . by the declaration of rights,"[126] and reinforces the conclusion that courts were not empowered to enforce the retained and unenumerated rights.

Ely finds Madison's explanation of the ninth amendment separating "the question of unenumerated powers from the question of unenumerated rights"[127] confused: "[T]he possibility that unenumerated rights will be disparaged is seemingly made to do service as an intermediate premise in an argument that unenumerated powers will be implied. . . ."[128] This "confusion" he attributes to "what we today would regard as a category mistake, a failure to recognize that rights and powers are not simply the absence of one another but that rights can cut across or 'trump' powers."[129] But

---

[123]J. Ely, *supra* note 114, at 40.

[124]The Federalist No. 78, at n.* (A. Hamilton) (Mod. Lib. ed. 1937) (quoting C. Montesquieu, The Spirit of the Laws (1748)). *See also* J. Wilson, *supra* note 21.

[125]J. Ely, *supra* note 114, at 34.

[126]1 Annals of Cong., *supra* note 28, at 457 (quoted at text accompanying *supra* note 50).

[127]J. Ely, *supra* note 114, at 35.

[128]*Id.* at 36.

[129]*Id.* Citing Hamilton's reply to the argument that the power of taxation could be used to inhibit freedom of expression, The Federalist No. 84, at 560 n.* (A. Hamilton) (Mod. Lib. ed. 1937), Ely concludes that "the possibility of a governmental act's being supported by one of the enumerated powers and at the same time violating one of the enumerated rights is one our forebears were capable of contemplating." J. Ely, *supra* note 114, at 202 n.86. Hamilton rejected the notion that "the imposition of duties upon publications" would be impeded by express "declarations in the State constitutions, in favor of the freedom of the press." He argued in support of his conclusion "that newspapers are taxed in Great Britain and yet it is notorious

whether the Founders were mistaken in logic is of no moment if they acted on that mistaken view.[130] That the framers premised that rights and powers were two sides of the same coin is hardly disputable. The exceptions "made in favor of particular *rights*," Madison stated, were to be regarded as "actual limitations on such *powers*."[131] The "great object" of a Bill of Rights, he said, was to limit . . . the *powers* of Government, *by excepting out* of the grant of power those cases in which the Government ought not to act, or could act only in a particular mode."[132] As Ely observes, "[w]hat is important" is that Madison "wished to forestall *both* the implication of unexpressed powers *and* the disparagement of unenumerated rights," employing the tenth amendment for the one and the ninth for the other.[133] By what logic do we derive "unexpected powers" to enforce "unenumerated rights" in the teeth of Madison's purpose to "foreclose . . . the implication of unexpressed powers," and his emphasis that the enumeration of "particular rights" was not to be construed to "enlarge the powers delegated by the Constitution," but rather "as actual limitations of such powers"?[134] Is it conceivable that Madison meant to confer "open-ended" power by "unenumerated rights" while limiting power by the enumeration of "particular rights"? Ely's conclusion also collides with his affirmation that the ninth amendment was not designed to add to article I, section eight "a general power to protect rights."

Finally Ely concludes, "[i]f a principled approach to judicial enforcement of . . . open-ended provisions cannot be developed,

---

that the press nowhere enjoys greater liberty than in that country." The Federalist No. 84, at 560 n.* (A. Hamilton) (Mod. Lib. ed. 1937).

Whether an *enumerated* power might override an "exception" in favor of an *enumerated* right need not presently concern us, although it is worth noting Madison's emphasis that *enumerated* rights were "excepted" "out of the grant of power"—that they were to be regarded "as actual limitations of such powers." Here the issue is whether there is an "unexpressed power" to enforce *unenumerated* rights "retained by the people."

[130]C. Hughes, The Supreme Court of the United States 186 (1928).

[131]1 Annals of Cong., *supra* note 28, at 435 (quoted at *supra* text accompanying note 47) (emphasis added).

[132]1 Annals of Cong., *supra* note 28, at 437 (quoted at *supra* text accompanying note 46) (emphasis added). *See also* 3 M. Farrand, *supra* note 22, at 256 (remarks of Rep. Pinckney) (quoted at *supra* note 39).

[133]J. Ely, *supra* note 114, at 36.

[134]1 Annals of Cong., *supra* note 28, at 435 (quoted at *supra* text accompanying note 47).

one that is not hopelessly inconsistent with our nation's commitment to representative democracy, responsible commentators must consider seriously the possibility that courts simply should stay away from them."[135] The notion that the framers, so fearful of the greedy expansiveness of power,[136] would make an "open-ended," *i.e.* unlimited, grant, which after the lapse of almost two hundred years is so "scary" that Ely would condemn it unless limited by a "principled" approach, verges on the "incredible."[137] Little less strange is the assumption that a Court which employed the allegedly "open-ended" terms of the fourteenth amendment[138] in

[135]J. Ely, *supra* note 114, at 41.

[136]*See supra* note 74 and accompanying text.

[137]I borrow the pejorative from Ely's description of my views. *See* J. Ely, *supra* note 114, at 198 n.66.

[138]For a critique of this theory, see R. Berger, Government by Judiciary: The Transformation of the Fourteenth Amendment 300–11 (1977). Ely has it that the framers of the fourteenth amendment issued "open and across-the-board *invitations* to import into the constitutional decision process considerations that will not be found in the amendment nor even . . . elsewhere in the Constitution." Ely, *supra* note 63, at 415 (emphasis added). For a critique of this view, see Berger, *Government by Judiciary: John Hart Ely's "Invitation,"* 54 Ind. L.J. 277 (1979).

The claim that the 1789 framers issued such an "invitation" through the medium of "open-ended" terms runs counter to Ely's own analysis. He remarks that the Founders "certainly didn't have natural law in mind when the Constitution's various open-ended delegations to the future were inserted and approved." J. Ely, *supra* note 114, at 39. He notes that "you can invoke natural law to support anything you want." *Id.* at 50. His "open-ended" theory would permit the imposition of personal, extra-constitutional values that found no favor in the shape of natural law.

The Founders, as Professor Philip Kurland observed, and as is well attested, were attached to a "written Constitution"—one of "fixed and unchanging meaning," except as changed by amendment. P. Kurland, Watergate and the Constitution 7 (1978). They conceived the judge's role as *policing* constitutional boundaries, not as taking over legislative functions within those boundaries, and still less as revision of the Constitution. *See* Berger, *Government by Judiciary: John Hart Ely's "Invitation,"* *supra*, at 287. As Elbridge Gerry stated, "[i]t was quite foreign from the nature of [the] office to make them judges of the policy of public measures." 1 M. Farrand, *supra* note 22, at 97–98. *See* 2 M. Farrand, *supra* note 22, at 75. "Vague and uncertain laws, and more especially Constitutions," wrote Samuel Adams, "are the very instruments of slavery." 3 S. Adams, Writings of Samuel Adams 262 (H. Cushing ed. 1904) (quoted in Berger, *Government by Judiciary: John Hart Ely's "Invitation,"* *supra*, at 288).

Such were the presuppositions that underlie Madison's reference to judicial protection of "stipulated rights." Ely's acknowledgment that the ninth amendment did not empower Congress to "create" additional rights, or add "a general power to protect rights" is at war with his view that the amendment is "open-ended."

disregard of the framers' unmistakable intention to exclude suffrage from its scope[139] will show greater respect for the self-denying "principles" which Ely now proffers.

Conclusion

The ninth amendment demonstrably was not custom-made to enlarge federal enforcement of "fundamental rights" in spite of state law; it was merely declaratory of a basic presupposition: all powers not "positively" granted are reserved to the people. It added no unspecified rights to the Bill of Rights; instead it demarked an area in which the "General Government" has no power whatsoever. To transform it into an instrument of control over state government by recourse to the fourteenth amendment blatantly perverts the meaning of the framers, both in 1789 and in 1866.

The newly discovered "meaning" of the ninth amendment is but another facet of the unremitting effort to rationalize the judicial takeover of government in areas which have found favor with activists. It was not ever thus. The shift has been described by an activist, Professor Stanley Kutler: through the late 1930s, academe "criticized vigorously the abusive powers of the federal judiciary" for "frustrating desirable social policies" and "arrogat[ing] a policymaking function not conferred upon them by the Constitution."[140] After 1937, these critics "suddenly found a new faith," a "new libertarianism promoting 'preferred freedoms' " protected by an "activist judiciary."[141] Now another activist, Professor Louis Lusky, defends "the Court's new and grander conception of its own place in the governmental scheme"[142] resting on "basic shifts in its approach to constitutional adjudication [including] . . . assertion of the power to *revise* the Constitution, *bypassing* the cumbersome amendment procedure prescribed by article V."[143] That "new and grander" role—conferred by the Court on the Court—pays little heed to the intention of the framers. When confronted by Justice Harlan's "irrefutable" demonstration that the fourteenth

---

[139]*See infra* notes 144 & 145 and accompanying text.

[140]Kutler, *Raoul Berger's Fourteenth Amendment: A History or Ahistorical?* 6 Hastings Const. L.Q. 511–12 (1979).

[141]*Id.* at 513.

[142]Lusky, *"Government by Judiciary": What Price Legitimacy?* 6 Hastings Const. L.Q. 403, 408 (1979).

[143]*Id.* at 406 (emphasis added).

amendment was not intended to "authorize Congress to set voter qualifications"[144]—it is safe to say that suffrage was *unmistakably excluded*[145]—Justices Brennan, White and Marshall "could not accept this thesis even if it were supported by historical evidence,"[146] and Justice Douglas dismissed it as "irrelevant."[147] This repudiated the traditional canon of construction reiterated by Justice Holmes: when a legislature "has intimated its will, however indirectly, that will should be recognized and obeyed. . . . [I]t is not an adequate discharge of duty for courts to say: We see what you are driving at, but you have not said it."[148] Still less is that will to be disobeyed when the framers have spoken with unmistakable clarity, any more than the Court may "revise" the express text. Posterity will honor Justice Harlan's comment:

> When the Court disregards the express intent and understanding of the Framers, it has invaded the realm of the political process to which the amending power was committed, and it has violated the constitutional structure which it is its highest duty to protect.[149]

Even the express text is thrust aside by one superheated activist, Professor Robert Cover:

---

[144]Oregon v. Mitchell, 400 U.S. 112, 350 (1970).

[145]Looking back in *Griswold,* Justice Harlan justly remarked that the reapportionment interpretations were "made in the face of irrefutable and still unanswered history to the contrary." 381 U.S. at 501 (Harlan, J., concurring). *See* R. Berger, *supra* note 59, at 52–98. Lusky considers that Harlan's demonstration is "irrefutable and unrefuted." Lusky, *supra* note 142, at 406. *See generally* Berger, *supra* note 42, at 794.

[146]Oregon v. Mitchell, 400 U.S. 112, 251 (1970).

[147]*Id.* at 140. Little wonder that Professor Paul Brest challenges the assumption "that judges and other public officials were bound by the text or original understanding of the Constitution." Brest, *The Misconceived Quest for the Original Understanding,* 60 B.U.L. Rev. 204, 224 (1980).

[148]Johnson v. United States, 163 F. 30, 32 (1st Cir. 1908) (quoted in Keifer & Keifer v. R.F.C., 306 U.S. 381, 391 n.4 (1939)). Judge Learned Hand stated in 1959 that "the purpose may be so manifest as to override even the explicit words used." Cawley v. United States, 272 F.2d 443, 445 (2d Cir. 1959). "The intention of the lawmaker is the law." Hawaii v. Mankichi, 190 U.S. 197, 212 (1903) (quoting Smythe v. Fiske, 90 U.S. (23 Wall.) 374, 380 (1874)). Those who dismiss out of hand the application of canons of statutory construction to constitutional interpretation are probably unaware that Justice Story, Edward Corwin, Julius Goebel and Harry Jones are to the contrary. *See* Berger, *supra* note 42, at 805.

[149]Oregon v. Mitchell, 400 U.S. 112, 203 (1970) (Harlan, J., concurring).

> [A] reading of the Constitution must stand or fall not upon the Constitution's *self-evident meaning*, nor upon the intentions of the 1787 or 1866 framers. . . . [I]t is for *us*, not the framers, to decide whether that end of liberty is best served by *entrusting* to judges a major role in defining our governing political ideas and in measuring the activity of the primary actors in majoritarian politics against that ideology.[150]

Of course Cover does not—and cannot—point to the source of this decision to "entrust" judges with the ultimate power to frame our "ideology"; he chooses instead to equate the wishes of the academic illuminati with the will of "We, the people." Widespread resistance to busing, as well as dissatisfaction with affirmative action, the Court's restrictions on death penalties, and State criminal law enforcement testify that the identification is imaginary. Were the values of the Justices superior to those of the commonality,[151] they would yet represent those of "Big Brother" and recall Robespierre: "If Frenchmen would not be free and virtuous voluntarily, then he would force them to be free and cram virtue down their throats."[152]

It is against this background that the Goldbergian resort to the ninth amendment is to be viewed; another bit of legal legerdemain whose purpose is to take from the people their right to self-government and put it in the hands of the Justices.[153]

---

[150]Cover, Book Review, New Republic, Jan. 14, 1978, at 27 (emphasis added). *See also* Brest, *The Misconceived Quest for the Original Understanding*, 60 B.U.L. Rev. 204, 224 (1980).

[151]Professor G. Edward White asks, "[W]hy should [the Court] not openly acknowledge that the source of [newly invented] rights is not the constitutional text but the enhanced seriousness of certain values in American society?" White, *Reflections on the role of the Supreme Court: the Contemporary Debate and the "Lessons" of History*, 63 Judicature 162, 168 (1979). *See also* Forrester, *Are We Ready for Truth in Judging?* 63 A.B.A.J. 1212 (1977).

[152]2 C. Brinton, J. Christoper & R. Wolff, A History of Civilization 115 (1st ed. 1955).

[153]Alfred Kelly, a devout activist, wrote that the Warren Court was "apparent[ly] determin[ed] to carry through a constitutional . . . revolution." Kelly, *Clio and the Court: An Illicit Love Affair*, 1965 Sup. Ct. Rev. 119, 158.

9. On Reading the Ninth Amendment: A Reply to Raoul Berger

Simeon C. R. McIntosh

Introduction

In his article on the ninth amendment in the *Cornell Law Review*,[1] Professor Raoul Berger sharply criticizes Justice Goldberg's interpretation of the amendment in his concurring opinion in *Griswold v. Connecticut*,[2] and has advanced, what I take is, in his opinion, the proper interpretation of the amendment. In this paper, I argue that Professor Berger's reading of the ninth amendment is deeply flawed because it rests on a rather naive and inadequate theory of constitutional interpretation. In sum, his theory is founded on an overly simplistic epistemology, one that seems oblivious of the fact that constitutional interpretation is, essentially, an hermeneutical enterprise[3] and does not consist in the mere empirical accounting

Excerpted, by permission, from 28 How. L. Rev. 913 (1985).

Editor's Note: In this excerpt, some footnotes have been edited and renumbered for consistency.

The author wishes to thank Jordan Paust, Houston Law School, and Winfried Brugger, Tübingen University, for their critical comments on an earlier draft of this paper.

[1]Berger, *The Ninth Amendment*, 66 Cornell L. Rev. 1 (1980–81).

[2]Griswold v. Connecticut, 381 U.S. 479 (1965). In *Griswold*, the Supreme Court invalidated a Connecticut statute forbidding the use of contraceptives, as applied to a married couple, on the ground that it violated a constitutional right of marital privacy. The opinion of the court, per Justice Douglas, found this right of marital privacy within the area of the penumbra created by specific guarantees in the Bill of Rights and made passing reference to the ninth amendment. *See Griswold*, 381 U.S. at 484 (Douglas, J., plurality opinion). However, it was Justice Goldberg who, in a concurring opinion, argued that such a right was more specifically protected under the ninth amendment. *See Griswold*, 381 U.S. at 486–91 (Goldberg, J., concurring).

[3]I say "hermeneutical" in the sense that constitutional interpretation involves our effort to find a theory of knowledge for the kind of data with which the cultural scientist deals, viz., texts, signs, symbols, etc., the products of man's deliberate ingenuity. In this respect, constitutional interpretation is not simply a methodolog-

of the framers' declarations of intention. What is more, his reading of the ninth amendment does not evidence a fundamental awareness that the amendment is part of a whole, a totality, a text. Consequently, it denies a basic hermeneutical premise, an operating ideal, that the text possesses some unifying insight, some inner dynamic, present in each of its parts. For although interpretation may begin with the study of a part, it is ultimately the whole we are seeking to understand, and it is in grasping the unifying insight of the whole that one understands or makes sense of the part. Constitutional interpretation, then, as an hermeneutical enterprise, is, essentially, a dialectical process, "a part-whole-part movement, a constant back and forth."[4] I wish to emphasize, therefore, that, particularly with respect to the understanding and application of the more important and open-textured clauses or sections of the Constitution, constitutional adjudication inevitably entails an expounding of the structure, the architectonic of the Constitution as a whole.

---

ical and practical endeavor but is essentially epistemological and theoretical. *See* McIntosh, *Legal Hermeneutics: A Philosophical Critique*, 35 Okla. L. Rev. 1, 50–72 (1982) [hereinafter cited as McIntosh, *Legal Hermeneutics*]; *see also* R. J. Howard, Three Faces of Hermeneutics 10 (1982).

[4]*See* R. J. Howard, *supra* note 3, at 10. Although it is unnecessary at this juncture to repeat my earlier argument on the importance of using hermeneutics in legal analysis, the following outline of the process might be useful to the reader:

Simply stated law is an interpretive process. . . . As a cognitive discipline, interpretation aims at knowledge—the understanding of rights and obligations created and confirmed through legal texts. This knowledge, however, will hardly be achieved through a methodology that too heavily structures the reader's way of seeing, allowing him to approach and control the text through canons of interpretation, as though the text consisted of natural objects obedient to laws which could be formulated and understood. In place of this methodology, a dialectical theory of interpretation is needed, one that allows the reader to question and, at once, be questioned by the "subject matter."

Stated generally, interpretation is a cognitive process whose proper object is our neighbors' mind, or, at least, a sign or expression whereby some mind manifest is its existence and its processes. . . . This understanding is made possible through our possession of language. . . .

It suffices, then, to say that all understanding (which also means all interpretation) is essentially linguistic.

McIntosh, *Legal Hermeneutics, supra* note 3, at 2–3.

In his opinion in *Griswold*, Justice Goldberg concluded that "the language and history of the ninth amendment[5] reveal that the framers of the Constitution believed that there are additional fundamental rights, protected from governmental infringement, which exist alongside those fundamental rights specifically mentioned in the first eight constitutional amendments."[6] But Professor Berger asks: "Who is to protect [these] undescribed rights?" He charges that Justice Goldberg, and others similarly inclined, would transform the ninth amendment into a bottomless well into which the judiciary can dip for the formation of undreamed of "rights" in their limitless discretion, something the founders would have rejected out of hand,[7] for this would constitute the most blatant form of judicial legislation, an obvious violation of the democratic ideal of separation of powers. What is more, Berger sees Justice Goldberg's reading of the ninth amendment as facilitating federal encroachment into local matters reserved to the states by the Constitution.

For Berger, the ninth amendment, which provides that "the enumeration in the Constitution, of certain rights, shall not be construed to deny or disparage others retained by the people," should be read in conjunction with the tenth amendment, which provides that "the powers not delegated to the United States by the Constitution, nor prohibited by it to the States, are reserved to the States respectively, or to the people," since, he believes, they are paired opposites of the same coin. He takes the words of James Madison to be conclusive:

---

[5]"The enumeration in the Constitution, of certain rights, shall not be construed to deny or disparage others retained by the people." U.S. Const. amend. IX.

[6]*Griswold*, 381 U.S. at 488 (Goldberg, J., concurring), *quoted in* Berger, *supra*, note 1, at 2.

[7]Berger, *supra* note 1, at 2. *But see* Paust, *Human Rights and the Ninth Amendment: A New Form of Guarantee*, 60 Conn. L. Rev. 231, 234–35, 245–52, & 260–62 (1975). Professor Jordan J. Paust is of the opposite opinion. He suggests that Madison, in common with others, feared that a specific enumeration of rights might someday be interpreted so as to deny or disparage others, and he (Madison) was persuaded by Jefferson and the general demands of the states that a bill of rights should be added to the Constitution along with some form of caveat to cover the danger. Paust further notes that Madison is supposed to have stated before the assemblage of the first House of Representatives that the argument that a specification of some rights might someday be misinterpreted to imply a denial of others was the best argument he had heard against the enumeration of any rights in the Constitution, but he felt confident that his new proposal—the predecessor to the ninth—would sufficiently guard against such attempted abuses of rights.

> If a line can be drawn between the powers granted and the rights retained, it would seem to be the same thing, whether the latter be secured by declaring that they shall not be abridged, or that the former shall not be extended. If no such line can be drawn, a declaration in either form would amount to nothing.[8]

It would seem intuitively obvious that the central problem raised in the interpretation of the ninth amendment would be that of ascertaining these unstipulated "rights" that are supposedly retained by the people. If this is true, then Madison's words would seem rather simplistic, for they would suggest that we may know what rights are retained simply by looking to see what powers have been granted. But granted to whom? Both to the federal government and the states? True, if there are rights retained by the people, then the federal government lacks the power to take away those rights, in the same sense that it lacks the power to take away rights that are stipulated in the first eight amendments. This conclusion, however, merely restates a factual proposition without providing an answer to the question. And what of the states? They, too, have powers reserved to them by the Constitution. Do they also lack the power to deny or disparage the "rights" retained by the people? This would seem the very question that Justice Goldberg had read *Griswold* as raising, but the fact that Professor Berger seems incognizant of this, by his preoccupation with the question of whether the federal government has any power to "protect" the "rights" retained by the people under the ninth amendment, reveals one of the disabling flaws in his essay: his conflation of the concepts of "rights" and "powers"—fundamental concepts of legal and political theory. I will return to this point later in my essay.

It is now common knowledge that there existed at the time of the adoption of the Constitution, a deep distrust of a strong central government, and, consequent upon the states' reluctance to adopt the Constitution, a Bill of Rights was drafted to serve as a qualification exclusively upon the powers of the federal government.

---

[8]Letter from James Madison to George Washington (Dec. 5, 1789), *reprinted in* 5 The Writings of James Madison 432 (G. Hunt ed. 1904), *quoted in* Berger, *supra* note 1, at 3. Note that Paust reads the historical record differently than Berger. He suggests that Madison, in common with others, feared that a specific enumeration of rights someday be interpreted so as to deny or disparage others, and that he was persuaded by Jefferson and the general demands of the states that a bill of rights should be added to the Constitution along with some form of caveat to cover the danger. *See* Paust, *supra* note 7, at 245.

"This declaration of rights . . . is intended to secure the people against the maladministration of the [federal] government."[9] The fact that the first sentence of Madison's fifth resolution, "No State shall violate the equal rights of conscience, or the freedom of the press, or the trial by jury in criminal cases,"[10] was rejected by the Senate, offers convincing proof, under Berger's analysis, that the Bill of Rights, of which the ninth amendment is a part, was to have no application to the states."[11]

Assuming all this to be true, the question still remains whether the Bill of Rights ought to be read as having no application to the states, since on this assumption, the framers would seem to have contradicted themselves. That is to say, if the federal government lacked the power to abridge the rights of the citizens which were secured by the Bill of Rights, were the states free to do so? Berger thinks that the founders had otherwise provided for the proper limitation on state authority, to wit, their reference in the tenth amendment to powers not "prohibited by [the Constitution] to the states." If by this he means that the tenth amendment is the source of limitations on the states' power to infringe those rights that people enjoy under the Constitution, then the tenth is indeed superfluous, for the limitation on state authority is the granting of the right itself. What is of greater consequence for me, however, is the fact that Berger's atomistic notion of constitutional interpretation would escape something that is central to any epistemological claim that interpretation, as concerned with the problem of understanding, can make: To grasp whatever contradictions there might be in the text, and resolve them in light of the most plausible reading which the text, taken as a whole, would allow.

According to Berger, the enumeration of rights in the first eight amendments was a cause for concern to those who feared that such enumeration might deliver those rights not enumerated into the hands of the federal government.[12] Hence the reason for the ninth amendment. Those rights, says Berger, that were not singled out, were not intended to be assigned into the hands of the federal

---

[9]Statement of Elbridge Gerry to the First Congress, *quoted in* 1 Annals of Congress 749 (Gales & Seaton eds. 1836), *reprinted in* Berger, *supra* note 1, at 5. *See also* Paust, *supra* note 7 at 245–47.

[10]1 Annals of Congress, *supra* note 9, at 749, *quoted in* Berger, *supra* note 1, at 5.

[11]Berger, *supra* note 1, at 5.

[12]*See id.* at 7.

government. But what does it mean to say that rights are "assigned into the hands of a government"? Do governments have rights in the sense in which we may speak of citizens as having rights? Berger reasons that Madison meant to bar the implication that unenumerated rights were "assigned to the federal government, for enforcement or otherwise," thus underscoring his principal theme that "the great object in view is to limit and qualify the powers of Government, by excepting out of the grant of power those cases in which the Government ought not to act, or to act only in a particular mode."[13]

However, Berger is in fact conceding that the enumerated rights were "assigned to the federal government, for enforcement or otherwise." This would appear to include enforcement against the states. The question therefore arises: Why not the unenumerated rights? The fact remains that the tenor of Madison's words would seem to reflect a Lockean version of the social contract theory. Jefferson's declaration in support of the ninth amendment seems of similar import: "[T]he purposes of society do not require a surrender of all our rights to our ordinary governors."[14] However, Berger would rather conclude from all this that the federal government's lack of power to "deny" the unenumerated rights entails a lack of power to enforce them against the states.[15] In sum, Berger's thesis is this: Not only are the undescribed rights retained by the people, but the federal government lacks the power to enforce them; its power of enforcement was to be confined to expressly stipulated rights.[16] On this reading, one must conclude that these unenumerated rights are either not rights in fact, or on the assumption that they do exist, then they are not a species of constitutional rights. This is indeed Berger's conclusion, for he opines that federal judicial power is limited to suits brought on such rights that are embodied in the Constitution. In other words, those rights retained by the people are not constitutional rights because they are not embodied in the Constitution.[17]

[13]1 Annals of Congress, *supra* note 9, at 437, *quoted in* Berger, *supra* note 1, at 7.

[14]Thomas Jefferson, *quoted in* Berger, *supra* note 1, at 5.

[15]Berger, *supra* note 1, at 5-6 & 23 (curiously, Berger's text and notes on this point focus on possible denials of those rights retained by the people and do not reach the crucial question concerning how those rights are to be protected).

[16]*See id.* at 8.

[17]*See id.* at 9.

Needless to say, this conclusion is inconsistent with the language of the ninth amendment which compels that certain unenumerated rights are not to be denied or disparaged. But, assuming, arguendo, that Berger has read Madison correctly on the question of the enforcement of rights retained by the people, then it would follow that Berger, like Madison, has confused two related, yet conceptually distinct, questions in constitutional adjudication: (1) whether the federal government has the power to regulate in a particular area of human affairs, and (2) whether a case in question is one for judicial review, as one arising under the Constitution or laws of the United States. Berger, I would submit, has conflated the federal government's legislative powers, on the one hand, with its judicial powers on the other. It is true that the judiciary is a coordinate branch of government, but its functions, limited to deciding cases and controversies,[18] are sufficiently distinct from those of the legislative branch. I think this is an important point, because an assertion that a particular matter falls within an area prohibited to the federal government does not lead to the conclusion that a case concerning the government's intrusion into that restricted area is not a proper subject for judicial review. Indeed, the very opposite conclusion would follow. Therefore, if we were to assume that the federal government lacks the power to regulate a matter covered by the ninth amendment, then it would follow that any attempt on the part of the federal government to regulate such a matter, in a manner that may constitute the denial or disparagement of rights retained by the people, should be the proper subject for judicial review and the ultimate enforcement of those rights. This argues that unless the very power that is denied the federal government to disparage rights retained by the people has been expressly given to the states, then it must follow that the states lack such power as well. If I am correct, then a state's infringement of those rights must also be a proper subject for judicial review. Thus the answer to the question, whether a state's alleged infringement of the rights retained by the people would give rise to cases arising under the Constitution, cannot turn on the fact that the federal government lacks the power to regulate in that area of human affairs thought to be covered by the ninth amendment. The answer rather depends on an answer to another question: whether the "rights" referred to in the ninth amendment (whatever they might be) are indeed protected under

[18]*See* U.S. Const. art. III, § 2.

the Constitution, and are therefore constitutional rights; or, are they rather outside the ambit of the Constitution, and are thus non-constitutional rights? The issue is now joined: Might Justice Goldberg indeed be correct that the ninth amendment must be read to say that there are additional fundamental rights, protected from governmental infringement, which exist alongside those fundamental rights specifically mentioned in the first eight constitutional amendments?

For me, Berger's most telling conclusion is that the "rights" retained by the people are not constitutional rights. In fact, he must ultimately deny that they are rights of any kind whatsoever, in any strong sense of the term. For one thing, his preoccupation with the question of any federal authority to enforce any so-called ninth amendments rights, underscores his confusion of the question of "encroachment" with that of "enforcement." For example, in support of his conclusion that it was the framers' intention that federal authority to enforce rights be confined expressly to "stipulated rights," he cites Madison, who opined that, "[T]he great mass of the people who opposed [the Constitution], disliked it because it did not contain effectual provisions against encroachments on particular rights."[19] Note that the passage refers to "encroachment" and not "enforcement." In constitutional theory the two are not one and the same. More important, however, is the fact that Berger does not see that his concession, that there is authority for the enforcement of stipulated rights, lends a disabling contradiction to his thesis on the ninth amendment "rights." That is to say, he is at least conceding that enforceability is a necessary condition for the existence of "legal rights." So when he chides Justice Goldberg for moving from the premise that the ninth amendment entails the existence of fundamental rights not specifically mentioned in the first eight amendments to the conclusion of a federal power to protect them,[20] it is Berger and not Justice Goldberg who is missing the point. For the power to protect (enforce) must indeed follow from the presumption that a right exists. Berger insists, however, that Justice Goldberg's conclusion is obviously wrong in light of Madison's disavowal of any implication that the unenumerated rights were "assigned" into the hands of the General Government,

[19]1 Annals of Congress, *supra* note 9, at 437, *quoted in* Berger, *supra* note 1, at 8.

[20]Berger, *supra* note 1, at 2.

least of all for the diminution of states' rights.[21] To recur to a point earlier stated, Berger seems to confuse the concepts of "rights" and "powers," and their proper use in constitutional theory. It is of greater importance to note here that Berger's conclusion, that the term "rights," as used in the ninth amendment, does not imply claims that are constitutionally protected, is the product of a rather simplistic theory of constitutional interpretation. I will address these problems in the sections that follow.

Rights and Powers: A Critique

In this section, I will discuss briefly the concepts of "rights" and "powers" to reveal the proper sense in which they are used in legal and political theory and, more importantly, to show that a better understanding of the ninth amendment results from the use of these terms in this sense and provides a basis for properly distinguishing the tenth amendment. This section allows for the assumption that Berger might indeed be correct that Madison understood the ninth amendment as barring any federal authority to protect (enforce) the "rights" thereunder, and, in which case, Madison was contradicting himself in thinking that he was, nonetheless, legislating for the acknowledgement of certain "rights" retained by the people. As I have earlier stated, I take it as appropriate to the task of interpretation to uncover contradictions in the text and resolve them in light of the most plausible reading that the text as a whole

---

[21]*Id.* at 10. Berger also quotes, with approval, Justice Black's assertion, in *Griswold*, to the effect that the ninth amendment was enacted to protect state powers against a federal invasion. *Griswold*, 381 U.S. at 519 (Black, J. dissenting). It would seem then, that for Berger, "states' rights" and "states' powers" are one and the same; hence his insistence that the ninth and tenth amendments are paired opposites of the same coin. Berger, *supra* note 1, at 3. However, the ninth refers to "rights" and the tenth to "powers." No matter. What is important to Berger is that he believes that his reading of the ninth amendment is faithful to the framers' (Madison's) intention, and, whether or not the founders may have been mistaken in their logic, at least they acted on that mistaken view and, thus, the text must be so read. Redlich, *Are There 'Certain Rights . . . Retained by the People,'* 37 N.Y.U. L. Rev. 787, 807 (1962) (on this point Redlich's argument proceeds along the same lines as Berger's). However, I insist that these concepts should be treated as separate and distinct words of art for the purposes of consitutional interpretation. If that distinction is accepted, then Berger's argument fails here. *See infra* text accompanying notes 22–44.

would allow. In this respect, I am no less faithful to the text and the "original intention."[22]

When I use the term "rights," I am speaking in the narrow sense of a claim created by a civil authority as opposed to other rights, such as natural rights, said to derive from man's rational nature. What, then, does it mean to say that someone, for example A, is the possessor of a legal right, that he has the right to X or to do X? Otherwise stated, what precisely are we seeking when we ask for an analysis of such notions as that of a legal right?[23]

In his seminal work on the fundamental conceptions applied in legal reasoning, Hohfeld defined a right (a right-claim, as he called it) in terms of its correlativity to a duty, the latter being of the same tenor as the former.[24] Thus, A's right-claim that B shall do or forbear from doing X is the correlative of B's duty to forbear. In short, rights and duties are sides of the same coin.[25] However, it would seem that there are several presuppositions entailed by the statement: "A has a right-claim against B." For one, it gives the right-holder the privilege or permission to do or not to do some thing. For example, if A is B's creditor, A might simply wish to cancel the debt. The possession of the right against B gives him this power or capacity to so alter their jural relation. Otherwise, A, in the event of B's default, may seek to have his right enforced by the society, specifically through its legal system. That is to say, he sues in court for the appropriate remedy. This argues that "a legal right is usually secured to its possessor by society," via a legal system in which

---

[22]The question of "original intention" is one that I believe has been sadly misconceived in American constitutional theory. I will discuss this at length in a forthcoming paper on constitutional theory. The beginnings of my analyses in this area can be seen in my article, McIntosh, *Legal Hermeneutics, supra* note 3.

[23]The point of this section is to show that states do not have moral rights, acknowledged by the Constitution in the same sense that individuals do. States, however, may have some "private" rights, e.g., state against state or contract rights deriving from contracts with private entities. *See* H.L.A. Hart, Essays on Bentham 163 (1982).

[24]W.H. Hohfeld, *Fundamental Conceptions as Applied in Legal Reasoning*, 26 Yale L.J. 710 (1917).

[25]Hohfeld's universe of jural correlatives is as follows: right-duty, privilege-no right, power-liability, immunity-disability. *Id.* at 710. The relationship between the correlatives is as explained by Hohfeld in an earlier article: "In other words, if x has a right against y that he shall stay off the former's land, the correlative (and equivalent) is that y is under a duty toward x to stay off the place." Hohfeld, *Some Fundamental Legal Conceptions as Applied in Judicial Reasoning*, 23 Yale L.J. 32 (1913).

citizens enjoy rights.[26] In sum, it would seem that the term legal right represents a cluster of legal liberties, claims, powers, and immunities, tied together by its defining core. "At the core of any legal right stand one or more legal advantages that define the essential content of the right. . . . At the core of my right to sell my car is my legal power of transferring ownership in my car to the second party of my choice. . . ."[27]

This tight correlativity between right and duty, in the sense of a correspondence between the "content" of the right and the "content" of the duty, has occasioned much criticism in philosophical literature.[28] On an ideal model of logical economy, a statement ascribing an active right to someone entails a statement ascribing an obligation to some other person or persons.[29] What about those general rights which are not necessarily rights against particular persons but merely "rights to" as opposed to "rights against"? They are, in short, "entitlements to." For example, does A's right to free speech support the entailment of a duty of the same tenor? It would seem not. This has led some to the conclusion that the pattern of relations between rights and obligations does not always hold.[30] Indeed, some duties do not necessarily correspond to rights, since they might not presuppose any special relations between particular individuals.[31] The truth of these criticisms need not lead us to deny, what Professor Braybrooke takes to be an obvious truth, that rights simply imply obligations and cannot be understood without accepting this implication.[32] It only means to say, then, that there are different kinds of rights. Though all may imply obligations, such implication need not always be in the nature of an exact correspondence of contents between the right and the obligation.[33] What must be appreciated here is the "open-texture" of the concept of a right, like the right of free speech and the obligation not to interfere that

---

[26]Wellman, *A New Conception of Human Rights*, in Human Rights 52 (E. Kamenka & A.E. Tay eds. 1978).

[27]*Id*. at 53.

[28]*See, e.g.*, Lyons, *Rights, Claimants and Beneficiaries*, 6 Amer. Phil. Quart. 173 (1969).

[29]Braybrooke, *The Firm but Untidy Correlativity of Rights and Obligations*, 1 Can. J. of Phil. 351, 353 (1971–72).

[30]*Id*.

[31]Lyons, *supra* note 28, at 173.

[32]Braybrooke, *supra* note 29, at 360.

[33]*Id*. at 362.

it entails. It is important to keep in mind that a general obligation not to interfere might not be exhausted by a finite set of particularized obligations.[34] However, it would be a grave error to surmise, because the situation with respect to the obligation is logically untidy, that no obligation is entailed. What, indeed, might be at stake here is a serious interpretative problem as to where the obligation lies, and what is its content, which at any given moment, cannot be fully and precisely exhibited because of the margin of open-texture.[35] Thus, if what I have said earlier about one possessing a legal right is generally sound, then it would be foolish to speak of a legal right without obligation, since obligation would seem logically linked with the attendant "power," "capacity" or further claim of the right-holder to have his right protected and enforced. I think this argument is supported by Kelsen's claim that efficacy or enforceability is a condition for the validity of a legal norm.[36]

This discussion, I believe, holds the deepest significance for my paper, indeed for any discussion of constitutional rights which, invariably, are not rights of citizens against citizens but are rights of citizens against the government. For American constitutional theory takes some rights as fundamental—rights against the State (the legislature) thereby limiting its power to make (or unmake) the ordinary law, where such would deny to individuals certain freedoms and benefits now regarded as essentials of human well-being, such as freedom of speech and association.[37] Of course, not all constitutional rights represent rights against the government, and, indeed, an eminent constitutional scholar has gone so far as to declare that the "Constitution does not confer private rights; rather they are antecedent and independent of it. The Constitution . . . only places limits on the infringement of private rights by governments, both the rights specified and all other[s] 'retained by the people.' "[38]

[34]*Id.* at 360.

[35]*Id.*

[36]*See generally* H. Kelsen, The Pure Theory of Law 213–14 (1967).

[37]H.L.A. Hart, *supra* note 23, at 190.

[38]Henkin, *Privacy and Autonomy,* 74 Colum. L. Rev. 1412 (1974). Professor Henkin, however, views the debate in different terms: "The judicial role which we know today blossomed during the period of our wildest national growth and an 'activist' Supreme Court cooperated in that growth by thwarting various status interferences with individual and corporate initiative in our terms by limiting the restrictions on private rights which the states sought to impose for the public good." *Id.* at 1411–12.

Whether Professor Henkin is correct or not, I think it is beyond question that those constitutional rights that we take to be fundamental also represent moral rights against the government or the State.[39] Above all, the point I wish to make here is that all constitutional rights—fundamental or not—are right-claims in a broadened Hohfeldian sense, and this feature of fundamentality that we attribute to some only signals the sense in which they trump the power of the State, or the quality of justification required where the State seeks to override them.[40]

The following summary might now be made. "The United States Constitution articulates a catalogue of freedoms or rights of the citizens in its first ten amendments. These amendments mostly have the character of prohibitions and commands addressed to the institutions which possess the legislative, executive, and judicial powers. They give the individual a right in the technical sense of the word only if he has the possibility of securing a legal remedy against the unconstitutional act of the institution, especially if he can put into motion a procedure leading to the annulment of the unconstitutional act. Since this possibility can be given only by positive law, then the rights themselves can only be such as are founded in a positive law."[41]

Now, it is widely believed that the Constitution was founded on some theory of natural law which was taken to be current in the eighteenth century.[42] Indeed, some believe that this theory of natural law is expressed in the ninth amendment. That is to say, by the language of the ninth amendment, the authors of the Constitution meant to say that there are certain rights which may neither be expressed in the Constitution nor in the positive legal order founded thereupon.[43]

> Nevertheless, the effect of this stipulation, from the point of view of positive law, is to authorize the state organs who have to execute the Constitution, especially the courts, to stipulate other rights

[39]R. Dworkin, Taking Rights Seriously 191 (1978).

[40]*Id.* at 191–97, and ch. 12.

[41]H. Kelsen, General Theory of Law and State 266 (1945).

[42]*Id. See also* Henkin, *supra* note 38, at 1413 n.7; E.S. Corwin, The "Higher Law" Background of American Constitutional Law (1974).

[43]H. Kelsen, *supra* note 41. *See also* Paust, *supra* note 7, at 234; Paust, *Human Dignity as a Constitutional Right: A Jurisprudentially Based Inquiry into Criteria and Content,* 27 How. L.J. 220 (1984).

than those established by the text of the Constitution. A right so stipulated is also granted by the Constitution, not directly, but indirectly, since it is stipulated by a law-creating act of an organ authorized by the Constitution. Such a right is thus no more "natural," (and thus no less "positive"), than any other right countenanced by the positive legal order.[44]

This argument, I believe, is a powerful corrective to Berger's claim about the "non-rights" of the ninth amendment. For if what Kelsen says is correct, then it would seem that the unenumerated rights are strikingly similar to the enumerated rights, in a manner we have generally ignored in constitutional debate. That is to say, both sets of rights have a recognizable basis in positive law, although the content of each set of rights must be further defined. For example, the contents of the rights enumerated in the first eight amendments are not specifically defined, although we might have some obvious instances in mind as to what might constitute a proper exercise of, for example, the right of free speech. Still, the fact remains, that in much of the more controversial or marginal cases, the normative content of the right is defined in an ongoing process of adjudication, wherein the individual who claims that his right has been violated by state or federal action, has exercised the "capacity" to put in motion a procedure to test the constitutionality of the act in question. The enumerated rights might seem to enjoy an obvious degree of determinacy, when compared to the unenumerated rights. However, such supposed determinacy can be quite deceiving. On the one hand, it may appear that the ninth amendment has introduced into American constitutional theory a hopeless indeterminacy without any criteria for its identification and application, but the ninth amendment holds no greater indeterminacy than any of its sister amendments; although, admittedly, this amendment presents some of the greatest challenges for constitutional adjudication and interpretation. I would hope to show, then, that the acknowledgement of "new" rights under the ninth amendment is in no way radically different from the judicial elaboration of such rights as the right to due process, or the right to the equal protection of the law.

. . .

[44]H. Kelsen, *supra* note 41.

On Reading The Ninth Amendment

It is submitted that the interpretation and application of the ninth amendment raise not only methodological, but also epistemological and theoretical, issues of fundamental importance. Given that the ninth amendment, unlike the first eight, or even the fourteenth amendment, allows no intimation even of the abstract rights with which it is concerned, and therefore suggests no criteria for the identification and application of the concrete rights to which it assumedly refers, the question arises as to how we may come to know what sorts of claims merit protection as ninth amendment rights and whether such claims can ever be said to be textually based. Otherwise stated, the question is whether any claim which is acknowledged as a ninth amendment right can be said to be one of objective ascertainable fact which can be rationally resolved by reference to the terms of the relevant positive law—the Constitution.

Still, some have suggested possible meanings. Indeed, one of the first scholars to have taken the ninth amendment seriously, suggests that it be read as a declaration and recognition of individualism and inherent rights, a basic statement of the inherent and natural rights of the individual. These inherent rights and liberties, it is significant to note, antedate and are socially of higher priority than constitutions. They may therefore be called pre-constitutional rights.[45] This sentiment has been echoed by other eminent constitutional scholars. To Professor Tom Grey, for example, the ninth amendment stands as the textual expression in the Federal Constitution of the notion of a "higher law," the principles of which are binding on legislators and judges.[46] Those who do not necessarily subscribe to a "higher law" theory, might allow that the ninth is a mandate to the Court and the federal judiciary to "create" new rights to meet the changing needs of the society.[47]

All this, however, would not placate those like Professor Berger who fear the jurisprudential implication of so open-ended a provision as the ninth amendment. Remember his charge regarding *Griswold*, that Justice Goldberg would transform the ninth amendment into a bottomless well in which the judiciary can dip for the

[45]B. Patterson, The Forgotten Ninth Amendment 20 (1955).
[46]*See* Grey, *Do We Have an Unwritten Constitution?* 27 Stan. L. Rev. 703, 715 (1965).
[47]*See* J. Ely, Democracy and Distrust 38 (1980).

formation of undreamed of "rights" in their limitless discretion. However, Berger's reading of the ninth amendment, I earlier stated, leads to the conclusion that ninth amendment rights are, in fact, non-rights. If, however, I have successfully debunked his claim and the ninth amendment does extend protection over some set of rights,[48] then the question to be resolved indeed turns on the sorts of claims that merit protection as ninth amendment rights. In other words, if we were to assume that Justice Goldberg was correct in his conclusion that the claimants in *Griswold* had a ninth amendment right to the privacy or autonomous choice for which they claimed protection, then what sorts of reasons might be advanced in support of that conclusion? What argument might one make to defend the particular liberty in question?

The interpretation of the ninth amendment necessarily entails the question of what rights or what sorts of rights, though not specifically given, are nonetheless worthy of constitutional protection. It would seem, then, that any case involving the interpretation and application of the ninth amendment inevitably falls in the category of the "hard case," which, it is charged, is a theory of adjudication stemming from a "simplistic and formalistic jurisprudential inheritance of the nineteenth century that can be generalized as 'legal positivism.' "[49] It is a theory that suggests that a case which cannot be brought under a clear rule of law, laid down by some institution in advance, leaves the judge with "discretion" to decide the case either way. Although the language of his opinion might tend to suggest that one or the other party had a pre-existing right to win the suit, that is indeed a fiction, for, in reality, he has legislated new legal rights, and then applied them retrospectively to the case at hand.[50] Against this position, I would argue that the methodological and jurisprudential issues raised by the interpretation and application of the ninth amendment must be resolved by a non-positivistic theory of adjudication. One that turns on the very fundamental question as to the nature and character of the constitutional text; one that takes account of the concept of justice embodied in the Constitution as developed by subsequent amend-

[48]Berger, *supra* note 1, at 2.

[49]Paust, *supra* note 7, at 236. Professor Paust sees the promise of the ninth amendment as providing a constitutional basis for the judicial enunciation and protection of human rights.

[50]R. Dworkin, *supra* note 39, at 81.

ments; and one that elucidates the political theory that can be said to justify the Constitution as a whole, thereby capturing the relationship between that set of abstract rights that the Constitution can be said to have legislated and the concrete rights thought to be required by the former.[51] The theory of adjudication suggested by legal positivism is simply inadequate to this task. For constitutional adjudication, which obviously includes adjudication involving the application of the ninth amendment, is ultimately the confirmation or denial of concrete legal rights that citizens (claimants) believe that they have.[52] Thus, if I am correct in my assumption that the ninth amendment does signal the existence of other constitutional rights, then I must make the further assumption that ninth amendment rights are those claims which cannot be said to derive from any of the other amendments, except by the most strained construction. However, the tenor of my arguments, thus far, would suggest that adjudication involving the ascertainment of rights under the ninth amendment would not be radically different from adjudication regarding any of the other amendments thought to be more specific. For the rights legislated in the first and fourteenth amendments, for example, do not carry "on their face" all instances that might possibly constitute freedom of expression, or the equal protection of the law. We therefore consider them to be abstract rights or "concepts," thereby allowing for their logical extensions in adjudication where, by "extensions," we mean all the individual instances—past, present, and future—that can be established as being subsumed under the concepts.[53] This argues that the concrete rights thought to be proper instantiations of freedom of expression or the equal protection of law are not necessarily or logically limited to the specific instances of these abstract rights that the framers may have had in mind. It follows, then, that in any of the more controversial cases of constitutional interpretation, cases where obviously the answers to the questions raised could not simply be "read off," the Court is necessarily faced with the sort of epistemological problem which entails a construal of the nature of the text as a whole, its structure, and its history. Constitutional adju-

---

[51]See generally id.

[52]Id. at 93; see also D.A.J. Richards, A Moral Criticism of Law ch. III (197–); McIntosh, A Poetic for Law: Constitutional Theory as Metaphor (forthcoming).

[53]See Hirsch, Meaning and Significance Re-interpreted, 11 Critical Inquiry 202, 207 (1984).

dication, then, is the sort of critical practice that invariably requires an abstracting from the text of those characteristics that can be said to be its defining, as opposed to its merely contingent, ones. In sum, we may say that the problems to be resolved in much of the more controversial cases involving the application of any of the so-called "open-ended" provisions of the Constitution are as much problems about the nature of the Constitution, read as an ordered whole, as they are problems about those concrete rights that can be said to be required by the relevant abstract rights.

It is important to point out that my theory of constitutional interpretation is in no way anti-intentionalist, and, in this respect, shares with Professor Berger's theory, an important premise about the critical practice of interpretation on the whole: namely, that the notion of "authorial intention" is a principal norm of textual interpretation. So the debate between myself and Professor Berger is also about our competing conceptions of "intention," and the conceptual standards by which it is established. For me, the intention of the text is the ultimate problem that all interpretation addresses, since, I believe, the construal of intention is logically implicit in any act of interpretation. However, it is the intention as expressed in the text, and not the author's declarations of intention, that we seek to uncover in interpretation. Such declarations, I have elsewhere argued, may have great evidentiary value, but it is not conceptually compelling for the reader to accept them.[54]

To interpret a text, i.e. the Constitution, is to situate it in a context and, thus, to construe it as someone's product directed to certain purposes, as the answer to a question, or to solve certain existential problems. The author's own declarations are certainly helpful in situating the text, for such statements may help us decide whether to view the text as a constitution, a novel, a poem, or maybe a letter to a sweetheart. However, if it is the case that interpretation is an act of critical inquiry, then it is never simply a matter of taking the author's words as conclusive statements compelling a certain reading. Rather, intention, as the object of knowledge, is established in terms of action-descriptions that are used by responsible agents themselves or that are realistically attributable to them.[55] That is to say, the act of interpretation entails such descriptions of the action

[54]See McIntosh, *Legal Hermeneutics, supra* note 3, at 50–72; Nehamas, *The Postulated Author: Critical Monism as a Regulative Ideal,* 8 Critical Inquiry 133, 144 (1981).

[55]Frederick Olafson, The Dialectic of Action 212 (1979).

in question that can reasonably be attributed to the author as a responsible rational agent, on the theory that the reader and the agent share a "common" language in the sense of a shared understanding of what is being done—in short, "a shared vocabulary of action-descriptions."[56]

Thus, the intention, the meaning of the text, is constituted in the act of reading, wherein the reader arrives at certain hypotheses, educated guesses, or possible interpretations, from which he establishes one as the most probable meaning of the text in light of all relevant evidence—both textual and extratextual.[57] So it is not what the author says the text means that concerns us; such would simply be just another interpretation. It is what the text means, at least what we can establish as its most plausible meaning in light of the public norms of the language of the text, which must be consistent with the conventions of the genre in which the text is formed. (For example, it is natural for us to assume that a text of positive law that uses the term "right" intends it in the sense in which it is generally understood in legal and political discourse.) Also, the reader would test his hypotheses in light of what he knows about the history of the time the text was written since, as I have stated, he understands the text to have been a response to certain existential problems which the author faced. Thus, it is proper to the task of interpretation for the reader to try to recuperate and reformulate the question that the text was supposedly an answer to. In this endeavor, the reader may understand the historical situation differently, or better, than the author understood it, in light of information that he now has, but which may not have been available to the author. No matter, what is important is that the reader is in a position to evaluate the author's own declarations in light of what he knows about the nature of the action that the author was engaged in. Above all, to make the validity of an interpretation depend on its being confirmed by the author's declarations of intention is to deny that interpretation is an act of critical inquiry, for instead of engaging in this critical task, we may simply refer to the author's declarations as though we were consulting the "Oracle." Someone like Berger, who equates the intention of the text with the author's declarations of intention, would no doubt charge that my theory of

---

[56]*Id.* at 218.

[57]*See* Marsh, *Historical Interpretation and the History of Criticism,* in Literary Criticism and Historical Understanding 4 (P. Damon ed. 1967).

constitutional interpretation gives short shrift to legislative history and, what is more, cannot render a true or correct interpretation of the Constitution. However, such a charge, as I have stated, only misconceives the conceptual nature of the problem of interpretation and the sense in which interpretive statements can never be empirically tested against the author's statements. Suffice it to say that my theory takes account of legislative history, the general historical context out of which the text emerged, and much more.

It has already been noted that our Constitution rests on a moral theory, namely, that citizens have moral rights against the State.[58] Moreover, as evidenced by such clauses as equal protection, and due process, or free speech, we may say, following Professor Dworkin, that the Constitution has fused legal and moral issues, thereby making the validity of a law depend on the answer to complex moral problems, like the problem of whether a particular statute respects the inherent equality of all men.[59] So although not all constitutional rights constitute moral rights, specifically moral rights against the State, we may yet say that the Constitution does acknowledge that citizens do have rights against the State and that these are abstract rights. This fact is of telling importance in constitutional adjudication, for it suggests that in many of the more important cases involving the application of any of the "open-ended" provisions that suggest one abstract right or another, the Court's decision cannot rest simply on an account of empirical historical evidence, since the problems involved are not simply empirical, but rather fundamental and conceptual. That is to say, the problems to be resolved in such cases are as much questions about the nature of the Constitution itself, read as an ordered generic whole, and the sort of abstract rights that the best theory of the Constitution can be said to justify, as they are questions about those concrete rights that can be said to be required by the former. Another way of putting the point is to say that constitutional adjudication inevitably entails the conceptual problem of the intentionality of a text of which the concept of justice is its forming principle. A judge, in an attempt to elucidate the nature of the Constitution and the political theory that justifies it, must ask himself whether there are fixed conceptions constituting the intention of the text

[58]R. Dworkin, *Liberalism*, in Public and Private Morality 147 (Stuart Hampshire ed. 1978).

[59]*Id*. at 185; *see also* D.A.J. Richards, *supra* note 52.

that he is limited to applying or whether he may consider the language of the Constitution, read as a whole, as providing some of the stipulated features of a general theory to be constructed.[60] Thus, the dialectical process of reasoning, that I claimed to be inevitable in constitutional interpretation,[61] would seem most evident in those instances where our reasoned judgment seems to endorse, for example, a denial of the equal protection of law, because either this judgment conflicts with what the framers may have thought was proper, or where the legislative history is simply not conclusive on the question. How, then, must such a case be decided, if not according to some theory of justice that we believe best captures the nature and the intention of the Constitution as a whole? In so doing, do we not explain the specific clause in question according to the most plausible reading that we believe the Constitution as a whole would allow?

What is especially peculiar to constitutional interpretation, I believe, is the extent to which the sort of inquiry that I argue for in this essay is required in all the more important cases. For in these cases, it would seem, the question about the concrete claim to be decided— (*Brown*, for example, and more recently, *Dronenburg v. Zeck*[62])—can never be resolved by squaring it against the legislative history of the amendment being applied. Rather the question is resolved by determining whether the abstract right(s) that can be said to have been legislated by the amendment imply the specific claim under consideration, in short, whether the concrete claim is a specification of the abstract right. In a general sense, the problem raised in such cases would seem rather consonant with the logical notion of the "extension" of a concept, where good interpretation requires that we be able to show why a case in point is, or is not, true (i.e. a proper instantiation) of the original concept. However, if we are pressed to further explain why a particular abstract right exists, since abstract rights are not necessarily explicitly stated, we must indeed fall back on some more general theory of justice that we believe best defines the Constitution. So we must put the following sort of question to ourselves: What political theory best explains a constitution that takes the concept of justice as its forming principle and specifies in some of its constituent parts certain moral rights

[60]*See generally* R. Dworkin, *supra* note 39.

[61]*See* McIntosh, *Legal Hermeneutics, supra* note 3, at 50–60; *see also supra* note 4.

[62]*Dronenburg v. Zeck,* 741 F.2d 1388, *reh'g denied,* 746 F.2d 1579 (D.C. Cir. 1984).

citizens have against the State? The point that I most wish to make here is that, sometimes, constitutional theory may require that we ask the more general question to answer the specific question raised by a particular case. Take the *Brown* case as an example. The more general question raised is whether the fourteenth amendment legislated equality as an abstract right. We put forth this question because, in our reasoned judgment, we take state enforced segregation of public schooling to be a denial of equality to blacks. Assuming that we are correct in our judgment, then the question remains whether a decision in accordance with our judgment is required by the intention of the fourteenth amendment and, concordantly, the intention of the Constitution. This procedure does not preclude consideration of the framers' declarations of intention; indeed, such consideration is invited. For what we want to know is not simply whether the framers wanted to outlaw segregation, but, more importantly, whether it was really their intention to grant the equal protection of the law to blacks. If, on the best reading of the legislative history, or other sources probative of the framers' intention, we were to arrive at a negative answer to this question, i.e. it was their intention not to grant the full equal protection of the law to blacks, then the further question arises as to whether the fourteenth amendment, read in accordance with the framers' declarations of intention, would not in fact be inconsistent with the concept of justice itself, which is the regulative and constitutive idea of the Constitution. So on the further assumption that it was also part of the framers' intention to have a coherent text, the inconsistency must be resolved.

If I am correct in my arguments for a more holistic theory of constitutional interpretation, then it would seem that the sort of conceptualizing that my theory calls for is especially required in the interpretation of the ninth amendment. This argues not only that the interpretation of the ninth amendment is in no way radically different from that of the first, fifth, or fourteenth amendments, for example, but also, that ninth amendment rights could not be substantively different from the sorts of rights covered by these other amendments. That is to say, since the interpretation and application of the ninth amendment is ultimately about the confirmation or denial of concrete legal claims that litigants believe they have, then the question, as to the validity of these claims, can only be answered in terms of a theory of justice that we believe best captures the nature of the Constitution itself. In other words, a judge, like Justice

Goldberg, who acknowledges a claim as meriting protection under the ninth amendment, is required to show why his conception of the Constitution requires that decision, and why it is the correct one. It means, then, that a refutation of his arguments cannot be secured simply by pointing to the fact that the framers expressed no opinions regarding marital privacy. Rather, a successful argument against his opinion must be the kind that attacks his theory of the Constitution itself.

In conclusion, therefore, this essay argues that ninth amendment rights would be those claims which cannot be said, except by the most strained construction, to derive from the more abstract rights legislated in the more so-called specific amendments. Rather, they are the concrete rights that can be said to be required by a theory of justice that best defines the Constitution. We should determine whether a claim merits protection under the ninth amendment by balancing the argument for its protection against the moral justification that the state can advance for denying protection. That is to say, ninth amendment rights, as rights retained by the people which may not be denied or disparaged, are rights against the State and are therefore moral rights. This means, then, that any claim for which protection is sought under the ninth amendment must be a moral claim. Therefore a state that wishes to deny such a claim must show that the claim is outweighed by other considerations on the grounds of principle—for example, that the autonomous choice à la *Griswold* has the consequence of infringing on the legitimate rights of others, or that the claimant is mistaken as to the moral force of her claim since it involves an act which, though not endangering the rights of others, is inimical to the claimant's own well-being, or that the act is simply immoral.

10. The History and Meaning of the Ninth Amendment*

Russell L. Caplan

I. Recalled to Life

After lying dormant for over a century and a half, the ninth amendment to the United States Constitution has emerged from obscurity to assume a place of increasing, if bemused, attention. The amendment provides: "The enumeration in the Constitution, of certain rights, shall not be construed to deny or disparage others retained by the people."[1] The meaning of the "almost unfathomable"[2] ninth amendment, "that old constitutional jester,"[3] has always been elusive. Justice Jackson confessed outright that "the Ninth Amendment rights which are not to be disturbed by the Federal Government are still a mystery to me."[4] Yet in this tumultuous century, rediscovery was perhaps inevitable for a constitutional amendment that speaks, however enigmatically, of basic human freedoms.

Ninth amendment analysis has proceeded in three stages. In the first stage, which lasted until 1965, the amendment received only perfunctory treatment from courts and commentators.[5] After World

---

Reprinted, by permission, from 73 Va. L. Rev. 223 (1983).

*Copyright © 1982 by Russell L. Caplan. Responsibility for this article remains solely with the author. Some of the ideas elaborated herein were included in Caplan, Book Review, 80 Mich. L. Rev. 656 (1982).

[1]U.S. Const. amend. IX.

[2]Dixon, *The* Griswold *Penumbra: Constitutional Charter for an Expanded Law of Privacy?* 64 Mich. L. Rev. 197, 207 (1965).

[3]J. Ely, Democracy and Distrust 33 (1980).

[4]R. Jackson, The Supreme Court in the American System of Government 74–75 (1955).

[5]During this first period there were only the most glancing judicial and scholarly references to the ninth amendment, with no explicit construction of the amendment by the Supreme Court in the seven cases that represent the sum total of the Court's pronouncements on the amendment prior to 1965. *See* Roth v. United States, 354 U.S. 476, 492 (1957); Woods v. Cloyd W. Miller Co., 333 U.S. 138, 144 (1948); United

War II, heightened concern for human rights inspired extolling of the "forgotten" ninth amendment for its value in the promotion of individual liberty.[6] Still, during this early period the ninth amendment was mostly a source of intermittent curiosity.

All that changed in 1965, when the United States Supreme Court ushered in the second stage of the ninth amendment's career with *Griswold v. Connecticut*.[7] In that case, the Court held unconstitutional Connecticut statutes that criminalized the use of, or assistance in the use of, contraceptives. In his opinion for the Court, Justice Douglas wrote that the statutes violated the right of marital privacy

---

Pub. Workers v. Mitchell, 330 U.S. 75, 94–95 (1947); Tennessee Elec. Power Co. v. TVA, 306 U.S. 118, 143–44 (1939); Ashwander v. TVA, 297 U.S. 288, 330–31 (1936); Scott v. Sandford, 60 U.S. (19 How.) 393, 511 (1857) (Campbell, J., concurring); Lessee of Livingston v. Moore, 32 U.S. (7 Pet.) 469, 511 (1833). *See also* J. Bayard, A Brief Exposition of the Constitution of the United States 154 (2d ed. 1834) (1st ed. 1833) (ninth and tenth amendments reflect "the care with which [the people] guarded against any unauthorized extension of [the new government's] power"); T. Cooley, The General Principles of Constitutional Law in the United States of America 34–35 (2d ed. 1891) (ninth amendment does not create but preserves existing rights); E. Corwin, The Constitution and What It Means Today 440 (14th ed. 1978) (ninth amendment safeguards unenumerated natural rights of a fundamental character); 3 J. Story, Commentaries on the Constitution of the United States 751–52 (1st ed. Boston 1833) (ninth amendment introduced to confirm framers' intent that rights not specified in the Bill of Rights were not thereby surrendered to the federal government); 2 J. Tucker, The Constitution of the United States 688 (1899) (ninth amendment "was meant to exclude the inference that the Federal government could touch any of the great fundamental rights of the people").

It was not until 1936 that a study devoted exclusively to the ninth amendment appeared. Kelsey, *The Ninth Amendment of the Federal Constitution*, 11 Ind. L.J. 309 (1936).

[6]*See* B. Patterson, The Forgotten Ninth Amendment (1955). Subtitled "A Call for Legislative and Judicial Recognition of Rights Under Social Conditions of Today," Patterson's book argues for the resuscitation of the ninth amendment as a source of additional federal and even state rights. For other works in a similarly effusive vein, see I. Brant, The Bill of Rights 66 & 77 (1965); Call, *Federalism and the Ninth Amendment*, 64 Dick. L. Rev. 121 (1960); Franklin, *The Relation of the Fifth, Ninth and Fourteenth Amendments to the Third Constitution*, 4 How. L.J. 170 (1958); Hamlin, *The Bill of Rights or the First Ten Amendments to the United States Constitution*, 68 Com. L.J. 233 (1963); Hennings, *The Executive Privilege and the People's Right to Know*, 19 Fed. B.J. 1, 6 (1959); Redlich, *Are There "Certain Rights . . . Retained by the People"?* 37 N.Y.U. L. Rev. 787 (1962). Others felt the ninth added little of significance to the Constitution. *See* E. Dumbauld, The Bill of Rights And What It Means Today 63–65 (1957) ("a dead letter in practice"); Dunbar, *James Madison and the Ninth Amendment*, 42 Va. L. Rev. 627 (1956); Rogge, *Unenumerated Rights*, 47 Calif. L. Rev. 787 (1959).

[7]381 U.S. 479 (1965).

created by the penumbral rights emanating from specific guarantees in the first, third, fourth, fifth, and ninth amendments.[8] But it was Justice Goldberg's concurring opinion, joined by Chief Justice Warren and Justice Brennan, that catapulted the ninth into sudden respectability. Justice Goldberg concluded that the right to marital privacy, although not expressly listed in the Constitution, is nonetheless protected by the ninth amendment.[9] "The language and history of the Ninth Amendment," he wrote, "reveal that the Framers of the Constitution believed that there are additional fundamental rights, protected from governmental infringement, which exist alongside those fundamental rights specifically mentioned in the first eight constitutional amendments."[10] Justice Goldberg was careful to add, however, that the ninth amendment does not constitute

> an independent source of rights protected from infringement by either the States or the Federal Government. Rather, the Ninth Amendment shows a belief of the Constitution's authors that fundamental rights exist that are not expressly enumerated in the first eight amendments and an intent that the list of rights included there not be deemed exhaustive.[11]

The considerable literature prompted by *Griswold* set about dissecting the general concept of privacy as a constitutional right and

---

[8]*Id.* at 482–86.

[9]*Id.* at 486–87 (Goldberg, J., Warren, C.J., Brennan, J., concurring).

[10]*Id.* at 488. *See also id.* at 490 & 495–96.

[11]*Id.* at 492. These unenumerated rights are derived from three sources: the "traditions and [collective] conscience of our people," "fundamental principles of liberty," and "experience with the requirements of a free society." *Id.* at 493 (citing authorities). In dissent, Justice Black rejected the reliance on unwritten fundamental rights as an illegitimate pretext for unrestrained judicial discretion and found in the ninth amendment "[no] such awesome veto powers over lawmaking, either by the States or by the Congress." *Id.* at 519 (Black, J., dissenting). Rather, "[t]hat Amendment was passed . . . to assure the people that the Constitution in all its provisions was intended to limit the Federal Government to the powers granted expressly or by necessary implication." *Id.* at 520. The ninth amendment was "enacted to protect state powers against federal invasion" and was not to be "used as a weapon of federal power to prevent state legislatures from passing laws they consider appropriate to govern local affairs." *Id. See also id.* at 529–30 (Stewart, J., dissenting); Black, *The Bill of Rights*, 35 N.Y.U. L. Rev. 865, 871 (1960) (ninth and tenth amendments "emphasize the limited nature of the Federal Government").

the role of the ninth amendment in defining that right.[12] Subsequent Supreme Court decisions, including *Richmond Newspapers, Inc. v. Virginia*,[13] *Planned Parenthood v. Danforth*,[14] *Buckley v. Valeo*,[15] and *Lubin v. Panish*,[16] have alluded to ninth amendment rights without further explaining precisely what unenumerated rights the ninth amendment might include. The sole exception is Justice Douglas' suggestion that "the right of the people to education or to work or to recreation . . . , like the right to pure air and pure water, may well be rights 'retained by the people' under the Ninth Amendment."[17]

As the Warren Court passed into history, the vanguard of a third stage, disenchanted with the civil liberties decisions of that Court's successor, began invoking the ninth amendment to justify an

[12]*See, e.g.*, Abrams, *What Are the Rights Guaranteed by the Ninth Amendment?* 53 A.B.A. J. 1033 (1967); Dirksen, *Individual Freedom Versus Compulsory Unionism: A Constitutional Problem*, 15 De Paul L. Rev. 259, 270–72 (1966) (right to work as a ninth amendment right); Franklin, *The Ninth Amendment as Civil Law Method and Its Implications for Republican Form of Government: Griswold v. Connecticut; South Carolina v. Katzenbach*, 40 Tul. L. Rev. 487 (1966); Kelly, *Clio and the Court: An Illicit Love Affair*, 1965 Sup. Ct. Rev. 119; Kirven, *Under the Ninth Amendment, What Rights Are the "Others Retained by the People"?* 14 S.D. L. Rev. 80 (1969); Kutner, *The Neglected Ninth Amendment: The "Other Rights" Retained by the People*, 51 Marq. L. Rev. 121 (1968); Rhoades & Patula, *The Ninth Amendment: A Survey of Theory and Practice in the Federal Courts Since Griswold v. Connecticut*, 50 Den. L.J. 153 (1973); *Symposium on Privacy*, 31 Law & Contemp. Probs. 251 (1966); *Comments on the Griswold Case*, 64 Mich. L. Rev. 197 (1965); *The Supreme Court, 1964 Term*, 79 Harv. L. Rev. 56, 162–65 (1965); Note, *The Ninth Amendment: Guidepost to Fundamental Rights*, 8 Wm. & Mary L. Rev. 101 (1966); Comment, *The Ninth Amendment*, 30 Alb. L. Rev. 89 (1966); Comment, *Ninth Amendment Vindication of Unenumerated Fundamental Rights*, 42 Temp. L.Q. 46 (1968); Comment, *The Uncertain Renaissance of the Ninth Amendment*, 33 U. Chi. L. Rev. 814 (1966) [hereinafter cited as *Uncertain Renaissance*].

[13]448 U.S. 555, 579 n.15 (1980) (Burger, C.J.); *id.* at 606 (Rehnquist, J., dissenting).

[14]428 U.S. 52, 60 (1976).

[15]424 U.S. 1, 59 n.67, 84 n.113 (1976) (*per curiam*).

[16]415 U.S. 709, 721 n.* (1974) (Douglas, J., concurring).

[17]Palmer v. Thompson, 403 U.S. 217, 233–34 (1971) (Douglas, J., dissenting). *See also* Doe v. Bolton, 410 U.S. 179, 210–11 (1973) (Douglas, J., concurring); Roe v. Wade, 410 U.S. 113, 152 (1973) (Blackmun, J.); Branzburg v. Hayes, 408 U.S. 665, 714 (1972) (Douglas, J., dissenting); Freeman v. Flake, 405 U.S. 1032, 1032 (1972) (Douglas, J., dissenting from denial of certiorari); Stanley v. Illinois, 405 U.S. 645, 651 (1972) (White, J.); Olff v. East Side Union High School Dist., 404 U.S. 1042, 1044 (1972) (Douglas, J., dissenting from denial of certiorari); McGautha v. California, 402 U.S. 183, 255 n.4 (1971) (Brennan, J., dissenting); Osborn v. United States, 385 U.S. 323, 341 (1966) (Douglas, J., dissenting).

expansive reading of individual rights. For Charles Black, the ninth amendment is a "fountain of law,"[18] and for John Hart Ely, it is "intended to signal the existence of federal constitutional rights beyond those specifically enumerated in the Constitution."[19] The rights that this cadre finds in the ninth amendment are generally those relating to marital or family privacy, in the manner of *Griswold.*

The central question in ninth amendment interpretation has been the existence and extent of the federal rights the amendment is supposed to encompass. The historical evidence set forth below, however, suggests that the ninth amendment is not a cornucopia

[18]C. Black, Decision According to Law 44 n.47 (1981). *See also* J. Ely, *supra* note 3, at 34–41; L. Tribe, American Constitutional Law 570 (1978) (ninth amendment "at least states a rule of construction pointing away from the reverse incorporation view that only the interests [specifically] secured by the Bill of Rights are encompassed within the fourteenth amendment, and at most provides a positive source of law for fundamental but unmentioned rights") (footnote omitted); Gibbons, *Symposium, Constitutional Adjudication and Democratic Theory,* Keynote Address, 56 N.Y.U. L. Rev. 260, 272–73 (1981); Henkin, *Infallibility Under Law: Constitutional Balancing,* 78 Colum. L. Rev. 1022, 1043 (1978); Kent, *Under the Ninth Amendment What Rights are the "Others Retained by the People"?* 29 Fed. B.J. 219 (1970); Moore, *The Ninth Amendment—Its Origins and Meaning,* 7 New Eng. L. Rev. 215 (1972); Paust, *Human Rights and the Ninth Amendment: A New Form of Guarantee,* 60 Cornell L. Rev. 231 (1975); Perry, *Interpretivism, Freedom of Expression, and Equal Protection,* 42 Ohio St. L.J. 261, 272–73 (1981); Ringold, *The History of the Enactment of the Ninth Amendment and Its Recent Development,* 8 Tulsa L.J. 1 (1972); Laycock, Book Review, 59 Tex. L. Rev. 343, 348–51 (1981); *Developments in the Law—The Constitution and the Family,* 93 Harv. L. Rev. 1156, 1173 n.100 & 1175 (1980); Comment, *Unenumerated Rights—Substantive Due Process, the Ninth Amendment, and John Stuart Mill,* 1971 Wis. L. Rev. 922.

For challenges to the expansionist trend, see M. Goodman, The Ninth Amendment (1981); Berger, *The Ninth Amendment,* 66 Cornell L. Rev. 1 (1980); Bork, *The Impossibility of Finding Welfare Rights in the Constitution,* 1979 Wash. U.L.Q. 695, 697; Monaghan, *Our Perfect Constitution,* 56 N.Y.U. L. Rev. 353, 365–67 (1981); *Forum: Equal Protection and the Burger Court,* 2 Hastings Const. L.Q. 645, 679 (1975) (remarks of Profs. Gunther & Choper); Note, *The Right of Privacy: A Black View of Griswold v. Connecticut,* 7 Hastings Const. L.Q. 777 (1980); Estreicher, Book Review, 56 N.Y.U. L. Rev. 547, 557–60 (1981); Van Alstyne, Book Review, 91 Yale L.J. 207 (1981).

[19]J. Ely, *supra* note 3, at 38. *See, e.g.,* State v. Abellano, 50 Hawaii 384, 393, 441 P.2d 333, 339 (1968) (Levinson, Richardson, JJ., concurring) (arguing that ninth amendment right of privacy should be basis for striking down a local ordinance prohibiting presence at, or participation in, a cockfighting exhibition: "[t]he Ninth Amendment is the place to which we must turn for protection of individual liberty from infringements not enumerated, and perhaps not contemplated, by the founding fathers.") (footnote omitted). *But see* Doe v. Bolton, 410 U.S. 179, 210 (1973) (Douglas, J., concurring) ("The Ninth Amendment obviously does not create federally enforceable rights.").

of undefined federal rights, but rather that it is limited to a specific function, well-understood at the time of its adoption: the maintenance of rights guaranteed by the laws of the states. These state rights represented entitlements derived from both natural law theory and the hereditary rights of Englishmen, but ninth amendment protection did not transform these unenumerated rights into constitutional, that is, federal, rights. It is therefore analytically incorrect, and historically ironic, to view the ninth amendment as creating rights that may be asserted against either a state or the federal government, because the amendment neither creates new rights nor alters the status of pre-existing rights. Instead, it simply provides that the individual rights contained in state law are to continue in force under the Constitution until modified or eliminated by state enactment, by federal preemption, or by a judicial determination of unconstitutionality.

II. The Enactment of the Ninth Amendment

A. State Law and Fundamental Law in the Revolutionary Era

Although the colonial governments eventually came to resemble the British model in differing degrees, they developed as individual political units, nearly sovereign republics.[20] John Adams' references in 1774 to Massachusetts as "our country" and to the Massachusetts delegation to the Continental Congress as "our embassy"[21] typified the colonial view of these sovereign governments as the primary guardians of individual liberties. Because they considered themselves the equals of native Englishmen, the colonists claimed enti-

---

[20]See W. Adams, The First American Constitutions 43–44 (1980); C. Rossiter, Seedtime of the Republic 13–18 (1953). See also Berger, supra note 18, at 3 & nn.21–22. The Articles of Confederation did not alter the situation. See M. Jensen, The Articles of Confederation 176 (1970); G. Wood, The Creation of the American Republic 1776–1787, at 357–58 (1969).

[21]Letter from John Adams to Abigail Adams (Sept. 18, 1774), reprinted in 1 Letters of Members of the Continental Congress 35 (E. Burnett ed. 1921). At the Constitutional Convention of 1787, Oliver Ellsworth of Connecticut, later the second Chief Justice, looked "for the preservation of his rights to the State Govts. From these alone he could derive the greatest happiness he expects in this life." 1 The Records of the Federal Convention of 1787, at 492 (M. Farrand ed. 1937) (footnote omitted) [hereinafter cited as Records].

tlement to the "rights of Englishmen" as contained in the English statutes and common law and enacted by the colonial legislatures.[22] In the wake of numerous measures passed by Parliament after the end of the Seven Years' War in 1763, notably the Stamp Act of 1765, this claim to the full rights of Englishmen grew more urgent. The Maryland Declaration of Rights, for example, adopted in 1776,[23] proclaimed:

> [T]he inhabitants of Maryland are entitled to the common law of England, and the trial by jury, according to the course of that law, and to the benefit of such of the English statutes, as existed at the time of their first emigration, and which, by experience, have been found applicable to their local and other circumstances, and of such others as have been since made in England, or Great Britain, and have been introduced, used and practised by the courts of law or equity; and also to acts of Assembly, . . . except such as may have since expired, or have been or may be altered by acts of Convention, or this Declaration of Rights—subject, nevertheless, to the revision of, and amendment or repeal by, the Legislature of this State. . . .[24]

The Maryland declaration was representative of the state constitutions,[25] which were "fundamental charters"[26] because they secured "the fundamental rights of individuals."[27]

---

[22]Statutory law consisted of the written charters and acts of Parliament, including the Magna Carta (1215), the Petition of Right (1628), the Habeas Corpus Act (1679), the Act of Rights (generally called the Bill of Rights) (1689), the Toleration Act (1689), the Mutiny Act (1689), and the Act of Settlement (1701). See 1 W. Blackstone, Commentaries *123–24.

The common law was derived from judicial reports and treatises. 1 W. Blackstone, *supra*, at *63–64. See Letter of "Novanglus" (John Adams) to the Inhabitants of the Colony of Massachusetts-Bay (Mar. 13, 1775), *reprinted in* 2 Papers of John Adams 327 (R. Taylor ed. 1977).

[23]Md. Declaration of Rights (1776), *reprinted in* 3 The Federal and State Constitutions, Colonial Charters and Other Organic Laws 1686 (F. Thorpe ed. 1909) [hereinafter cited as Federal and State Constitutions].

[24]*Id.* at art. III, *reprinted in* 3 Federal and State Constitutions, *supra* note 23, at 1686–87. Colonial charters and other major documents are collected in Foundations of Colonial America (W. Kavenagh ed. 1973). *See also* The Bill of Rights: A Documentary History (B. Schwartz ed. 1971); Sources of Our Liberties (R. Perry & J. Cooper eds. 1959). Complete state constitutions are assembled in Federal and State Constitutions, *supra* note 23.

[25]Earlier resolutions and declarations include: Resolutions of the Stamp Act Congress (Oct. 19, 1765), *reprinted in* Documents of American History 57 (H. Commager

The colonists premised their fight for independence, when the time came, on the natural law–social contract theory expounded by numerous writers, foremost among them John Locke.[28] Under that theory, individuals are born into a "state of nature," that is, without organized government, and agree out of "strong Obligations of Necessity, Convenience, and Inclination"[29] to live in political communities.[30] In so contracting, individuals must give up some of their natural rights so that the rest of those rights may be more effectively

---

3d ed. 1943); Declaration and Resolves of the First Continental Congress (Oct. 14, 1774), *reprinted in* 1 Journals of the Continental Congress 1774–1789, at 67–73 (W. Ford ed. 1904) [hereinafter cited as Journals]; Virginia Stamp Act Resolutions (May 30, 1765), *reprinted in* Documents of American History, *supra*, at 56; Resolutions of the Freeholders of Albemarle County (July 26, 1774), *reprinted in* 1 The Papers of Thomas Jefferson 117 (J. Boyd ed. 1950).

[26]The Federalist No. 44, at 301 (J. Madison) (J. Cooke ed. 1961).

[27]1 Records, *supra* note 21, at 493 (quoting Rufus King of Massachusetts). George Mason of Virginia averred that "in the state government . . . it was necessary that the great rights of human nature should be secure from the encroachments of the legislature." 3 J. Elliot, The Debates in the Several State Conventions on the Adoption of the Federal Constitution 444–45 (2d ed. Philadelphia 1836). Patrick Henry declared that the 1776 Virginia bill of rights, drafted by Mason, "secures the great and principal rights of mankind," (*id.* at 461) and equated "[t]he rights of the people" with the safeguards of English statutory and common law. *Id.* at 513. *See id.* at 587–88. *Cf.* Weimer v. Bunbury, 30 Mich. 201, 214 (1874) (Cooley, J.) ("the bills of rights in the American constitutions have not been drafted for the introduction of new law, but to secure old principles against abrogation or violation").

[28]Other natural law theorists such as Hugo Grotius, Emmerich de Vattel, Samuel von Pufendorf and Jean-Jacques Burlamaqui were also well known to the colonists. *See, e.g.,* 1 Records, *supra* note 21, at 437–38; 4 J. Elliot, *supra* note 27, at 278–79; G. Wood, *supra* note 20, at 355. J. Rousseau, Du Contrat Social (1st ed. 1762), was less influential, because the notion of a general will superior to any individual will was not congenial to a group of sovereign colonies. *See infra* text accompanying note 86. The law of nature was considered, ultimately, to be the will of God. *See* J. Locke, The Second Treatise of Government, *reprinted in* Two Treatises of Government § 13, at 293, § 195, at 413 (P. Laslett ed. 1970) (1st ed. 1690) [hereinafter cited as Second Treatise]. *See also* 1 W. Blackstone, *supra* note 22, at *38–43; J. Locke, The First Treatise of Government, *reprinted in* Two Treatises of Government, *supra*, §§ 126–27, at 251–52, § 137, at 259–60.

[29]Second Treatise, *supra* note 28, § 77, at 336.

[30]*Id.* § 77, at 336–37, § 87, at 341–42, § 89, at 343. The Massachusetts Constitution, drafted by John Adams, stated: "The body politic is formed by a voluntary association of individuals: it is a social compact, by which the whole people covenants with each citizen, and each citizen with the whole people, that all shall be governed by certain laws for the common good." Mass. Const. preamble (1780), *reprinted in* 3 Federal and State Constitutions, *supra* note 23, at 1889.

secured.[31] The sole legitimate purpose of government, therefore, is the good of the contracting parties—the public.[32] Accordingly, government has a right only to act for the benefit of the governed, to protect its citizens from rebellion within and invasion without.[33] As a part or consequence of this right to govern in pursuance of the public good, then, the government preserves individual rights.

In the *Second Treatise of Government*, Locke defined political power as "*a Right* of making Laws . . . for the Regulating and Preserving of Property, and of employing the force of the Community, in the Execution of such Laws, and in the defence of the Commonwealth from Foreign Injury, and all this only for the Publick Good."[34] Locke defined the supreme political power in a state, the legislative power, as "that which has a right to direct how the Force of the Commonwealth shall be imploy'd for preserving the Community and the Members of it."[35] Under this natural law theory, individuals have a right to be governed by representatives whom they have chosen. The government so chosen, as a creature of the people and instituted solely for their benefit, has the concomitant or derivative *right* to govern.

The colonists based their demand for the twofold right of self-determination—the right of the contractual state to govern and its citizens to be so governed[36]—on this theory. James Otis' 1764

---

[31]Second Treatise, *supra* note 28, § 87, at 341–42, § 95, at 348–49, § 98, at 350–51, § 123, at 368. *See* Boddie v. Connecticut, 401 U.S. 371, 374 (1971); The Federalist No. 2, at 8 (J. Jay) (J. Cooke ed. 1961).

[32]Second Treatise, *supra* note 28, § 124, at 368–69, § 131, at 371.

[33]*Id.* § 131, at 371. This right later found expression in the guarantee clause of the Constitution. *See infra* note 65.

[34]Second Treatise, *supra* note 28, § 3, at 286 (emphasis in original).

[35]*Id.* § 143, at 382 (emphasis deleted). *See also id.* § 135, at 375 (legislative power "can never have a right to destroy, enslave, or designedly to impoverish the Subjects"); *id.* § 150, at 386 (legislative is the supreme power "by the right it has to make Laws for all the parts and for every Member of the Society"). *Cf.* 1 W. Blackstone, *supra* note 22, at *52 ("wherever the supreme authority in any state resides, it is the right of that authority to make laws").

[36]The concept of self-government in the name of the common good has remained inherently ambiguous, for it ignores conflicts between the rights of the individual and the needs of the collective. *See* W. Adams, *supra* note 20, at 219–20 & 223; G. Wood, *supra* note 20, at 53–65. The twofold meaning of the term is especially conspicuous in article IV of the 1780 Massachusetts Declaration of Rights: "The people of this commonwealth have the sole and exclusive right of governing themselves, as a free, sovereign, and independent state; and do, and forever hereafter

pamphlet, *The Rights of the British Colonies Asserted and Proved*,[37] was an influential example. Quoting, paraphrasing, or alluding to Locke on almost every page, Otis wrote that it is the duty of government "to provide for the security, the quiet, and happy enjoyment of life, liberty, and property. There is no one act which a government can have a *right* to make that does not tend to the advancement of the security, tranquillity, and prosperity of the people."[38]

The right of self-government was characteristically expressed as the exclusive right of each colony to regulate its own "internal police"[39] or "internal polity."[40] The fourth of the Virginia Stamp Act

---

shall, exercise and enjoy every power, jurisdiction, and right, which is not, or may not hereafter be, by them expressly delegated to the United States of America, in Congress assembled." 3 Federal and State Constitutions, *supra* note 23, at 1890. Although the "exclusive right" of the people to govern themselves in the first clause refers to the prerogatives of the commonwealth exercisable as against external powers, the meaning of "every . . . right" enjoyed by the people in the second clause more naturally denotes individual liberties. The Massachusetts provision, adapted by John Adams from article II of the Articles of Confederation, *infra* text accompanying note 53, was copied almost exactly by New Hampshire in its bill of rights four years later. The corresponding phrase, however, in article VII of the New Hampshire bill read "enjoy every . . . right pertaining thereto," the additional last two words emphasizing the distinct yet interdependent nature of the two kinds of rights. *See* 4 Federal and State Constitutions, *supra* note 23, at 2454.

[37]J. Otis, The Rights of the British Colonies Asserted and Proved (1764), *reprinted in* 1 Pamphlets of the American Revolution, 1750–1776, at 408 (B. Bailyn ed. 1965).

[38]*Id.* at 425 (emphasis in original). It followed for Otis that "[n]o legislative, supreme or subordinate, has a right to make itself arbitrary." *Id.* at 446 (emphasis deleted). *See* Second Treatise, *supra* note 28, § 135, at 375–76.

[39]*See* Galloway Plan, *infra* text accompanying note 42; Dickinson draft of Articles of Confederation, *infra* text accompanying note 47; Md. Declaration of Rights, art. II, *reprinted in* 3 Federal and State Constitutions, *supra* note 23, at 1686 ("the people of this State ought to have the sole and exclusive right of regulating the internal government and police thereof"). *See also* N.C. Declaration of Rights, art. III, *reprinted in* 5 *id.* at 2801; Pa. Declaration of Rights, art. III, *reprinted in id.* at 3082; Vt. Declaration of Rights, art. IV, *reprinted in* 6 *id* at 3740.

Judge Cooley explained this "police power" in his Treatise on Constitutional Limitations:

The police of a State, in a comprehensive sense, embraces its system of internal regulation, by which it is sought not only to preserve the public order and to prevent offences against the State, but also to establish for the intercourse of citizen with citizen those rules of good manners and good neighborhood which are calculated to prevent a conflict of rights, and to insure to each the uninterrupted enjoyment of his own, so far as is reasonably consistent with a like enjoyment of rights by others.

T. Cooley, A Treatise on the Constitutional Limitations Which Rest Upon the Leg-

Resolutions, written by Patrick Henry and approved by the House of Burgesses on May 30, 1765, stated:

> *Resolved,* That His Majesty's liege people of this his most ancient and loyal Colony have without interruption enjoyed the inestimable right of being governed by such laws, respecting their internal polity and taxation, as are derived from their own consent, with the approbation of their sovereign, or his substitute; and that the same hath never been forefeited or yielded up, but hath been constantly recognized by the kings and people of Great Britain.[41]

As America edged towards independence, a conciliatory "Plan of a proposed Union between Great Britain and the Colonies" was submitted by Joseph Galloway of Pennsylvania to the First Continental Congress on September 28, 1774. Galloway's Plan of Union, which was defeated by one vote, provided:

> That a British and American legislature, for regulating the administration of the general affairs of America, be proposed and estab-

---

islative Power of the States of the American Union 572 (1st ed. Boston 1868) (footnote omitted). *See id.,* n.1 (citing similar definitions in 4 W. Blackstone. *supra* note 22, at *162). *See also* Barbier v. Connolly, 113 U.S. 27, 31 (1885) (police power promotes "health, peace, morals, education, and good order of the people"); New York v. Miln, 36 U.S. (11 Pet.) 102, 132, 139 & 141–42 (1837); Gibbons v. Ogden, 22 U.S. (9 Wheat.) 1, 209–10 (1824); 2 Records, *supra* note 21, at 629. The definition is verified by Alexander Hamilton's criticism of the Articles of Confederation: "The confederation in my opinion should give Congress complete sovereignty; except as to that part of internal police, which relates to the rights of property and life among individuals and to raising money by internal taxes. It is necessary, that every thing, belonging to this, should be regulated by the state legislatures." Letter from Alexander Hamilton to James Duane (Sept. 3, 1780), *reprinted in* 2 The Papers of Alexander Hamilton, at 407–08 (H. Syrett & J. Cooke eds. 1961); *see id.* at 402. *See generally* W. Adams, *supra* note 20, at 135–37 & 288.

[40]*See* 1774 Declaration and Resolves of the Continental Congress (original draft), *infra* text accompanying note 43; Fourth Virginia Stamp Act Resolution, *infra* text accompanying note 41; Virginia Instructions to the Continental Congress (Aug. 1, 1774), *reprinted in* Documents of American History, *supra* note 25, at 79 ("The original constitution of the American colonies posses[ed] their assemblies with the sole right of directing their internal polity"). *See also* Mecklenburg County Resolutions (North Carolina), *reprinted in* Documents of American History, *supra* note 25, at 98 ("internal Government"); Resolutions of the Virginia Convention Calling for Independence, May 15, 1776, *reprinted in* 1 J. Boyd, *supra* note 25, at 291 ("internal concerns"); Letter from Alexander Hamilton to George Clinton (Feb. 13, 1778), *reprinted in* 1 The Papers of Alexander Hamilton, *supra* note 39, at 427 ("internal government"). *See generally* W. Adams, *supra* note 20, at 21.

[41]Documents of American History, *supra* note 25, at 56.

lished in America, including all the said colonies; within, and under which government, each colony shall retain its present constitution, and powers of regulating and governing its own internal police, in all cases what[so]ever.[42]

Phrases reminiscent of Henry's and Galloway's appear in the very first resolutions passed by the First Continental Congress, the "Declaration and Resolves" adopted on October 14, 1774. Congress, meeting at Carpenters' Hall in Philadelphia, approved eleven resolutions declaring that the colonists' rights had been infringed by Parliament. The original draft of the first resolution, by Major John Sullivan of New Hampshire, asserted:

> That the power of making laws for ordering or regulating the internal polity of these Colonies, is, within the limits of each Colony, respectively and exclusively vested in the Provincial Legislature of such Colony; and that all statutes for ordering or regulating the internal polity of the said Colonies, or any of them, in any manner or in any case whatsoever, are illegal and void.[43]

The version approved by Congress expressed the same ideas in more familiar language: "That [the inhabitants of the English Colonies in North America] are entitled to life, liberty, & property, and they have never ceded to any sovereign power whatever, a right to dispose of either without their consent."[44]

The resolution for independence, introduced in the Continental Congress by Richard Henry Lee of Virginia on June 7, 1776, called for "a plan of confederation,"[45] and the Congress appointed a committee to draw up the plan.[46] Sullivan's original version of the first 1774 resolution influenced the wording of article III of the original draft of the Articles of Confederation, which was largely the work of the committee chairman, John Dickinson:

---

[42]1 Journals, *supra* note 25, at 49.

[43]*Id.* at 67. There is evidence that the draft is attributable at least in part to John Dickinson of Pennsylvania. 2 Papers of John Adams, *supra* note 22, at 155 n.1.

[44]1 Journals, *supra* note 25, at 67. The 1774 resolutions were referred to as "the American Bill of rights" in the credentials of the Massachusetts delegates to the Second Continental Congress. 2 *id.* at 13 (1905).

[45]5 *id.* at 425 (1906).

[46]*Id.* at 431–33 (June 11, 1776) ("*Resolved*, That a committee be appointed to prepare and digest the form of a confederation to be entered into between these colonies[.]" *Id.* at 433).

Each Colony shall retain and enjoy as much of its present Laws, Rights and Customs, as it may think fit, and reserves to itself the sole and exclusive Regulation and Government of its internal police, in all matters that shall not interfere with the Articles of this Confederation.[47]

Congress amended Dickinson's proposed article III on the motion of Thomas Burke of North Carolina.[48] Burke's amendment retained

[47]Id. at 547. This draft was reported to Congress on July 12, 1776. Id. Dickinson also followed article III of the plan of confederation which was submitted by Benjamin Franklin on July 21, 1775, though never formally voted on by Congress. 2 Journals, supra note 25, at 196. Franklin proposed: "That each Colony shall enjoy and retain as much as it may think fit of its own present Laws, Customs, Rights, [and] Privileges, and peculiar Jurisdictions within its own Limits; and may amend its own Constitution as shall seem best to its own Assembly or Convention." Id. Significantly, Franklin juxtaposed the rights retained by the colonies with the administration of their respective constitutions, the compendiums of their internal laws. This article Franklin had borrowed from his Albany Plan of Union of 1754, "by virtue of which," its preamble stated, "one general government may be formed in America, including all the said colonies, within and under which government each colony may retain its present constitution. . . ." Documents of American History, supra note 25, at 43. A second draft of the Dickinson Articles, reported on August 20, 1776, contained minor changes (5 Journals, supra note 25, at 675), and was not considered by Congress because of the demands placed on its members by the conduct of the Revolution.

[48]Burke recalled that his proposed second article occasioned two days debate. It stood originally the third article; and expressed only a reservation of the power of regulating the internal police, and consequently resigned every other power. It appeared to me that this was not what the States expected, and, I thought, it left it in the power of the future Congress or General Council to explain away every right belonging to the States and to make their own power as unlimited as they please. I proposed, therefore, an amendment, which held up the principle, that all sovereign power was in the States separately, and that particular acts of it, which should be expressly enumerated, would be exercised in conjunction, and not otherwise; but that in all things else each State would exercise all the rights and power of sovereignty, uncontrolled.
7 Journals, supra note 25, at 123 n.4 (1907) (reprinting a letter from Thomas Burke to Governor Caswell (May 23, 1777), from 11 N.C. Colonial Records 477). See generally M. Jensen, supra note 20, at 161–76; G. Wood, supra note 20, at 358. Observing that his amendment received the votes of 11 of the 13 states, Burke wrote to the governor of his home state: "I was much pleased to find the opinion of accumulating powers to Congress so little supported. . . . In a word, Sir, I am of opinion, the Congress should have power enough to call out and apply the common strength for the common defense: but not for the partial purposes of ambition." Letter from Thomas Burke to Richard Caswell (April 29, 1777), reprinted in 7 Journals, supra note 25, at 123 n.4 (1907). See id. at 112 n.1 (Burke "refused to say what his State could not do,

the core right of the states to self-government and bolstered it with additional rights at the expense of Congress, so that the states remained independent not only of Great Britain but also of each other.[49] Hence Burke's amendment augmented each state's right to order its internal polity because it left to the states "every power, jurisdiction and right"[50] not expressly yielded to Congress.[51] By the time Congress approved the final version of the "Articles of Confederation and Perpetual Union" on November 15, 1777,[52] Dickinson's article III had become Burke's article II and provided: "Each state retains its sovereignty, freedom and independence, and every power, jurisdiction and right, which is not by this confederation expressly delegated to the United States, in Congress assembled."[53]

The Articles of Confederation recognized that the country's fundamental law consisted of the states' fundamental laws. The states retained the right of self-government and, consequently, the right to enact and maintain laws regarding individual liberties. These fundamental rights were drawn from the English constitution[54] and

---

declaring he thought she could do every thing which she had not precluded herself from by plain and express declaration: to yield up any of her rights was not in his power, and very far from his inclination"). A marginal inscription on a printed copy of the Articles in the handwriting of Charles Thomson, Secretary of the Continental Congress, indicates that Burke's amendment was agreed to by Congress on April 25, 1777, 9 id., frontispiece.

[49]Burke wrote: "The inequality of the States, and yet the necessity of maintaining their separate independence, will occasion dilemmas almost inextricable." Letter from Thomas Burke to Richard Caswell (April 29, 1777), reprinted in 7 Journals, supra note 25, at 123 n.4 (1907).

[50]9 Journals, supra note 25, at 908 (1907).

[51]See W. Adams, supra note 20, at 282.

[52]9 Journals, supra note 25, at 907 (1907).

[53]Id. at 908, Article II provoked no comment in the ratification documents submitted by the states to Congress. 1 The Documentary History of the Ratification of the Constitution 97–137 (M. Jensen ed. 1976). The Articles became effective on March 1, 1781. Id. at 97.

[54]By "constitution" the Americans originally meant, as did the English, not a basic charter of government, but rather "that assemblage of laws, customs and institutions which form the general system; according to which the several powers of the state are distributed, and their respective rights are secured to the different members of the community." C. Inglis, The True Interest of America 18 (1776) (quoted in G. Wood, supra note 20, at 261). See B. Bailyn, The Ideological Origins of the American Revolution 67–68 (1967). Thus Blackstone did not distinguish between England's constitution and its system of laws as a whole. 1 W. Blackstone, supra note 22, at *50–52. Presaging the famous aphorism of Chief Justice Hughes that the Constitution

consisted of both "natural" and "civil" rights.[55] The phrase "retained rights" was not itself a term of art, but the concept did recur in two particular contexts: rights that individuals in a state of nature[56] bring

---

is what the judges say it is (C. Hughes, Addresses of Charles Evans Hughes 185 (2d ed. 1916)), James Wilson of Pennsylvania remarked, "The British constitution is just what the British Parliament pleases." 2 J. Elliot, *supra* note 27, at 432. The statutes listed at *supra* note 22, however, are considered the foundation of England's constitution. R. Moore, Modern Constitutions 30–55 (1957).

Under the impact of worsening relations with the Crown in the 1760's and 1770's, the colonists held England to have violated the principles of natural justice inherent in its own constitution. "The Colonies adopt the common Law," said Roger Sherman of Connecticut in 1774, "not as the common Law, but as the highest Reason." 2 Diary and Autobiography of John Adams 129 (L. Butterfield ed. 1961). Eventually these principles were extracted from the existing governmental arrangements and fixed as standards beyond the power of ordinary legislation to alter. By 1776, Tom Paine had called for a "Continental Charter, or Charter of the United Colonies . . . [s]ecuring freedom and property . . . [and] the free exercise of religion." T. Paine, Common Sense 40 (Dolphin ed. 1960) (1st ed. 1776). This disengagement and recodification was the genesis first of the state constitutions and bills of rights, and later of their federal counterparts. *See generally* J. Gough, Fundamental Law in English Constitutional History 160–213 (1955); Corwin, *The Progress of Constitutional Theory Between the Declaration of Independence and the Meeting of the Philadelphia Convention*, 30 Am. Hist. Rev. 511 (1925).

[55]When Madison introduced his proposed constitutional amendments in Congress, he distinguished between the "natural rights. retained" such as freedom of speech, 5 The Writings of James Madison 389 n.1 (G. Hunt ed. 1904) (emphasis deleted, punctuation in original) [hereinafter cited as Writings], i.e., "those rights which are retained when particular powers are given up to be exercised by the Legislature," 1 Annals of Cong. 454 (Gales & Seaton eds. 1834) (remarks of Rep. Madison) [hereinafter cited as Annals], and positive rights, which as Madison explained, "may seem to result from the nature of the compact. Trial by jury cannot be considered as a natural right, but a right resulting from a social compact which regulates the action of the community, but is as essential to secure the liberty of the people as any one of the pre-existent rights of nature." *Id. See also* 1 B. Schwartz, *supra* note 24, at 349 (demand in 1778 by Essex County, Massachusetts, for state bill of rights, distinguishing between "alienable" and "unalienable" rights); 1 W. Blackstone, *supra* note 22, at *42–44; Second Treatise, *supra* note 28, §§ 87–89, at 341–43; T. Paine, Candid and Critical Remarks on a Letter Signed Ludlow (1777), *reprinted in* 1 B. Schwartz, *supra* note 24, at 315–16; T. Paine, The Rights of Man, *reprinted in* Reflections on the Revolution in France by Edmund Burke & The Rights of Man by Thomas Paine 305–06 (Dolphin ed. 1961) (1st ed. 1791) [hereinafter cited as Rights of Man].

Political liberty is accordingly the capacity to exercise natural rights retained in civil society and is to be afforded maximum scope. *See* Boyd v. United States, 116 U.S. 616, 626–35 (1886); B. Bailyn, *supra* note 54, at 77; Letter III of "Fabius" (John Dickinson), *reprinted in* Pamphlets on the Constitution of the United States 176 (P.

with them on entering civil society,[57] and rights kept by the states in forming a union.[58] These two usages of the concept are related, for, in the view of Luther Martin of Maryland at the 1787 Convention, "the separation from [Great Britain] placed the 13 States in a state of nature towards each other; [and] they would have remained in that state till this time, but for the confederation."[59] Article II of

---

Ford ed. 1968) (1st ed. 1888).

The distinction between natural, universally valid law and positive or enacted law boasted a venerable lineage, descended as it was from the Corpus juris civilis of Justinian (see Inst. Just. 1.2) and ultimately from Aristotle's division of political justice into "natural" justice, universal truths existing independently of particular human notions of right and wrong, and "legal" or "statutory" justice, which is valid only by enactment and so varies with time and place. The Nicomachean Ethics of Aristotle, bk. 5, ch. 7, at 124–25 (D. Ross trans. 1925). Early in its history the Supreme Court observed, "The right to appropriate [abandoned property] is one of universal law, well known to the civil law, the common law, and to all law: it existed in a state of nature, and is only modified by society, according to the discretion of each community." Hawkins v. Barney's Lessee, 30 U.S. (5 Pet.) 457, 467 (1831). The distinction between natural law and positive law less universally applicable was used again to determine which constitutional protections were suitable to the territories outside the continental mainland that were annexed and administered by the United States. See Hawaii v. Mankichi, 190 U.S. 197, 217–18 (1903); Downes v. Bidwell, 182 U.S. 244, 282–83 (1901); Thayer, Our New Possessions, 12 Harv. L. Rev. 464, 473, 478–82 (1899).

[56]The term "state of nature" denoted for the colonists the absence of an operating government. At the Continental Congress Patrick Henry announced: "Government is dissolved. . . . We are in a State of Nature, Sir." 2 Diary and Autobiography of John Adams, supra note 54, at 124. Cf. Second Treatise, supra note 28, §§ 89–94, at 343–48 (state of nature exists in absence of laws that are binding on every member of a community, as in the case of absolute monarchies).

[57]See, e.g., 1 Annals, supra note 55, at 454 (remarks of Rep. Madison); Rights of Man, supra note 55, at 306.

[58]See 1 Annals, supra note 55, at 454; infra text accompanying notes 95 & 100–01; infra note 148.

[59]1 Records, supra note 21, at 324. See also id. at 437. The analogy between individuals in a state of nature entering into civil society and sovereign states entering into a federal union was expressly stated in the letter of transmittal which the Philadelphia Convention submitted over Washington's signature to Congress together with the draft Constitution on September 17, 1787 (see 2 Records, supra note 21, at 666–67) and which was later sent with the proposed Constitution to the state ratification conventions: "It is obviously impracticable in the Federal Government of these States to secure all rights of independent sovereignty to each, and yet provide for the interest and safety of all. Individuals entering into society must give up a share of liberty to preserve the rest." 1 Annals, supra note 55, at vii. See also Ogden v. Saunders, 25 U.S. (12 Wheat.) 213, 346 (1827) (Marshall, C.J., dissenting); Letter III

the Articles of Confederation therefore maintained the rights of individuals as well as the rights and powers of the states, and was accordingly a direct ancestor not only of the tenth amendment, which reserves powers to the states,[60] but of the ninth amendment as well.[61]

B. *From Philadelphia to Adoption of the Bill of Rights*

Scarcely any attention was paid to framing a bill of rights at the Constitutional Convention of 1787.[62] On August 20, Charles Pinckney of South Carolina submitted to the Committee of Detail a number of proposals that amounted to a bill of rights, but the provisions were never brought to the floor for consideration.[63] George Mason suggested, five days before the convention ended, that the Constitution be prefaced with a bill of rights,[64] but Roger Sherman's response expressed the prevailing view at Philadelphia: "The State Declarations of Rights are not repealed by this Constitution; and

---

of "Fabius" (John Dickinson), *supra* note 55, at 174–77; Second Treatise, *supra* note 28, § 145, at 383.

[60]The tenth amendment reads: "The powers not delegated to the United States by the Constitution, nor prohibited by it to the States, are reserved to the States respectively, or to the people." U.S. Const. amend. X. *See infra* notes 163 & 168.

[61]The records of the debates in the state ratification conventions uniformly show that article II rights included individual rights as set out in the state constitutions, bills of rights, and the common law. *See infra* note 100.

[62]Washington wrote to Lafayette: "[T]here was not a member of the convention, I believe, who had the least objection to [a bill of rights, but such a bill,] where the people evidently retained every thing which they did not in express terms give up, was considered nugatory as you will find to have been more fully explained by Mr. Wilson and others[.]" Letter from George Washington to Marquis de Lafayette (April 28, 1788), *reprinted in* 29 The Writings of George Washington 478 (J. Fitzpatrick ed. 1939). For Wilson's argument, see *infra* text accompanying notes 67–69. *See generally* 2 J. Elliot, *supra* note 27, at 435–36; G. Wood, *supra* note 20, at 536; Uncertain Renaissance, *supra* note 12, 816. For the history of the enactment of the Bill of Rights, see generally 1 J. Goebel, History of the Supreme Court of the United States 413–56 (1971); R. Rutland, The Birth of the Bill of Rights 1776–1791 (1955); Storing, *The Constitution and the Bill of Rights, in* Essays on the Constitution of the United States 32 (M. Harmon ed. 1978).

[63]*See* 2 Records, *supra* note 21, at 340–42. *See also id.* at 612–19 (bill of rights not considered in Report of the Committee of Stile & Arrangement).

[64]*See id.* at 587–88.

being in force are sufficient."[65] The motion was then considered and unanimously defeated. Yet the delegates discovered, on returning home, that ratification of the Constitution would almost certainly require the addition of a bill of rights.[66]

Advocates of a bill of rights were concerned that individual liberties would be lost under a Constitution that did not expressly declare them reserved. The federalists countered that imperfect protection of personal freedoms would result instead if a bill were added. Although they eventually acceded to a bill of rights, the federalists initially opposed adding such a bill on two grounds. First, it would be impossible or highly impractical to specify every right reserved by the people that was not inconsistent with the express and implicit powers granted the federal government. At the Pennsylvania ratification convention, James Wilson, who would later serve with Ellsworth on the United States Supreme Court, said that "in a government consisting of enumerated powers, such as is proposed for the United States, a bill of rights would not only be unnecessary, but, in my humble judgment, highly imprudent.

[65]*Id.* at 588. Mason's terse reply to Sherman, "The Laws of the U.S. are to be paramount to State Bills of Rights"(*id.*), anticipates the antifederalist argument that the Constitution superseded and hence abrogated the existing state bills of rights. *See infra* note 75 and accompanying text. The exchange between Mason and Sherman also suggests that at the Philadelphia Convention, a proposed bill of rights was understood to mean preservation of the rights contained in the state charters.

A proposal that "a Republican Constitution & its existing laws ought to be guarantied to each State by the U. States" (2 Records, *supra* note 21, at 47), which would have "perpetuat[ed]" the existing Constitutions of the States" (*id.* at 48), was intended, as James Wilson explained, "merely to secure the States agst. dangerous commotions, insurrections and rebellions." *Id.* at 47. The provision for repromulgation of the state constitutions was omitted on Wilson's motion, which gave the guarantee clause essentially its final form. *See id.* at 48–49. The clause presently states: "The United States shall guarantee to every State in this Union a Republican Form of Government, and shall protect each of them against Invasion; and . . . against domestic Violence." U.S. Const. art. IV, § 4. *See generally* W. Wiecek, The Guarantee Clause of the U.S. Constitution (1972).

[66]Elbridge Gerry of Massachusetts commented, "The ratification of the constitution in several States would never have taken place, had [the people] not been assured that the objections would have been duly attended to by Congress." 1 Annals, *supra* note 55, at 464. *See also id.* at 734 (remarks of Rep. Page); *id.* at 448–50 (remarks of Rep. Madison).

In all societies, there are many powers and rights which cannot be particularly enumerated."[67] The federalists' second argument was that an enumeration of rights, necessarily incomplete, could give rise to the presumption that all rights left unspecified would be forfeited to the federal government. Wilson reasoned that, because a bill of rights constitutes "*an enumeration of the powers* reserved[,] . . . every thing that is not enumerated is presumed to be given. The consequence is, that an imperfect enumeration would throw all implied power into the scale of the government, and the rights of the people would be rendered incomplete."[68] Wilson acknowledged that a constitution constructed to enumerate the powers of government, rather than to reserve rights to the people, could also be incomplete, but contended that such a scheme would be preferable: "[A]n omission in the enumeration of the powers of government is neither so dangerous nor important as an omission in the enumeration of the rights of the people."[69] To the same effect, Alexander Hamilton wrote six months[70] later in *The Federalist* that a bill of rights "would

[67]2 J. Elliot, *supra* note 27, at 436. Madison knew that "no language is so copious as to supply words and phrases for every complex idea." The Federalist No. 37, at 236 (J. Madison) (J. Cooke ed. 1961).

[68]2 J. Elliot, *supra* note 27, at 436 (emphasis in original).

[69]*Id.* at 436–37. *See id.* at 87–88; 4 *id.* at 149; G. Wood, *supra* note 20, at 539–40. The jurisdiction of the proposed federal government, wrote Madison, "extends to certain enumerated objects only, and leaves to the several States a residuary and inviolable sovereignty over all other objects." The Federalist No. 39, at 256 (J. Madison) (J. Cooke ed. 1961). *See also* 3 J. Elliot, *supra* note 27, at 438–39 & 455. Writing to Jefferson, Madison claimed: "My own opinion has always been in favor of a bill of rights; provided it be so framed as not to imply powers not meant to be included in the enumeration." Letter from James Madison to Thomas Jefferson (Oct. 17, 1788), *reprinted in* 5 Writings, *supra* note 55, at 271. *See also* 3 J. Elliot, *supra* note 27, at 620, 626–27.

This argument foreshadows the insistence of later commentators that "law can never make us as secure as we are when we do not need it. Those freedoms which are neither challenged nor defined are the most secure." A. Bickel, The Morality of Consent 60 (1975). *See also* W. Douglas, We the Judges 259 (1956); 2 J. Kent, Commentaries on American Law *11; Frankfurter, *John Marshall and the Judicial Function*, 69 Harv. L. Rev. 217, 235–36 (1955).

[70]The date given in 2 J. Elliot, *supra* note 27, at 436, for Wilson's statement at the Pennsylvania ratification convention, October 28, 1787, is apparently a misprint, as the Pennsylvania convention did not begin until November 20, 1787. 1 The Documentary History of the Ratification of the Constitution, *supra* note 53, at 22. Assuming that Wilson actually spoke on November 28, 1787, Hamilton's writing of May 28, 1788 (*see* The Federalist No. 84 (A. Hamilton)), would be six months later.

even be dangerous" because it "would contain various exceptions to powers which are not granted; and on this very account, would afford a colourable pretext to claim more than were granted."[71] Rhetorically, Hamilton asked, "Why for instance, should it be said, that the liberty of the press shall not be restrained, when no power is given by which restrictions may be imposed?"[72]

Hamilton pressed his argument that enumeration was unnecessary to protect retained rights. His argument is noteworthy because it explains Hamilton's position in 1788 on the issue of unenumerated rights, the same type of rights as those that would come within the purview of the ninth amendment after adoption of the Bill of Rights.[73] Hamilton's analysis in *The Federalist No. 83* suggests that unenumerated rights are to be identified with the state constitutions, statutes, and common law. The specific antifederalist argument that Hamilton chose to rebut was the contention that, because the Constitution provides for jury trials in criminal but not civil cases,[74] trial by jury in civil cases would be eliminated unless it were specifically protected.[75] Hamilton answered that "trial by jury is in no case

[71]The Federalist No. 84, at 579 (A. Hamilton) (J. Cooke ed. 1961).

[72]*Id.* Hamilton accurately distinguished the Constitution, in which the public retains all powers not surrendered to the federal government, from the bills of rights that English kings had granted to their subjects, in which the monarch retained all prerogatives not conceded. *Id.* at 578. See G. Wood, *supra* note 20, at 561, 601; McIlwain, *The Fundamental Law Behind the Constitution of the United States,* in The Constitution Reconsidered 3 (C. Read ed. 1938).

[73]Although there was no single antifederalist "position" on every issue concerning the proposed Constitution, e.g., the composition of the legislature, the strength of the executive, and even whether the Constitution should be ratified, on the question of adding a bill of rights Elbridge Gerry's description is fair: "[T]he federalists were for ratifying the constitution as it stood, and the [antifederalists,] not until amendments were made." 1 Annals, *supra* note 55, at 759. *See generally* Anti-Federalists versus Federalists: Selected Documents (J. Lewis ed. 1967); J. Main, The Antifederalists (1961); R. Rutland, The Ordeal of the Constitution (1966); H. Storing, The Complete Anti-Federalist (1981); The Antifederalist Papers (M. Borden ed. 1965); The Antifederalists (C. Kenyon ed. 1966); The States Rights Debate: Antifederalism and the Constitution (A. Mason ed. 1964). These federalists are to be distinguished from the political party of the same name which flourished in the ensuing decade.

[74]U.S. Const. art. III, § 2.

[75]The Federalist No. 83, at 559 (A. Hamilton) (J. Cooke ed. 1961). The antifederalists argued that this could be accomplished in two ways: under the supremacy clause or under the necessary and proper clause. *See, e.g.,* 1 J. Elliot, *supra* note 27, at 381–82 (supremacy clause); 2 *id.* at 374 (same); 3 *id.* at 513 (same); 3 *id.* at 439 & 441–42 (necessary and proper clause). *See generally* G. Wood, *supra* note 20, at 539–43. James

abolished by the proposed constitution,"[76] and because most civil controversies would involve issues arising under state law, "they will remain determinable as heretofore by the state courts only, and in the manner which the state constitutions and laws prescribe."[77] Hamilton added that "no general rule could have been fixed upon by the convention which would have corresponded with the circumstances [as to jury trials in civil cases] of all the states," with only dubious gains to be made in "taking the system of any one state for a standard."[78] Hence the most judicious solution was reached

---

Wilson's concise rebuttal was that the Constitution does not abolish but rather "presupposes the existence of state governments." 2 J. Elliot, *supra* note 27, at 439. *See generally* The Federalist No. 46 (J. Madison). "The Constitution, in all its provisions," Chief Justice Chase was to say, "looks to an indestructible Union, composed of indestructible States." Texas v. White, 74 U.S. (7 Wall.) 700, 725 (1868).

The right to trial by jury was especially valued, since jurisdiction to enforce the Stamp Act had been given to the admiralty courts, which had no jury. Parliament intentionally chose those courts to decide cases under the Act, which required duties on, inter alia, newspapers, diplomas, legal documents and playing cards, because jurors were often sympathetic to those engaged in the extensive smuggling business which continued throughout the century. *See* E. Morgan & H. Morgan, The Stamp Act Crisis 24 (1953). *See also* 4 J. Elliot, *supra* note 27, at 147; J. Otis, *supra* note 37, at 461–62. As John Adams reported, admiralty judges served only during the king's pleasure and took commissions on all monetary penalties assessed, so that they were "under a pecuniary temptation always against the subject." Instructions of the Town of Braintree, Massachusetts, on the Stamp Act, Oct. 14, 1765, *reprinted in* Documents of American History, *supra* note 25, at 57. Adams concluded that "this part of the act . . . is directly repugnant to the Great Charter itself." *Id.* The right of subjects to have a voice in the imposition of taxes dates back at least as early as 1215, for chapters 12 and 14 of the Magna Carta required the consent of an assembly of feudal lords before the king could levy taxes. Magna Carta, chs. 12 & 14, *reprinted in* G. Davis, Magna Carta 26 (1977).

[76]The Federalist No. 83, at 561 (A. Hamilton) (J. Cooke ed. 1961). See *id.* at 560 (Constitution's "specification of particulars evidently excludes all pretension to a general legislative authority").

[77]*Id.* See 4 J. Elliot, *supra* note 27, at 144–45 (remarks of Richard Spaight and James Iredell). The omission of such a provision, said Iredell, "arose from the difficulty of establishing one uniform, unexceptionable, mode." *Id.* at 144. Iredell, a future Supreme Court Justice, added: "It is not to be presumed that the Congress would dare to deprive the people of this valuable privilege. Their own interest will operate as an additional guard, as none of them could tell how soon they might have occasion for such a trial themselves." *Id.* at 145.

[78]The Federalist No. 83, at 566 (A. Hamilton) (J. Cooke ed. 1961).

by "leaving the matter as it has been left, to legislative regulation."[79] Hamilton thereupon rejected a proposed amendment stating that "trial by jury shall be as heretofore"[80] because such a statement would be too uncertain, necessarily depending on the pre-constitutional law governing civil jury trials, which differed in each state.[81] For Hamilton, there was no pre-constitutional federal law, only the common law and statutes of the individual states.

Even though the Bill of Rights came to include a provision for trial by jury in civil cases,[82] Hamilton's analysis is important because it shows that enforceable rights beyond those enumerated in the Constitution (or in the form of federal statutes) would exist only in the governments of the various states. Thus, if a bill of rights were adopted in which certain key rights were reserved and "other" rights were incorporated by reference in a residuary clause, recourse to the existing constitutions, statutes, and common law of the states would be necessary to ascertain those unenumerated rights. For

---

[79]*Id.* at 567. A month earlier, Washington had written that as to trial by jury, "it was only the difficulty of establishing a mode which should not interfere with the fixed modes of any of the States, that induced the Convention to leave it, as a matter of future adjustment." Letter from George Washington to Marquis de Lafayette (April 28, 1788), *supra* note 62, at 478–79. At the Virginia ratification convention, Edmund Randolph said: "The trial by jury in criminal cases is secured; in civil cases it is not so expressly secured as I should wish it; but it does not follow that Congress has the power of taking away this privilege, which is secured by the constitution of each state, and not given away by this Constitution." 3 J. Elliot, *supra* note 27, at 68.

[80]The Federalist No. 83, at 567 (A. Hamilton) (J. Cooke ed. 1961).

[81]*Id.* Hamilton wrote:
Now it is evident, that though trial by jury, with various limitations, is known in each state individually, yet in the United States, *as such*, it is at this time altogether unknown, because the present federal government has no judiciary power whatever; and consequently there is no proper antecedent or previous establishment to which the term *heretofore* could relate.
Id. (emphasis in original).
In his State House speech of October 6, 1787, James Wilson told his fellow Pennsylvanians that, when the matter of jury trials in civil cases was debated at the Constitutional Convention, it was found "impracticable . . . to have made a general rule" owing to the "want of uniformity" in the practices of the "thirteen independent sovereignities [sic]." 1 J. McMaster & F. Stone, Pennsylvania and the Federal Constitution 1787–1788, at 144–45 (1888). With Hamilton, Wilson concluded that "it could not with any propriety be said that, 'The trial by jury shall be as heretofore,' since there has never existed any federal system of jurisprudence, to which the declaration could relate." *Id.* at 145.

[82]U.S. Const. amend. VII.

the federalists, the Bill of Rights was a concession to skeptics, merely making explicit the protection of rights that had always been implicit. The unenumerated rights retained under the ninth amendment were to continue in force as before, as the operative laws of the states. Unenumerated rights were not federal rights, as were the enumerated rights, but represented the persistence of the "legislative regulation" of the states.

Some years later, in his *Report on the Virginia Resolutions,*[83] Madison confirmed Hamilton's position on the nonexistence of pre-constitutional federal rights. In his *Report,* Madison refuted the assertion, made in defense of the Sedition Act, that federal courts had jurisdiction over common law crimes such as seditious libel, inasmuch as the common law is "a part of the law of these states, in their united and national [i.e., collective] capacity."[84] Madison stressed at some length that before the Revolution, the common law "was the separate law of each colony within its respective limits, and was unknown to them as a law pervading and operating through the whole, as one society."[85] The common law "was not the same in any two of the colonies; in some, the modifications were mate-

---

[83]*See* 4 J. Elliot, *supra* note 27, at 546; 6 Writings, *supra* note 55, at 347. In this report, written in 1799–1800 and adopted by the Virginia legislature on January 11, 1800 (*id.*), Madison attempted to vindicate the resolutions passed by Virginia against the Alien and Sedition Acts and articulated the principles guiding state governments in the protection of civil liberties against encroaching and unconstitutional federal legislation.

[84]4 J. Elliot, *supra* note 27, at 561.

[85]*Id.* George Mason, who had wanted the Constitution to enact the common law, *see infra* note 103, admitted that the common law "stands here upon no other foundation than its having been adopted by the respective acts forming the constitutions of the several States." 2 Records, *supra* note 21, at 637. *See* Allen v. State Bd. of Elections, 393 U.S. 544, 596 (1969) (Black, J., dissenting) ("the separate Colonies were passing laws in their legislative bodies before they themselves created this Union"); Smith v. Alabama, 124 U.S. 465, 478 (1888); Lane County v. Oregon, 74 U.S. (7 Wall.) 71, 76 (1868); Wheaton v. Peters, 33 U.S. (8 Pet.) 591, 658 (1834) ("It is clear, there can be no common law of the United States. . . . The common law could be made a part of our federal system, only by legislative adoption."); United States v. Worrall, 2 U.S. (2 Dall.) 384, 394 (1798) (Chase, Circuit Justice) ("the United States, as a federal government, have no common law. . . . The common law, therefore, of one state, is not the common law of another; but the common law of England, is the law of each state, so far as each state has adopted it") 1 W. Blackstone, *supra* note 22, at *105 ("the common law of England, as such, has no allowance or authority" in the American colonies). *See generally* M. Horwitz, The Transformation of American Law, 1780–1860, at 11–30 (1977).

rially and extensively different. There was no common legislature, by which a common will could be expressed in the form of a law."[86] Madison concluded that "no support or color can be drawn . . . for the doctrine that the common law is binding on these states as one society,"[87] an arrangement left unaffected by article II of the Articles of Confederation.[88]

After the Constitution was transmitted to the states on September 28, 1787, the states held conventions to which specially elected delegates were sent in order to decide on ratification. Several state ratification conventions produced declarations of rights and proposed amendments to incorporate into the Constitution.[89] At the conventions, the antifederalists pointed out that article II of the Articles of Confederation had embraced individual as well as state rights, and argued that a bill of rights was necessary to guarantee individuals the same protection under the proposed Constitution. The antifederalists were concerned to establish, by specific enumeration, certain important rights as constitutionally protected, so that the federal government could not abridge those rights. They also wished to avoid the possibility that other rights under state law would be rendered a nullity under the proposed Constitution, and therefore sought to obtain a declaration that defeated such a construction. At the North Carolina convention, delegate Samuel Spencer, favoring a bill of rights, argued:

> [A]s the government was not to operate against states, but against individuals, the rights of individuals ought to be properly secured.

[86]4 J. Elliot, *supra* note 27, at 561–62. In Massachusetts, for example, the legislature possessed "full power and authority . . . to make, ordain, and establish, all manner of . . . orders, laws, statutes, and ordinances, . . . as they shall judge to be for the good and welfare of this commonwealth." Mass. Const., pt. II, ch. 1, § 1, art. 4, *reprinted* in 3 Federal and State Constitutions, *supra* note 23, at 1894. *See* The Federalist No. 84, at 578 (A. Hamilton) (J. Cooke ed. 1961) (discussing similar provision in New York constitution). *See generally* W. Nelson, Americanization of the Common Law (1975).

[87]4 J. Elliot, *supra* note 27, at 562. A limited federal common law was recognized by the Supreme Court in Swift v. Tyson, 41 U.S. (16 Pet.) 1, 19 (1842) ("general principles and doctrines of commercial jurisprudence"), which was overruled by Erie R. R. v. Tompkins, 304 U.S. 64, 78 (1938) ("There is no federal general common law.").

[88]*See* 4 J. Elliot, *supra* note 27, at 563.

[89]A total of eight states submitted proposed amendments: Massachusetts, New Hampshire, New York, North Carolina, Pennsylvania, Rhode Island, South Carolina, and Virginia. *See* 1 J. Elliot, *supra* note 27, at 319–37; 2 *id.* at 545–46.

In order to constitute this security, it appears to me there ought to be such a clause in the Constitution as there was in the Confederation, expressly declaring, that every power, jurisdiction, and right, which are not given up by it, remain in the states. Such a clause would render a bill of rights unnecessary. But as there is no such clause, I contend that there should be a bill of rights, ascertaining and securing the great rights of the states and people[90]

Patrick Henry and George Mason, leading the antifederalists at the Virginia ratifying convention, shared Spencer's understanding. Henry declared "a bill of rights indispensably necessary; [and] that a general positive provision should be inserted in the new system, securing to the states and the people every right which was not conceded to the general government."[91] A bill of rights would include "all the rights which are dear to human nature—trial by jury, the liberty of religion and the press, &c."[92] These rights are found, said Henry, in the state constitutions.[93]

Two days after Henry spoke, on June 14, 1788, George Mason, who had refused to sign the Constitution and carried the fight for a bill of rights to Richmond, urged an amendment similar to article II, which had "never been complained of, but approved by all." Mason asked, "Why not, then, have a similar clause in this Constitution, in which it is the more indispensably necessary than in the Confederation, because of the great augmentation of power

[90]4 id. at 163. Cf. 2 id. at 131 (remarks of Samuel Adams at the Massachusetts Convention).

[91]3 id. at 150.

[92]Id. at 314.

[93]Henry remarked:

It is alleged that several states, in the formation of their government, omitted a bill of rights. To this I answer, that they had the substance of a bill of rights contained in their constitutions, which is the same thing. I believe that Connecticut has preserved it, by her Constitution, her royal charter, which clearly defines and secures the great rights of mankind—secures to us the great, important rights of humanity; and I care not in what form it is done.

Id. at 317. Madison would later ask his associates in Congress to approve a bill of rights by urging them to "expressly declare the great rights of mankind secured under this constitution." 1 Annals, supra note 55, at 449. In 1787, six states lacked a separate "declaration of rights," the formal title for a bill of rights: Connecticut, Georgia, New Jersey, New York, Rhode Island, and South Carolina. These states nevertheless incorporated similar guarantees into their constitutions or relied on their colonial charters. See J. Main, The Sovereign States, 1775–1783, at 143–85 (1973).

vested in the former?"[94] Mason later in the debate reportedly "still thought that there ought to be some express declaration in the Constitution, asserting that rights not given to the general government were retained by the states."[95] Mason feared that without a clause resembling article II in the Constitution, "many valuable and important rights would be concluded to be given up by implication."[96] It was necessary, said Mason, to reserve "certain great and important rights, which the people [of Virginia], by their bill of rights, declared to be paramount to the power of the legislature."[97]

Henry picked up Mason's argument and proceeded to identity the "great" and "unalienable" rights as those contained in the common law and state bill of rights.[98] "If you intend to reserve your unalienable rights," Henry argued, "you must have the most express stipulation; for, if implication be allowed, you are ousted of those rights."[99] Like Mason, he took the plausible position that, because article II had expressly provided for retention of rights by the states,[100] the absence of a similar provision in the new Constitution, "by a natural and unavoidable implication," surrendered those rights to the general government.[101] Henry expounded on the necessity for a bill of rights that would continue the protection afforded by the English common law:

> You have a bill of rights to defend you against the state government, which is bereaved of all power, and yet you have none against Congress, though in full and exclusive possession of all

[94]3 J. Elliot, *supra* note 27, at 442.

[95]*Id.* at 444.

[96]*Id.*

[97]*Id.*

[98]*See id.* at 445–49.

[99]*Id.* at 445.

[100]As noted previously, the rights retained by the states under the Articles of Confederation included not only rights of the state governments as against the central government or against each other, but also the individual liberties preserved by state law. This is apparent from the speeches of George Mason and Patrick Henry at the Virginia convention. *See supra* text accompanying notes 91–97. At that convention, William Grayson questioned "whether rights not given up were reserved. A majority of the states, he observed, had expressly reserved certain important rights by bills of rights, and that in the Confederation there was a clause declaring expressly that every power and right not given up was retained by the states." 3 J. Elliot, *supra* note 27, at 449. *See also infra* note 148.

[101]*See* 3 J. Elliot, *supra* note 27, at 445–46.

power! . . . What barriers have you to oppose to this most strong, energetic government? To that government you have nothing to oppose. All your defence is given up. This is a real, actual defect. It must strike the mind of every gentleman. When our government was first instituted in Virginia, we declared the common law of England to be in force.[102]

"That paper," said Henry, meaning the proposed Constitution, "ought to have declared the common law in force."[103] Unmistakably identifying rights retained by the people with state bills of rights and the common law, Henry concluded: "If you will, like the Virginian government, give them knowledge of the extent of the rights retained by the people, and the powers of themselves, they will, if they be honest men, thank you for it."[104]

The retained rights envisioned by the framers, however, included not only those established by common law and statute as of the Constitution's adoption,[105] but also those to be subsequently established by state legislation. Consequently, the demand for explicit reenactment of the common law drew replies that shed light on the framers' decision not simply to declare in either the Constitution or the Bill of Rights that the common law, or even state law in general, remained in effect. George Nicholas and Edmund Randolph agreed that such a declaration would mean that the common law would be frozen as of the date of adoption and hence would be immune to any alteration that the state legislatures might deem appropriate."[106] Of course the common law "is not excluded," said Nicholas, "[b]ut now it can be changed or modified as the legislative body may find necessary for the community."[107] The common law, added Randolph, "ought not to be immutably fixed. . . . It would, in many respects, be destructive to republican principles, . . . [for instance,]

[102]Id. at 446.

[103]Id. at 447. In his pamphlet, Objections to this Constitution of Government, George Mason criticized the Constitution because "[t]here is no Declaration of Rights . . . [n]or are the people secured even in the enjoyment of the benefit of the common law." See 2 Records, supra note 21, at 637.

[104]See 3 J. Elliot, supra note 27, at 448. See also Henry's remarks, quoted supra note 27.

[105]Pursuant to article VII, the Constitution went into effect on June 21, 1788, when New Hampshire became the ninth state to ratify. 1 J. Elliot, supra note 27, at 325–27.

[106]See 3 J. Elliot, supra note 27, at 450–51 (Nicholas) & 469–70 (Randolph).

[107]Id. at 451.

the *writ of burning heretics* would have been revived by it."[108] As Rufus King had said at the Massachusetts convention several months earlier: "[I]f the present constitution of this state had been guarantied by the United States . . . , it must have precluded the state from making any alteration in it, should they see fit so to do."[109]

In his *Report on the Virginia Resolutions,* Madison squarely denied that the Constitution incorporated a federal common law. "If the common law had been understood to be a law of the United States, it is not possible to assign a satisfactory reason why it was not expressed in the enumeration."[110] Like Randolph, Madison argued that explicit enactment would have made the common law immune to reform. The entire common law, "with all its incongruities, barbarisms, and bloody maxims, would be inviolably saddled on the good people of the United States."[111] Further, "whether the common law be admitted as of legal or of constitutional obligation, it would confer on the judicial department a discretion little short of a legislative power."[112] Because the common law "relates to every subject of legislation, and would be paramount to the constitutions and laws of the states," the legislative sovereignty of the states would be reduced to nothing and replaced by a national, uniform,

---

[108]*Id.* at 469–70 (emphasis in original).

[109]2 *id.* at 101. See *supra* note 65 (repromulgation of state constitutions provision omitted from guarantee clause).

[110]4 J. Elliot, *supra* note 27, at 565. The term "Laws of the United States" designates federal law, as in U.S. Const. art. III, § 2, cl. 1 and *id.,* art. VI, cl. 2 (the supremacy clause). *See also* The Federalist No. 33, at 207 (A. Hamilton) (J. Cooke ed. 1961) ("laws of the Union"). State or common law, by contrast, is signified by "rights of the people," a phrase derived from English sources, especially the Bill of Rights of 1689, the full title of which is "An Act Declareing the Rights and Liberties of the Subject, and Settling the Succession of the Crowne," *reprinted in* T. Taswell-Langmead, English Constitutional History 449 (11th ed. 1960). The section in the 1689 Bill of Rights providing that "it is the right of the subjects to petition the King" (*id.* at 451) was restated a hundred years later in the first amendment's "right of the people . . . to petition the Government." U.S. Const. amend. I. In the Declaration of Independence, the indictment of the King for his "invasions on the rights of the people" alludes to the English statutory and common law as transplanted to the colonies: "depriving us in many cases, of the benefits of Trial by Jury." *See generally infra* text accompanying note 129; *infra* notes 134 & 155.

[111]4 J. Elliot, *supra* note 27, at 565.

[112]*Id.* at 566. That is to say, if the common law were deemed to have "a constitutional obligation, this power in the judges would be permanent and irremediable by the legislature. On the other supposition, the power would not expire until the legislature should have introduced a full system of statutory provisions." *Id.*

and immutable system of law.[113] Madison listed the problems besetting any effort to declare the common law as the national law of the United States:

> Is it to be the common law with or without the British statutes?
>
> . . . .
>
> If with these [statutory] amendments, what period is to be fixed for limiting the British authority over our laws?
>
> . . . .
>
> Is, again, regard to be had to the various changes in the common law made by the local codes of America?
>
> . . . .
>
> Is the law to be different in every state, as differently modified by its code; or are the modifications of any particular state to be applied to all?
>
> And on the latter supposition, which among the state codes forms the standard?[114]

"Questions of this sort," Madison added, "might be multiplied with as much ease as there would be difficulty in answering them."[115] These problems were precisely the sorts of difficulties noted by Hamilton, Washington, Iredell, Wilson, and Randolph in drafting a constitutional provision relating to jury trials in civil cases that would be equally well-tailored for each state.[116]

On June 25, 1788, Virginia ratified the Constitution and sent to Congress a set of proposed amendments, including one which stated that the rights and powers protected under state law and not yielded to Congress would be preserved under the new Constitution, and another which provided that the enumerated limitations on the powers of Congress did not imply that Congress kept all other powers not expressly denied it:

---

[113]*Id.*

[114]*Id.* at 565.

[115]*Id.*

[116]*See supra* notes 77, 79 & 81; *supra* text accompanying note 81. This is why it was reckoned impossible to specify in writing all the individual rights currently in force: those rights are comprehended within the common law, which is different in each state and always changing. As Chief Justice Marshall said, "A constitution, to contain an accurate detail of all the subdivisions of which its great powers will admit, and of all the means by which they may be carried into execution, would partake of the prolixity of a legal code, and could scarcely be embraced by the human mind." McCulloch v. Maryland, 17 U.S. (4 Wheat.) 316, 407 (1819). *See also* The Federalist No. 84, at 579 (A. Hamilton) (J. Cooke ed. 1961).

1st. That each state in the Union shall respectively retain every power, jurisdiction, and right, which is not by this Constitution delegated to the Congress of the United States, or to the departments of the federal government.

17th. That those clauses which declare that Congress shall not exercise certain powers, be not interpreted, in any manner whatsoever, to extend the powers of Congress; but that they may be construed either as making exceptions to the specified powers where this shall be the case, or otherwise, as inserted merely for greater caution.[117]

The first proposed amendment was approved by the Virginia convention on the strength of the arguments by Henry and Mason for preserving the guarantees of article II of the Articles of Confederation in the new Constitution. The seventeenth proposed amendment was passed to ensure that the rule of construction against enhancement of congressional power, as expounded by Hamilton in *The Federalist No. 83*,[118] would in fact be controlling.[119]

New York ratified the Constitution a month after Virginia and also included several proposed amendments, prefaced by a declaration combining the substance of the first and seventeenth Virginia

[117]3 J. Elliot, *supra* note 27, at 659 & 661. The amendments adopted by the Virginia convention were almost identical to those proposed at the convention by Patrick Henry, who moved for the circulation of his amendments to the other ratification conventions. *See id.* at 593. North Carolina's 1st and 18th proposed amendments reproduced Virginia's 1st and 17th verbatim, with minor alterations in punctuation. *See* 4 *id.* at 244 & 246.

[118]*See supra* note 76.

[119]Justice Joseph Story, appointed to the Supreme Court by President Madison, wrote:

[The ninth amendment] was manifestly introduced to prevent any perverse or ingenious misapplication of the well-known maxim, that an affirmation in particular cases implies a negation in all others; and, *e converso*, that a negation in particular cases implies an affirmation in all others. . . . The amendment was undoubtedly suggested by the reasoning of the Federalist on the subject of a general bill of rights.

2 J. Story, *supra* note 5, at 651 (5th ed. 1891) (footnotes omitted). *See* 1 Annals, *supra* note 55, at 456 (remarks of Rep. Madison); *see also id.* at 442 (remarks of Rep. Jackson, espousing the repudiated maxim).

amendments.[120] Pennsylvania's first proposed amendment, submitted in September 1788, likewise borrowed from article II of the Articles of Confederation. Instead, however, of reciting the "power, jurisdiction, and right" triad of that article, the Harrisburg convention expanded the "right" component to disclose the bifurcated nature of the rights retained by the states:

> That Congress shall not exercise any powers whatever, but such as are expressly given to that body by the Constitution of the United States: nor shall any authority, power, or jurisdiction, be assumed or exercised by the executive or judiciary departments of the Union, under color or pretence of construction or fiction; but all the rights of sovereignty, which are not by the said Constitution expressly and plainly vested in the Congress, shall be deemed to remain with, and shall be exercised by, the several states in the Union, according to their respective constitutions; and that *every reserve of the rights of individuals, made by the several constitutions of the states in the Union, to the citizens and inhabitants of each state respectively, shall remain inviolate,* except so far as they are expressly and manifestly yielded or narrowed by the national Constitution.[121]

Sensing that ratification would hinge on enacting a bill of rights, distressed at the prospect of another constitutional convention already rumored,[122] and spurred by Jefferson's persistent exhortations to

---

[120]The declaration read, in pertinent part:
That the powers of government may be reassumed by the people whensoever it shall become necessary to their happiness; that every power, jurisdiction, and right, which is not by the said Constitution clearly delegated to the Congress of the United States, or the departments of the government thereof, remains to the people of the several states, or to their respective state governments, to whom they may have granted the same; and that those clauses in the said Constitution, which declare that Congress shall not have or exercise certain powers, do not imply that Congress is entitled to any powers not given by the said Constitution; but such clauses are to be construed either as exceptions to certain specified powers, or as inserted merely for greater caution.
1 J. Elliot, *supra* note 27, at 327. Rhode Island's declaration of rights, submitted with that state's ratification in 1790, contained a nearly identical provision. *See* 1 *id.* at 334 & 336.

[121]2 *id.* at 545 (emphasis added).

[122]"The friends of the Constitution," Madison wrote to Jefferson, ". . . are generally agreed that the System should be revised. But they wish the revisal to be carried no farther than to supply additional guards for liberty, . . . and are fixed in opposition to the risk of another Convention, whilst the purpose can be as well

append a bill of rights,[123] Madison became convinced of the need "to give satisfaction to the doubting part of our fellow-citizens"[124] and, after ratification of the Constitution, personally shepherded his proposed amendments through a somewhat indifferent House of Representatives.[125] As the "Father of the Constitution"—an honor

---

answered, by the other mode provided for introducing amendments." Letter from James Madison to Thomas Jefferson (Dec. 8, 1788), *reprinted* in 14 The Papers of Thomas Jefferson, *supra* note 25, at 340. *See* 1 Annals, *supra* note 55, at 450; R. Ketcham, James Madison 234 (1971); Letter from James Madison to Thomas Jefferson (Aug. 23, 1788), *reprinted* in 13 The Papers of Thomas Jefferson, *supra* note 25, at 540. The New York, North Carolina, and Pennsylvania conventions had recommended a second constitutional convention, as had the Rhode Island and Virginia legislatures. *See, e.g.,* 1 Annals, *supra* note 55, at 446; 2 J. Elliot, *supra* note 27, at 544; Smith, *The Movement Towards a Second Constitutional Convention* in 1788, in Essays in the Constitutional History of the United States in the Formative Period 1775–1789, at 46 (J. Jameson ed. 1889).

[123]Madison had protested to Jefferson that "there is great reason to fear that a positive declaration of some of the most essential rights could not be obtained in the requisite latitude." Letter from James Madison to Thomas Jefferson (Oct. 17, 1788), *reprinted* in 5 Writings, *supra* note 55, at 271. By letter from Paris came Jefferson's answer: "Half a loaf is better than no bread. If we cannot secure all our rights, let us secure what we can." Letter from Thomas Jefferson to James Madison (March 15, 1789), *reprinted* in 14 The Papers of Thomas Jefferson, *supra* note 25, at 660. Jefferson's letter also contained what seems to have been the clinching argument for Madison: "The legal check which [a declaration of rights] puts into the hands of the judiciary." *Id.* at 659. A few months later, Madison argued in Congress that "independent tribunals of justice will consider themselves in a peculiar manner the guardians of those rights." 1 Annals, *supra* note 55, at 457. The major correspondence between Madison and Jefferson is reprinted in 1 The Bill of Rights: A Documentary History, *supra* note 24, at 592–623. *See* D. Malone, Jefferson and the Rights of Man 175–77 (1951); G. Wood, *supra* note 20, at 542–43. Washington urged Congress in his first inaugural address to move quickly to propose amendments attesting "a reverence for the characteristic rights of freemen and a regard for the public harmony." The First Inaugural Address (April 30, 1789), *reprinted* in 30 The Writings of George Washington, *supra* note 62, at 295. Although Madison's apprehension as to securing rights of satisfactory amplitude could suggest the ninth amendment was intended to justify eventual inclusion of other rights, necessarily federal on this theory, for which he could not at the moment obtain support, the historical record is devoid of such an expressed purpose. *See* Abrams, *supra* note 12, at 1035; Kelly, *supra* note 12, at 153; Uncertain Renaissance, *supra* note 12, at 824–25.

[124]1 Annals, *supra* note 55, at 449. By proposing the amendments Madison fulfilled a pledge he had made at the Virginia convention to press for a bill of rights, 3 J. Elliot, *supra* note 27, at 627, a promise which gained the necessary votes at Richmond for ratification.

[125]*Id.* One member of the House claimed that his constituents "would not value [the proposed amendments] more than a pinch of snuff; they went to secure rights

he stoutly disclaimed[126]—Madison was assigned the task of producing a set of amendments based on the proposals submitted by the state conventions.[127]

In the speech he delivered to the House of Representatives on June 8, 1789, Madison explained and defended his proposed amendments[128] by referring to the widespread apprehension that the rights enjoyed and protected under state and common law would be lost under the new Constitution:

> I believe that the great mass of the people who opposed [the Constitution], disliked it because it did not contain effectual provisions against encroachments on particular rights, and those safeguards which they have been long accustomed to have interposed between them and the magistrate who exercises the sovereign power.[129]

Madison gave short shrift to the notion that unwritten "natural" law made enumeration of retained rights unnecessary:

> It would be a sufficient answer to say, that this objection lies against such provisions under the State Governments, as well as under the General Government; and there are, I believe, but few gentlemen who are inclined to push their theory so far as to say that a declaration of rights in those cases is either ineffectual or improper.[130]

Madison next rejected the argument that a federal bill of rights was unnecessary because the state bills of rights were sufficient to

---

never in danger." *Id.* at 805 (remarks of Rep. Livermore). First elected in 1788, Madison served four terms in the House of Representatives. R. Ketcham, *supra* note 122, at 276–77.

[126]"You give me a credit to which I have no claim, in calling me '*the* writer of the Constitution of the U.S.' This was not, like the fabled Goddess of Wisdom, the offspring of a single brain. It ought to be regarded as the work of many heads & many hands." Letter from James Madison to William Cogswell (March 10, 1834), *reprinted* in 9 Writings, *supra* note 55, at 533.

[127]Madison had been present at the Virginia convention as a delegate. *See, e.g.*, 3 J. Elliot, *supra* note 27, at 616–20 & 626–27; R. Ketcham, *supra* note 122, at 235 & 249–64 (1971).

[128]*See* 1 Annals, *supra* note 55, at 448–59, *reprinted* in B. Patterson, *supra* note 6, at 107–18; 2 The Bill of Rights: A Documentary History, *supra* note 24, at 1023–34; The Mind of the Founder 161–75 (M. Meyers ed. 1981): 5 Writings, *supra* note 55, at 370–89.

[129]1 Annals, *supra* note note 55, at 450.

[130]*Id.* at 455.

protect the rights of the people. The importance of the rights at issue mandated additional security: "some states have no bills of rights, there are others provided with very defective ones, and there are others whose bills of rights are not only defective, but absolutely improper; [and do not secure some rights] in the full extent which republican principles would require."[131]

In order to guarantee that rights protected under state law would not be construed as supplanted by federal law merely because they were not expressly listed in the Constitution, Madison offered the final clause of his fourth resolution, which became the ninth amendment. Madison's draft of the ninth amendment borrowed heavily from the first proposed Virginia amendment in its first half and the seventeenth Virginia amendment in its second half:

> The exceptions here or elsewhere in the constitution, made in favor of particular rights, shall not be so construed as to diminish the just importance of other rights retained by the people, or as to enlarge the powers delegated by the constitution; but either as actual limitations of such powers, or as inserted merely for greater caution.[132]

Madison explained the need for this amendment by adducing the early federalist argument that specification of some rights "would disparage those rights which were not placed in that enumeration; and it might follow, by implication, that those rights which were not singled out, were intended to be assigned into the hands of the

---

[131]*Id.* at 456. This is why a federal bill of rights, protecting what Madison called "the most essential rights" (Letter from James Madison to Thomas Jefferson (Oct. 17, 1788), quoted *supra* note 123), was needed in addition to the blanket preservation of state laws afforded by the ninth amendment. *See also* 3 J. Elliot, *supra* note 27, at 626 ("our essential rights").

[132]1 Annals, *supra* note 55, at 452. The ninth amendment's descent from the 1st Virginia proposed amendment (and therefore from article II of the Articles of Confederation), as well as from the usually acknowledged 17th Virginia amendment, has not been noted in previous studies of the ninth, probably on the assumption that article II refers exclusively to rights pertaining more particularly to the state governments than to individual citizens. For sources tracing the ninth amendment's antecedents to the 17th, but omitting the 1st Virginia proposed amendment, see Dunbar, *supra* note 6, at 631–32; Rogge, *supra* note 6, at 789; Note, *supra* note 12, at 104; Uncertain Renaissance, *supra* note 12, at 820 n.25. The connection with the 1st Virginia amendment is nonetheless confirmed by a letter of Madison's. *See infra* accompanying note 138.

General Government, and were consequently insecure."[133] Madison called this objection "one of the most plausible arguments I have ever heard urged against the admission of a bill of rights into this system,"[134] but replied that such an inference "may be guarded against" by the insertion of his fourth resolution.[135] Madison believed, moreover, that the argument respecting an implicit surrender of rights was not a threat unique to a federal bill of rights. In the notes Madison prepared for his House speech, he made the point, left out of the speech, that if a federal bill of rights may be construed to disparage other, unenumerated rights, the same objection may be raised against state bills of rights that omit important safeguards.[136]

Madison's explanation of the ninth amendment's protective role nevertheless did not satisfy Edmund Randolph, Governor of Virginia and reluctant supporter of the Constitution at his state's convention, who wrote to Washington that the ninth amendment "is exceptionable to me, in giving a handle to say, that Congress have endeavored to administer an opiate, by an alteration, which is merely plausible."[137] In his own letter to Washington—demonstrating, incidentally, that the ninth amendment was indeed based on the first Virginia proposed amendment as well as on the seventeenth—Madison recounted Randolph's opposition to the measure when the proposed amendments came up for ratification by the Virginia legislature:

> His principal objection was pointed agst. the 'retained,' in the eleventh proposed amendment [the ninth amendment], and his argument if I understood it was applied in this manner—that as the rights declared in the first ten of the proposed amendments were not all that a free people would require the exercise of, and that as there was no criterion by which it could be determined whether any other particular right was retained or not, it would be more safe and more consistent with the spirit of the 1st & 17th amendts. proposed by Virginia that this reservation agst constructive power, should operate rather as a provision agst extending

---

[133] 1 Annals, *supra* note 55, at 456.

[134] *Id.* Significantly, Madison identified the rights contained in state bills of rights with the "rights of the people." *Id.*

[135] *Id.*

[136] *See* 5 Writings, *supra* note 55, at 390 n.1.

[137] Letter from Edmund Randolph to George Washington (Dec. 6, 1789), *reprinted in* 4 J. Sparks, Correspondence of the American Revolution 298 (1853). *See generally* Dunbar, *supra* note 6, at 633–35; Rogge, *supra* note 6, at 792–93.

the powers of Congs. by their own authority, than a protection to rights reducible to no definite certainty.[138]

Randolph, in order to guard against the nullification of state law, thus preferred an amendment drafted as a limitation on the powers of the central government, rather than as a reservation of individual rights. Madison, however, professed to "see not the force of this distinction,"[139] on the theory that individual rights and governmental powers composed two mutually exclusive and collectively exhaustive categories. Consequently, "it would seem to be the same thing, whether [rights] be secured by declaring that they shall not be abridged, or that [powers] shall not be extended."[140]

Madison's distinction between powers and rights assumed a sharply definable boundary between governmental and individual discretion. For Madison, a power was a delegated capacity allowing the government to perform certain kinds of acts.[141] With rights, said Madison, "the great object in view is to limit and qualify the powers of Government, by excepting out of the grant of power those cases in which the Government ought not to act, or to act only in a particular mode."[142] To the extent, however, that a government can

[138]Letter from James Madison to George Washington (Dec. 5, 1789), *reprinted* in 5 Writings, *supra* note 55, at 431 (emphasis in original).

[139]*Id*. At this juncture, Madison added: "If the [Virginia House of Delegates] should agree to the Resolution for rejecting the two last [amendments], I am of opinion it will bring the whole into hazard again, as some who have been decided friends to the ten first think it would be unwise to adopt them without the 11th & 12th." *Id*. This was Madison's own view. *See* Letter from James Madison to Thomas Jefferson (Oct. 17, 1788), quoted *supra* note 69.

[140]5 Writings, *supra* note 55, at 432. Reprising one of the federalists' anti-amendment arguments in the House, Madison said "the constitution is a bill of powers, the great residuum being the rights of the people." 1 Annals, *supra* note 55, at 455. *See id*. at 454.

[141]One of Madison's proposed amendments provided that "[t]he powers delegated by this constitution are appropriated to the departments [legislative, executive, and judicial] to which they are respectively distributed. . . ." 1 Annals, *supra* note 55, at 453. The amendment drew on similar provisions in the 1774 resolutions (1 Journals, *supra* note 25, at 70), and the Virginia constitution of 1776. 7 Federal and State Constitutions, *supra* note 23, at 3814–15.

[142]1 Annals, *supra* note 55, at 454. Madison "seems to have thought of rights under two main headings. One, as stipulating agreed upon methods by which in particular cases the government shall exercise its powers [e.g., trial by jury]. . . . Secondly, he thought of another class of rights as declarations of areas totally outside the province of government." Dunbar, *supra* note 6, at 635. *See* Rogge, *supra* note 6, at 788 n.5;

exercise powers beyond the express and implied powers allotted to it, thus blurring the demarcation of powers and rights,[143] Randolph's criticism had merit. Madison, distrustful of attempts to weaken the federal government, had in any event conceded the issue the previous year by writing that "in case the Congress shall misconstrue [the necessary and proper clause], and exercise powers not warranted by its true meaning[,] . . . the people . . . can by the election of more faithful representatives, annul the acts of the usurpers."[144]

Notwithstanding Randolph's misgivings, the House select committee (the "Committee of Eleven") formed to review the proposed amendments[145] revised and approved the ninth amendment. On July 28, 1789, the select committee, which consisted of one representative from each state then in the Union and included Madi-

---

Uncertain Renaissance, *supra* note 12, at 818–19 n.20. Although Madison's contemporaries did not always strictly observe the distinction (*see, e.g., supra* text accompanying note 69 (bill of rights as enumeration of powers)), it is Madison's consistent usage, which eliminated the ambiguous concept of state rights as referring to both governmental and personal rights, replacing it with the clearer power/right dichotomy, that was adopted with the Bill of Rights. To say that the ninth amendment was "enacted to protect state *powers* against federal invasion" (*Griswold*, 381 U.S. at 520 (Black, J., dissenting) (emphasis added)), is to employ terminology incompatible with Madison's usage and make the ninth amendment indistinguishable from the tenth. *See infra* text accompanying notes 168–70. Justice Black was correct, however, in asserting that the ninth amendment protects rights under state law from "federal invasion." *Griswold*, 381 U.S. at 520 (Black, J., dissenting).

[143]Wrote one antifederalist: "I say, that a declaration of those inherent and political rights ought to be made in a *Bill of Rights*, that the people may never lose their liberties by construction. If the liberty of the press be an inherent political right, let it be so declared, that no despot however great shall *dare to gain say it*." A Confederationist, Pennsylvania Herald and General Advertiser (Oct. 27, 1787), *reprinted in* 1 H. Storing, *supra* note 73, at 64–65 (emphasis in original). *See generally* Holmes v. Jennison, 39 U.S. (14 Pet.) 540, 557 (1840) (argument for plaintiff); Dunbar, *supra* note 6, at 633–35; Rogge, *supra* note 6, at 792–93.

[144]The Federalist No. 44, at 305 (J. Madison) (J. Cooke ed. 1961). Madison did, however, take issue with Chief Justice Marshall's generous reading of the clause in McCulloch v. Maryland, 17 U.S. (4 Wheat.) 316, 421 (1819) ("Let the end be legitimate, . . . and all means which are appropriate, . . . which are not prohibited, but consist with the letter and spirit of the constitution are constitutional."). Letter from James Madison to Spencer Roane (Sept. 2, 1819), *reprinted in* 8 Writings, *supra* note 55, at 448–52 ("Does not the Court also relinquish by this doctrine all controul on the Legislative exercise of unconstitutional power?" *Id.* at 449.).

[145]*See* 1 Annals, *supra* note 55, at 690–91 & 803.

son,[146] reported the amendments back to the House.[147] The sole recorded debate in the House concerning the ninth amendment is the following:

> The eighth clause of the fourth proposition was taken up, which was, "The enumeration in this Constitution of certain rights shall not be construed to deny or disparage others retained by the people."
>
> Mr. *Gerry* said, it ought to be "deny or impair," for the word "disparage" was not of plain import; he therefore moved to make that alteration, but not being seconded, the question was taken on the clause, and it passed in the affirmative.[148]

Before its passage by a House Committee of the whole on August 24,[149] the phrase "the Constitution" was substituted for "this Constitution," and a comma was added. During Senate consideration of the amendments, from September 2 through 9, the second comma was added, so that the amendment received its final form in the joint resolution of Congress proposing a bill of rights for ratification by the state legislatures.[150]

[146]*Id.*

[147]*See id.* at 699.

[148]*Id.* at 783 (proceedings of August 17, 1789). In the original printed committee report the first letter of "Constitution" is capitalized, although this feature is absent from the Annals. One other pertinent comment is recorded:

> Mr. *Hartley* observed, that it had been asserted in the convention of Pennsylvania, by the friends of the constitution, that all the rights and powers that were not given to the Government were retained by the States and the people thereof. This was also his own opinion; but as four or five States had required to be secured in those rights by an express declaration in the constitution, he was disposed to gratify them; he thought every thing that was not incompatible with the general good ought to be granted, if it would tend to obtain the confidence of the people in the Government; and, upon the whole, he thought these words were as necessary to be inserted in the declaration of rights as most in the clause.

Id. at 760.

[149]*See id.* at 808–09. The House approved the amendments as revised by the Senate on September 24. *See id.* at 948.

[150]*See id.* at 90. There is no record of deliberations concerning the ninth amendment in the Senate, which conducted its sessions in secret until 1793. G. Haynes, The Senate of the United States, Its History and Practice 44 (1938). In the summary of the Senate proceedings, there is a notation that while considering article 15 (which became the ninth amendment), the Senate rejected another proposed amendment on the subject of taxation. *See* 1 Annals of Congress, *supra* note 55, at 78 (proceedings of September 7, 1789). The Senate approved the amendments, as revised, on September 9. *See id.* at 80.

Of the 186 proposed amendments submitted by the states to the first Federal Congress,[151] the House approved 17 articles,[152] including article 15, which was Madison's original version of the ninth amendment in his fourth resolution. On September 25, 1789, the House and Senate by joint resolution concurred on twelve amendments, of which Madison's resolution was article 11, to be presented to the states.[153] The first two articles[154] failed to win the approval of the states, and article 11 became the ninth amendment with Virginia's assent on December 15, 1791, when the Bill of Rights was ratified by the necessary three-fourths of the states.

III. The Other Rights Retained by the People

By the provision which ultimately became the ninth amendment, Madison intended to assure the antifederalists that the Constitution would leave intact those individual rights contained in the state constitutions, statutes, and common law. All of the "certain rights" enumerated in the Constitution and Bill of Rights were derived from state law,[155] and so the "others," that is, "those rights which

---

[151]See Ringold, supra note 18, at 4. A number of these amendments were duplications. See, e.g., supra notes 117 & 120; supra text accompanying notes 120–21.

[152]See 1 Annals, supra note 55, at 808–09.

[153]See id. at 90.

[154]These articles provided for a specific ratio of representation in the House of Representatives according to population and prohibited Congress from making a change in its members' salary that would be effective before the next election of representatives. See id. at 451; 1 J. Elliot, supra note 27, at 338; H. Taylor, The Origin and Growth of the American Constitution 228 (1911).

[155]See supra text accompanying note 129. The rights set out in the main body of the Constitution, e.g., prohibitions against suspending habeas corpus and against bills of attainder and ex post facto laws (see U.S. Const. art. I, § 9, cls. 2–3), are rooted in the common law. See The Federalist No. 84, at 576–77 (A. Hamilton) (J. Cooke ed. 1961). Chief Justice Taft wrote: "The language of the Constitution cannot be interpreted safely except by reference to the common law and to British institutions as they were when the instrument was framed and adopted." Ex parte Grossman, 267 U.S. 87, 108–09 (1925). See also United States v. Wong Kim Ark, 169 U.S. 649, 654 (1898); Robertson v. Baldwin, 165 U.S. 275, 281 (1897) (Bill of Rights was "not intended to lay down any novel principles of government, but simply to embody certain guaranties and immunities which we had inherited from our English ancestors"); Moore v. United States, 91 U.S. 270, 274 (1875); Murray's Lessee v. Hoboken Land & Improvement Co., 59 U.S. (18 How.) 272, 276–77 (1855) (content of fifth amendment due process ascertained from pre–1776 English common law and statutory sources). The specific English common law and statutory precursors of the

were not singled out" for enumeration were those state laws not selected for inclusion.[156] Appropriately, Madison's discussion of the ninth amendment in his House speech immediately followed his analysis of the protection afforded by state bills of rights.[157]

The meaning of the ninth amendment is therefore entwined with the meaning of the Bill of Rights as a whole, the amendment's purpose is to preserve individual rights that had long been protected by the states. The Bill of Rights preserved those rights in two ways: by offering explicit federal protection to the rights expressly included and—in the single case of the ninth amendment—by shielding the rights not listed against the inference that they were repealed or otherwise adversely affected by ratification of the Constitution. If natural law is embedded in the ninth amendment, it is because at the time the ninth was adopted natural law was an integral part of justiciable state law.[158] Both Hamilton and Madison

---

Bill of Rights are traced in H. Taylor, *supra* note 154, at 230–43. Madison had attempted to win over the New York antifederalists by demonstrating the similarities in governmental structure between the proposed federal Constitution and the state constitutions. *See* The Federalist No. 39, at 250, 252–53; *id.* No. 57, at 389–90; *id.* No. 63, at 429–30 (J. Madison) (J. Cooke ed. 1961). *See also* 2 J. Elliot, *supra* note 27, at 126–28 (James Bowdoin's arguments for the Constitution at the Massachusetts convention).

[156]Against this conclusion may be cited the comment that "the Bill of Rights presumes the existence of a substantial body of rights not specifically enumerated but easily perceived in the broad concept of liberty and so numerous and so obvious as to preclude listing them." L. Tribe, *supra* note 18, at 570. *See also* 2 J. Story, Commentaries on the Constitution of the United States 626–27 & 651 (5th ed. 1891). This need not suggest, however, that this body of rights must be unwritten, federal rights.

[157]*See supra* text accompanying notes 131–35.

[158]This is evident from one of James Wilson's Philadelphia law lectures delivered in 1790–91, entitled "Of the Natural Rights of Individuals," in 2 The Works of the Honourable James Wilson, L.L.D. 453 (B. Wilson ed. 1804) (Lockean exposition of the role of civil government in protecting natural rights, with reference exclusively and extensively to the provisions of the common law and none at all to the ninth amendment). From the presence of natural law elements, one commentator concluded:

A right "retained" by the people [via the ninth amendment] is not embodied in the Constitution, and a suit brought on such a right does not "arise" thereunder [for purposes of federal jurisdiction]. . . . With Leslie Dunbar, I would hold that the ninth amendment "is an affirmation that rights exist independently of government, that they constitute an area of no-power."

Berger, *supra* note 18, at 9 (quoting Dunbar, *supra* note 6, at 641). *See also* Redlich, *supra* note 6, at 807. Such a conclusion flies in the face of the ninth amendment's

are clear that unenumerated rights refer to the laws of the several states, not to anterior, transcendent federal norms.[159] Ninth amendment rights, therefore, because they are state rather than federal in character, cannot form a basis for holding acts of Congress unconstitutional.[160] Nor is it logically possible to "incorporate" the ninth

---

admonition not to "deny or disparage" those other rights; contrary to this interpretation, the lack of federal cognizance does not mean that those rights are totally unenforceable at law. See Berger, *supra* note 18, at 9 n.50 (quoting Dunbar, *supra* note 6, at 643 (enumeration is the criterion for determining rights judicially enforceable as positive law)). Rather, since the intent of the ninth was to keep state rights intact, such rights are still part of state law and to be protected by the courts. See *supra* text accompanying notes 77 & 79. Elbridge Gerry's recommended substitution of "impair" for "disparage" (*supra* text accompanying note 148) may well have been intended to stress that the amendment's effect was legal, instead of merely hortatory or rhetorical.

It has been aptly observed that if the ninth amendment embodied natural law exclusively, the amendment presumably would have been cited in such expositions of natural law doctrine as Loan Ass'n v. Topeka, 87 U.S. (20 Wall.) 655, 662–63 (1874); Slaughter-House Cases, 83 U.S. (16 Wall.) 36, 76–80 (1872); and Calder v. Bull, 3 U.S. (3 Dall.) 386, 387–89 & 399 (1798). Dunbar, *supra* note 6, at 640 n.47. Other cases that could have cited the ninth amendment in such a context include Bradwell v. Illinois, 83 U.S. (16 Wall.) 130, 141–42 (1872) (Bradley, J., concurring); Ogden v. Saunders, 25 U.S. (12 Wheat.) 213, 345–48 (1827) (Marshall, C.J., dissenting); Terrett v. Taylor, 13 U.S. (9 Cranch) 43, 51 (1815) (Story, J.); Fletcher v. Peck, 10 U.S. (6 Cranch) 87, 143 (1810) (Johnson, J., concurring).

[159]See *supra* text accompanying notes 81 (Hamilton) & 85–88 (Madison); see also *supra* note 81 (Hamilton and James Wilson). It is therefore insignificant that Madison made no reference to the ninth amendment in his Report on the Virginia Resolutions, *supra* note 83. See Dunbar, *supra* note 6, at 635–37 & 637 n.38; Rogge, *supra* note 6, at 794–95. In the Report Madison denied the constitutionality of the Sedition Act, which prohibited the writing or publication of "any false, scandalous and malicious writing or writings against the government of the United States." 1 Stat. 596 (1798). Madison addressed the contention that under the necessary and proper clause the express power of Congress to "suppress Insurrections," U.S. Const. art. I, § 8, cl. 15, could be construed to "imply a power to prevent insurrections, by punishing whatever may lead or tend to them." 4 J. Elliot, *supra* note 27, at 568. The right Madison saw threatened was freedom of the press (*id.* at 569–73), and he accordingly dealt with the first amendment. The ninth would have been irrelevant to his thesis.

[160]See U.S. Const. art. VI, cl. 2 (the supremacy clause). In any event, Hamilton's rejection of the proposal stating that "trial by jury shall be as heretofore" as "destitute of a precise meaning" (The Federalist No. 83, at 567 (A. Hamilton) (J. Cooke ed. 1961)), suggests that the ninth amendment's similar catch-all phraseology would have rendered it equally vague and hence unavailable as a check on Congress. See *supra* text accompanying note 81. It may well be counterdemocratic to strike down a statute on the basis of a constitutional text so devoid of content. See Cahn, *The Parchment Barriers,* 32 Am. Scholar 21 (1962–63), *reprinted in* Confronting Injustice

amendment through the fourteenth to apply as a prohibition against the states,[161] because the ninth amendment was designed not to circumscribe but to protect the enactments of the states.

Finally, the ninth amendment is not redundant with the tenth amendment.[162] Certainly, both amendments were aimed at quelling fears of federal encroachment on state prerogatives.[163] Like the ninth amendment, which was "inserted merely for greater caution,"[164] the tenth, said Madison when he introduced it, "may be deemed unnecessary; but there can be no harm in making such a

---

104 (L. Cahn ed. 1962). *But see* United Pub. Workers v. Mitchell, 330 U.S. 75, 94–96 (1947) (right to political activity without congressional interference implicates first, ninth, and tenth amendments); Rogge, *supra* note 6, at 793 (framers intended ninth to be used by federal judiciary and state legislatures to judge validity of acts of Congress).

[161]Justice Goldberg argued that "the Ninth Amendment is relevant in a case dealing with a *State's* infringement of a fundamental right." Griswold v. Connecticut, 381 U.S. at 493 (Goldberg, J., concurring) (emphasis in original). A similar argument is contained in the renowned fourth footnote of the *Carolene Products* case, where Justice Stone asserted his theory of incorporation: "the first ten amendments . . . are deemed equally specific when held to be embraced within the Fourteenth." United States v. Carolene Prods. Co., 304 U.S. 144, 152 n.4 (1938). *See also* C. Black, *supra* note 18, at 47; B. Patterson, *supra* note 6, at 36–43; L. Tribe, *supra* note 18, at 570; Redlich, *supra* note 6, at 808; Ringold, *supra* note 18, at 24. Justice Black's position, however (see *supra* note 142) makes clear the incongruity of applying the incorporation doctrine to the ninth amendment, a doctrine which is equally incongruous as applied to the tenth amendment. *See infra* note 163.

Patterson finds it significant that the Supreme Court has regarded the Bill of Rights as comprising only the first eight amendments (*see, e.g.,* Palko v. Connecticut, 302 U.S. 319, 323 (1937); *cf.* Eilenbecker v. Plymouth County, 134 U.S. 31, 34 (1890)), thus ostensibly leaving the ninth available as a source of rights against state governments as well as against the federal government. B. Patterson, *supra* note 6, at 23, 25–26 & 37. The ninth amendment, however, as well as the tenth, belongs to the Bill of Rights. *See* 3 J. Story, *supra* note 5, at 721.

[162]Commentators who find the ninth and tenth amendments redundant include Redlich, *supra* note 6, at 808–12 (urging that the *Griswold* statutes be struck down under the ninth and tenth amendments), and E. Dumbauld, *supra* note 6, at 138 (ninth and tenth amendments are both reservations for the benefit of the states).

[163]"I find," said Madison, "from looking into the amendments proposed by the State conventions, that several are particularly anxious that it should be declared in the constitution, that the powers not therein delegated should be reserved to the several States." 1 Annals, *supra* note 55, at 458.

[164]1 Annals, *supra* note 55, at 452 (Madison's proposed text of ninth amendment). *See supra* note 132 and accompanying text.

declaration."[165] Though not in sequence in Madison's draft,[166] the ninth and tenth amendments both derived from article II of the Articles of Confederation[167] and were paired in the final version of the Bill of Rights, probably because of their analogous residual purposes. Yet the ninth amendment is not superfluous, for it preserves the rights existing under state laws already "on the books" in 1791 plus those rights which the states would thereafter see fit to enact.[168] The tenth, by contrast, permits the states, by virtue of the powers delegated to them by the people,[169] to continue to exer-

[165]*Id.* at 459. *See id.* at 458. The arguments of the federalists as to the nature of delegated and retained powers are now so entrenched in our constitutional system that it has become possible to say the tenth amendment "states but a truism that all is retained which has not been surrendered." United States v. Darvy, 312 U.S. 100, 124 (1941).

[166]Madison had intended the amendments as insertions in the main text of the Constitution to show that their status is equal to that of the original document. *See* 1 Annals, *supra* note 55, at 735. The House of Representatives, however, at the suggestion of Roger Sherman, decided to collect them separately, for convenience in adding later amendments. *See* 1 Annals, *supra* note 55, at 734–35.

[167]*See supra* note 100.

[168]Unlike the tenth amendment, which encompasses all governmental activities, including the structure of governmental institutions and powers such as taxation, the ninth reserves state law only with regard to individual rights. Under the tenth amendment, of course, the states can define their own powers, limiting their regulations to certain areas or qualifying the powers that are in fact exercised. This is, in the Madisonian formulation, tantamount to reserving rights. *See supra* text accompanying notes 141–42; The Federalist No. 84, at 578 (A. Hamilton) (J. Cooke ed. 1961) ("a declaration of rights . . . under our [state] constitutions must be intended as limitations of the power of the government itself"). Under the clauses in a number of state constitutions patterned after the ninth amendment (*see* J. Ely, *supra* note 3, at 203 n.87; F. Stimson, The American Constitution 90–91 (1908) (state exemplars, like ninth amendment, protect natural rights anterior to federal and state law)), the statutory and common-law rights of the respective state codes are similarly preserved. Although the state provisions offer the same protection in their own states as does the ninth amendment, the ninth is still of value because it is not replicated in every state constitution. In any event, Madison had endorsed such redoubled security. *See supra* text accompanying note 131.

[169]In accordance with social contract theory, the people retain the power to form governments and to change or end them upon violation of the "contract" to preserve and further their well-being. At the Constitutional Convention Madison stated that "[t]he people were in fact, the fountain of all power. . . . They could alter constitutions as they pleased." 2 Records, *supra* note 21, at 476. "[W]ho but the people can delegate powers?" asked Edmund Pendleton at the Virginia ratification convention. "Who but the people have a right to form government?" *See* 3 J. Elliot, *supra* note 27, at 37. *See also* 2 *id.* at 434–35; *id.* at 456 (James Wilson acknowledging Lockean

cise their allocated functions. The ninth amendment looks to the past, to established rights that have been or shall have been "retained"; the tenth amendment looks to the future, allowing the states to legislate, to revise their constitutions, and in general to engage in appropriate governmental operations.[170]

---

source of doctrine); Second Treatise, *supra* note 28, § 141, at 380 (legislative power "but a delegated Power from the People"). Fittingly, then, the last four words of the Bill of Rights—"or to the people"—added to Madison's draft on the motion of Charles Carroll of Maryland (1 Annals, *supra* note 55, at 790) are not synonymous or an appositional phrase with "the States respectively," as suggested in 1 W. Crosskey, Politics and the Constitution in the History of the United States 705 (1953), and J. Taylor, Construction Construed, and Constitutions Vindicated 48 (Richmond 1820) ("states' rights" tract). Rather, they reflect the principle articulated by Justice Story: "[Because the Constitution is] an instrument of limited and enumerated powers, it follows irresistibly, that what is not conferred, is withheld, and belongs to the state authorities, if invested by their constitutions of government respectively in them; and if not so invested, it is retained by the people, as a part of their residuary sovereignty." 3 J. Story, *supra* note 5, at 752 (emphasis omitted; footnote omitted). Indeed, Carroll's phrase was meant to replace a Jeffersonian preface which Madison had composed to head the Constitution, declaring in part that "all power is originally invested in, and consequently derived from, the people. . . . [T]he people have an indubitable, unalienable, and indefeasible right to reform or change their Government, whenever it be found adverse or inadequate to the purposes of its institution." 1 Annals, *supra* note 55, at 451. See United Pub. Workers v. Mitchell, 330 U.S. 75, 95–96 (1947); McCulloch v. Maryland, 17 U.S. (4 Wheat.) 316, 404–05 (1819); 2 J. Elliot, *supra* note 27, at 437, 443 & 502; G. Wood, *supra* note 20, at 535; *supra* note 120.

Hence it is unlikely that the powers reserved to the people in the tenth amendment form a pocket of individual freedom exercisable against an existing scheme of government, as argued in Ely, *Democracy and the Right to Be Different*, 56 N.Y.U. L. Rev. 397, 402 (1981), and Redlich, *supra* note 6, at 807. Such discretion would be not a power but a right. See *supra* note 142 and accompanying text. Reserved powers comprise the residual capacity of a people to form or re-form a government, not the particular liberties enjoyed *under* a government. "And thus the community may be said . . . to be always the supreme power, but not as considered under any form of government, because this power of the people can never take place till the government be dissolved." Second Treatise, *supra* note 28, § 149, at 385 (quoted in J. Otis, *supra* note 37, at 434). Said Madison: "My idea of the sovereignty of the people is, that the people can change the constitution if they please; but while the constitution exists, they must conform themselves to its dictates." 1 Annals, *supra* note 55, at 767. See 35 The Writings of George Washington, *supra* note 62, at 224 (Washington's Farewell Address of Sept. 19, 1796).

[170]Such a Janus-like relationship between the ninth and tenth amendments was suggested by Dean Roscoe Pound. See Pound, Introduction to B. Patterson, *supra* note 6, at iv & vi–vii (ninth and tenth amendments read together are authority for federal constitutional amendments or for state legislation to define and secure addi-

In sum, the available historical evidence concerning the ninth amendment indicates that by 1789, "natural" and other fundamental rights were regarded as secured by the statutory and common law of the several states. This was the understanding embodied in article II of the Articles of Confederation and Virginia's first proposed constitutional amendment, which amendment in turn was an immediate progenitor of the ninth amendment itself. The prospect of losing rights protected by state law, which had hitherto been the preeminent resort of popular liberty, became the critical issue in the ratification of the 1787 Constitution. Like the rest of the Bill of Rights, the ninth amendment was drafted in order to allay concern that the Constitution might abolish rights traditionally guaranteed by state law, and the amendment's stated purpose was to leave unimpaired the individual rights not included in the federal Constitution or Bill of Rights. These "other" rights were understood to refer to the common law, along with the state constitutions and statutes engrafted onto it. Accordingly, the ninth amendment embraces those individual liberties protected by state laws.

IV. Epilogue

In retrospect, the ninth amendment was probably destined for eclipse by the twin forces of constitutionalization and federalization that have been almost continually at work throughout the nation's history. The states, receding from the front ranks as defenders of individual freedom, eventually came to be regarded as obstacles to liberty. The civil rights revolution of the past fifty years was largely propelled by a federal judiciary overturning state laws by means of expansive readings of constitutional protections.[171] Further, it was

---

tional inherent rights). Only the tenth amendment's reservation of power to the people, however, applies to federal constitutional amendments (see supra note 169) because the ninth refers to unenumerated, state rights.

[171]See, e.g., G. Calabresi, A Common Law for the Age of Statutes 8–15 (1982); A. Miller, The Supreme Court and American Capitalism (1968); J. Pole, The Pursuit of Equality in American History 253–92 (1978); Cox, The New Dimensions of Constitutional Adjudication, 51 Wash. L. Rev. 791 (1976); Michelman, The Supreme Court, 1968 Term— Foreword: On Protecting the Poor Through the Fourteenth Amendment, 83 Harv. L. Rev. 7 (1969); Monaghan, supra note 18.

The constitutionalizing trend can be traced at least to the Reconstruction amendments. Unlike the two amendments preceding them, which adjusted the machinery of the federal government, the Reconstruction amendments enacted nationwide social reform. See H. Hyman, A More Perfect Union (1975); Bickel, The Original Understanding and the Segregation Decision, 69 Harv. L. Rev. 1, 56–65 (1955) (framers of the fourteenth amendment chose "language capable of growth," id. at 63).

the federal government which presided over the country's transformation from a watchman state of limited reach to a welfare state both expansive and intrusive.[172] For a long time only the federal government was thought to have the resources and political impetus necessary to redeem all the promises of the Constitution.[173] As a result, the conventional assumption has been that the rights retained by the people under the ninth amendment are federal rights not enumerated elsewhere in the Constitution.

Among these supposed unenumerated federal rights, the right of privacy has been particularly associated with the ninth amendment in recent decades. Yet historically, this right is a relatively new amalgam of two distinct kinds of rights: constitutional rights primarily involving freedom of expression and certain procedural guarantees, and property rights customarily regarded as belonging

---

[172]*See, e.g.,* United States v. E.C. Knight Co., 156 U.S. 1, 19 (1895) (Harlan, J., dissenting) (advocating expansive role for federal antitrust laws); A. Miller, The Assault on Privacy (1971); J. Rosenberg, The Death of Privacy (1969); A. Westin, Privacy and Freedom (1967); T. White, American in Search of Itself 103–36 (1982).

[173]*See, e.g.,* Slaughter-House Cases, 83 U.S. (16 Wall.) at 82; M. Harrington, The Other America 166–67 (1968). Dissatisfaction with recent Supreme Court civil liberties rulings has prompted in some circles a reconsideration of the protections afforded by the state constitutions to their citizens, to an extent restoring the states to their original role as the indispensable first-line guardians of individual rights. *See* Brennan, *State Constitutions and the Protection of Individual Rights,* 90 Harv. L. Rev. 489 (1977); Walinski & Tucker, *Expectations of Privacy: Fourth Amendment Legitimacy through State Law,* 16 Harv. C.R.–C.L. L. Rev. 1 (1981); *Developments in the Law—The Interpretation of State Constitutional Rights,* 95 Harv. L. Rev. 1324 (1982); Note, *Free Speech, the Private Employee, and State Constitutions,* 91 Yale L.J. 522 (1982); Margolick, *State Judiciaries Are Shaping Law that Goes Beyond Supreme Court,* N.Y. Times, May 19, 1982, at A1, col. 1. *See also* Michelman, States' Rights and States' Roles: Permutations of "Sovereignty," in *National League of Cities v. Usery,* 86 Yale L.J. 1165, 1172 (1977) (*National League of Cities'* broad concept of "state sovereignty" reflects "the state's role of providing for the interests of its citizens in receiving important social services"); Tribe, *Unraveling National League of Cities: The New Federalism and Affirmative Rights to Essential Government Services,* 90 Harv. L. Rev. 1065, 1076 (1977) (*National League of Cities* "suggest[s] the existence of protected expectations—of rights—to basic government services," i.e., from state governments). For an early statement, see Hart, *The Power of Congress to Limit the Jurisdiction of Federal Courts: An Exercise in Dialectic,* 66 Harv. L. Rev. 1362, 1401 (1953), *reprinted in* P. Bator, P. Mishkin, D. Shapiro, & H. Wechsler, Hart & Wechsler's The Federal Courts and the Federal System 359 (2d ed. 1973) ("In the scheme of the Constitution, [the state courts] are the primary guarantors of constitutional rights, and in many cases they may be the ultimate ones.").

to the common law of tort.[174] In fact, the phrase popularized by Justice Brandeis to describe the right of privacy, the "right to be let alone,"[175] was taken from a treatise on tort law.[176] The idea of privacy as now understood, moreover, did not develop until the mid-eighteenth century[177] and did not fully mature until the late nineteenth.[178] Privacy as an all-encompassing constitutional right[179] was

[174]"There are, of course, guarantees in certain specific constitutional provisions which are designed in part to protect privacy at certain times and places with respect to certain activities. . . . [But] I get nowhere . . . by talk about a constitutional 'right of privacy' as an emanation from one or more constitutional provisions." Griswold v. Connecticut, 381 U.S. at 508–10 (Black, J., dissenting) (footnote omitted). See Whalen v. Roe, 429 U.S. 589, 599–600 (1977); Paul v. Davis, 424 U.S. 693, 713 (1976); Roe v. Wade, 410 U.S. 113, 167 n.2 (1973) (Stewart, J., concurring); Beaney, The Constitutional Right to Privacy in the Supreme Court, 1962 Sup. Ct. Rev. 212; Gerety, Redefining Privacy, 12 Harv. C.R.–C.L. L. Rev. 233 (1977); Henkin, Privacy and Autonomy, 74 Colum. L. Rev. 1410, 1418–19 (1974); Posner, The Uncertain Protection of Privacy by the Supreme Court, 1979 Sup. Ct. Rev. 173, revised and reprinted in R. Posner, The Economics of Justice 310–47 (1981).

[175]Olmstead v. United States, 277 U.S. 438, 478 (1928) (Brandeis, J., dissenting); Warren & Brandeis, The Right to Privacy, 4 Harv. L. Rev. 193, 195 (1890).

[176]To Cooley, Law of Torts 29 (2d ed. 1888). See generally Time, Inc. v. Hill, 385 U.S. 374, 412 (1967) (Fortas, J., dissenting); Griswold v. Connecticut, 381 U.S. at 510 n.1 (Black, J., dissenting). Compare Warren & Brandeis, supra note 175, at 195 ("[W]ith the advance of civilization, [it became] clear to men that only a part of the pain, pleasure, and profit of life lay in physical things. . . . [T]he next step which must be taken [by the judges of the common law is] . . . securing to the individual what Judge Cooley calls the right 'to be let alone' ") (citing T. Cooley, supra) with Olmstead v. United States, 277 U.S. at 478 (1928) (Brandeis, J., dissenting) ("The makers of our Constitution . . . knew that only a part of the pain, pleasure and satisfactions of life are to be found in material things. . . . They conferred, as against the Government, the right to be let alone. . . .") (no reference to Cooley).

[177]See D. Flaherty, Privacy in Colonial New England 92–97, 104–10 & 164–88 (1972) (in early American history, absence of well-established social mores proscribing intrusion of the community into personal matters). See generally F. Braudel, The Structures of Everyday Life (1981); R. Sennett, The Fall of Public Man (1977).

[178]See G. White, Tort Law in America 173 (1980) ("Privacy became important when America became more heterogeneous, crowded, urbanized, and socially mobile: it was a respite from the pressures of living in a complex world."); Godkin, The Rights of the Citizen. IV.—To His Own Reputation, 8 Scribner's Magazine 58 (1890); Nizer, The Right of Privacy, A Half Century's Developments, 39 Mich. L. Rev. 526, 526–28 (1941). The right of privacy "is a modern demand, growing out of the conditions of life in the crowded communities of to-day." Pound, Interests of Personality, 28 Harv. L. Rev. 343, 362–63 (1915). The year in which the Warren and Brandeis article appeared, 1890, is the same year that, for the historian Frederick Jackson Turner,

accordingly not a part of the legal tradition inherited from England by the colonies which would have been secured in either a state or federal bill of rights.[180]

The ninth amendment, therefore, has become obscure precisely because of its own success. Its actual significance taken for granted as obvious, its role in the ratification controversy forgotten, the amendment uniquely fulfills one of the aspirations Madison held for a bill of rights. "The political truths declared in that solemn manner," he wrote to Jefferson, "acquire by degrees the character of fundamental maxims of free Government, and as they become incorporated with the national sentiment, counteract the impulses of interest and passion."[181] That character, to the point of being "still a mystery," the ninth amendment has attained.

---

marked the closing of the American frontier. See F. Turner, *The Significance of the Frontier in American History,* in The Frontier in American History 1–38 (1920).

[179]Kutner, *supra* note 12, at 137.

[180]Regulation of personal conduct in the colonies, enforced with varying degrees of enthusiasm, reflected contemporary English attitudes towards controlling aspects of individual behavior. See D. Flaherty, *supra* note 177, at 180–84; C. Hill, Society and Puritanism in Pre-Revolutionary England 126–38 (1964). *See also* 1 Foundations of Colonial America, *supra* note 24, at 410–12; 2 *id.* at 1184–85, 1334–35, & 1337–38; 3 *id.* at 2078–80, 2273–76, & 2314–17 (early colonial ordinances legislating morality in numerous areas of individual and social conduct). *See generally* State v. Nelson, 126 Conn. 412, 425, 11 A.2d 856, 862 (1940).

The enactment of such laws, including those at issue in *Griswold,* renders problematic Justice Goldberg's criteria for discerning unenumerated fundamental rights. *See supra* note 11. *See* Goldberg, *Can We Afford Liberty?* 117 U. Pa. L. Rev. 665, 667 (1969) (discussing individual privacy in terms of the fourth and fifth amendments, with no mention of the ninth).

[181]Letter from James Madison to Thomas Jefferson (Oct. 17, 1788), *reprinted in* 5 Writings, *supra* note 55, at 273.

11. Federalism and Fundamental Rights: The Ninth Amendment

Calvin R. Massey

I. Introduction

Two decades after its emergence from 175 years of constitutional hibernation, the ninth amendment continues to perplex those who seek meaning within it. The amendment was largely ignored by litigants and judges until Justice Goldberg, joined by Chief Justice Warren and Justice Brennan, fastened upon it as a basis for concurring in the Court's invalidation of state prohibition of contraceptive use in 1965.[1] As the nation prepares to enter its third century of constitutional interpretation, and issues of personal liberty and the proper distribution of political power between state and federal government occupy a central place on the judicial agenda, it is appropriate to examine, once again,[2] this "almost unfathomable"[3] constitutional provision.

Reprinted, by permission, from 38 Hastings L.J. 305 (1987).

[1]Griswold v. Connecticut, 381 U.S. 479 (1965). Justices Harlan and White each concurred separately in the Court's judgment. *Id.* at 499 & 502. Justices Black and Stewart dissented. *Id.* at 507 & 527. Justice Douglas authored the Court's opinion, in which he dared not venture as far as Justice Goldberg, preferring merely to include the ninth amendment among the provisions of the Bill of Rights that have "penumbras, formed by emanations from [such] guarantees."*Id.* at 484.

Only seven Supreme Court cases prior to Griswold dealt in any fashion with the ninth amendment: Roth v. United States, 354 U.S. 476, 492–93 (1957); Woods v. Cloyd W. Miller Co., 333 U.S. 138, 144 (1948); United Pub. Workers v. Mitchell, 330 U.S. 75, 94–96 (1947) ; Tennessee Elec. Power Co. v. TVA, 306 U.S. 118, 143–44 (1939); Ashwander v. TVA, 297 U.S. 288, 330–31 (1936); Dred Scott v. Sandford, 60 U.S. (19 How.) 393, 511 (1857) (Campbell, J., concurring); Lessee of Livingston v. Moore, 32 U.S. (7 Pet.) 469, 551 (1833) (in which the Court's reference to the "ninth article of amendment" is unclear and may refer to the ninth proposed amendment, the seventh amendment enacted).

[2]The earliest scholarly study of the ninth amendment seems to be Kelsey, *The Ninth Amendment of the Federal Constitution,* 11 Ind. L.J. 309 (1936). In the years from 1791 to 1936, only passing references were made to the ninth amendment by com-

When approaching the ninth amendment, problems seem to be legion. Is it superfluous? Is it merely a rule of construction? On its face it would seem to be so, for the amendment provides simply that "The enumeration in the Constitution, of certain rights, shall not be construed to deny or disparage others retained by the people."[4] Is it, as Dunbar and Berger contend, a declaration of an area in which government has "no power"?[5] What was intended by its framers? Does it incorporate "natural law" theories of individual rights? If so, how can those rights be divined in any principled way? May it be enforced by the courts? Does it operate to prohibit

---

mentators. *See, e.g.*, J. Bayard, A Brief Exposition of the Constitution of the United States 184 (2d ed. 1834) (ninth amendment reflective of intent to prevent "unauthorized extension" of federal government's power); T. Cooley, Constitutional Law 36–37 (3d ed. 1898) (ninth amendment does not create rights but recognizes existing rights and operates to preserve them); S. Miller, Lectures on the Constitution 650 (1891) (ninth amendment serves as a "just" rule of construction which would exist even in its absence); J. Story, Commentaries on the Constitution of the United States 751–52 (1st ed. 1833) (amendment confirms that unenumerated rights not surrendered to federal government); 2 H. Tucker, The Constitution of the United States 688–89 (1899) (ninth amendment excludes inference that federal government could invade "great fundamental rights of the people").

A mass of literature pertaining to the ninth amendment has now developed. Some of the recent works are: C. Black, Decision According to Law (1981); J. Ely, Democracy and Distrust 34–41 (1980); M. Goodman, The Ninth Amendment (1981); Berger, *The Ninth Amendment*, 66 Cornell L. Rev. 1 (1980); Caplan, *The History and Meaning of the Ninth Amendment*, 69 Va. L. Rev. 223 (1983); Gibbons, Keynote Address, *Symposium: Constitutional Adjudication and Democratic Theory*, 56 N.Y.U. L. Rev. 260, 272–73 (1981); Monaghan, *Our Perfect Constitution*, 56 N.Y.U. L. Rev. 353, 365–67 (1981); Note, *The Right of Privacy: A Black View of Griswold v. Connecticut*, 7 Hastings Const. L.Q. 777 (1980); Estreicher, Book Review, 56 N.Y.U. L. Rev. 547 (1981) (reviewing J. Ely, *supra*); Van Alstyne, *Slouching Toward Bethlehem with the Ninth Amendment* (Book Review), 91 Yale L.J. 207 (1981) (reviewing C. Black, *supra*).

[3]Dixon, *The Griswold Penumbra: Constitutional Charter for an Expanded Law of Privacy?*, 64 Mich. L. Rev. 197, 207 (1965).

[4]U.S. Const. amend. IX. At least two commentators have thought the amendment was nothing more than a rule of construction. E. Dumbauld, The Bill of Rights 63 (1957), concludes that the ninth amendment "was designed to obviate the possibility of applying the maxim *expressio unius est exclusio alterius* (the expression of one [right] is the exclusion of alternative [rights]) in interpreting the Constitution." Justice Story believed that the ninth amendment "was manifestly introduced to prevent any perverse or ingenious misapplication of the well-known maxim, that an affirmation in particular cases implies a negation in all others." J. Story, *supra* note 2, at 951.

[5]Berger, *supra* note 2, at 9; Dunbar, *James Madison and the Ninth Amendment*, 42 Va. L. Rev. 627, 635–36 (1956).

state, as well as federal, action?[6] Is it overridden by explicit constitutional grants of power to the federal government?[7] Answers to these vexing questions are not easy. Indeed any answer proposed will inevitably implicate other areas of constitutional interpretation. Because of the enigmatic nature of the amendment and its helix-like intertwining with other powers and guarantees specified in the Constitution, it is uncommonly difficult to find within it a coherent package of guaranteed rights susceptible to judicial protection without reference to unmanageable, standardless, and amorphous extrinsic sources. Yet, there is a thread that, when followed faithfully, produces a comprehensive, principled, and historically consistent theory of both the content of the ninth amendment and the enforceability of its guarantees.

II. Historical Background

The ninth amendment cannot be properly understood without an appreciation of the historical circumstances which gave rise to its adoption. The Articles of Confederation reflected revolutionary America's deep distrust of centralized authority and strong predilection to retain separate sovereignty for each of the newly independent former colonies. Under the Articles of Confederation, Congress was unable to levy taxes or tariffs and required unanimity of the constituent states to exercise what little authority was vested in it.[8] As a result, the American "nation" formed by the Articles was fragmented by state jealousies, rival tariffs, artificial barriers to

---

[6]There is no direct holding on the applicability of the ninth amendment to the states. Lessee of Livingston v. Moore, 32 U.S. (7 Pet.) 469, 551–52 (1833), denied generally that the Bill of Rights extended to the states. *See also* Barron v. Baltimore, 32 U.S. (7 Pet.) 242 (1833), decided in the same term. *But see* Griswold v. Connecticut, 381 U.S. 479 (1965); *infra* text accompanying notes 110–25.

[7]Justice Reed certainly thought so.

[W]hen objection is made that the exercise of a federal power infringes upon rights reserved by the Ninth and Tenth Amendments, the inquiry must be directed toward the granted power under which the action of the Union was taken. If granted power is found, necessarily the objection of invasion of those rights, reserved by the Ninth and Tenth Amendments, must fail.

United Pub. Workers v. Mitchell, 330 U.S. 75, 95–96 (1947).

[8]9 Journals of the Continental Congress 1774–1789, at 90 (P. Ford ed. 1904) [hereinafter Journals]; *see also* 1 A. Beveridge, Life of John Marshall 304 (1916).

trade, and lack of a national currency or credit.[9] These conditions effectively plunged the nation into economic depression as well as social and economic isolation.[10]

The Constitutional Convention proposed to remedy this situation by the creation of a strong national government.[11] But this radical proposal was not received with anything like acclamation by the early citizens of our nation. In Pennsylvania, for example, the ratification convention was selected by less than ten percent of the eligible voters. This condition came about because the pro-ratification forces called the elections in such a way and on such short notice that, as a practical matter, the citizens of Pennsylvania were disenfranchised in selecting their representatives for the ratification convention.[12] Similarly, in Massachusetts public opinion was so overwhelmingly against the Constitution that some forty-six towns refused to send a delegate to the state ratification convention. Had those forty-six communities

---

[9]Examples of protective tariffs enacted by states and directed against their fellow states include Virginia's imposition of duties on articles imported by land or sea and providing for forfeiture upon violation. Va. Stat. at Large, ch. 14, at 46 (1785). Pennsylvania imposed similar duties on American, non-Pennsylvania manufacturers. 1785 Pa. Laws 99.

"The financial situation was chaos." 1 A. Beveridge, *supra* note 8, at 295. Each state issued its own paper currency which was virtually worthless and unacceptable outside its state of issuance. *Id.* at 296. Interstate trade was predictably strangled. New Yorkers discounted New Jersey money at an "unconscionable" rate, 3 J. Jay, Correspondence and Public Papers (H. Johnston ed. 1890), and New Jersey merchants adjusted prices accordingly if buyers tendered New York currency. *Id. See generally* 1 A. Beveridge, *supra* note 8, at 295–311.

[10]*See generally* 1 A. Beveridge, *supra* note 8, at 250–311.

[11]In writing Washington in April 1787, Madison declared that

the national Government should be armed with positive and compleat authority in all cases which require uniformity; such as the regulation of trade. . . . Over and above this positive power, a negative *in all cases whatsoever* on the legislative acts of the States, as to heretofore exercised by the Kingly prerogative, appears to me to be absolutely necessary, and to be the least possible encroachment on the State jurisdictions. Without this defensive power, every positive power that can be given on paper will be evaded and defeated. The States will continue to invade the National jurisdiction, to violate treaties and the law of nations & to harass each other with rival and spiteful measures dictated by mistaken views of interest.

2 The Writings of James Madison 345–46 (G. Hunt ed. 1904) (emphasis in original) [hereinafter Madison Writings]. This ultra-nationalist view sheds light on Madison's real desires when introducing the ninth amendment. *See infra* text accompanying notes 25–31.

[12]1 A. Beveridge, *supra* note 8, at 327.

been represented, it is a virtual certainty that Massachusetts would have refused to ratify the new Constitution.[13] In Virginia, perhaps the most pivotal state of all, it was acknowledged that, south of the James River, public opinion was at least nine to one against adoption of the new Constitution.[14] In New York, public opinion was also overwhelmingly against ratification.[15] In all probability, apart from Delaware, Rhode Island, and New Jersey, which regarded the new Constitution as a way of achieving enhanced economic and political leverage,[16] public opinion throughout the original states was substantially opposed to adoption of the new document.[17] Opposition to the Constitution's adoption was rooted in a deep fear of national power.[18] This sentiment, pervasive throughout the early American states, ultimately compelled proposal and adoption of the first ten amendments to the Constitution.[19] Indeed, ratification was obtained in part by the promise that a bill of rights would be promptly appended to the newly adopted Constitution.[20]

The purpose of the demanded bill of rights was to provide certainty that the newly created federal government would be disabled from intruding upon the elementary and fundamental rights of the citizenry.[21] There does not appear to have been disagreement over this objective. Rather, dispute centered upon the wisdom of including any enumeration of rights within the Constitution. Those who preferred the unamended version of the Constitution argued that any enumeration of rights would necessarily be imperfect and would create the inference that no rights existed except those itemized. The federal

[13]*Id.* at 340 & n.4. Massachusetts ratified the Constitution by a vote of 187 to 168. *Id.* at 348; 2 J. Elliot, Debates in the Several State Conventions on the Adoption of the Federal Constitution 178–81 (2d ed. 1836).

[14]1 A. Beveridge, *supra* note 8, at 367, 468–70; 3 J. Elliot, *supra* note 13, at 587–96; 5 Madison Writings, *supra* note 11, at 120–22 & 302.

[15]1 A. Beveridge, *supra* note 8, at 379.

[16]*Id.* at 325.

[17]*Id.* at 307–09 & 324–25; 5 J. Marshall, Life of Washington 132 (1st ed. 1807).

[18]1 A. Beveridge, *supra* note 8, at 342–47 ("National Government would destroy . . . liberties . . . [and was thought to be] a kind of foreign rule.").

[19]*See generally* Patrick Henry's two remarkable speeches on the penultimate day of the Virginia convention, June 24, 1788, *reprinted in* 3 J. Eliot, *supra* note 13, at 587–625; *see also infra* notes 26 & 58.

[20]1 Annals of Cong. 464 (J. Gales & W. Seaton eds. 1836) (remarks of Elbridge Gerry) [hereinafter Annals of Cong.].

[21]*See infra* note 59.

government possessed only certain enumerated powers, according to this argument, and thus could have no valid claim to interfere with the exercise of the citizens' rights. Adherents to this view, including Alexander Hamilton and James Wilson of Pennsylvania, contended that it was better to imperfectly enumerate the powers of the federal government with the implication that powers not enumerated were reserved to the people, than to attempt an imperfect enumeration of rights reserved to the people, with the implication that rights not so reserved were impliedly delegated to the federal government.[22]

The opposition contended that any creation of a government by the people carried with it a delegation to that government of all rights not expressly reserved for the people.[23] Whatever its wisdom, the latter argument was the stronger and, accordingly, James Madison assumed responsibility for introducing into the first Congress constitutional amendments responsive to demands for an articulated bill of rights.[24] In an attempt to deal with the concern that any enumeration of rights would imply that the enumeration was exhaustive, Madison introduced his fourth resolution which, after considerable revision, became the ninth amendment:

> The exceptions here or elsewhere in the Constitution, made in favor of particular rights, shall not be so construed as to diminish the just importance of other rights retained by the people, or as to enlarge the powers delegated by the Constitution; but either as actual limitations of such powers, or as inserted merely for greater caution.[25]

A close comparison of Madison's resolution and its ancestors[26] with the final draft of the ninth amendment reveals a subtle shift

[22]See The Federalist No. 84 (A. Hamilton); 2 J. Elliot, supra note 13, at 436–37.

[23]3 J. Elliot, supra note 13, at 445–49 (Patrick Henry's remarks urging the Virginia convention to consider issues of fundamental rights before considering ratification of the Constitution).

[24]1 Annals of Cong., supra note 20, at 438.

[25]Id. at 435.

[26]Madison's resolution owed much to Virginia's 17th proposed amendment, North Carolina's 18th proposed amendment, the third article of Rhode Island's declaration of rights, and New York's act of ratification. Virginia's 17th proposed amendment provided: "That those clauses which declare that Congress shall not exercise certain powers, be not interpreted, in any manner whatsoever, to extend the powers of Congress; but that they be construed either as making exceptions to the specified powers where this shall be the case, or otherwise, as inserted merely for greater caution." 3 J. Elliot, supra note 13, at 661. North Carolina's 18th proposed amendment

of focus. Madison's original resolution contained within it a clause that enjoined interpreters of the Constitution from enlarging the powers delegated by the Constitution to the federal government. This focus on powers is missing in the final version which deals only with the rights retained by the people.[27] The tenth amendment provides the focus missing in the ninth on limitation of powers of the federal government.[28] This division of powers and rights into separate amendments allows contemporary analysis of the concepts of peoples' rights and governmental powers without reference

---

was identical. 4 *id.* at 246. New York's act of ratification provided:

> That the powers of government may be reassumed by the people whensoever it shall become necessary to their happiness; that every power, jurisdiction, and right, which is not by the said Constitution clearly delegated to the Congress of the United States, or the departments of the government thereof, remains to the people of the several states, or to their respective state governments, to whom they may have granted the same; and that those clauses in the said Constitution, which declare that Congress shall not have or exercise certain powers, do not imply that Congress is entitled to any powers not given by the said Constitution; but such clauses are to be construed either as exceptions to certain specified powers, or as inserted merely for greater caution.

1 *id.* at 327. The third article of Rhode Island's declaration of rights, proclaimed as a part of the state's act of ratification, was virtually identical. *Id.* at 336.

Caplan contends that Virginia's 17th proposed amendment is derived from article II of the Articles of Confederation: "Each state retains its sovereignity, freedom and independence, and every power, jurisdiction and right, which is not by this confederation expressly delegated to the United States, in Congress assembled." 9 Journals, *supra* note 8, at 908; *see* Caplan, *supra* note 2, at 236, 254 n.132.

[27]Berger contends that Madison perceived the reservation of rights in the ninth amendment and limitation upon governmental powers in the tenth amendment to be indivisibly related. Berger, *supra* note 2, at 3. Dunbar contends that Madison was attempting to reserve rights while simultaneously preserving power in the central government. Dunbar, *supra* note 5, at 635; *see also* The Federalist No. 44 (J. Madison).

The progenitors of the ninth amendment dealt with limitations of powers. *See supra* note 26; *infra* notes 57–58. Madison's gradual elimination of the original focus of the proposed amendments—restriction of any implication of congressional power beyond the express grant of the Constitution—was consistent with Madison's commitment, at the time, to a strong federal system. *See* 1 A. Beveridge, *supra* note 8, at 312; Dunbar, *supra* note 5, at 634–35; *supra* note 11.

[28]"The powers not delegated to the United States by the Constitution, nor prohibited by it to the States, are reserved to the States respectively, or to the people." U.S. Const. amend X.

to each other although the amendments articulate very related concerns.[29]

Madison conceived of rights as of two varieties. "[T]he great object in view is to limit and qualify the powers of Government, by excepting out of the grant of power those cases in which the Government ought not to act, or to act only in a particular mode."[30] Thus, some rights are procedural, delimiting the manner in which the government may exercise its powers. Examples include the right to a trial by jury and due process assurances of notice and opportunity to be heard. Other rights are substantive prohibitions upon the ability of government to exercise its powers at all. For example, Madison thought government should be disabled from any regulation of the press, however abusive its content.[31] These twin springs of individual rights form the source of the rights preserved by the ninth amendment. Identification of their source, however, does little to solve the problem of defining their content.

III. The Nature of Ninth Amendment Rights

In general, two broad, and contradictory, viewpoints exist concerning the content of the ninth amendment. One maintains that

---

[29]Madison regarded individual rights and governmental powers as separate and mutually exclusive categories. In a letter to Washington he rejected Edmund Randolph's preference for an amendment limiting the federal government's powers rather than reserving individual rights: "If a line can be drawn between the powers granted and the rights retained, it would seem to be the same thing, whether the latter be secured by declaring that they shall not be abridged, or that the former shall not be extended. If no such line can be drawn, a declaration in either form would amount to nothing." Madison Writings, *supra* note 11, at 432. But Madison's observation may have obscured his desire both to retain power in the central government at the expense of the states, *see supra* note 11, and to ensure that the Constitution contained "effectual provisions against the encroachments on particular [individual] rights." 1 Annals of Cong., *supra* note 20, at 433; *see also* Dunbar, *supra* note 5, at 635; The Federalist No. 44 (J. Madison). *But see* J. Ely, *supra* note 2, at 35–36 (accusing Madison of "confusion" attributable to a "failure to recognize that rights and powers are not simply the absence of one another but that rights can cut across or 'trump' powers."); *see also* C. Black, Structure and Relationship in Constitutional Law (1969), in which Professor Black forcefully illustrates the importance of construing any portion of the Constitution by reference to other portions of the document which set forth the powers and structure of the federal government.

[30]1 Annals of Cong., *supra* note 20, at 454; *see also infra* notes 47 & 82.

[31]4 J. Elliot, *supra* note 13, at 567, 571 & 573. Madison did acknowledge the common-law power to infringe press freedom by means of actions for libel. *Id.*

the amendment is a bottomless well from which can be extracted any hitherto unarticulated private right. This view comes in two dimensions: one has its philosophical underpinnings in natural law theories of individual rights[32]; the other is a modern construct of activist egalitarians.[33] The contradictory position is that the ninth amendment is merely declaratory of a truth that the people possess unspecified rights.[34] This position holds that these "rights" may neither be invaded nor protected by government. As two commentators have put it, the amendment merely declares an area in which government has "no power."[35] Or, as another member of this school asserts, "it simply provides that the individual rights contained in state law are to continue in force under the Constitution until modified or eliminated by state enactment, by federal preemption, or by a judicial determination of unconstitutionality."[36]

[32]B. Patterson, The Forgotten Ninth Amendment (1955), is perhaps most representative of this genre. Patterson's thesis is that the ninth amendment protects "the inherent natural rights of the individual." *Id.* at 19. Patterson does not identify the source of these rights; presumably he finds them in natural law theories of immutable and inalienable rights. Although this may be a theoretical source, as Dunbar suggests, "they could just as well be ascribed to the doctrine of 'the rights of Englishmen,' or to the consensus of the American people." Dunbar, *supra* note 5, at 640; *see infra* text accompanying notes 75–81. Professor Corwin argues that the ninth amendment illustrates natural law theories and contends that the Constitution would not be "regarded as complete" without recognition of transcendental rights. Corwin, *The "Higher Law" Background of American Constitutional Law* (pt. 1), 42 Harv. L. Rev. 149, 153 (1928); *see also* Towe, *Natural Law and the Ninth Amendment*, 2 Pepperdine L. Rev. 270 (1975); Van Loan, *Natural Rights and the Ninth Amendment*, 48 B.U.L. Rev. 1 (1968).

[33]*See, e.g.,* C. Black, *supra* note 2, at 44–68; J. Ely, *supra* note 2, at 34–41; L. Tribe, American Constitutional Law 570 (1978); Gibbons, *supra* note 2, at 272–73; Henkin, *Infallibility Under Law: Constitutional Balancing*, 78 Colum. L. Rev. 1022, 1043 (1978); Kent, *Under the Ninth Amendment What Rights Are the "Others Retained by the People"?* 29 Fed. B.J. 219 (1970); Moore, *The Ninth Amendment—Its Origins and Meaning*, 7 New Eng. L. Rev. 215 (1972); Paust, *Human Rights and the Ninth Amendment: A New Form of Guarantee*, 60 Cornell L. Rev. 231 (1975); Perry, *Interpretivism, Freedom of Expression, and Equal Protection*, 42 Ohio St. L.J. 261, 272–73 (1981); Ringold, *The History of the Enactment of the Ninth Amendment and Its Recent Developments*, 8 Tulsa L.J. 1 (1972).

[34]*See, e.g.,* M. Goodman, The Ninth Amendment (1981); Berger, *supra* note 2; Bork, *The Impossibility of Finding Welfare Rights in the Constitution*, 1979 Wash. U.L.Q. 695, 697; Caplan, *supra* note 2; Dunbar, *supra* note 5; Monaghan, *supra* note 2, at 365–67; Van Alstyne, *supra* note 2.

[35]Berger, *supra* note 2, at 9; Dunbar, *supra* note 5, at 641.

[36]Caplan, *supra* note 2, at 228.

Each of these conceptions of the amendment's content is flawed. The notion that the ninth amendment provides a judicially enforceable constitutional guarantee for individual inherent rights seemingly involves the courts in an open-ended exercise in noninterpretive judicial review.[37] To the extent that this activity would further erode public support for the judiciary, lasting damage to the fragile balance of power in our tripartite system might be incalculable.[38] The efficacy of judicial review is dependent upon public acquiescence.[39] To endanger this keystone principle by foraging for inherent rights among the moral controversies of the day would seem to be foolhardy indeed. Those who urge the judiciary to use the ninth amendment as a catapult for extending constitutional protection to all manner of personal preference no doubt believe that the result will be an expansion of personal liberty. But should the judicial role as bulwark against majoritarian excesses[40] be ruptured by this aggressive strategy, a far more likely result will be a shrinkage of human liberty. Moreover, once license is granted to incorporate extrinsic values into the ninth amendment, there is no easy way to limit such imported values to those expansive of personal liberty.[41] Even Dean Ely, an advocate of this view, admits that

[37]See generally M. Perry, The Constitution, The Courts and Human Rights (1982). Perry defines noninterpretive review as judicial review which does not engage in interpretation of the Constitution itself, but which uses wholly extrinsic sources to find or make law. These extrinsic sources may be as fleeting as current public opinion or as nebulous as the sitting justices' private subjective values. Id. at 37–60. By contrast, interpretive review seeks legitimacy by deriving law from the constitutional text. Id. at 61–90.

[38]Consider the periodic attempts to strip the federal courts of jurisdiction to hear cases involving school prayer, school busing, or any other area in which the courts have rendered unpopular decisions. See Ex parte McCardle, 74 U.S. (8 Wall.) 506 (1868) (in which Congress successfully stripped the Supreme Court of appellate jurisdiction over Reconstruction actions of the military authorities); A. Cox, The Role of the Supreme Court in American Government 99–118 (1976); P. Murphy, Congress and the Court (1962); L. Tribe, Constitutional Choices 47–65 (1985). For an unequivocal assertion of congressional power over federal court jurisdiction, see C. Black, supra note 2, at 17–19 & 37–39.

[39]A. Cox, supra note 38, at 103–18; A. Bickel, The Least Dangerous Branch (1962).

[40]A. Bickel, supra note 39, at 16–23.

[41]For example, the ninth amendment could be read as preservative of Lochner-era individual inherent rights. See Lochner v. New York, 198 U.S. 45 (1905). One commentator would probably do just that. See B. Patterson, supra note 32, at 58, where he reveals his belief that the inherent rights protected by the ninth amendment consist, in part, of individual "protection" against public assistance and other gov-

the amendment "seems open-textured enough to support almost anything one might wish to argue, and that can get pretty scary."[42] Exclusive reliance upon natural law provides an uncertain buoy for those adrift in the sea of "open texture." Natural law theories of human rights have been criticized as sufficiently indeterminate to provide little guidance within the boundless dimensions of the ninth amendment as seen by the expansionists.[43] Indeed, the modern activist egalitarians reject natural law foundations for their open-ended interpretation[44] though it is not historically accurate to do so.[45] The American Revolution had its intellectual underpinnings in Lockean theory,[46] and the constitutional framers, though not fettered by natural law, clearly relied upon natural law principles in formulating constitutional guarantees.[47] Though there is little

---

ernmental transfer payments. Those Americans who owe their continued existence to public assistance would be surprised to learn that their ninth amendment rights were thereby violated.

[42]J. Ely, *supra* note 2, at 34.

[43]*See* Towe, *supra* note 32, at 273–74 (collecting arguments asserting that natural law arguments are impossible to prove and merely provide a euphemistic disguise for naked subjective preferences).

[44]*See* J. Ely, *supra* note 2, at 50. ("[Y]ou can invoke natural law to support anything you want."); *cf.* C. Black, *supra* note 2, at 44 & 49 (advocating an expansive reading of the ninth amendment based on the utilitarian principle of facilitating judicial outcomes not otherwise attainable).

[45]*See infra* notes 82–85 and accompanying text.

[46]Lockean theory posits that men are born into a "state of nature," without government, and agree out of "strong obligations of necessity, convenience and inclination" to constitute governments. The social contract thus made necessarily involves parting with some individual (natural) rights in order to secure the remainder more effectively. J. Locke, Two Treatises of Government § 77, at 336–37 (P. Laslett 2d ed. 1967) (3d ed. 1698). Lockean theory was generally accepted by such esteemed commentators as Blackstone. 1 W. Blackstone, Commentaries *42–44 & *121–22; *see also infra* notes 50–57 & 198–200 and accompanying text.

[47]Though the framers distinguished between natural law and positive law, they were anything but meticulous in maintaining that distinction when debating the necessity of a Bill of Rights. Madison identified freedom of speech as a natural right but trial by jury as a positive right, resulting from the social compact. 5 Madison Writings, *supra* note 11, at 389 & n.1; 1 Annals of Cong., *supra* note 20, at 454. More importantly, Madison concluded that the positive or civil right to a jury trial was "as essential to secure the liberty of the people as any one of the pre-existent rights of nature." *Id.* at 454. In urging adoption of a Bill of Rights, both George Mason and Patrick Henry referred to "great and important" rights of humanity, without neatly dividing them into natural and positive categories. 3 J. Elliot, *supra* note 13, at 317 & 444; *cf. infra* note 129.

intimation in the 175 years prior to *Griswold v. Connecticut*[48] that the ninth amendment was thought to be a repository of natural law,[49] its foundation in Lockean political theory requires an understanding of those actuating notions.

Writing as rough contemporaries in the seventeenth century, John Locke and Thomas Hobbes found different answers to a common problem. Hobbes, the defender of absolute sovereign power, regarded humans as uniformly selfish in a world without external authority to restrain their passions. Accordingly, life in this condition was "solitary, poore, nasty, brutish and short."[50] To escape this gloomy fate and to acquire security and order, Hobbes would exact a price consisting of the surrender of liberty and property to an absolute sovereign. While the individuals in this Hobbesian social contract would be somewhat better off, the big winner from this exchange would no doubt be the sovereign. Being a legal monopolist, the sovereign would exact monopoly rents—most of the benefits of political union would be expropriated by and for the sovereign.

Locke, by contrast, sought to devise a set of institutional arrangements which would allow individuals to escape the perils of social disorder without having to surrender their entire stock of individual rights. His goal was to vest the individuals composing the society with all the benefits created by political union. Locke's sovereign

---

[48]381 U.S. 479 (1965).

[49]None of the seven cases prior to *Griswold* carry any suggestion that the ninth amendment raised natural law notions of individual rights to the level of a constitutional guarantee. *See* cases cites *supra* note 1. Indeed the cases seem to adumbrate a rule confining the ninth amendment to hortatory dimensions.

[Moreover,] were the amendment ever to be adopted into the armory of natural law, one would have expected it to have occurred in such classic connections as the opinion of Chase, J., in Calder v. Bull, 3 U.S. (3 Dall.) 386 (1798), or in the argument of former Justice Campbell in Slaughter-House Cases, 83 U.S. (16 Wall.) 36 (1872), or in the opinion of Miller, J., in Loan Ass'n v. Topeka, 87 U.S. (20 Wall.) 655 (1874). But it does not, not even when Mr. Justice Miller in the later case speaks of "Implied reservations of individual rights, without which the social compact could not exist, and which are respected by all governments entitled to the name." *Id.* at 663.

Dunbar, *supra* note 5, at 640 n.47; *see also* Caplan, *supra* note 2, at 261 n.158. It is possible, as Dunbar indicates, that these cases did not recognize the ninth amendment as a repository of natural law because they involved state, rather than federal, action.

[50]T. Hobbes, Leviathan ch. 13 (1651).

was to be prevented from expropriating the benefits of the social contract. To accomplish this, Locke posited that the sovereign merely succeeded to the private rights given up to it by the contracting individual members of society. Thus, the state itself had no claim to new and independent rights as against the persons under its control. As a modern commentator has put it: "The state can acquire nothing by simple declaration of its will but must justify its claims in terms of the rights of the individuals whom it protects."[51] Of course, since "the central purpose of government is to maintain peace and order within the territory,"[52] the Lockean sovereign succeeds to private rights of self-defense in order to curb illegitimate, power-based intrusions upon the rights of others.[53] This police power attribute of sovereignty insures that the state can effectively provide peace and order to the individual members of the society but, critically, the power's theoretical outer limits are the limits of self-defense in private hands. The state cannot prohibit what could not legitimately be resisted or prohibited by private action prior to the Lockean compact.

Lockean thought was the dominant political theory at the time of the Constitution's adoption.[54] Constitutional limitations upon the federal government's power and express diffusion of its exercise were intended to guarantee the liberties of the individuals forming the society by dividing the potential power of the state to seize

---

[51]R. Epstein, Takings: Private Property and the Power of Eminent Domain 12 (1985).

[52]*Id.* at 16.

[53]An apt illustration of this principle is to be seen in the interplay of the law relative to possession of and trespass upon real property. At early common law, the essence of possession was the legal concept of the right of "seisin," a term connoting "peace and quiet." 2 F. Pollock & F. Maitland, The History of English Law Before the Time of Edward I 29–30 (2d ed. 1959). To vindicate this right, the law of trespass was created. Since allowing "men to make forcible entries on land . . . is to invite violence," the trespass laws' protection of possession "is a prohibition of self-help in the interest of public order." *Id.* at 31 & 41.

[54]Not only did Blackstone adopt the Lockean theory of the state, *see supra* note 46, but the constitutional framework of limited and separated powers provides evidence of intent to disable the sovereign from seizing the benefits of political union. *See* R. Epstein, *supra* note 51, at 16; Corwin, *The "Higher Law" Background of American Constitutional Law* (pt. 2), 42 Harv. L. Rev. 365, 394–409 (1929).

those liberties for itself.[55] The Constitution specifies precise measures to divide and check the exercise of power but is generally silent about protection of individual substantive rights. The elaborate devices created to limit power were, of course, intended to serve some substantive end. The procedural safeguards in the original Constitution implicitly protected against encroachments upon individual entitlements. It was for this reason that Hamilton and Wilson opposed adoption of the Bill of Rights.[56] With this conceptual understanding it is possible to see the function to be discharged by the Bill of Rights. It "identifies the ends of government, the rights that the system of limited jurisdiction, indirect voting, and separation of power is designed to protect."[57] It is this theoretical substantive end which the ninth amendment was intended to serve that must be kept in mind when examining its specific content.

Construing the ninth amendment as a mere declaration of a constitutional truism, devoid of enforceable content, renders its substance nugatory and assigns to its framers an intention to engage in a purely moot exercise. This view is at odds with the contextual historical evidence[58] and the specific, articulated concerns of its framers,[59] and violates the premise of *Marbury v. Madison* that the

[55]Locke desired a separation of executive and legislative functions. J. Locke, *supra* note 46, §§ 143–144, at 382–83. Montesquieu is generally credited with the doctrine of separation of powers. 1 C. Montesquieu, The Spirit of the Laws, bk. 11, at 149–51 (1748).

[56]*See supra* text accompanying notes 21–22.

[57]R. Epstein, *supra* note 51, at 18.

[58]*See supra* text accompanying notes 8–24. Too much cannot be made of the public opposition to the Constitution's adoption. It was this opposition, which viewed the central government as "foreign," that compelled the first Congress to propose the Bill of Rights. *See, e.g.*, Elbridge Gerry's assertion in Congress:

[A] great body of our constituents opposed the Constitution as it now stands, . . . [and] are apprehensive of the enormous power of [the federal] Government. . . . The ratification of the Constitution in several states would never have taken place had they not been assured that the objections would be duly attended to by Congress.

1 Annals of Cong., *supra* note 20, at 446–47; *see also supra* note 18.

[59]The draftsmen of the ninth amendment knew what they were about: limiting the delegated powers of the federal government. "This declaration of rights, I take it, is intended to secure the people against the maladministration of the [new central] government." 1 Annals of Cong., *supra* note 20, at 749 (remarks of Elbridge Gerry). Even the nationalist Madison admitted that "the abuse of powers of the General Government may be guarded against in a more secure manner than is now done [by the unamended Constitution]." *Id.* at 449–50.

Constitution contains judicially discoverable and enforceable principles.[60]

If the ninth amendment merely declares certain areas to be off limits for the exercise of the federal government's power, by what mechanism is that government to be prevented from ignoring its constitutionally defined boundaries? Berger contends that ninth amendment rights are not judicially enforceable because they do not arise under the Constitution but find their source wholly outside the Constitution.[61] This conclusion is premised, in part, upon the language chosen by Madison for introducing the ninth amendment in the House of Representatives.[62] Madison asserted that if the Bill of Rights were

> incorporated into the Constitution, independent tribunals of justice will consider themselves in a peculiar manner the guardians of those rights; they will be an inpenetrable bulwark against every assumption of power in the legislative or executive; they will be naturally led to resist every encroachment upon rights expressly stipulated for in the constitution by the declaration of rights.[63]

Berger contends that Madison's assertion, coupled with his belief that constitutional opponents were motivated in their opposition by the absence in the Constitution of "effectual provisions against encroachments on particular rights,"[64] is a sure indicator that only the specified rights were to be judicially enforced.[65] Rights were enumerated solely to make them susceptible of judicial enforcement. The inevitable corollary conclusion to this proposition is that ninth amendment rights, whatever their substance, are not capable

---

[60]5 U.S. (1 Cranch) 137, 166–67 & 117–78 (1803); *see also* L. Tribe, *supra* note 33, at 20–23 (Constitution contains principles enforceable through judicial review); H. Wechsler, Principles, Politics and Fundamental Law 4–10 (1961) (contending that Constitution's status as supreme law demands that it contain discoverable, enforceable values); Scharpf, *Judicial Review and the Political Question: A Functional Analysis*, 75 YALE L.J. 517, 517–19 (1966); Van Alstyne, *A Critical Guide to Marbury v. Madison*, 1969 DUKE L.J. 1, 16–29 (surveying arguments advanced by Chief Justice Marshall in *Marbury* for judicial review).

[61]Berger, *supra* note 2, at 9.

[62]*Id.* at 8; *see supra* text accompanying note 26.

[63]1 Annals of Cong., *supra* note 20, at 440.

[64]*Id.* at 433.

[65]Berger, *supra* note 2, at 8–9; *cf.* Dunbar, *supra* note 5, at 643 (judicial enforcement is the practical effect of enumeration; ninth amendment rights are defendable only through political action).

of judicial enforcement. As a practical matter, then, they may be freely invaded by a Congress vigorously exercising its express or implied powers.[66] This conclusion meets an immediate and formidable obstacle in the language of the ninth amendment itself. If the reserved rights are not to be denied or disparaged by the enumeration of other rights, but only the enumerated rights may be judicially enforced, the reserved rights necessarily shrivel. If this is not disparagement, or "impairment" as Elbridge Gerry would have preferred,[67] then the concept has been drained of all meaning.

Moreover, Berger makes too much of "Madison's disclaimer of intention 'to enlarge the powers delegated by the Constitution' by nonenumeration of 'other rights.' "[68] Madison's fourth resolution sets forth a rule of construction that enumeration of rights should "not be construed as to . . . enlarge the powers delegated by the constitution; but either as actual limitations of such powers, or as inserted merely for greater caution."[69] Madison's language readily supports the conclusion that the ninth amendment cannot be used as a springboard for enabling Congress, under Article I, section 8,[70] to create additional rights.[71] But delegated powers are not enlarged

[66]When the rule of McCulloch v. Maryland, 17 U.S. (4 Wheat.) 316 (1819), the supremacy clause, the post–1937 expansion of the commerce clause, and the attenuation of the tenth amendment are read together, an interpretation of the ninth amendment which denies judicial enforcement of those rights "retained by the people" is the amendment's death sentence. That, perhaps, is the logical extension of the evolution of constitutional jurisprudence in a direction which dismisses federalism as an antiquarian relic to be discarded for lack of modern relevance. A comprehensive treatment of federalism, setting forth a modern federal theory, is beyond the scope of this article. For ninth amendment rights to have real flesh, whether one subscribes to Berger's view of enforceability or to the view set forth in the text accompanying note 58 above to note 74 below, may require a radical change of thought in constitutional interpretation concerning the proper scope of the powers of Congress, at least with respect to the states.

[67]1 Annals of Cong., *supra* note 20, at 754.

[68]Berger, *supra* note 2, at 8; *see also supra* text accompanying notes 62–63.

[69]1 Annals of Cong., *supra* note 20, at 435.

[70]U.S. Const. art. I, § 8 enumerates the powers delegated to Congress and concludes with a grant of power to Congress "To make all Laws which shall be necessary and proper for carrying into Execution the foregoing Powers, and all other Powers vested by this Constitution in the Government of the United States, or in any Department or Officer thereof."

[71]Both Berger, a principal advocate of a limited, declaratory reading of the ninth amendment, and Ely, an activist egalitarian, agree on this point. Berger, *supra* note 2, at 8–10; J. Ely, *supra* note 2, at 37. Madison's disclaimer, coupled with the explicit text of the necessary and proper clause, disposes of any such notion.

by treating the ninth amendment's declaration of reserved rights to be, itself, a constitutional right. The amendment is, after all, a part of the Constitution and declares its purpose to be to prevent denial or disparagement of its unspecified rights. It would be richly ironic to find this piece of the constitutional text undeserving of judicial protection, for it would declare the principle that the rights thereby reserved were simply reserved for oblivion whenever the federal government chose to eradicate or ignore them.[72] Rather, proceeding from the familiar maxim, "for every wrong there is a remedy."[73] it would seem logical to assume the existence of some enforceable remedy whenever the federal government exceeds its delegated powers by invading a reserved right. This remedy, of course, can have meaning only to the extent that the ninth amendment has substantive sources or content discernible by principled means of interpretation not reliant upon the importation of wholly subjective values.[74]

In drafting the ninth amendment, surely its authors had in mind some bundle of rights worthy of constitutional protection. Perhaps the surest indication of the kind of rights with which they were

---

[72]By inference, Caplan would seem to adopt this topsy-turvy view. He contends that the ninth amendment merely perpetuates any individual rights rooted in state law until "eliminated . . . by federal preemption." Caplan, *supra* note 2, at 228. Caplan relies on the supremacy clause. U.S. Const. art. VI, cl. 2, for this conclusion.

Of course, there are constitutional guarantees that escape judicial review by application of the murky doctrine of nonjusticiability. *See, e.g.,* the guarantee clause, U.S. Const. art. IV, § 4, cl. 1 ("The United States shall guarantee to every State in this Union a Republican Form of Government. . . ."). Since Luther v. Borden, 48 U.S. (7 How.) 1 (1849), the guarantee clause has been consigned to this constitutional purgatory. L. Tribe, *supra* note 33, § 3–16. *But see* Note, *The Rule of Law and the States: A New Interpretation of the Guarantee Clause,* 93 Yale L.J. 561 (1984); *infra* text accompanying notes 118–25; *see also* Ludecke v. Watkins, 335 U.S. 160, 168–70 (1948) (refusal to determine the duration of a state of war); Clark v. Allen, 331 U.S. 503, 514 (1947) (refusal to determine whether treaty abrogated); Coleman v. Miller, 307 U.S. 433 (1939) (refusal to determine whether a state has properly ratified a constitutional amendment). It is possible that the tenth amendment has also slipped into this nether world. *See* Garcia v. San Antonio Metro. Transit Auth., 105 S. Ct. 1005 (1985).

[73]Cal. Civ. Code § 3523 (West 1984). Maxims of jurisprudence and rules of statutory construction are not inapplicable when wrestling with constitutional meaning. *See* Berger, *"Government by Judiciary": Judge Gibbons' Argument Ad Hominem,* 59 B.U.L. Rev. 783, 804–06 (1977) (citing eminent jurists and commentators who believe such canons to be applicable to constitutional interpretation).

[74]*See supra* notes 37–42 and accompanying text.

concerned lies in the fact that the ninth amendment was proposed, considered, and adopted as a part of the Bill of Rights.[75] This was no accident; it was the logical product of a century and a half of colonial government. From the beginning of English settlement in North America, colonists believed themselves the equals of native Englishmen and entitled to the "rights of Englishmen" as established by English statutory and common law.[76] The colonists did not believe these were static rights but asserted them to be capable of limitation, amplification, or revision by their colonial legislatures.[77] Moreover, they did not wholly trust the English statutory enactments, preferring to enact existing guarantees as part of colonial organic law.[78] Accordingly, during the Virginia ratification debates, Patrick Henry declared that George Mason's 1776 Virginia Bill of Rights "secures the great and principal rights of mankind," such "rights of the people" being those secured by English and American statutory law and the common law of England as imported to America.[79] A federal Bill of Rights, then, was a plain statement of these great and principal rights of mankind. It was not an exhaustive list; the ninth amendment reminds us of this fact.

[75]Divining meaning from constitutional text by its context and from structurally related constitutional concepts is at the heart of Professor Black's thesis. *See* C. Black, *supra* note 29, at 3–32.

[76]T. Curry, The First Freedoms 64, 66 (1986); *see also* 1 Blackstone, Commentaries *63–64, *104–05 & *123–24. Among the important statutory sources of the "rights of Englishmen" were the Magna Carta (1215), Petition of Rights (1628), Habeas Corpus Act (1679), Declaration of Rights (1689), Toleration Act (1689), Mutiny Act (1689), and Settlement Act (1701). *See generally* F. McDonald, Novus Ordo Seclorum: The Intellectual Origins of the Constitution 9–55 (1985); H. Taylor, The Origin and Growth of the American Constitution 230–43 (1911).

[77]*See, e.g.,* Maryland Declaration of Rights (1776), *reprinted in* 3 Federal and State Constitutions, Colonial Charters and Other Organic Laws 1686 (F. Thorpe ed. 1909) [hereinafter Federal and State Constitutions].

[78]The Magna Carta established that personal liberty and private rights to property were beyond the royal grasp and could be taken only as provided by the law of the land. This early statement of due process had been confirmed by Parliament in 1773. *Cf.* 1 Blackstone, Commentaries *137–38. (Since Blackstone's first edition was published in 1765, it contains no reference to the 1773 statutory enactment. Later editions contain the reference. *See, e.g., id.* at *139–40 (J. Chitty ed. 1826).) It had also been incorporated into Maryland law (1639), Massachusetts' Body of Liberties (1641), the West New Jersey Charter (1676), New York's "Charter of Libertyes and Privilidges" (1683), and even the Northwest Ordinance (1787). 5 Federal and State Constitutions, *supra* note 77, at 2549.

[79]3 J. Elliot, *supra* note 13, at 461, 513 & 587–88.

Since the source of the first eight amendments was the inherited "rights of Englishmen" as adapted to colonial circumstances and secured by state charters and statutes, it would seem a safe point of departure to assume that the unenumerated rights of the ninth amendment were intended to be the remaining such "rights of Englishmen." But, of course, after successful revolt from British rule, Americans possessed only rights of Americans. To be sure, the rights of Americans might have a source in the traditional fount of common law but, to the extent such rights were of statutory dimension, the relevant statutes were those enacted by the states.[80] Indeed, the sentiment of many of the framers was to look to the states as the source of protection of their cherished liberties.[81] It was this source that was drawn upon to compose a federal Bill of Rights.

This stream of rights had two branches. The framers understood and observed a distinction between "natural" rights and "civil" or "positive" rights.[82] Positive rights had their source in state common, constitutional, and statutory law; natural rights stemmed from Lockean notions concerning the "unalienable"[83] rights of the people. But, because both forms were considered to be "essential to

[80]Caplan makes a persuasive case that the ninth amendment was intended only to preserve from federal encroachment rights secured by state law. See Caplan, *supra* note 2, at 228–59. He concludes that "the ninth amendment embraces those individual liberties protected by state laws." *Id.* at 265.

[81]Oliver Ellsworth, for example, trusted "for the preservation of his rights to the State Govts. From these alone he could derive the greatest happiness he expects in this life." 1 The Records of the Federal Convention of 1787, at 492 (M. Farrand ed. 1937) [hereinafter Records]. In recommending against inclusion of a Bill of Rights in the Federal Constitution, Roger Sherman declared: "The State Declarations of Rights are not repealed by this Constitution; and being in force are sufficient." 2 *id.* at 588. James Wilson asserted in 1791 that "our [colonial] assemblies were chosen by ourselves: they were the guardians of our rights, the objects of our confidence, and the anchor of our political hopes." 1 Works of James Wilson 292 (R. McCloskey ed. 1967).

[82]Madison perceived a distinction between natural rights, "those rights which are retained when particular powers are given up to be exercised by the Legislature," and positive rights, those which "may seem to result from the nature of the compact." 1 Annals of Cong., *supra* note 20, at 954; *see supra* note 47. This distinction was also seen by Blackstone. 1 Blackstone, Commentaries *42–44 & *121–22. Indeed its roots can be traced to Aristotle. See Caplan, *supra* note 2, at 237 n.55.

[83]See 1 The Bill of Rights: A Documentary History 349 (B. Schwartz ed. 1971); Declaration of Independence para. 1 (U.S. 1776) ("We hold these Truths to be self-evident, that all Men are . . . endowed by their Creator with certain unalienable rights. . . .").

secure the liberty of the people,"[84] the package of rights expressly enumerated in the first eight amendments contains both natural and positive rights.[85] It is a fair inference, then, that the unenumerated rights of the ninth amendment were thought to consist of both varieties. If this be so, the distinction between "natural" and "positive" rights cannot account for the selection of the rights worthy of enumeration in the first eight amendments. Some other rationale must be supplied for the specification of those rights, else we reach the unlikely conclusion that the thoughtful, learned framers were actuated by caprice.

The framers enumerated certain rights for a purpose other than insuring their judicial enforceability.[86] Madison observed, when introducing the Bill of Rights in Congress, that it was necessary to enumerate certain rights of the people because some states had no bill of rights and other states' declarations were defective.[87] Moreover, Madison was unwilling to rely on natural law as wholly preservative of the peoples' liberties:

> It would be a sufficient answer to say, that this objection lies against such provisions [declarations of rights] under the State Governments, as well as under the General Government; and there are, I believe, but few gentlemen who are inclined to push their theory so far as to say that a declaration of rights in those cases is either ineffectual or improper.[88]

Rights were enumerated in the federal Constitution to provide a clear barrier to federal action[89]; the specific guarantees selected for

[84]1 Annals of Cong., *supra* note 20, at 454 (Madison's remarks).

[85]*See supra* note 47. *Compare* U.S. Const. amend. I (freedom of speech, a natural right) *with* U.S. Const. amend. VII (trial by jury, a positive right).

[86]Madison undoubtedly thought enumeration would lead to judicial enforceability. *See supra* text accompanying notes 62–63. Yet, he also entertained larger hopes for the entire Bill of Rights. "The political truths declared in that solemn manner acquire by degrees the character of fundamental maxims of free Government, and as they become incorporated with the national sentiment, counteract the impulses of interest and passion." 5 Madison Writings, *supra* note 11, at 273. One of those political truths for which Madison held such high hopes was that unenumerated rights retained by the people were of equal constitutional dignity with the specified rights.

[87]1 Annals of Cong., *supra* note 20, at 452; *see also infra* text accompanying note 121.

[88]1 Annals of Cong., *supra* note 20, at 455.

[89]*See supra* note 59.

enumeration were derived from similar specific guarantees then in existence under state charters, constitutions, or declarations of rights.[90] The inclusion of the ninth amendment was, in part, an attempt to be certain that rights protected by state law were not supplanted by federal law simply because they were not enumerated.[91] But the ninth amendment was intended to do more than secure unenumerated state-based rights from federal invasion; it was also to serve as a barrier to encroachment upon natural rights retained by the people.[92]

Thus, the ninth amendment protects two distinct categories of rights: positive rights, having their source in state law, and natural rights, grounded in conceptions of inalienable rights of man.[93] The difference compels differing analytical treatment of their content and enforceability. If the reserved positive rights of the ninth amendment may be determined by reference to state law, either existing in 1788 or later created, there is no genuine theoretical obstacle to their judicial enforcement. Concern that the substance of these rights is so amorphous as to endanger the validity of judicial process by license to import subjective personal values is eliminated by looking only to state law to provide the boundaries of reserved positive rights. Unfortunately, judicial enforcement of reserved natural rights implicates precisely these concerns.[94]

IV. Positive Rights

Application of state law positive rights, secured by the ninth amendment, as a barrier to action by the federal government poses

[90]*See supra* note 87 & *infra* note 121.

[91]*See* Caplan, *supra* note 2, at 254.

[92]Madison feared that enumeration of rights "would disparage those rights which were not placed in that enumeration; and it might follow, by implication, that those rights which were not singled out, were intended to be assigned into the hands of the General Government, and were consequently insecure." 1 Annals of Cong., *supra* note 20, at 456. This inference could be "guarded against" by the ninth amendment. *Id.* The fact that Madison had the same fear with respect to state bills of rights indicates that he appreciated that certain rights were "natural [and] . . . retained by the people" (5 Madison Writings, *supra* note 11, at 390 & n.1), and were properly beyond the powers of government.

[93]This division is wholly consistent with Madison's conception of rights as procedural, or positive, and substantive, or natural. *See supra* notes 30–31 and accompanying text.

[94]*See infra* notes 126–32 and accompanying text.

substantial apparent conflict with the supremacy clause.[95] How-ever, once it is conceded that the state-based rights guaranteed by the ninth amendment are federal rights, the conflict partially vanishes, for the rights preserved are federal in character though state in origin. This starting point finds support in the amendment's text, which enjoins a construction of the Constitution that would "deny or disparage" the unenumerated rights. To conclude that ninth amendment rights are capable of invasion by means of the supremacy clause[96] is to both deny and disparage them, for no one contends that the rights secured by the first eight amendments may be preempted by simple congressional action.[97]

Even though ninth amendment positive rights are federal in character, their state origin poses practical problems in finding a comfortable fit between the supremacy clause and the ninth amendment. Two extreme alternatives may be quickly dismissed. First, Congress could be conceded the power to preempt a state-based ninth amendment right. As discussed above, this conclusion repudiates the amendment's text and ignores whatever effect the later amendment may have been intended to have on the earlier supremacy clause. Second, Congress could be denied any power to preempt a state-based ninth amendment right under any circumstances. While this conclusion would elevate ninth amendment rights to equal status with the enumerated rights, a result commanded by the amendment itself, it raises an ugly specter of back-door nulli-fication. If congressional action can be effective only if the states implicitly consent by their failure to enact contrary legislation (which

[95]This Constitution, and the Laws of the United States which shall be made in Pursuance thereof; and all Treaties made, or which shall be made, under the Authority of the United States, shall be the supreme Law of the Land; and the Judges in every State shall be bound thereby, any Thing in the Constitution or Laws of any State to the Contrary notwithstanding.
U.S. Const. art. VI, cl. 2. Supremacy clause problems are confined to evaluation of ninth amendment positive rights. Since the source of natural rights lies in conceptions of inalienable rights of the people not transferable to government upon making the social compact, such rights do not present any state challenge to federal authority. See supra text accompanying notes 30–31 & 54–55; infra notes 128–32.

[96]See supra note 7 & 72.

[97]This is the fundamental error of Justice Reed in United Pub. Workers v. Mitchell, 330 U.S. 75, 95–96 (1947); see supra note 7. By assuming that the ninth amendment can be invaded by congressional action and that the first eight amendments cannot, Justice Reed made a distinction fatally disparaging to ninth amendment rights. Unless its text be ignored, the ninth amendment forbids the distinction.

would provide a source for the federal rights reserved by the ninth amendment) the ghost of John C. Calhoun has arisen in a new and powerful form.[98] This would be a disturbing and radical result at odds with much of American history and the settled understanding of the proper place of the states and Congress.

Can there be any rationally explicable middle ground? The fundamental problem is to differentiate among state rights in a way that does not "deny or disparage" ninth amendment rights. The understanding of the ninth amendment's framers provides a helpful departure for formulation of a usable standard. The framers were unwilling to declare in the Constitution that common law, or even state law, remained in effect because they thought that to do so would freeze the common law at the date of its adoption, thereby preventing that highly organic mechanism from undergoing further change.[99] Rufus King also thought that constitutional guarantees of state law would prevent the states from later altering their laws.[100] The common law was in an anomalous position: it was "not excluded"[101] but neither was it "understood to be a law of the United States."[102] It was not expressly adopted, for to do so would mummify it in place; it was not excluded because, when all was said and done, it was still a source of the "great and principal rights of mankind."[103] Clearly, the framers intended to permit the later evolution of common and statutory law within the several states. Simultaneously, in adopting the ninth amendment, they preserved the

---

[98]Calhoun, of course, as Vice-President in Andrew Jackson's first term, originated the doctrine of nullification in response to the Tariff of 1828. He asserted the constitutional right of a state to void federal law within its own borders whenever the state independently determined such law to be unconstitutional. Following enactment of the Tariff of 1832, South Carolina's enthusiastic adoption of nullification with respect to application of the tariff in South Carolina threatened the continued existence of the Union. See generally R. Remini, Andrew Jackson and the Course of American Freedom, 1822–1832, at 137, 160, 232–37, 381 & 387–89 (1981); R. Remini, Andrew Jackson and the Course of American Democracy, 1833–1845, at 8–44 (1984).

[99]3 J. Elliot, supra note 13, at 450–51 (G. Nicholas, Virginia) & 469–70 (E. Randolph, Virginia).

[100]In the Massachusetts ratification convention, King declared that "if the present constitution of this state had been guaranteed by the United States . . . , it must have precluded the state from making any alteration in it, should [Massachusetts] see fit so to do." 2 id. at 101.

[101]3 id. at 451 (G. Nicholas).

[102]4 id. at 565 (J. Madison, Report on the Virginia Resolutions).

[103]3 id. at 461 (P. Henry); see supra text accompanying notes 72–79.

constitutionally guaranteed dignity of personal rights which have their source in such state laws.[104]

Two principles then suggest themselves as possible alternative vehicles for sorting out the claims of a state-based ninth amendment right when they conflict with otherwise legitimate federal legislative action. First, if the asserted federal ninth amendment right is predicated upon state action taken prior to the Constitution's adoption,[105] the claimed ninth amendment right is secured against congressional invasion. This conclusion finds support in the general fear of federal encroachment that prompted adoption of the ninth amendment—not all of the great and principal rights of man were specified in the first eight amendments; failure to preserve inviolate the unspecified rights would hazard them to loss by action of an aggressive central government.[106] If the ninth amendment was to preserve against federal action unspecified rights whose source was in state constitutional, common, or statutory law it is readily inferable that the framers intended thereby to displace the federal preemptive power, at least with respect to ninth amendment rights which could be identified by reference to then existing state sources.

A second, and more radical, alternative is to conclude that the framers intended to permit the states to continue to develop sources of ninth amendment rights after the Constitution's adoption. To reconcile this conclusion with the supremacy clause it is necessary to assume that, from the clean slate of constitutional adoption, both the federal Congress and the states possessed concurrent authority to modify personal positive rights.[107] To be sure, congressional authority is limited to its delegated powers; state authority is limited by constitutional prohibitions, including the supremacy clause. A principle of priority in time then suggests itself as a vehicle for sorting out the conflicting claims of a state-based ninth amendment

---

[104]In evaluating the proposed Constitution during the Philadelphia convention, George Mason concluded that "[t]he laws of the U.S. are to be paramount to State Bills of Rights." 2 Records, *supra* note 81, at 588. For this, among other reasons, Mason opposed the Constitution's ratification by Virginia and, once adoption became inevitable, urged the adoption of a federal Bill of Rights.

[105]July 2, 1788. 1 J. Elliot, *supra* note 13, at 332.

[106]*See supra* notes 58 & 59 and accompanying text.

[107]*Cf.* The Federalist No. 82 (A. Hamilton) (concluding that concurrent jurisdiction exists with respect to personal positive rights); Brown v. Gerdes, 321 U.S. 178, 188 (1944) (Frankfurter, J., concurring) (federal rights may be vindicated in a state forum unless Congress has conferred exclusive jurisdiction upon federal courts.)

right and otherwise legitimate federal legislative action. If the state-law source of the asserted federal ninth amendment right predates the congressional action which would invade the right, the congressional action must yield. If the contrary condition exists, Congress will be deemed to have preempted the field. Such an approach allows for the natural development of democratic institutions in the twin arenas of the Capitol and the state houses. When the people, through their spokespersons, declare a right to be of sufficient importance to be worthy of legal articulation, it becomes preserved through the ninth amendment. But if the right is merely quiescent, and Congress has exercised otherwise legitimate authority to regulate state and personal behavior in a way which would preclude exercise of the inchoate right, it is waived until and unless the federal democracy changes its legislative determination. This proposal may be more nearly consistent with the framers' desire to ensure the continued evolution of state common law[108] but poses enormous practical problems that, in all likelihood, doom it as a seriously workable constitutional mechanism.[109]

Limiting ninth amendment positive rights to those having a clear textual foundation in state sources in existence at the time of the Constitution's adoption avoids the mischief inherent in splitting

---

[108]*See supra* text accompanying notes 99–104.

[109]The foremost problem is the difficulty of establishing priority of action between Congress and the several states. Perhaps some rights are of dubious ancestry; rules governing burden of proof could dispose of these questionable claims. Later-admitted states would object that reckoning their citizens' rights by dates of admission to the Union contradicts the principle of equal status of the states. This problem could be avoided by permitting a later-admitted state to assert the priority of earlier states if it has vested its citizens with a reserved ninth amendment right in existence, by reference to sister state sources, prior to its own admission. A cottage industry of legal historians would spring up, bringing greater expense to litigants but providing the valuable benefits of enhanced public understanding of the roots of assumed liberties.

Perhaps most nettlesome would be the issue of the uniform (or nonuniform) character of this federal ninth amendment right. Since it derives its content from state sources, it is logical to view the federal right as one varying in content with the state citizenship of the claimant. For example, a Californian possesses a state constitutional right to privacy. Cal. Const. art. I, § 1(1849, amended 1972). Assuming, hypothetically, the absence of a federal constitutional right of privacy, should a Californian be able to assert a federal right not available to an Alabaman? By contrast, what good reason demands that an Alabaman be able to assert a federal right that owes its existence to timely action by the citizens of California? The practical problems thus illustrated reveal this alternative to be hopelessly unworkable.

supremacy clause hairs. Moreover, it permits the asserted ninth amendment right to be uniform in character, a result unlikely to be achieved were the "priority in time" alternative adopted. Since, under this proposal, a federal ninth amendment positive right finds its substance in state action prior to 1788, its boundaries are defined by the pre–1788 organic law of all of the original states, taken together. A ninth amendment right thus derived is identical for all citizens, whatever their state citizenship, and operates to block federal action invasive of this right.

Commentators agree that the ninth amendment operates, if at all, against federal action.[110] Disagreement begins when attempts are made to apply the amendment as a barrier to state action.[111] Most such attempts have utilized the incorporation doctrine, by which specific guarantees of the Bill of Rights have been held applicable to the states through the fourteenth amendment.[112] Superficially, it would appear that it is not "logically possible to 'incorporate' the ninth amendment through the fourteenth to apply as a prohibition against the states, because the ninth amendment was designed not to circumscribe but to protect the enactments of the states."[113] But if one considers that the federal character of ninth amendment positive rights derives from state action, application of the ninth amendment to the states would merely amount to a

---

[110]J. Ely, *supra* note 2; Berger, *supra* note 2.

[111]*Compare* Berger, *supra* note 2, at 23–24 and Caplan, *supra* note 2, at 264 *with* Redlich, *Are There "Certain Rights . . . Retained by the People"?* 37 N.Y.U. L. Rev. 787, 806 (1962) (suggesting application of ninth amendment to states through fourteenth amendment) and C. Black, *supra* note 2; *see also* Griswold v. Connecticut, 381 U.S. 479, 493 (1981) (Goldberg, J., concurring):

> [T]he Ninth Amendment, in indicating that not all such liberties are specifically mentioned in the first eight amendments, is surely relevant in showing the existence of other fundamental personal rights, now protected from state, as well as federal, infringement. In sum, the Ninth Amendment simply lends strong support to the view that the "liberty" protected by the Fifth and Fourteenth Amendments from infringement by the Federal Government or the States is not restricted to rights specifically mentioned in the first eight amendments.

[112]*See, e.g.,* Duncan v. Louisiana, 391 U.S. 145 (1968); Washington v. Texas, 388 U.S. 14 (1967); Klopfer v. North Carolina, 386 U.S. 213 (1967); Pointer v. Texas, 380 U.S. 400 (1965); Gideon v. Wainwright, 372 U.S. 335 (1963); Mapp v. Ohio, 367 U.S. 643 (1961); In re Oliver, 333 U.S. 257 (1948); Fiske v. Kansas, 274 U.S. 380 (1927); Chicago, Burlington & Quincy R.R. v. Chicago, 166 U.S. 226 (1897).

[113]Caplan, *supra* note 2, at 261–62 (footnote omitted).

federally enforced right to make the states abide by their own law. For a government to abide by its own law is of the essence of due process.[114] Since the fourteenth amendment demands that states not "deprive any person of life, liberty, or property, without due process of law,"[115] it is no grotesque distortion of either the ninth or fourteenth amendments to read into them a requirement that a state observe its own law.[116] Moreover, this result is hightly compatible with Madison's observation that positive rights secured by the Bill of Rights are procedural in nature.[117]

However, if incorporation is deemed undesirable, a state may still be required to enforce its own law through the guarantee clause.[118] This approach would require a substantial modification in the accepted understanding of that clause. Since *Luther v. Borden*[119] the guarantee clause has evaded judicial review because it has been

[114]"The words 'due process of law,' were undoubtedly intended to convey the same meaning as the words 'by the law of the land,' in Magna Charta." Murray's Lessee v. Hoboken Land & Improvement Co., 9 U.S. (18 How.) 272, 276 (1855) (citing 2 E. Coke, Institutes *45 & *50); *see also* Corwin, *supra* note 54, at 378.

[115]U.S. Const. amend. XIV, § 1.

[116]In order to give full effect to such a guarantee it would be helpful to discard the current erroneous understanding of the eleventh amendment, which reads: "The Judicial power of the United States shall not be construed to extend to any suit in law or equity, commenced or prosecuted against one of the United States by Citizens of another State, or by Citizens or Subjects of any Foreign State." U.S. Const. amend. XI. The current doctrine, based on Hans v. Louisiana, 134 U.S. 1 (1890), holds that a citizen may not sue his own state directly in federal court, Employees v. Missouri Pub. Health & Welfare Dep't, 411 U.S. 279 (1973), nor even invoke federal jurisdiction to compel his own state to observe its own law. Pennhurst State School & Hosp. v. Halderman, 465 U.S. 89 (1984). The current doctrine proceeds from the mistaken assumption that the eleventh amendment was intended to constitutionalize state sovereign immunity as a result of the profound "shock of surprise" created by Chisholm v. Georgia, 2 U.S. (2 Dall.) 419 (1793), which held Georgia amenable to suit by a South Carolina creditor. *Hans*, 134 U.S. at 11. The doctrine ignores the plain language of the eleventh amendment, the history of its adoption, and the century of judicial interpretation of its text prior to the 1890 *Hans* decision. *See generally Pennhurst*, 465 U.S. at 125 (Brennan, J., dissenting); Gibbons, *The Eleventh Amendment and State Sovereign Immunity: A Reinterpretation*, 83 Colum. L. Rev. 1889 (1983); Massey, *The Pennhurst Decision: Ignoring the History of the 11th Amendment*, L.A. Daily J., Oct. 5, 1984, at 13.

[117]*See supra* text accompanying notes 30–31.

[118]"The United States shall guarantee to every State in this Union a Republican Form of Government. . . ." U.S. Const. art. IV, § 4, cl. 1.

[119]48 U.S. (7 How.) 1 (1849).

consigned to the nether world of nonjusticiability. But reading the clause as a federal constitutional guarantee "that the states either observe their own constitutions and laws or change them by legally valid procedures"[120] is a peculiarly well-suited vehicle for enforcing state compliance with the state laws which form the content of ninth amendment positive rights. When introducing the Bill of Rights, Madison explained its necessity, in part, by observing that "some states have no bills of rights," and those that did had failed to secure rights to "the full extent which republican principles would require."[121] This contemporaneous expression is a plain indication that both the specific and unenumerated rights which compose the Bill of Rights form part of the core understanding of the meaning of republican government. Moreover, conformity to law is at the heart of any conception of republican government.[122] This reading of the guarantee clause modifies but in no way distorts the established conception of the clause,[123] helps effectuate the ninth amendment without damaging other constitutional values,[124] and conforms to the constitutional duty to decide cases and controversies.[125]

V. Natural Rights

Since the "great and principal rights of mankind"[126] protected by the ninth amendment include both positive and natural rights, it is necessary to confront the amorphous goblin of natural law in order to define natural ninth amendment rights without reference to sources wholly extrinsic to the Constitution.[127] Madison's contention that "natural rights [are] retained"[128] by the people is consistent with the theory that natural rights find their source in the immutable, inalienable rights of mankind, possessed apart from and

---

[120]Note, *supra* note 72, at 561.

[121]1 Annals of Cong., *supra* note 20, at 452.

[122]*See* the authorities collected in Note, *supra* note 72, at 566 n.34.

[123]*Id.* at 565–73.

[124]*Cf.* C. Black, *supra* note 29, at 33–51 (constitutional interpretation should take place within whole context of legal and political structures created by the Constitution).

[125]U.S. Const. art. III, § 2; Marbury v. Madison, 5 U.S. (1 Cranch) 137 (1803).

[126]3 J. Elliot, *supra* note 13, at 461 (Patrick Henry).

[127]*See supra* notes 37–49 and accompanying text.

[128]5 Madison Writings, *supra* note 11, at 389 n.1.

transcendent to government.[129] It is the transcendent authority of these rights that makes them important to confront; it is their gossamer nature that makes them virtually impossible to discern by application of neutral principles. If they be paramount to legislative action, it is no accident that the framers selected the phrase "retained by the people"[130] to describe these rights. Positive rights acquired substance by the social compact; hence their retention by the people was ceded to the government as part of the initial governmental contract.[131] Natural rights could not, by definition, be so ceded. Hence it is logically anomalous to conclude that the people's assertion of a retained natural right against state action infringing that right is not proper.[132]

[129]W. Friedmann, Legal Theory 117–27 (5th ed. 1967). That this notion was central to the framers' intellectual understanding of their government can be seen from the Declaration of Independence, which echoed earlier colonial declarations of rights: "We hold these truths to be self-evident, that all men are created equal, that they are endowed by their Creator with certain unalienable Rights, that among these are Life, Liberty and the Pursuit of Happiness—That to secure these Rights, Governments are instituted among Men, deriving their just powers from the consent of the governed." Declaration of Independence para. 1 (U.S. 1776). At the Constitutional Convention, Madison observed that the people are "the fountain of all power." 2 Records, *supra* note 81, at 476. Edmund Pendleton echoed Madison during the Virginia ratification convention: "Who but the people have a right to form government?" 3 J. Elliott, *supra* note 13, at 37. As early as 1775, Alexander Hamilton proclaimed his allegiance to natural law principles. 1 The Works of Alexander Hamilton 61–64 & 87 (H. Lodge ed. 1904). Indeed, Hamilton went so far as to proclaim: "The Sacred Rights of Mankind are not to be rummaged for among old parchments or musty records. They are written, as with a sunbeam, in the whole volume of human nature, by the hand of Divinity itself, and can never be erased or obscured by mortal power." *Id.* at 113, *see also* McCulloch v. Maryland, 17 U.S. (4 Wheat.) 316, 404–05 (1819).

[130]U.S. Const. amend. IX.

[131]*See supra* notes 47 & 82.

[132]This conclusion encounters difficulty when it is recalled that the enumerated rights (among them some natural rights) were not originally intended to be enforceable against the states: "Had congress engaged in the extraordinary occupation of improving the constitutions of the several states by affording the people additional protection from the exercise of power by their own governments in matters which concerned themselves alone, they would have declared this purpose in plain and intelligible language." Barron v. Mayor of Baltimore, 32 U.S. (7 Pet.) 243, 250 (1833). Establishment of the incorporation doctrine as a fixture of constitutional law removes most of these difficulties. Incorporation implicitly recognizes that the paramount nature of the enumerated rights overrides state attempts to rescind their guarantees. *See supra* note 112 and accompanying text.

The hard task is finding principled substance in these natural rights. When it is recalled that the objective in erecting a constitutional barrier to the denial of retained, unenumerated rights was to preserve the great and principal rights of man, it becomes apparent that it is possible to borrow from existing constitutional theory to put flesh on these skeletal rights. The doctrine of fundamental rights, long a part of equal protection analysis,[133] seems most conceptually akin to Patrick Henry's great and principal rights.[134] Moreover, to be consistent with Lockean political theory, such fundamental rights must be seen to be precisely coterminous with private rights not subject to invasion by legitimate private action. Yet, for purposes of finding those paramount fundamental rights protected by the ninth amendment against state or federal invasion, some limiting principles are prudent. An asserted fundamental right should have textual foundation in the Constitution, however implicit or attenuated.[135] It should have some historical authenticity in the organic law of the nation, the states, the colonies, or the common law. It should be consistent with the theoretical construct of natural rights, so far as that subject can provide meaning.[136] It should be a right generally recognized by a significant portion of contemporary society as one inextricably connected with the inherent dignity of the individual.[137]

[133]See, e.g., Shapiro v. Thompson, 394 U.S. 618 (1969); Harper v. Virginia State Bd. of Elections, 383 U.S. 663 (1966); Reynolds v. Sims, 377 U.S. 533, 561–62 (1964); cf. Yick Wo v. Hopkins, 118 U.S. 356, 370 (1885).

[134]Natural law is long-established in American law. See W. Friedmann, supra note 129, at 136–51; see also supra notes 46 & 49–57 and accompanying text; infra notes 198–99. If fundamental rights have any philosophical foundation, it is upon the rock of natural law which has actuated so much of American legal thought. See supra note 129; Corwin, supra note 32, at 152; Corwin, The Debt of American Constitutional Law to Natural Law Concepts, 25 Notre Dame Law. 258 (1950).

[135]In this connection, the utility of finding constitutional meaning in "structure and relationship" is germane. See C. Black, supra note 29. This limitation is plainly not required by the ninth amendment, which indeed would seemingly preclude reliance upon textual foundations other than the amendment itself. The proposed limitation is prudential only, intended to limit judicial resort to personal values and subjective preferences. See supra notes 37–42 and accompanying text.

[136]At the very least, an asserted fundamental right ought to be plainly inferable from the analytical arguments advanced by natural law scholars.

[137]No suggestion is made that an asserted right must command a majority. Given the anti-majoritarian nature of judicial review, this is unlikely. Rather, the right, even if highly controversial, should be recognized to exist in concepts of inherent

A. The Right of Privacy

The right of privacy, particularly as manifested in intimate choices regarding marital sex and procreation, is the constitutional right most closely associated with the ninth amendment.[138] Where, if at all, does this right fit analytically into the constitutional template constructed thus far? First, privacy would not seem to be a positive or civil right. It is not manufactured by operation of the social compact, as Madison thought of the right to trial by jury.[139] That is, in parting with unfettered personal autonomy in order to create government, a right of privacy was not thereby created as a regulation upon the procedural action of the community. Rather, a substantive right of privacy would seem to exist independently of the acts of civil authorities. A right of privacy is thus at least consistent with the theoretical understanding of natural rights, although justifying a right of privacy as a ninth amendment right solely by reference to natural law theory is tautological. Fortunately, there are more secure anchors. Privacy has historical authenticity. Its roots may be traced back from *Griswold* to *Olmstead v. United States*[140] to the nineteenth-century torts commentator, Judge Cooley, who described the right as the "right to be let alone."[141] Cooley, in turn, in all likelihood distilled the right from the package of fundamental personal rights conceived by Blackstone to consist of the inviolate nature of the person[142] and recognized by the Anglo-American adage, "a man's home is his castle."[143]

Privacy also has a textual foundation in the Constitution. The first amendment secures basic freedoms of thought, expression, and association; the third and fourth preserve inviolate the

---

human dignity. A contemporary paradigmatic example is the asserted right of a woman to freely terminate her pregnancy.

[138]No doubt this association is primarily due to Justice Goldberg's concurrence in Griswold v. Connecticut, 381 U.S. 479, 486 (1965); *see also* Roe v. Wade, 410 U.S. 113 (1973); Doe v. Bolton, 410 U.S. 179 (1973); *infra* text accompanying notes 145–62.

[139]*See supra* notes 47 & 82.

[140]277 U.S. 438, 478 (1928) (Brandeis, J., dissenting); see Caplan, *supra* note 2, at 266 n.176.

[141]T. Cooley, Law of Torts 29 (2d ed. 1888).

[142]1 W. Blackstone, Commentaries *119–20 & *130.

[143]This maxim has roots in English law that are recorded in decisional law as early as 1605. Semayne's Case, 5 Co. Rep. 91, 77 Eng. Rep. 194 (K.B. 1605). According to Corwin, the adage may have existed as early as Justinian's Digest. *See* Corwin, *supra* note 54, at 371 n.19.

individual home and person. While this textual warrant is concededly attenuated, it is safe to derive from the context and intent of these enumerated rights a concern that individuals, in their homes and with respect to their persons and effects, remain free from unwarranted governmental intrusion.[144] Although privacy, as manifested in the right of a woman to determine whether or not to continue her pregnancy, is undoubtedly a subject of great public controversy, there can be no question that a significant portion of our contemporary society regards this right as one inherent in the dignity of the individual. By application of these criteria it can thus be seen that privacy is a fundamental right of constitutional stature. Possessed of this status, it should be confidently asserted against rival governmental claims, whether federal or state.

By contrast, current constitutional privacy jurisprudence is unnecessarily muddled. Rather than grounding privacy rights squarely amid the unenumerated natural rights secured by the ninth amendment, it uses as its constitutional anchor the due process clauses of the fifth and fourteenth amendments. This due process source was first identified in *Meyer v. Nebraska*[145] as the constitutional agent which secured the liberty "to marry, establish a home and bring up children."[146] Two years later *Pierce v. Society of Sisters*[147] concluded that the same due process clause protected

---

[144]Professor Caplan, however, asserts that "privacy as now understood . . . did not develop until the mid-eighteenth century and did not fully mature until the nineteenth. Privacy as an all-encompassing constitutional right was accordingly not a part of the legal tradition inherited from England by the colonies which would have been secured in either a state or federal bill of rights. "Caplan, *supra* note 2, at 267 (footnotes omitted). It is noteworthy that Professor Caplan's cited authorities all deal with the colonial experience in Puritan New England. A tradition of far less governmental intrusion in private affairs existed in Rhode Island, New York, Pennsylvania, and, for a time, Maryland. *See* T. Curry, *supra* note 76, at 29–77. Moreover, Caplan's conclusion in this instance rests on the dubious assumption that ninth amendment rights are static.

[145]262 U.S. 390 (1923). *Meyer* was not the first case to allude to a constitutionally protected privacy right. As early as 1886, the fourth and fifth amendments were held to "apply to all invasions on the part of the government and its employes of the sanctity of a man's home and the privacies of life. It is not the breaking of his doors, and the rummaging of his drawers, that constitutes the essence of the offense; but it is the invasion of his indefeasible right of personal security, personal liberty and private property. . . ." Boyd v. United States, 116 U.S. 616, 630 (1886).

[146]*Meyer*, 262 U.S. at 399.

[147]268 U.S. 510 (1925).

"the liberty . . . to direct the upbringing and education of children."[148] It is no accident that the Court selected the due process clauses as the vehicle to secure these felt liberties. The doctrinal mainstream of the Court in the 1920s was still in the channels of substantive due process; locating these natural liberties among the substance of due process liberties was both consistent and logical. But, as the Court has repudiated substantive due process while reaffirming the constitutional legitimacy of privacy rights, it has created for itself unnecessary doctrinal difficulties coupled with infirm restraints upon the privacy right. A juxtaposition of two cases from the Court's 1985 Term, *Bowers v. Hardwick*[149] and *Thornburgh v. American College of Obstetricians and Gynecologists*[150] highlights the quagmire into which the Court has slipped. Before comparing *Bowers* and *Thornburgh*, however, it will be useful to sketch the evolution of the doctrine.

Skinner v. Oklahoma[151] used equal protection as the mechanism to strike down an Oklahoma statute permitting involuntary sterilization on the ground that the statute intruded upon "the basic civil rights of man"[152] and was wholly artificial in its application. The Court emphasized the fundamental nature of the right involved, marriage and procreation, as the basis for the strict scrutiny to which the statute was subjected. *Skinner* thus adumbrates the role which fundamental rights play in modern equal protection analysis. Similarly, in *Prince v. Massachusetts*[153] the Court reaffirmed, on due process grounds, that there is a "realm of family life which the state cannot enter"[154] without compelling justification. In the highly charged atmosphere of racial discrimination, the Warren Court concluded, in *Loving v. Virginia*,[155] that a state statute barring racially mixed marriage was offensive to the liberty of marriage secured by

[148]*Id*. at 534–35.
[149]106 S. Ct. 2841 (1986).
[150]106 S. Ct. 2169 (1986).
[151]316 U.S. 535 (1942).
[152]*Id*. at 541.
[153]321 U.S. 158 (1944).
[154]*Id*. at 166.
[155]388 U.S. 1 (1967).

the due process clauses.[156] During the same period, the Court decided *Griswold*, in which the liberty interest protected was characterized in a concurrence by Justice White as the right "to be free of regulation of the intimacies of the marriage relationship."[157] Similarly, *Eisenstadt v. Baird*[158] invalidated a Massachusetts statute prohibiting contraceptive use by either married or unmarried couples. The *Eisenstadt* Court specifically dismissed marriage as a prerequisite for assertion of the liberty interest there advanced, characterizing the protected right as the "decision whether to bear or beget a child."[159] The watershed cases of *Roe v. Wade*[160] and *Doe v. Bolton*[161] held that "a woman's decision whether or not to terminate her pregnancy" is among the liberty interests protected by the due process clause.[162]

To reach these conclusions the Court has first characterized the claimed liberty interests as fundamental rights deserving of heightened judicial protection.[163] In sifting the fundamental from the incidental the Court has used, as its sieve, concepts acquired from due process jurisprudence. Justice White, for example, categorizes fundamental rights as either those "implicit in the concept of ordered liberty, such that 'neither liberty nor justice would exist if [they] were sacrificed' "[164] or those "deeply rooted in the Nation's history and traditions."[165]

Application of this doctrine during this past Term has produced confusing, inconsistent results. In *Bowers v. Hardwick*[166] the Court, by a five to four margin, concluded that a Georgia statute making private, consensual anal or oral sex a felony did not violate the

---

[156]The Court struck down the statute on equal protection grounds as well as finding that the law deprived the Lovings of due process by denying them the "freedom of choice to marry" that had "long been recognized as one of the vital personal rights essential to the orderly pursuit of happiness by free men." *Id.* at 12.

[157]Griswold v. Connecticut, 381 U.S. 479, 502–03 (1965) (White, J., concurring).

[158]405 U.S. 438 (1972).

[159]*Id.* at 453.

[160]410 U.S. 113 (1973).

[161]410 U.S. 179 (1973).

[162]*Roe v. Wade,* 410 U.S. at 153.

[163]*Bowers,* 106 S. Ct. at 2843.

[164]*Id.* at 2844 (quoting Palko v. Connecticut, 302 U.S. 319, 325–26 (1937)).

[165]*Id.* (quoting Moore v. City of East Cleveland, 431 U.S. 494, 503 (1977)).

[166]106 S. Ct. 2841 (1986).

constitutional privacy right as applied to homosexuals. To reach this conclusion Justice White distinguished the earlier privacy cases as limited to rights of family, marriage, or procreation, then proceeded to dismiss any claimed right to engage in private, consensual anal or oral sex as both unrelated to these identified rights and not deserving of characterization as a fundamental right. In reaching the latter result, Justice White relied heavily on the historical facts that sodomy was a common-law crime, had been made criminal by each of the original states when the Bill of Rights was adopted in 1791, and was subject to criminal penalties in thirty-two of the thirty-seven states in existence when the fourteenth amendment was adopted in 1868. Perhaps most unfortunate was Justice White's express refusal to evaluate the ninth amendment rights asserted in Hardwick's initial complaint but, apparently, not explicitly urged upon the Court at oral argument.[167]

Even viewed as a due process case, Justice White's reasoning in *Bowers* cannot withstand minimal, much less close, scrutiny. Assuming, *arguendo*, that the fundamental rights secured by prior privacy case law are limited to those revolving around family, marriage, or procreation, Justice White's conclusory implication that no nexus can be found between anal or oral sexual activity and these identified rights is erroneous. *Moore v. City of East Cleveland*[168] reminds us not to "close our eyes to the basic reasons why certain rights associated with the family have been accorded shelter under the Fourteenth Amendment's Due Process Clause."[169] As Justice Blackmun noted, "[w]e protect those rights not because they contribute, in some direct and material way, to the general public welfare, but because they form so central a part of an individual's life."[170] To Justice Stevens, "the concept of privacy embodies the 'moral fact that a person belongs to himself and not to others nor to society as a whole.' "[171] Because "sexual intimacy is 'a sensitive, key relationship of human existence, central to family life, community welfare,

---

[167]*Compare id.* at 2846 & n.8 *with id.* at 2849–50 (Blackmun, J., dissenting).

[168]431 U.S. 494 (1977).

[169]*Id.* at 501.

[170]*Bowers*, 106 S. Ct. at 2851 (Blackmun, J., dissenting).

[171]*Thornburgh*, 106 S. Ct. at 2187 n.5 (Stevens, J., concurring) (quoting Fried, Correspondence, 6 Phil. & Pub. Aff. 288–89 (1977)), *quoted in Bowers*, 106 S. Ct. at 2851 (Blackmun, J., dissenting).

and the development of human personality,' "[172] and the "ability independently to define one's identity . . . is central to any concept of liberty,"[173] only "the most willful blindness"[174] can conclude that there is no linkage between existing privacy guarantees and the right to engage in private, consensual oral or anal sex.

Moreover, because the Court chose to hem itself in by selective, and artificially limited, tests of fundamental liberties, Justice White was able to offer, as conclusive evidence of its lack of fundamental status, the historical fact that sodomy was generally criminal in 1791 and 1868. This mechanical assembly fails adequately to explain *Loving v. Virginia*, in which the Court invalidated a Virginia statute outlawing interracial marriage despite uncontroverted proof that the statute (and others like it) had long historical roots.[175] The result in this case serves to further illustrate the bankruptcy of the due process analytical framework in the context of fundamental liberties associated with privacy.[176]

---

[172]*Bowers*, 106 S. Ct. at 2851 (Blackmun, J., dissenting) (quoting Paris Adult Theatre I v. Slayton, 413 U.S. 49, 63 (1973)).

[173]Roberts v. United States Jaycees, 468 U.S. 609, 619 (1984).

[174]*Bowers*, 106 S. Ct. at 2851 (Blackmun, J., dissenting).

[175]388 U.S. 1, 3 (1967); *see Bowers*, 106 S. Ct. at 2854 n.5 (Blackmun, J., dissenting). In other settings, the Court has vindicated fundamental rights despite impressive historical prohibition of the claimed right. For example, since the Middle Ages, English law had provided for the removal of an indigent from the community. This scheme persisted and finally resulted in the 1662 Law of Settlement and Removal. This act was the model for similar colonial statutes. Removal of a pauper was upheld by the Supreme Court of Pennsylvania in Fallowfield Township v. Marlborough Township, 1 U.S. (1 Dall.) 32 (1776), and quashed on a technicality in Upper Dublin Overseers of the Poor v. Germantown Overseers of the Poor, 2 U.S. (2 Dall.) 213 (1793). The Supreme Court generally validated state laws inhibiting the free movement of indigents in City of New York v. Miln, 36 U.S. (11 Pet.) 102, 142–43 (1837). Yet in Edwards v. California, 314 U.S. 160 (1941), the Court struck down a California statute, which had existed in some version since 1860, prohibiting the introduction into California of any indigent. Mr. Justice Byrnes rejected these historical buttresses because they "no longer fit the facts." *Id.* at 174. *Edwards* was decided under the commerce clause, but the right involved—freedom of movement—is a fundamental right. *See* Shapiro v. Thompson, 394 U.S. 618 (1969).

[176]The *Bowers* majority chose to skate by the fact that the Georgia statute at issue prohibits, on its face, all oral or anal sex, wherever it may occur, whether between married or unmarried heterosexuals or unmarried homosexuals. Ga. Code Ann. § 16-6-2 (1984). Thus, the statute is facially suspect when analyzed in light of the most orthodox privacy precedents.

In its October 1986 Term, the Court has created further confusion in whatever

Whatever conceptual scaffolding is erected, there is an uneasy disharmony between *Bowers* and *Thornburgh*, decided just nineteen days apart. In *Thornburgh*, the Court, again by a five to four margin, invalidated key portions of Pennsylvania's 1982 Abortion Control Act,[177] which imposed restrictions upon the availability of abortions. In concluding that a state may not "intimidate women into continuing pregnancies"[178] by erecting powerful psychological and legal barriers to an abortion, the Court reaffirmed the constitutional foundation of *Roe v. Wade*. In doing so, Justice Blackmun observed:

> Our cases long have recognized that the Constitution embodies a promise that a certain private sphere of individual liberty will be kept largely beyond the reach of the government. . . . Few decisions are more personal and intimate, more properly private, or more basic to individual dignity and autonomy, than a woman's decision—with the guidance of her physician and within the limits specified in *Roe*—whether to end her pregnancy. A woman's right to make that choice freely is fundamental. Any other result, in our view, would protect inadequately a central part of the sphere of liberty that our law guarantees equally to all.[179]

---

doctrine *Bowers* established. In Oklahoma v. Post, 715 P.2d 1105 (Okla. Crim. App. 1986), *cert. denied*, 55 U.S.L.W. 3249 (Oct. 14, 1986) (No. 85-2071), the Oklahoma Court of Criminal Appeals held that a man's criminal conviction for consensual oral and anal sex with a woman must be set aside because "the right to privacy, as formulated by the Supreme Court, includes the right to select consensual adult sex partners." *Id.* at 1109. The Oklahoma court, writing prior to *Bowers*, relied on Carey v. Population Servs. Int'l, 431 U.S. 678 (1977), Eisenstadt v. Baird, 405 U.S. 438 (1972), and Stanley v. Georgia, 394 U.S. 557 (1969), to reach this conclusion. The court also explicitly relied, in part, on Justice Goldberg's *Griswold* concurrence emphasizing the relevance of the ninth amendment to the *Griswold* holding. The Oklahoma court was careful to limit its decision to consensual adult heterosexual sex, specifically disavowing any application of the decision to homosexual activity.

Following *Bowers*, one would suppose that the Supreme Court would have granted certiorari, if only to correct summarily Oklahoma's presumably erroneous notion of constitutional privacy rights. Its refusal to do so merely leads to further confusion. Is *Bowers* now to be read as a denial only to homosexuals of the right to select consensual sex partners? Does the Court wish to permit the states latitude to formulate independent notions of the limits of the privacy right? If so, the desire is inefficacious without further explication of the grossly disparate results in *Post* and *Bowers*.

[177]18 Pa. Cons. Stat. §§ 3201–3220 (1983).

[178]*Thornburgh*, 106 S. Ct. at 2178.

[179]*Id.* at 2184–85 (citations omitted).

Noteworthy by its absence is any mention of the precise constitutional bedrock upon which these liberties are grounded. By implication, of course, the due process clauses clothe these liberties with constitutional protection. But, it is possible that Justice Blackmun, who briefly flirted with the ninth amendment as an alternative source for protecting the right claimed by Hardwick,[180] at least may be thinking about application of the ninth amendment to privacy rights. If so, he may be alone, for Justices Stevens, White, and Rehnquist plainly view the due process clauses as the doctrinal source of the liberty interest protected by *Thornburgh*.[181]

B. Privacy and the Ninth Amendment

Would it make any difference if these issues were analyzed as claimed unenumerated natural rights under the ninth amendment? The initial inquiry, which has already been decided affirmatively within the due process framework, is whether a privacy right, however manifested, is constitutionally protected. As discussed above,[182] privacy as an abstraction fits neatly into the template proposed for evaluation of prospective unenumerated natural rights. Let us now examine the specific claimed rights in *Thornburgh* and *Bowers* through the ninth amendment lens.

In *Thornburgh*, the reconstructed ninth amendment claim is that a woman has an unenumerated natural right to choose whether to continue her pregnancy, without interference from the state in that decision. This right finds textual warrant in several places: the fourth amendment's guarantee of "[t]he right of the people to be secure in their persons," the first amendment's guarantee of free association,[183] and the third amendment's limited guarantee of the inviolability of the home.[184]

---

[180]*Bowers*, 106 S. Ct. at 2849 (Blackmun, J., dissenting).

[181]*Thornburgh*, 106 S. Ct. at 2185 (Stevens, J., concurring); *id.* at 2194 (White, J., dissenting).

[182]*See supra* text accompanying notes 133–44.

[183]In speaking of "free association," I am loosely construing the specific guarantees of the first amendment. Taken together, the animating impulse of the first amendment is to ensure freedom of thought, expression, assembly or association, and political participation. Thought, expression, and association form the heart of individual autonomy and are essential attributes of "the fundamental interest all indi-

The right has historical authenticity. To be sure, it is disingenuous to claim that a woman's right to control her pregnancy has been expressly recognized since the nation's formation. Such an inquiry is hollow because abortion, like computers and video machinery, was simply not a part of the landscape in the late eighteenth century.[185] To attempt to disprove the claimed right in such fashion is "to use history as drunks use lampposts—more for support than for illumination."[186] The proper historical inquiry is one which seeks to determine "what history teaches are the traditions from which [the nation's constitutional jurisprudence] developed as well as the traditions from which it broke. That tradition is a living thing."[187] And that tradition is not slavishly devoted to fidelity to past practice. In promoting the unratified Constitution, Madison observed:

> [T]he glory of the people of America [is] that whilst they have paid a decent regard to the opinions of former times and other nations, they have not suffered a blind veneration for antiquity, for custom, or for names, to overrule the suggestions of their own good sense, the knowledge of their own situation, and the lessons of their own experience.[188]

---

viduals have in controlling the nature of their intimate associations with others." *Bowers*, 106 S. Ct. at 2852 (Blackmun, J., dissenting).

[184]"No Soldier shall, in time of peace be quartered in any house, without the consent of the Owner, nor in time of war, but in a manner to be prescribed by law." U.S. Const. amend. III. Though this amendment may seem to be an antiquarian relic, its substance provides further evidence of "original intent" that individual privacy be protected and preserved.

[185]Abortion performed before "quickening"—recognizable movement of the fetus—was not a common-law crime. 3 E. Coke, Institutes *50; 1 W. Blackstone, Commentaries *125–26. Although Lord Coke believed that abortion after quickening was "a great misprision, and no murder" (3 E. Coke, Institutes *50) and Blackstone styled the offense less severe than manslaughter (1 W. Blackstone, Commentaries *125–26), some modern scholars believe abortion was never a common-law crime, whenever performed. *See* authorities collected in *Roe v. Wade,* 410 U.S. at 135 n.26. The first American legislation criminalizing abortion was enacted by Connecticut in 1821. *See id.* at 138 n.29.

[186]Abrams, *Mr. Meese Caricatures the Constitution,* N.Y. Times, July 25, 1986, at A31, col. 6.

[187]Poe v. Ullman, 367 U.S. 497, 543 (1961) (Harlan, J., dissenting), *quoted in Thornburgh,* 106 S. Ct. at 2189 (Stevens, J., concurring).

[188]The Federalist No. 14 at 52 (J. Madison) (6th ed. 1847).

To this spirit Madison attributed the Constitution's innovations "in favor of private rights and public happiness."[189] Without such resolution, "the people of the United States . . . must at best have been laboring under the weight of some of those forms which have crushed the liberties of the rest of mankind."[190] Thus, the historical authenticity to be sought is the historical current of constitutional thought. Viewed in this fashion, it is plainly evident that "the balance struck by this country"[191] has been moving inexorably toward greater security and freedom, whether economic or personal, for the female majority of this society.

The right claimed in *Thornburgh* is wholly consistent with the theory of natural rights. It is not a right created by or dependent upon the original grant of power from private citizens to the representative government. Nor could the right legitimately be invaded by private action prior to the creation of the representative government which succeeded to those private rights. Pregnancy is a uniquely personal condition, inextricably linked with a woman's most imtimate choices of association. To suggest that a woman's rights concerning this condition flow from or can be conditioned by the Lockean sovereign is to pervert horribly the political theory that actuated the framers and that is embodied in the Constitution.[192]

Despite the emotion which the subject generates, a woman's right of choice to continue her pregnancy unassailably turns on competing conceptions of the inherent dignity of the individual. Even its opponents frame their opposition in such terms, choosing to concentrate on the inherent dignity of the embryonic individual rather than on that of the acknowledged individual faced with the personal anguish of decision.

The ninth amendment right asserted in *Bowers* is, most abstractly, the right of individuals to control the nature of their intimate associations with others. More concretely, it is a right to engage in private, consensual sex acts without interference or limitations imposed by the state. It is not limited to homosexuality, as the *Bowers* majority characterized the claim. The textual foundation for the claimed right is found most strongly in the fourth amendment,

[189]*Id.*

[190]*Id.*

[191]Poe v. Ullman, 367 U.S. 497, 543 (1961) (Harlan, J., dissenting), *quoted in Thornburgh*, 106 S. Ct. at 2189 (Stevens, J., concurring).

[192]*See supra* notes 50–57; *infra* notes 198–99 and accompanying text.

but powerful support is to be enlisted from the first and third amendments.[193]

Several sources provide historical support for the claimed right. First, as the *Bowers* majority implicitly acknowledged, oral and anal sex (or sodomy, to use the Court's preferred label) has existed as long as humans have recorded history. The fact that sodomy has also been consistently criminal is of no more force in *Bowers* than was the consistent historic criminality of racially mixed marriages in *Loving v. Virginia*.[194] Second, the privacy right has plainly evolved in the direction of more extensive protection for the individual's intimate sexual choices. It is this moving target of tradition which the Court should seek to hit, not some static bull's-eye of historic public moral condemnation.[195] Indeed, the focus on historic public condemnation of sodomy only serves to remind the reader that, behind the public posture, the condemned behavior has persisted for millenia. It is a strange historical authenticity that focuses on the reflections of history and fails to examine the deep pool of human nature from which the reflections shine.

The right to engage freely in private, consensual sex is a paradigmatic natural right. Can it be seriously contended that the social compact creates the right to have sexual relations? What private right, to which the state is the successor, could be asserted to circumscribe private, consensual sexual behavior? Whatever arguments may be made concerning the efficacy of natural rights theory, sex is one right which is undeniably, and powerfully, natural.

Similarly, only the most withered of souls would contend that an individual's personal choices of intimate relations are other than inextricably linked to the inherent dignity of the individual. Even though the right litigated in *Bowers* was seen to be morally loathsome to many, a moment's objectivity on the part of the moral

---

[193]*See supra* notes 182–84 and accompanying text.

[194]The historical status of a claimed right (in 1791, 1868, or at any other time) is most relevant to claims that the right is a ninth amendment civil or positive right and of little or no relevance to claims that it is a natural right. *See supra* notes 86–94 and accompanying text.

[195]The *Bowers* majority acknowledged this evolution of public choice, yet drew a contrary conclusion from the facts. Although the past 25 years have marked the abandonment of criminal penalties for sodomy by 27 states, the *Bowers* majority persisted in labelling "facetious" any argument that a right to engage in private, adult, consensual sex was historically authentic. *Bowers,* 106 S. Ct. at 2845; *cf. supra* note 176.

condemnors would lead to an admission that an individual's choice of when to have private sex, with whom, and in what fashion, is at the heart of the definition of individual freedom.

The analytical apparatus used to test the sufficiency of an asserted ninth amendment natural right bears many similarities to the criteria employed in evaluating claimed fundamental rights in the context of due process. However, the text of the ninth amendment, its historical genesis, and the structural role it plays in the Constitution provide important and crucial differences. Viewed most literally, the amendment enjoins constitutional interpreters from denying or disparaging unenumerated rights on the basis of the absence of a textual warrant. Thus, contemporary concern about the absence of an explicit textual foundation for an asserted fundamental right such as privacy[196] becomes of no consequence when the claimed right is advanced as an unenumerated natural right protected by the ninth amendment. Nevertheless, prudential concerns mandate some textual foundation apart from the ninth amendment itself.[197] The significant difference from due process analysis is that the textual fidelity required to support a claimed ninth amendment natural right is minimal. When the claimed right is consistent with the theoretical construct of natural rights and a significant portion of contemporary society acknowledges that the right is inherent in the concept of individual dignity, textual fidelity is absolutely supplied by the ninth amendment itself.

The historical genesis of the ninth amendment provides ample support for the conclusion that contemporary expositors of the Constitution ought to be generous in their acceptance of claimed natural rights. The limiting principles suggested are prudential only, are not mandated by the Lockean political theory which actuated the Constitution and Bill of Rights, are not required by the text of

---

[196]Justice White best expressed this concern in his opinions in both *Thornburgh*, 106 S. Ct. at 2194 (White, J., dissenting), and *Bowers*, 106 S. Ct. at 2846. The necessity for an "explicit textual warrant" for the right asserted in *Thornburgh* was argued by Solicitor General Fried in the federal government's amicus brief in support of Pennsylvania: "There is no explicit textual warrant in the Constitution for a right to abortion. . . . [T]he further afield interpretation travels from its point of departure in the text, the greater the danger that constitutional adjudication will be like a picnic to which the framers bring the words and the judges the meaning." Brief for the United States as Amicus Curiae in Support of Appellant at 24, *Thornburgh, reprinted in* L.A. Daily J., Aug 20, 1985, at 1, col. 6.

[197]*See supra* notes 133–37 and accompanying text.

the amendment, and were probably not even considered by the framers. Nevertheless, they are appropriate minimal standards to winnow the substantial from the frivolous.

The structural role played by the ninth amendment is often conveniently overlooked. It is a counterweight to the vast momentum generated by governmental power. This is an important, even vital, structural role that is only partially filled by other constitutional guarantees and prohibitions. Indeed, by its terms the amendment is the final counterweight, to be used against governmental intrusion upon the people when all else fails. It is precisely this role which the ninth amendment should play in privacy jurisprudence. It is perhaps due to its absence from the text that the constitutional right of privacy assumes such a tortured shape.

Moreover, the ninth amendment springs from and helps effectuate John Locke's conception of representative government, which is so deftly embodied in the entire Constitution. Lockean theory posits that each man is his own master. In the Lockean state of nature, no political control of any kind is exerted upon the individual.[198] Yet, upon formation of government, some individual rights are ceded to the state for the purpose of more fully securing the liberty of all. Thus "[r]epresentative government begins with the premise that the state's rights against its citizens are no greater than the sum of the rights of the individuals whom it benefits in any given transaction. The state *qua* state has no independent set of entitlements. . . ."[199] Because the state possesses only limited rights

---

[198]This is not to say that in the theoretical state of nature there are no social controls. Even a politically unorganized society is likely to have a common language, culture, or tradition, and ethical conceptions of right and wrong. These social controls are not enforced by the state, however, and this distinction is significant in contemplating the implications of Lockean theory.

[199]R. Epstein, *supra* note 51, at 331. Locke's view of legislative power was as follows: First, It is not nor can possibly be absolutely arbitrary over the lives and fortunes of the people. For it being but the joint power of every member of society given up to that person, or assembly, which is legislator, it can be no more than those persons had in a state of nature before they entered into society, and gave it up to the community. For nobody can transfer to another more power than he has in himself; and nobody has absolute arbitrary power over himself, or over any other to destroy his own life, or to take away the life or property of another.

J. Locke, Of Civil Government § 135 (1690). Epstein's view of the governmental powers vested in the Lockean state is forcefully clear: "The sovereign has no absolute power to generate rights. The state can acquire nothing by simple declaration of its

derived entirely from individual constituents, it cannot regulate individual behavior in any greater fashion than could the individual members of society regulate the behavior of their fellows. To be sure, one purpose of the state is to assume and enforce community powers of self-help to prevent individuals from seizing, through force or fraud, what is not rightfully their own. Accordingly, the Lockean state is empowered to curb rape, murder, pillage, plunder, and other conduct that uses force or deceit to deprive others of what is justly their own. Viewed in light of Lockean political theory, there is no room for state intervention in matters so basic to personal autonomy as sex and procreation. Absent force or fraud, one's choice of a sex partner and sex practices is not susceptible to regulation by private action, to which the state is but the successor. Similarly, so long as a fetus is regarded as simply one who would be a citizen,[200] a woman's choice concerning pregnancy lacks any element of force which could provide a theoretical justification for state intervention.

Only by ignoring the fundamental political theory embodied in the Constitution can the state be ceded power to intervene in this private arena. The ninth amendment, in current constitutional jurisprudence, is an ill-tended sentry post on the frontier of representative government. Restoration of its intended function would serve as a welcome reminder that "[t]he state is not the source of individual rights or of social community"[201] but, rather, that the state merely possesses private rights of action which it can exercise for the community benefit. Since individuals lack private-law means of prohibiting private behavior that is not forcibly or deceitfully intrusive upon others, the state is similarly lacking in power. That fundamental nugget of political theory is at the heart of any conception of unenumerated natural rights. It is that vision of representative government that the ninth amendment serves and imposes as an outer boundary upon government action.

VI. Conclusion

The ninth amendment was born amid the heightened concern for both state sovereignty and individual liberty that marked the

---

will but must justify its claims in terms of the rights of the individuals whom it protects. . . ." R. Epstein, *supra* note 51, at 12; *see also* Corwin, *supra* note 54, at 383–94.

[200]*Thornburgh*, 106 S. Ct. at 2188 (Stevens, J., concurring).

[201]R. Epstein, *supra* note 51, at 333.

adoption of the Bill of Rights. It was specifically intended as a catch-all to preserve for the people their great and fundamental rights that were not enumerated in the first eight amendments or elsewhere in the Constitution. Its text mandates treatment of these unspecified rights on a par with the enumerated rights. The framers recognized the source of these unenumerated rights to be largely state common, constitutional, and statutory law. But, because they conceived of both enumerated and unenumerated rights as consisting of positive and natural rights, they recognized an additional, transcendent source of these rights.

Ninth amendment rights are enforceable against the federal government because it is textually logical to do so and because it is not inconsistent with the framers' intent. Since ninth amendment positive rights are state-based, but federal in character, they pose unique potential conflicts with the supremacy clause. The conflicts are resolvable in part by limiting their state foundation to pre–1788 state law. Natural, or fundamental, ninth amendment rights pose no such conflict with federal action.

While the ninth amendment was not intended to bar state action, to do so is consistent with and efficacious of the due process and republican government guarantees of the Constitution, for in the case of positive rights it would merely compel the states to observe their own laws. Natural or fundamental ninth amendment rights are enforceable against the states because the theoretical understanding of the ninth amendment reservation, in this instance, is to vest these rights in the people, rather than in any government. Being paramount by nature, such rights pose no real conflict with the apparently conflicting original intent of the framers.

Divining fundamental rights in a principled fashion poses problems of noninterpretive judicial review. To eliminate or minimize these problems, courts must recognize as fundamental only those rights which have some textual foundation in the Constitution, can claim historical authenticity in traditional sources of our organic law, are consistent with the theoretical understanding of natural rights, and command recognition as inherent in personal dignity by a substantial portion of contemporary society. As a guide, courts should keep in mind the Lockean principle which the ninth amendment was intended to effectuate: the state can only exercise coercive powers which its constituent members could legitimately exercise in self-defense.

The result of this reading of the ninth amendment is to revive the amendment as a keystone of federalism and as a source of substantive, fundamental personal liberties. Without corresponding changes in other constitutional sources of regulation of federal-state relations, the ninth amendment will not revolutionize federalism. It will, however, provide new life to the states as protectors of the liberties of their citizens against federal encroachment. At the same time, assertion of fundamental ninth amendment rights will operate to prevent the federal or state governments from invading the reserved personal liberties of the people. It is a challenging amendment; it should not languish in desuetude because of the challenge it poses.

12. On Reading and Using the Ninth Amendment

Charles L. Black, Jr.

For the reader's convenience, I will set out the brief text of the Ninth Amendment to the Constitution of the United States: "The enumeration in the Constitution, of certain rights, shall not be construed to deny or disparage others retained by the people."

This sentence stands at the end of a very short "enumeration" of rights—an "enumeration" nobody could possibly think anywhere near sufficient for guarding even the values it patchily and partially shields. The Ninth Amendment language was put where it is by people who believed they were enacting for an indefinite future. All sorts of other language may have been used around this language. But this was the language chosen to become "valid to all Intents and Purposes, as Part of [the] Constitution." What does it seem to be saying?

It could be read as saying that nobody really ought to deny, in discourse of a mixed moral and political tenor, that a number of rights exist, beyond the enumerated ones. But this is quite unbelievable. Virtually all of the Constitution, including the amendments preceding and later following this one, is *law*, sparely stated in the language of law. Attention here should be focused especially on the first eight amendments, together with which the Ninth Amendment entered the Constitution. These are austere, preemptory directions to law-making and law-enforcing officials, from Congress, through courts of law, down to magistrates issuing search warrants and military officers quartering troops. In the Constitution as a whole, and in this immediate context, the insertion of a precept of moral philosophy would not merely have changed the subject abruptly, but would have put the content of this amendment in

Reprinted, by permission, from *Power and Policy in Quest of Law: Essays in Honor of Eugene Rostow*, ed. M. McDougal & W.N. Reisman (Boston: Martinus Nijhoff, 1985), p. 187.

quite a different world from that of the Constitution, and of the "enumerated" rights just set out.

The amendment could be read as saying no more than that the bare fact of "enumeration" of other rights should not, in and of itself, give rise to the inference that no other rights exist, but that the forbidding of the drawing of this one inference in no way prejudices the question whether there really are, in addition to the enumerated rights, any "others retained by the people." I guess a computer, fed the words, would have to print this out as a logical possibility. I submit that it is not a serious psychological possibility that anyone totally neutral on the question of the existence of rights not "enumerated" would bother to set up this kind of directive as to what course the non-logic of *expressio unius* may take, leaving it quite open that the very same conclusion—no non-enumerated rights—may be reached by some other path of reasoning. The Ninth Amendment seems to be guarding something; such bother is not likely to be taken if the question is thought to be quite at large whether there is anything out there to be guarded.

It should be noted, in passing, that the most one could get out of even this computer print is that the language of the Ninth Amendment does not *affirmatively imply* the existence of unenumerated rights; even a computer would have to print out that this language implies that such rights *may* exist—if you also fed into that computer the assumption: "The utterers of this language were not talking just to hear their heads rattle." This, while not strictly an existence proof, would be a proof of the serious possibility of the existence of rights not enumerated; even this might be enough to legitimate a further quest. But the Constitution is not a computer program, and I submit that preponderance of reason leaves us with the conclusion, about as well-supported as any we can reach in law, that the Ninth Amendment declares as a matter of law—of constitutional law, overriding other law—that some other rights are "retained by the people," and that these shall be treated as *on an equal footing* with rights enumerated.

This would have to mean that these rights "not enumerated" may serve as the substantive basis for judicial review of governmental actions; any other conclusion would not only do violence to expectations naturally shaped by the command that these other rights not be "denied or disparaged" in respect to the enumerated rights, but would also lead one back around to the inadmissible idea, discussed above, that this amendment, placed where it is, is merely a directive for the course of moral philosophy or of purely political argument. Nor does it make any difference whether the possibility of judicial review was immediately present to everyone's mind at just the moment the Ninth Amendment passed Congress, or was ratified by the last necessary state. The idea that constitutional rights were to form the substantive basis of such review was so much in the air (and in the laws) that it is unlikely it was overlooked by the *major et senior pars*. But in any case the direction of the Ninth Amendment—that non-enumerated rights not be "denied or disparaged," as against enumerated rights—was directed literally at the future, at the corpus of law-to-be, and affirmative settlement of the question (if, as I doubt, it was a real question in 1790) of the rightness of judicial review, on the basis of *any* right "enumerated' in the Constitution, would settle the rightness of judicial review on the basis of those rights not enumerated, though "retained by the people," because anything else would "deny or disparage" these latter, in a quite efficacious way.

The only hitch is, in short, that the rights not enumerated are not enumerated. We are not told what they are. So the question is, "What do you do when you are solemnly told, by an authority to which you owe fidelity, to protect a designated set of things in a certain way, but are, in the very nature of the case, not told what particular things this set comprises?"

There are two possible courses to follow. One is to throw up your hands and say that no action is possible, because you haven't been told exactly how to act. The other is to take the Ninth Amendment as a command to use any rational methods available to the art of law, and with these in hand to set out to discover what it is you are to protect.

The first of these leads right back around, yet again, to a *practical* "denial and disparagement" of the rights not enumerated; it leads, indeed, to something a shade more imbecile than taking the amendment as a direction of the course of moral philosophy, for it disclaims any power even to discover what rights are not to be "denied or disparaged" in out-of-court discourse. But at least you stay out of trouble.

The second course gets you into deep troubles. First is the trouble of deciding, by preponderance of reason, what *methods* are to be seen as legitimate, in our legal culture, for making out the shape of the rights not named. Then there is the trouble—since no known legal method produces anything like certain results—of deciding where the preponderance of reason lies on the merits of *any particular claim of right*, when that claim is weighed by the methods you have decided are legitimate. And the worst of it is that these troubles will never be done with, or even lessened. The methods of law are not a closed canon. The problems they must solve are infinite and unforeseeable. The solutions will never have the quality of the Pythagorean Theorem; time may even bring the conviction that some solutions, though confidently arrived at, were wrong, and must be revised.

Altogether, it's a lot of troubles. Maybe we ought to give up, and let the Ninth Amendment—and the priceless rights it refers to— keep gathering dust for a third century.

But there is one thing to note about the very real troubles that face us when we turn to the search that the Ninth Amendment seems to command. *These are the troubles not of the Ninth Amendment itself, but of law.* If they put one off the Ninth Amendment enterprise, maybe one ought to give up law altogether, try something else. But that course has its own problems. To turn to medicine, to music, to history—even to mathematical physics—is to accept the burden of troubles rather closely analogous to those of Ninth Amendment law, or of law as a whole. For my part, too old to train for anything else, I would accept the challenge of Ninth Amendment law, as the same old (and forever new) challenge of law. (I shall explain, below, my use of the terms "Ninth Amendment law" and "Ninth Amendment right.")

What methods are legitimate for finding and giving shape to the non-enumerated rights guarded by the Ninth Amendment?

Let me start with a rejection. Some people, faced with this question, would try to dig up every scrap of paper that happens to have survived since the eighteenth century, and to piece together some sort of "intent," with very little weight given to the transcendently relevant piece of paper, the one on which the duly enacted text of the Ninth Amendment was written.

I am one who thinks that, in a general way, our legal culture carries this sort of thing much too far. We sometimes treat statements made informally in one House of Congress as the exact equivalent, in everything but name, of formal statutory language; if it is right to do that, what are the formalities for? In the very teeth of Madison's quite sound and reiterated insistence that the records of the 1787 Convention, not being publicly known until decades after the government was formed, ought not to be used to establish the public meaning of the Constitution's text, we sometimes seem to treat these records as all but superior in authority to that text itself. If we had to choose between our style of getting drunk on collateral and sometimes casual evidences of "intent," and leaving the stuff altogether alone, as the British do, I would choose the latter course—though I think sometimes a very cautious use of such material may be warranted.

But if there ever was a case where informal collateral evidence of "intent" must be useless, it is in regard to the finding of the rights that belong in the class of "others retained by the people." This language of the Ninth Amendment is apt for referring to things you haven't thought of or quite agreed upon; such language would be hopelessly inapt as a sort of coded-message reference to a closed class of "rights" you *have* thought of and agreed upon. If the decoded message read that rights A, B, C, D, *and no others*, were not to be "denied or disparaged," then the peculiar result would have been reached that we would have two kinds of "enumeration," the second kind being a coded enumeration, and that these *two* kinds of "enumeration" exhausted the class of rights to be protected, so that other rights, not thus "enumerated," *could* be "denied or disparaged." The informally arrived at "enumeration" would thus be given an *"expressio unius"* force explicitly denied to the formal "enumeration" elsewhere. Something would have gone wrong here; doubtless the Greeks had a word for that kind of paradox. I am content to say that it seems to me to have no place in the robust common-sense world of the best work on American constitutional law.

If, on the other hand, the decoded message of the Ninth Amendment turned out to be that rights A, B, C, and D are not to be denied or disparaged, but that this class is *not* closed, then we are right where we were, with (in effect) *another* amendment "enumerating" rights A, B, C, and D, and a Ninth Amendment still commanding that rights not "enumerated" shall not be denied or disparaged.

Some pause might be given if we found a real consensus uniting the *major pars* of the relevant eighteenth-century people, that some identifiable claim to a "right" was *not* to be looked on as guarded by the Ninth Amendment. But this would be a pause only. "Due process" is an evolving concept: "cruel and unusual punishment" is an evolving concept; the language of the Ninth Amendment seems even more apt than these to be mentioning an evolving set of rights, not to be bounded even by a negative eighteenth-century judgment based on eighteenth-century evaluations and social facts as then seen. And one would have to remember that even the arbitrary blackballing of one "right" or several "rights," on the basis of "intent" evidence, would in no way impair the generality of the Ninth Amendment's command as to the other rights not enumerated.

I have treated this issue of collaterally evidenced "intent" quite abstractly; I don't know of any corpus of actual evidence that would enable or oblige one to treat it more concretely.

To me, the upshot is that we have to take this language as it comes to us. We are its inheritors; it "belongs in usufruct to the living," as Jefferson said of the earth. If we regard it (as I do) as directing us to do our best to discover for ourselves what unenumerated rights are to be given sanction, so that we may obey the Ninth Amendment command against their denial or disparagement, there is really no dearth of sound and well-tested methods for obeying this command, and so moving in the direction of a rational and coherent corpus juris of human rights.

This statement gains a great deal of plausibility, or more, from the fact that we have for a very long time been protecting unnamed rights. We have done this, sometimes, under the guise of treating the language of the Constitution as highly metaphoric or otherwise figurative, as when we see "speech" or "press" in picketing and black armbands, or see the making of a noise near someone's land as a "taking." But the *appropriateness* of any such metaphoric extension can be explored only by asking, for example, "Is the wearing of a black armband so similar, in relevant respects, to speech, that it ought to be treated as speech is treated?" And when we ask this question we recognize an old friend—the common law method of arguing from the established to the not yet established, weighing similarities and differences, and deciding where the balance lies. Sometimes, as in the common law, this method creates a whole new heading, as with the "freedom of association" now generally recognized as arising, by the discernment of functional equivalence or analogy, from the First Amendment rights literally "enumerated." This is how (for one example more) we achieved the result of applying the double jeopardy clause to cases where *imprisonment* is the penalty, though, if you read the Fifth Amendment, you find that, as named or "enumerated," this protection applies only to "jeopardy of life or limb." If, in time of peace, government attempted the "quartering" of sailors or government civilian employees in houses without the consent of the owners, or if consent was had from the "owner" of an apartment house but not from a tenant in possession under a lease, rational legal discourse could be addressed to the questions all these actions would raise in confrontation with the Third Amendment. You could, of course, talk as though the questions were whether a sailor is "really" a soldier, whether the tenant of an apartment is "really" the owner of a house—but even in this disguise these questions could be rationally addressed only by adding to them the phrase "in preponderantly relevant respects," or some such language. And this would lead right into the eternal question, "Is this a difference that *ought to make a difference?*" This question sounds familiar, because it is, first, a question repeated infinite times in the quest for rational justice, and, secondly, because it is the question continually asked—and answered in each case as best it may be—by the common law, the matrix of all our particular legal methodology. The issue is not whether the use of this method would be a bizarre innovation; the issue is whether any quest for decent law, with its parts rationally related, can possibly do without it.

Nor need this method of "analogy" be used only for small motions, like the supplying of the hiatus in the double jeopardy clause. The seeking of consistent rationality is a requirement of all good law, at every level of generality. If the central meaning of the equal protection clause is—as it surely is—the forbidding of discrimination against *blacks,* then the propriety of applying that clause to discrimination against *women* can be reasoned about by marshalling the similarities (the genetic and indelible character of the trait, the maintenance of the discriminatory regime by social stereotypes, and so on) in confrontation with the differences (for example, absence of whole-family discrimination stretching back through history). And, since this is both a real and a complicated case, the Nineteenth Amendment would also serve as a starting point for the eternal similarity-difference reasoning of law questing for justice: If women may not be excluded from voting, may they be excluded from office-holding? From jury service? And so on.

I must resist the impulse towards—and am really glad to eschew—any attempt here and now to build a corpus juris of human rights on this basis, or on the others to be mentioned below. In a proper and profound sense, that corpus will never be built; it will always be building, like the common law. If this method is not rational, then neither is the common law. And neither is any other attempt to give due effect to similarities and differences between already decided and newly presented cases and problems.

There is another generative principle in our legal system, the principle that law may be generated by due attention to the sound requirements arising out of social or political structures and relations. This is how we got the warranty of fitness for human consumption in the sale of food; this is also how, in some states, we have recently gotten that warranty extended to bind the manufacturer and packager or canner, when structures and relationships changed in the food trade. This is how we got the insurer's right of subrogation, and the testimonial privilege for communications between penitent and priest. This how we got the obligation of parents to care for their children. Our law—and, I venture to say, *all* law—has been and is continually being shaped and reshaped by this generative principle. It is the principle from which we first derived the right—not literally "enumerated"—to move from one state to another.

Now, if we had only these two master methods—the method of similarity-difference reasoning from the committed to the not yet committed, and the method of reasoning from structures and relationships—we would have the means of building towards a rationally consistent, comprehensive and fairly serviceable law of human rights. There is no question here of discerning that these rights are in any designative sense "mentioned" or "incorporated" in the Ninth Amendment, or that they derive from that amendment; the language of the amendment suggests—or commands, as I think—a quest outside itself, a quest for rights *nowhere* enumerated, not the mere tracing out of its references, which are purposefully of total vagueness.

But methods, in any mature and subtle legal culture, are never a closed class. Law ought to be seen to contain not only the means of striving toward rational consistency, not only the means of keeping the rules of legal decision in tune with the society's structures and relationships, but also the means—the methods—for reaching toward higher goals. Herein is the very best of what was so beautifully called, by Lon Fuller, "The Law in Quest of Itself." With the carefulness that is a condition of law's rationality, we may be able to discern and validate "other rights retained by the people" as latent in, and therefore susceptible of being drawn from, the noblest of the concepts to which our nation is committed.

The two best sources for such concepts are the Declaration of Independence and the Preamble to the Constitution. To illustrate, I will take the concept that is common to these, the concept of "liberty." If we are committed to anything, it is to the idea of "liberty." If that commitment doesn't really refer to anything except a good inner feeling, we ought to shut up about it.

There is of course an enormous area wherein the concept or idea of "liberty" solves no problems. But it would be very careless to conclude from this that the concept has no problem-solving power at all, no power to generate "unenumerated rights" by rational operations. "Loyalty to one's friends" and "kindness to one's children" are quite vague in some ranges. But we cannot and do not conclude from this that we can never identify actions, and broad classes of actions, which constitute disloyalty to one's friends, or unkindness to one's children. If concepts like these were really totally vague, through their entire range, society would fall to pieces— or, rather, would never have formed itself. A serious dedication to "liberty" seems to resemble these other concepts in that, while it is vague in much of its range, we can still identify some things that are inconsistent with this serious dedication to "liberty."

It seems to me that a serious *and thoroughly general* commitment to liberty is inconsistent with restrictions or deprivations grossly out of proportion, in their impact on persons, to the benefits that may reasonably be anticipated by the society that imposes them. Every term in this formula is vague in a good part of its range. But, again, there is likely to be no difficulty in identifying at least some instances in which most people would agree that the gross dispro-portion is visible—sometimes even grotesque. If this is so, then at least some "unenumerated" rights may be generated by the pro-portionality principle, and so pass into the corpus juris of human rights.

Indeed, this principle seems supported even by the kind of ana-logic reasoning discussed above, for the idea of proportionality is seen several times in the first eight amendments: "*excessive* bail," "*excessive* fines," "*unreasonable* searches and seizures." The idea of proportionality is just below the surface at other points; it is a part, for example, of the now-accepted definition of "cruel and unusual punishment." In absolute terms, this is not much—but it is quite a lot in a Bill of Rights of some 500 words in all.

The actual judgment of gross disproportionality must be made case by case and field by field; that is in the very nature of the test itself. And in this area, perhaps more than in most others, continual shifting and readjustments, at the borderland, would be bound to occur, because knowledge and insight, both as to the harshness of impact on individuals and as to the benefit reasonably to be anticipated by society, must change from time to time.

This proportionality standard would none the less have power. It could for example, easily explain the judgment, controversial in its own time, that nullified state anti-contraceptive laws; the state that came to bar in that case scarcely made a serious effort to establish any very likely or very large beneficial effect of the prohibition it had imposed, as weighed against the crushing effect the statute would have, if enforced, on the personal lives of citizens. Many past decisions, looked on as highly problematic in their days, would easily yield to justification on proportionality grounds, and such grounds are in fact very near the surface—sometimes virtually explicit—in a good range of such cases.

"Liberty," with the "proportionality" rule it seems to me to generate, is only one instance of such a well-authenticated and generative value. The "pursuit of happiness" as an "inalienable right," the promotion "of the general welfare" and the establishment of "justice" as goals of our political association—these may assert their power in time. Even the dogmata of the Catholic Church have unfolded gradually; we can scarcely expect any more of our constitutional law—and the history of that law amply shows that it is utterly idle to think all questions can be answered at once. We may come to see, for example, that the *effective* "pursuit of happiness" is not really possible to those hobbled and hamstrung by physical and intellectual malnutrition in childhood, and in young adulthood doomed to exclusion from rewarding or even remunerative work, through no fault of their own.

It is time to sum up what I have tried to say.

Of course, no "rights" are "Ninth Amendment rights," in the sense of their being simply referred to or "incorporated" in the general language of that amendment, and so deriving both their shape and their positive force from it. On overwhelming preponderance of reason, it seems to me, the amendment *recognizes the existence* of such rights, and, by its command that they not be denied or disparaged, commands in the same breath (as the command of the end commands the means) that they be sought for and given shape by use of whatever rational means may be available within our legal culture—because the abstention from this search and shaping would be the most efficacious possible denial and disparagement. (When I say, anywhere, "Ninth Amendment rights," or "Ninth Amendment law," I mean to symbolize this relation.)

We possess powerful tools for this work. We can reason from analogy, functional similarity, common underlying values, and the like, using "enumerated" rights as points of departure. We can shape rules that arise out of the structures and relationships of our society—our political society chiefly, but not necessarily that society alone. As to both these methods, they are of a rationality and utility demonstrated beyond a doubt, because they are the methods of the common law, one of the most creative legal systems the world has seen. And it must be repeated that we have already used and currently do use both of them for the shaping of constitutional rights *not* enumerated; all we need to do is cease to duck our heads in embarrassment about this entirely creditable fact, and let these methods loose, for the work of law-finding that they surely can perform.

We are committed, moreover to certain root values: "liberty," "equality," the right to "the pursuit of happiness," and others as well. This commitment is unusually clear in our case; it was undertaken in the organic act that made us an independent nation, and in the words in which we first stated the goals of our political organization, as that structure stands today. Commitment to these values is too vague for use in law, *in part of their range*. But as to some other parts of that range, it is possible to deduce rights usable in constitutional law; I have tendered a vastly important rule of "proportionality" as an example of this, and have suggested one or two others.

In these methods, we have ample means of making out—*for ourselves*, because it has not been done for us positively or negatively, early or late—what it is that the Ninth Amendment is guarding against denial and disparagement. What can and should result is a systematic corpus of the law and equity of human rights, under our Constitution. We will not all agree with every conclusion on which the legal system as a whole settles; this disagreement will exist because the methods we have to use do not produce demonstrable certainty. In other words, we are dealing with *law*, and our systematic corpus of constitutionally guarded human rights will have the characteristics of all law. If we build this corpus, we will do so fallibly; the product will have flaws. If we do not build it, we will have attained certainty—the certainty of unflawed injustice.

I think I ought to repeat that, unless we are to see a massive overruling of cases, some of which are now in their second century, *we are going to be protecting rights not named in the Constitution.* We do that already, under a variety of explanations, the most bizarre of which is doubtless the concept of *"substantive due process."* That teasingly paradoxical phrase is the competition to a frank acceptance of the invitation to use our sanctioned legal methods in an unembarrassed and never-to-be-finished building of a well-joined edifice of binding human-rights law.

I have a final thought about the general shape of that edifice of law—and in that thought may be contained not only a vision of a goal but also a further methodologic canon. There doubtless never was, historically, a "social contract." But our legal system very often *implies* or *postulates* "contracts" that we know were never actually entered into, for the purpose of doing justice and equity. These have been named "quasi-contracts"; we have constructed them when it seemed that a person ought equitably to be treated *as though* bound by a "contract," and the terms of these quasi-contracts have been settled by asking, "What, under the circumstances, ought this person be *taken* to have agreed to do, in order that justice be done?" There is no reason why a Social Quasi-contract might not be given shape, binding the government (and, in proper cases, one's fellow citizens) to forbearances and actions. We would have to ask, for example, "What are the terms of the quasi-contract that this political society ought to be *treated* as having entered into, when it commands and forces its members to abstain from violence and fraud in their attempt to feed their children and themselves? Or when it drafts them into its armies?"

The resultant scope and tenor of this Social Quasi-contract would, obviously, overlap largely with the protections and affirmative assurances resulting from the methods already discussed. This reinforcement of one line of reasoning by another equally valid is a characteristic of all well-developed and complex systems; mathematics is the paradigm. And we might remember, also, that the line is not always easily drawn, in private law, between the contract implied-in-law—the true quasi-contract—and the contract implied-in-fact. A nation that declares itself founded, partly, to "promote the general welfare," may be thought to have undertaken, by implication-in-fact, that welfare is to be generally diffused. The Social Quasi-contract may be thought to contain much the same term, for reasons already hinted at. And so on. The "citizenship" concept and promise, textually locked into the Fourteenth Amendment, may be a bridge between these two modes. We should make the most of these resonances; where they are audible, they powerfully confirm the rightness of any conclusion.

This invocation of the private-law concept of quasi-contract, as a conceivable part of the constitutional law of human rights, should strongly remind us that our Constitution is a part of the "Law of the Land"—by express command of Article VI, and by an implication that would have been a necessary one even if Article VI had not contained the phrase. It is an integral part of the legal system within which it has been placed. There is no reason why it ought not use the methods of that system—of its "Law and Equity," as Article III irresistibly implies. In one aspect, the unitary thesis of this article has been that the construction of a general system of human-rights constitutional law not only demands but deserves the use of the full methodologic set of tools, small and large, that are contained within and accepted by the legal system with which the Constitution is united and blended.

At least no one can say there is no worthy work for law or lawyers in the decades to come, if we have courage to take that work upon us—the courage to enter and cultivate the field that the Ninth Amendment fences and guards.

Notes

In this essay I have tried to bring together, into one structure, various thoughts on warrantable legal methods for the rational development of an open-edged corpus juris of human-rights constitutional law—and therefore of an ever-productive *system* of the rights that are referred to in the Ninth Amendment. I have drawn upon, and tried to make more precise and to place in their mutual relations, some of the ideas in earlier writings of my own, mainly Structure and Relationship in Constitutional Law (1969), *The Unfinished Business of the Warren Court*, 46 Wash. L. Rev. 3 (1970), and Decision According to Law (1981)—as well as my recent book review, *A Round Trip to Eire: Two Books on the Irish Constitution*, 91 Yale L.J. 391 (1981). This process of combination has naturally engendered some new ideas; even two musical tones, sounded together, produce a third.

Such obligations as I am conscious of have been acknowledged in those earlier writings. I have tried so to construct the present essay as to make it readable by itself.

Appendix A: Roger Sherman's Draft of the Bill of Rights

Following is a working draft of the Bill of Rights written by Roger Sherman, representative from Connecticut, in July 1789. If his colleagues on a House committee that was considering amendments approved his proposal, their names were evidently to precede his opening words. The last two lines of Article 4 end with blank spaces in the original, and the word in brackets in the last paragraph follows a deletion and appears to have been intended for deletion also.

Report as their Opinion, That the following articles be proposed by Congress to the legislatures of the Several States to be adopted by them as amendments of the Constitution of the united States, and when ratified by the legislatures of three fourths (at least) of the Said States in the union, to become a part of the Constitution of the united States, pursuant to the fifth Article of the said Constitution.

1. The powers of government being derived from the people, ought to be exercised for their benefit, and they have an inherent and unalienable right to change or amend their political Constitution, when ever they judge such change will advance their interest & happiness.

2. The people have certain natural rights which are retained by them when they enter into Society, Such are the rights of Conscience in matters of religion; of acquiring property and of pursuing happiness & Safety; of Speaking, writing and publishing their Sentiments with decency and freedom; of peaceably assembling to consult their common good, and of applying to Government by petition or remonstrance for redress of grievances. Of these rights therefore they Shall not be deprived by the Government of the united States.

3. No person Shall be tried for any crime whereby he may incur loss of life or any infamous punishment, without Indictment

Reprinted from the New York Times, July 29, 1987.

by a grand Jury, nor be convicted but by the unanimous verdict of a Petit Jury of good and lawful men freeholders of the vicinage or district where the trial Shall be had.

4. After a census Shall be taken, each State Shall be allowed one representative for every thirty thousand Inhabitants of the description in the Second Section of the first Article of the Constitution, until the whole number of representatives shall amount to   but never to exceed

5. The militia shall be under the government of the laws of the respective States, when not in the actual Service of the united States, but such rules as may be prescribed by Congress for their uniform organization & discipline shall be observed in officering and training them, but military Service shall not be required of persons religiously scrupulous of bearing arms.

6. No soldier shall be quartered in any private house in time of Peace, nor at any time, but by authority of law.

7. Excessive bail shall not be required, not excessive fines imposed, nor cruel & unusual punishments inflicted in any case.

8. Congress Shall not have power to grant any monopoly or exclusive advantages of commerce to any person or Company; nor to restrain the liberty of the Press.

9. In suits at common law in courts acting under the authority of the united States, issues of fact shall be tried by a Jury if either party request it.

10. No law Shall be passed for fixing a compensation for the members of Congress except the first Shall take effect until after the next election of representatives posterior to the passing such law.

11. The legislative, executive and judiciary powers vested by the Constitution in the respective branches of the Government of the united States, shall be exercised according to the distribution therein made, so that neither of said branches shall assume or exercise any of the powers peculiar to either of the other branches.

And the powers not delegated to the Government of the united States by the Constitution, nor prohibited by it to the particular States, are retained by the States respectively, nor shall [any] the exercise of power by the Government of the united States particular instances here in enumerated by way of caution be construed to imply the contrary.

Appendix B: Amendments to the United States Constitution Proposed by State Ratification Conventions[1]

Massachusetts[2]

. . .

And as it is the opinion of this Convention, that certain amendments and alterations in the said Constitution would remove the fears, and quiet the apprehensions, of many of the good people of this commonwealth, and more effectually guard against an undue administration of the federal government,—the Convention do therefore recommend that the following alterations and provisions be introduced into the said Constitution:—

I. That it be explicitly declared that all powers not expressly delegated by the aforesaid Constitution are reserved to the several states, to be by them exercised.

II. That there shall be one representative to every thirty thousand persons, according to the census mentioned in the Constitution, until the whole number of the representatives amounts to two hundred.

III. That Congress do not exercise the powers vested in them by the 4th section of the 1st article, but in cases where a state shall neglect or refuse to make the regulations therein mentioned, or shall make regulations subversive of the rights of the people to a free and equal representation in Congress, agreeably to the Constitution.

IV. That Congress do not lay direct taxes but when the moneys arising from the impost and excise are insufficient for the public exigencies, nor then until Congress shall have first made a requisition upon the states to assess, levy, and pay, their respective proportions of such requisition, agreeably to the census fixed in the

[1]Source: Debates in the Several State Conventions on the Adoption of the Federal Constitution (J. Elliot ed. 1836) [hereinafter Elliot's Debates].

[2]Elliot's Debates 322–23.

353

said Constitution, in such way and manner as the legislatures of the states shall think best; and in such case, if any state shall neglect or refuse to pay its proportion, pursuant to such requisition, then Congress may assess and levy such state's proportion, together with interest thereon at the rate of six per cent-per annum, from the time of payment prescribed in such requisition.

V. That Congress erect no company of merchants with exclusive advantages of commerce.

VI. That no person shall be tried for any crime by which he may incur an infamous punishment, or loss of life, until he be first indicted by a grand jury, except in such cases as may arise in the government and regulation of the land and naval forces.

VII. The Supreme Judicial Federal Court shall have no jurisdiction of causes between citizens of different states, unless the matter in dispute, whether it concerns the realty or personalty, be of the value of three thousand dollars at the least; nor shall the federal judicial powers extend to any actions between citizens of different states, where the matter in dispute, whether it concerns the realty or personalty, is not of the value of fifteen hundred dollars at least.

VIII. In civil actions between citizens of different states, every issue of fact, arising in actions at common law, shall be tried by a jury, if the parties, or either of them, request it.

IX. Congress shall at no time consent that any person, holding an office of trust or profit under the United States, shall accept of a title of nobility, or any other title or office, from any king, prince, or foreign state.

. . .

New Hampshire[3]

. . .

And as it is the opinion of this Convention, that certain amendments and alterations in the said Constitution would remove the fears and quiet the apprehensions of many of the good people of this state, and more effectually guard against an undue administration of the federal government,—the Convention do therefore recommend that the following alterations and provisions be introduced in the said Constitution:—

[3]Elliot's Debates 326.

I. That it be explicitly declared that all powers not expressly and particularly delegated by the aforesaid Constitution are reserved to the several states, to be by them exercised.

II. That there shall be one representative to every thirty thousand persons, according to the census mentioned in the Constitution, until the whole number of representatives amount to two hundred.

III. That Congress do not exercise the powers vested in them by the fourth section of the first article but in cases when a state shall neglect or refuse to make the regulations therein mentioned, or shall make regulations subversive of the rights of the people to a free and equal representation in Congress; nor shall Congress in any case make regulations contrary to a free and equal representation.

IV. That Congress do not lay direct taxes but when the moneys arising from impost, excise, and their other resources, are insufficient for the public exigencies, nor then, until Congress shall have first made a requisition upon the states to assess, levy, and pay, their respective proportions of such requisition, agreeably to the census fixed in the said Constitution, in such way and manner as the legislature of the state shall think best; and in such case, if any state shall neglect, then Congress may assess and levy such state's proportion, together with the interest thereon, at the rate of six per cent-per annum, from the time of payment prescribed in such requisition.

V. That Congress shall erect no company of merchants with exclusive advantage of commerce.

VI. That no person shall be tried for any crime by which he may incur an infamous punishment, or loss of life, until he first be indicted by a grand jury, except in such cases as may arise in the government and regulation of the land and naval forces.

VII. All common-law cases between citizens of different states shall be commenced in the common-law courts of the respective states; and no appeal shall be allowed to the federal court, in such cases, unless the sum or value of the thing in controversy amount to three thousand dollars.

VIII. In civil actions between citizens of different states, every issue of fact, arising in actions at common law, shall be tried by jury, if the parties, or either of them, request it.

IX. Congress shall at no time consent that any person, holding an office of trust or profit under the United States, shall accept any title of nobility, or any other title or office, from any king, prince, or foreign state.

X. That no standing army shall be kept up in time of peace, unless with the consent of three fourths of the members of each branch of Congress; nor shall soldiers, in time of peace, be quartered upon private houses, without the consent of the owners.

XI. Congress shall make no laws touching religion, or to infringe the rights of conscience.

XII. Congress shall never disarm any citizen, unless such as are or have been in actual rebellion.

. . .

New York[4]

We, the delegates of the people of the state of New York, duly elected and met in Convention, having maturely considered the Constitution for the United States of America, agreed to on the 17th day of September, in the year 1787, by the Convention then assembled at Philadelphia, in the commonwealth of Pennsylvania, (a copy whereof precedes these presents,) and having also seriously and deliberately considered the present situation of the United States,— Do declare and make known,—

That all power is originally vested in, and consequently derived from, the people, and that government is instituted by them for their common interest, protection, and security.

That the enjoyment of life, liberty, and the pursuit of happiness, are essential rights, which every government ought to respect and preserve.

That the powers of government may be reassumed by the people whensoever it shall become necessary to their happiness; that every power, jurisdiction, and right, which is not by the said Constitution clearly delegated to the Congress of the United States, or the departments of the government thereof, remains to the people of the several states, or to their respective state governments, to whom they may have granted the same; and that those clauses in the said Constitution, which declare that Congress shall not have or exercise certain powers, do not imply that Congress is entitled to any powers not given by the said Constitution; but such clauses are to be construed either as exceptions to certain specified powers, or as inserted merely for greater caution.

[4]1 Elliot's Debates 327–31.

That the people have an equal, natural, and unalienable right freely and peaceably to exercise their religion, according to the dictates of conscience; and that no religious sect or society ought to be favored or established by law in preference to others.

That the people have a right to keep and bear arms; that a well-regulated militia, including the body of the people *capable of bearing arms*, is the proper, natural, and safe defence of a free state.

That the militia should not be subject to martial law, except in time of war, rebellion, or insurrection.

That standing armies, in time of peace, are dangerous to liberty, and ought not to be kept up, except in cases of necessity; and that at all times the military should be under strict subordination to the civil power.

That, in time of peace, no soldier ought to be quartered in any house without the consent of the owner, and in time of war only by the civil magistrate, in such manner as the laws may direct.

That no person ought to be taken, imprisoned, or disseized of his freehold, or be exiled, or deprived of his privileges, franchises, life, liberty, or property, but by due process of law.

That no person ought to be put twice in jeopardy of life or limb, for one and the same offence; nor, unless in case of impeachment, be punished more than once for the same offence.

That every person restrained of his liberty is entitled to an inquiry into the lawfulness of such restraint, and to a removal thereof if unlawful; and that such inquiry or removal ought not to be denied or delayed, except when, on account of public danger, the Congress shall suspend the privilege of the writ of *habeas corpus*.

That excessive bail ought not to be required, nor excessive fines imposed, nor cruel or unusual punishments inflicted.

That (except in the government of the land and naval forces, and of the militia when in actual service, and in cases of impeachment) a presentment or indictment by a grand jury ought to be observed as a necessary preliminary to the trial of all crimes cognizable by the judiciary of the United States; and such trial should be speedy, public, and by an impartial jury of the county where the crime was committed; and that no person can be found guilty without the unanimous consent of such jury. But in cases of crimes not committed within any county of any of the United States, and in cases of crimes committed within any county in which a general insurrection may prevail, or which may be in the possession of a foreign enemy, the inquiry and trial may be in such county as the Congress shall by law direct; which county, in the two cases last mentioned, should be as near as conveniently may be to that county in which the crime may have been committed;—and that, in all criminal prosecutions, the accused ought to be informed of the cause and nature of his accusation, to be confronted with his accusers and the witnesses against him, to have the means of producing his witnesses, and the assistance of counsel for his defence; and should not be compelled to give evidence against himself.

That the trial by jury, in the extent that it obtains by the common law of England, is one of the greatest securities to the rights of a free people, and ought to remain inviolate.

That every freeman has a right to be secure from all unreasonable searches and seizures of his person, his papers, or his property; and therefore, that all warrants to search suspected places, or seize any freeman, his papers, or property, without information, upon oath or affirmation, of sufficient cause, are grievous and oppressive; and that all general warrants (or such in which the place or person suspected are not particularly designated) are dangerous, and ought not to be granted.

That the people have a right peaceably to assemble together to consult for their common good, or to instruct their representatives, and that every person has a right to petition or apply to the legislature for redress of grievances.

That the freedom of the press ought not to be violated or restrained.

That there should be, once in four years, an election of the President and Vice-President, so that no officer, who may be appointed by the Congress to act as President, in case of the removal, death, resignation, or inability, of the President and Vice-President, can in any case continue to act beyond the termination of the period for which the last President and Vice-President were elected.

That nothing contained in the said Constitution is to be construed to prevent the legislature of any state from passing laws at its discretion, from time to time, to divide such state into convenient districts, and to apportion its representatives to and amongst such districts.

That the prohibition contained in the said Constitution, against *ex post facto* laws extends only to laws concerning crimes.

That all appeals in causes determinable according to the course of the common law, ought to be by writ of error, and not otherwise.

That the judicial power of the United States, in cases in which a state may be a party, does not extend to criminal prosecutions, or to authorize any suit by any person against a state.

That the judicial power of the United States, as to controversies between citizens of the same state, claiming lands under grants from different states, is not to be construed to extend to any other controversies between them, except those which relate to such lands, so claimed, under grants of different states.

That the jurisdiction of the Supreme Court of the United States, or of any other court to be instituted by the Congress, is not in any case to be increased, enlarged, or extended, by any faction, collusion, or mere suggestion; and that no treaty is to be construed so to operate as to alter the Constitution of any state.

Under these impressions, and declaring that the rights aforesaid cannot be abridged or violated, and that the explanations aforesaid are consistent with the said Constitution, and in confidence that the amendments which shall have been proposed to the said Constitution will receive an early and mature consideration,—We, the said delegates, in the name and in the behalf of the people of the state of New York, do, by these presents, assent to and ratify the said Constitution. . . .

And the Convention do, in the name and behalf of the people of the state of New York, enjoin it upon their representatives in Congress to exert all their influence, and use all reasonable means, to obtain a ratification of the following amendments to the said Constitution, in the manner prescribed therein; and in all laws to be passed by the Congress, in the mean time, to conform to the spirit of the said amendments, as far as the Constitution will admit.

That there shall be one representative for every thirty thousand inhabitants, according to the enumeration or census mentioned in the Constitution, until the whole number of representatives amounts to two hundred, after which that number shall be continued or increased, but not diminished, as the Congress shall direct, and according to such ratio as the Congress shall fix, in conformity to the rule prescribed for the apportionment of representatives and direct taxes.

That the Congress do not impose any excise on any article (ardent spirits excepted) of the growth, production, or manufacture of the United States, or any of them.

That Congress do not lay direct taxes but when the moneys arising from the impost and excise shall be insufficient for the public exigencies, nor then, until Congress shall first have made a requisition upon the states to assess, levy, and pay, their respective proportions of such requisition, agreeably to the census fixed in the said Constitution, in such way and manner as the legislatures of the respective states shall judge best; and in such case, if any state shall neglect or refuse to pay its proportion, pursuant to such requisition, then Congress may assess and levy such state's proportion, together with interest at the rate of six per centum per annum, from the time of payment prescribed in such requisition.

That the Congress shall not make or alter any regulation, in any state, respecting the times, places, and manner, of holding elections for senators and representatives, unless the legislature of such state shall neglect or refuse to make laws or regulations for the purpose, or from any circumstance be incapable of making the same, and then only until the legislature of such state shall make provision in the premises; provided, that Congress may prescribe the time for the election of representatives.

That no persons, except natural-born citizens, or such as were citizens on or before the 4th day of July, 1776, or such as held commissions under the United States during the war, and have at any time since the 4th day of July, 1776, become citizens of one or other of the United States, and who shall be freeholders, shall be eligible to the places of President, Vice-President, or members of either house of the Congress of the United States.

That the Congress do not grant monopolies, or erect any company with exclusive advantages of commerce.

That no standing army or regular troops shall be raised, or kept up, in time of peace, without the consent of two thirds of the senators and representatives present in each house.

That no money be borrowed on the credit of the United States without the assent of two thirds of the senators and representatives present in each house.

That the Congress shall not declare war without the concurrence of two thirds of the senators and representatives present in each house.

That the privilege of the *habeas corpus* shall not, by any law, be suspended for a longer term than six months, or until twenty days after the meeting of the Congress next following the passing the act for such suspension.

That the right of Congress to exercise exclusive legislation over such district, not exceeding ten miles square, as may, by cession of a particular state, and the acceptance of Congress, become the seat of government of the United States, shall not be so exercised as to exempt the inhabitants of such district from paying the like taxes, imposts, duties, and excises, as shall be imposed on the other inhabitants of the state in which such district may be; and that no person shall be privileged within the said district from arrest for crimes committed, or debts contracted, out of the said district.

That the right of exclusive legislation, with respect to such places as may be purchased for the erection of forts, magazines, arsenals, dock-yards, and other needful buildings, shall not authorize the Congress to make any law to prevent the laws of the states, respectively, in which they may be, from extending to such places in all civil and criminal matters, except as to such persons as shall be in the service of the United States; nor to them with respect to crimes committed without such places.

That the compensation for the senators and representatives be ascertained by standing laws; and that no alteration of the existing rate of compensation shall operate for the benefit of the representatives until after a subsequent election shall have been had.

That the Journals of the Congress shall be published at least once a year, with the exception of such parts, relating to treaties or military operations, as, in the judgment of either house, shall require secrecy; and that both houses of Congress shall always keep their doors open during their sessions, unless the business may, in their opinion, require secrecy. That the yeas and nays shall be entered on the Journals whenever two members in either house may require it.

That no capitation tax shall ever be laid by Congress.

That no person be eligible as a senator for more than six years in any term of twelve years; and that the legislatures of the respective states may recall their senators, or either of them, and elect others in their stead, to serve the remainder of the time for which the senators so recalled were appointed.

That no senator or representative shall, during the time for which he was elected, be appointed to any office under the authority of the United States.

That the authority given to the executives of the states to fill up the vacancies of senators be abolished, and that such vacancies be filled by the respective legislatures.

That the power of Congress to pass uniform laws concerning bankruptcy shall only extend to merchants and other traders; and the states, respectively, may pass laws for the relief of other insolvent debtors.

That no person shall be eligible to the office of President of the United States a third time.

That the executive shall not grant pardons for treason, unless with the consent of the Congress; but may, at his discretion, grant reprieves to persons convicted of treason, until their cases can be laid before the Congress.

That the President, or person exercising his powers for the time being, shall not command an army in the field in person, without the previous desire of the Congress.

That all letters patent, commissions, pardons, writs, and processes of the United States, shall run in the name of *the people of the United States,* and be tested in the name of the President of the United States, or the person exercising his powers for the time being, or the first judge of the court out of which the same shall issue, as the case may be.

That the Congress shall not constitute, ordain, or establish, any tribunals of inferior courts, with any other than appellate jurisdiction, except such as may be necessary for the trial of cases of admiralty and maritime jurisdiction, and for the trial of piracies and felonies committed on the high seas; and in all other cases to which the judicial power of the United States extends, and in which the Supreme Court of the United States has not original jurisdiction, the causes shall be heard, tried, and determined, in some one of the state courts, with the right of appeal to the Supreme Court of the United States, or other proper tribunal, to be established for that purpose by the Congress, with such exceptions, and under such regulations, as the Congress shall make.

That the court for the trial of impeachments shall consist of the Senate, the judges of the Supreme Court of the United States, and the first or senior judge, for the time being, of the highest court of general and ordinary common-law jurisdiction in each state; that the Congress shall, by standing laws, designate the courts in the respective states answering this description, and, in states having no courts exactly answering this description, shall designate some other court, preferring such, if any there be, whose judge or judges may hold their places during good behavior; provided, that no more than one judge, other than judges of the Supreme Court of the United States, shall come from one state.

That the Congress be authorized to pass laws for compensating the judges for such services, and for compelling their attendance; and that a majority, at least, of the said judges shall be requisite to constitute the said court. That no person impeached shall sit as a member thereof; that each member shall, previous to the entering upon any trial, take an oath or affirmation honestly and impartially to hear and determine the cause; and that a majority of the members present shall be necessary to a conviction.

That persons aggrieved by any judgment, sentence, or decree, of the Supreme Court of the United States, in any cause in which that court has original jurisdiction, with such exceptions, and under such regulations, as the Congress shall make concerning the same, shall, upon application, have a commission, to be issued by the President of the United States to such men learned in the law as he shall nominate, and by and with the advice and consent of the Senate appoint, not less than seven, authorizing such commissioners, or any seven or more of them, to correct the errors in such judgment, or to review such sentence and decree, as the case may be, and to do justice to the parties in the premises.

That no judge of the Supreme Court of the United States shall hold any other office under the United States, or any of them.

That the judicial power of the United States shall extend to no controversies respecting land, unless it relate to claims of territory or jurisdiction between states, and individuals under the grants of different states.

That the militia of any state shall not be compelled to serve without the limits of the state, for a longer term than six weeks, without the consent of the legislature thereof.

That the words *without the consent of the Congress,* in the seventh clause of the ninth section of the first article of the Constitution, be expunged.

That the senators and representatives, and all executive and judicial officers of the United States, shall be bound by oath or affirmation not to infringe or violate the constitutions or rights of the respective states.

That the legislatures of the respective states may make provision, by law, that the electors of the election districts, to be by them appointed, shall choose a citizen of the United States, who shall have been an inhabitant of such district for the term of one year immediately preceding the time of his election, for one of the representatives of such state.

North Carolina[5]

. . .

"*Resolved*, That a declaration of rights, asserting and securing from encroachment the great principles of civil and religious liberty, and the unalienable rights of the people, together with amendments to the most ambiguous and exceptionable parts of the said Constitution of government, ought to be laid before Congress, and the convention of the states that shall or may be called for the purpose of amending the said Constitution, for their consideration, previous to the ratification of the Constitution aforesaid on the part of the state of North Carolina."

Declaration of Rights

1. That there are certain natural rights, of which men, when they form a social compact, cannot deprive or divest their posterity, among which are the enjoyment of life and liberty, with the means of acquiring, possessing, and protecting property, and pursuing and obtaining happiness and safety.

2. That all power is naturally vested in, and consequently derived from, the people; that magistrates, therefore, are their trustees and agents, and at all times amenable to them.

3. That government ought to be instituted for the common benefit, protection, and security, of the people; and that the doctrine of non-resistance against arbitrary power and oppression is absurd, slavish, and destructive to the good and happiness of mankind.

4. That no man or set of men are entitled to exclusive or separate public emoluments or privileges from the community, but in consideration of public services, which not being descendible, neither ought the offices of magistrate, legislator, or judge, or any other public office, to be hereditary.

5. That the legislative, executive, and judiciary powers of government should be separate and distinct, and that the members of the two first may be restrained from oppression by feeling and participating the public burdens: they should, at fixed periods, be reduced to a private station, return into the mass of the people, and

[5]4 Elliot's Debates 242–47.

the vacancies be supplied by certain and regular elections, in which all or any part of the former members to be eligible or ineligible, as the rules of the constitution of government and the laws shall direct.

6. That elections of representatives in the legislature ought to be free and frequent, and all men having sufficient evidence of permanent common interest with, and attachment to, the community, ought to have the right of suffrage; and no aid, charge, tax, or fee, can be set, rated, or levied, upon the people without their own consent, or that of their representatives so elected; nor can they be bound by any law to which they have not in like manner assented for the public good.

7. That all power of suspending laws, or the execution of laws, by any authority, without the consent of the representatives of the people in the legislature, is injurious to their rights, and ought not to be exercised.

8. That, in all capital and criminal prosecutions, a man hath a right to demand the cause and nature of his accusation, to be confronted with the accusers and witnesses, to call for evidence, and be allowed counsel in his favor, and a fair and speedy trial by an impartial jury of his vicinage, without whose unanimous consent he cannot be found guilty, (except in the government of the land and naval forces;) nor can he be compelled to give evidence against himself.

9. That no freeman ought to be taken, imprisoned, or disseized of his freehold, liberties, privileges, or franchises, or outlawed or exiled, or in any manner destroyed, or deprived of his life, liberty, or property, but by the law of the land.

10. That every freeman, restrained of his liberty, is entitled to a remedy to inquire into the lawfulness thereof, and to remove the same if unlawful; and that such remedy ought not to be denied nor delayed.

11. That, in controversies respecting property, and in suits between man and man, the ancient trial by jury is one of the greatest securities to the rights of the people, and ought to remain sacred and inviolable.

12. That every freeman ought to find a certain remedy, by recourse to the laws, for all injuries and wrongs he may receive in his person, property, or character; he ought to obtain right and justice freely without sale, completely and without denial, promptly and without delay; and that all establishments or regulations contravening these rights are oppressive and unjust.

13. That excessive bail ought not to be required, nor excessive fines imposed, nor cruel and unusual punishments inflicted.

14. That every freeman has a right to be secure from all unreasonable searches and seizures of his person, his papers and property; all warrants, therefore, to search suspected places, or to apprehend any suspected person, without specially naming or describing the place or person, are dangerous, and ought not to be granted.

15. That the people have a right peaceably to assemble together, to consult for the common good, or to instruct their representatives; and that every freeman has a right to petition or apply to the legislature for redress of grievances.

16. That the people have a right to freedom of speech, and of writing and publishing their sentiments; that freedom of the press is one of the greatest bulwarks of liberty, and ought not to be violated.

17. That the people have a right to keep and bear arms; that a well-regulated militia, composed of the body of the people, trained to arms, is the proper, natural, and safe defence of a free state; that standing armies, in time of peace, are dangerous to liberty, and therefore ought to be avoided, as far as the circumstances and protection of the community will admit; and that, in all cases, the military should be under strict subordination to, and governed by, the civil power.

18. That no soldier, in time of peace, ought to be quartered in any house without the consent of the owner, and in time of war, in such manner only as the laws direct.

19. That any person religiously scrupulous of bearing arms ought to be exempted, upon payment of an equivalent to employ another to bear arms in his stead.

20. That religion, or the duty which we owe to our Creator, and the manner of discharging it, can be directed only by reason and conviction, not by force or violence; and therefore all men have an equal, natural, and unalienable right to the free exercise of religion, according to the dictates of conscience; and that no particular religious sect or society ought to be favored or established by law in preference to others.

Amendments to the Constitution

1. That each state in the Union shall respectively retain every power, jurisdiction, and right, which is not by this Constitution

delegated to the Congress of the United States, or to the departments of the federal government.

2. That there shall be one representative for every thirty thousand according to the enumeration or census mentioned in the Constitution, until the whole number of representatives amounts to two hundred; after which that number shall be continued or increased as Congress shall direct, upon the principles fixed in the Constitution, by apportioning the representatives of each state to some greater number of the people, from time to time, as the population increases.

3. When Congress shall lay direct taxes or excises, they shall immediately inform the executive power of each state of the quota of such state, according to the census herein directed, which is proposed to be thereby raised; and if the legislature of any state shall pass any law which shall be effectual for raising such quota at the time required by Congress, the taxes and excises laid by Congress shall not be collected in such state.

4. That the members of the Senate and House of Representatives shall be ineligible to, and incapable of holding, any civil office under the authority of the United States, during the time for which they shall respectively be elected.

5. That the Journals of the proceedings of the Senate and House of Representatives shall be published at least once in every year, except such parts thereof relating to treaties, alliances, or military operations, as in their judgment require secrecy.

6. That a regular statement and account of receipts and expenditures of all public moneys shall be published at least once in every year.

7. That no commercial treaty shall be ratified without the concurrence of two thirds of the whole number of the members of the Senate. And no treaty, ceding, contracting, restraining, or suspending, the territorial rights or claims of the United States, or any of them, or their, or any of their, rights or claims of fishing in the American seas, or navigating the American rivers, shall be made, but in cases of the most urgent and extreme necessity; nor shall any such treaty be ratified without the concurrence of three fourths of the whole number of the members of both houses respectively.

8. That no navigation law, or law regulating commerce, shall be passed without the consent of two thirds of the members present in both houses.

9. That no standing army or regular troops shall be raised or kept up in time of peace, without the consent of two thirds of the members present in both houses.

10. That no soldier shall be enlisted for any longer term than four years, except in time of war, and then for no longer term than the continuance of the war.

11. That each state respectively shall have the power to provide for organizing, arming, and disciplining its own militia, whensoever Congress shall omit or neglect to provide for the same; that the militia shall not be subject to martial law, except when in actual service in time of war, invasion, or rebellion; and when not in the actual service of the United States, shall be subject only to such fines, penalties, and punishments, as shall be directed or inflicted by the laws of its own state.

12. That Congress shall not declare any state to be in rebellion, without the consent of at least two thirds of all the members present in both houses.

13. That the exclusive power of legislation given to Congress over the federal town and its adjacent district, and other places purchased or to be purchased by Congress of any of the states, shall extend only to such regulations as respect the police and good government thereof.

14. That no person shall be capable of being President of the United States for more than eight years in any term of fifteen years.

15. That the judicial power of the United States shall be vested in one Supreme Court, and in such courts of admiralty as Congress may from time to time ordain and establish in any of the different states. The judicial power shall extend to all cases in law and equity arising under treaties made, or which shall be made, under the authority of the United States; to all cases affecting ambassadors, other foreign ministers, and consuls; to all cases of admiralty and maritime jurisdiction; to controversies to which the United States shall be a party; to controversies between two or more states, and between parties claiming lands under the grants of different states. In all cases affecting ambassadors, other foreign ministers, and consuls, and those in which a state shall be a party, the Supreme Court shall have original jurisdiction. In all other cases before mentioned, the Supreme Court shall have appellate jurisdiction as to matters of law only, except in cases of equity, and of admiralty and maritime jurisdiction, in which the Supreme Court shall have appellate jurisdiction both as to law and fact, with such exceptions, and

under such regulations, as the Congress shall make: but the judicial power of the United States shall extend to no case where the cause of action shall have originated before the ratification of this Constitution, except in disputes between states about their territory, disputes between persons claiming lands under the grants of different states, and suits for debts due to the United States.

16. That, in criminal prosecutions, no man shall be restrained in the exercise of the usual and accustomed right of challenging or excepting to the jury.

17. That Congress shall not alter, modify, or interfere in, the times, places, or manner, of holding elections for senators and representatives, or either of them, except when the legislature of any state shall neglect, refuse, or be disabled, by invasion or rebellion, to prescribe the same.

18. That those clauses which declare that Congress shall not exercise certain powers be not interpreted in any manner whatsoever to extend the power of Congress; but that they be construed either as making exceptions to the specified powers, where this shall be the case, or otherwise as inserted merely for greater caution.

19. That the laws ascertaining the compensation of senators and representatives for their services, be postponed in their operation until after the election of representatives immediately succeeding the passing thereof, that excepted which shall first be passed on the subject.

20. That some tribunal other than the Senate be provided for trying impeachments of senators.

21. That the salary of a judge shall not be increased or diminished during his continuance in office, otherwise than by general regulations of salary, which may take place on a revision of the subject at stated periods of not less than seven years, to commence from the time such salaries shall be first ascertained by Congress.

22. That Congress erect no company of merchants with exclusive advantages of commerce.

23. That no treaties which shall be directly opposed to the existing laws of the United States in Congress assembled shall be valid until such laws shall be repealed, or made conformable to such treaty; nor shall any treaty be valid which is contradictory to the Constitution of the United States.

24. That the latter part of the 5th paragraph of the 9th section of the 1st article be altered to read thus: "Nor shall vessels bound to a particular state be obliged to enter or pay duties in any other; nor,

when bound from any one of the states, be obliged to clear in another."

25. That Congress shall not, directly or indirectly, either by themselves or through the judiciary, interfere with any one of the states in the redemption of paper money already emitted and now in circulation, or in liquidating and discharging the public securities of any one of the states, but each and every state shall have the exclusive right of making such laws and regulations, for the above purposes, as they shall think proper.

26. That Congress shall not introduce foreign troops into the United States without the consent of two thirds of the members present of both houses.

. . .

Pennsylvania[6]

After free discussion, and mature deliberation, had upon the subject before them, the following resolutions and propositions were adopted—

The ratification of the federal Constitution having formed a new era in the American world, highly interesting to all the citizens of the United States, it is not less the duty than the privilege of every citizen to examine with attention the principles and probable effect of a system on which the happiness or misery of the present as well as future generations so much depends. In the course of such examination, many of the good citizens of the state of Pennsylvania have found their apprehensions excited that the Constitution, in its present form, contains in it some principles which may be perverted to purposes injurious to the rights of free citizens, and some ambiguities which may probably lead to contentions incompatible with order and good government. In order to remedy these inconveniences, and to avert the apprehended dangers, it has been thought expedient that delegates, chosen by those who wish for early amendments in the said Constitution, should meet together for the purpose of deliberating on the subject, and uniting in some constitutional plan for obtaining the amendments which they may deem necessary.

We, the conferees, assembled for the purpose aforesaid, agree in opinion,—

[6] 2 Elliot's Debates.

That a federal government, only, can preserve the liberties and secure the happiness of the inhabitants of a country so extensive as these United States; and experience having taught us that the ties of our union, under the Articles of Confederation, were so weak as to deprive us of some of the greatest advantages we had a right to expect from it, we are fully convinced that a more efficient government is indispensably necessary. But although the Constitution proposed for the United States is likely to obviate most of the inconveniences we labored under, yet several parts of it appear so exceptionable to us, that we are clearly of opinion considerable amendments are essentially necessary. In full confidence, however, of obtaining a revision of such exceptionable parts by general convention, and from a desire to harmonize with our fellow-citizens, we are induced to acquiesce in the organization of the said Constitution.

We are sensible that a large number of the citizens both of this and the other states, who gave their assent to its being carried into execution previous to any amendments, were actuated more by fear of the dangers that might arise from delays, than by a conviction of its being perfect; we therefore hope they will concur with us in pursuing every peaceable method of obtaining a speedy revision of the Constitution in the mode therein provided; and, when we reflect on the present circumstances of the Union, we can entertain no doubt that motives of conciliation, and the dictates of policy and prudence, will conspire to induce every man of true federal principles to give his support to a measure which is not only calculated to recommend the new Constitution to the approbation and support of every class of citizens, but even necessary to prevent the total defection of some members of the Union.

. . .

The amendments proposed are as follows, viz.:—

I. That Congress shall not exercise any powers whatever, but such as are expressly given to that body by the Constitution of the United States; nor shall any authority, power, or jurisdiction, be assumed or exercised by the executive or judiciary departments of the Union, under color or pretence of construction or fiction; but all the rights of sovereignty, which are not by the said Constitution expressly and plainly vested in the Congress, shall be deemed to remain with, and shall be exercised by, the several states in the Union, according to their respective constitutions; and that every reserve of the rights of individuals, made by the several constitutions of the states in the Union, to the citizens and inhabitants of each state respectively, shall remain inviolate, except so far as they are expressly and manifestly yielded or narrowed by the national Constitution.

Article 1, section 2, paragraph 3.

II. That the number of representatives be, for the present, one for every twenty thousand inhabitants, according to the present estimated numbers in the several states, and continue in that proportion until the whole number of representatives shall amount to two hundred; and then to be so proportioned and modified as not to exceed that number, until the proportion of one representative for every thirty thousand inhabitants shall amount to the said number of two hundred.

Section 3. III. That senators, though chosen for six years, shall be liable to be recalled, or superseded by other appointments, by the respective legislatures of the states, at any time.

Section 4. IV. That Congress shall not have power to make or alter regulations concerning the time, place, and manner of electing senators and representatives, except in case of neglect or refusal by the state to make regulations for the purpose; and then only for such time as such neglect or refusal shall continue.

Section 8. V. That when Congress shall require supplies, which are to be raised by direct taxes, they shall demand from the several states their respective quotas thereof, giving a reasonable time to each state to procure and pay the same; and if any state shall refuse, neglect, or omit to raise and pay the same within such limited time, then Congress shall have power to assess, levy, and collect the quota of such state, together with interest for the same, from the time of such delinquency, upon the inhabitants and estates therein, in such manner as they shall by law direct; provided that no poll tax be imposed.

Section 8. VI. That no standing army of regular troops shall be raised or kept up in time of peace, without the consent of two thirds of both houses in Congress.

Section 8. VII. That the clause respecting the exclusive legislation over a district not exceeding ten miles square be qualified by a proviso that such right of legislation extend only to such regulations as respect the police and good order thereof.

Section 8. VIII. That each state, respectively, shall have power to provide for organizing, arming, and disciplining the militia thereof, whensoever Congress shall omit or neglect to provide for the same.

That the militia shall not be subject to martial law, but when in actual service, in the time of war, invasion, or rebellion; and when not in the actual service of the United States, shall be subject to such fines, penalties, and punishments, only, as shall be directed or inflicted by the laws of its own state: nor shall the militia of any state be continued in actual service longer than two months, under any call of Congress, without the consent of the legislature of such state, or, in their recess, the executive authority thereof.

Section 9. IX. That the clause respecting vessels bound to or from any one of the states be explained.

Article 3, section 1. X. That Congress establish no other court than the Supreme Court, except such as shall be necessary for determining causes of admiralty jurisdiction.

Section 2, paragraph 2. XI. That a proviso be added at the end of the second clause of the second section of the third article, to the following effect, viz.: Provided, that such appellate jurisdiction, in all cases of common-law cognizance, be by a writ of error, and confined to matters of law only; and that no such writ of /error shall be admitted, except in revenue cases, unless the matter in controversy exceed the value of three thousand dollars.

Article 6, paragraph 2. XII. That to article 6, clause 2, be added the following proviso, viz: Provided always that no treaty, which shall hereafter be made, shall be deemed or construed to alter or affect any law of the United States, or of any particular state, until such treaty shall have been laid before and assented to by the House of Representatives in Congress.

Rhode Island[7]

We, the delegates of the people of the state of Rhode Island and Providence Plantations, duly elected and met in Convention, having maturely considered the Constitution for the United States of America, agreed to on the seventeenth day of September, in the year one thousand seven hundred and eighty-seven, by the Convention then assembled at Philadelphia, in the commonwealth of Pennsylvania, (a copy whereof precedes these presents,) and having also seriously and deliberately considered the present situation of this state, do declare and make known,—

[7]1 Elliot's Debates 334–37.

I. That there are certain natural rights of which men, when they form a social compact, cannot deprive or divest their posterity,—among which are the enjoyment of life and liberty, with the means of acquiring, possessing, and protecting property, and pursuing and obtaining happiness and safety.

II. That all power is naturally vested in, and consequently derived from, the people; that magistrates, therefore, are their trustees and agents, and at all times amenable to them.

III. That the powers of government may be reassumed by the people whensoever it shall become necessary to their happiness. That the rights of the states respectively to nominate and appoint all state officers, and every other power, jurisdiction, and right, which is not by the said Constitution clearly delegated to the Congress of the United States, or to the departments of government thereof, remain to the people of the several states, or their respective state governments, to whom they may have granted the same; and that those clauses in the Constitution which declare that Congress shall not have or exercise certain powers, do not imply that Congress is entitled to any powers not given by the said Constitution; but such clauses are to be construed as exceptions to certain specified powers, or as inserted merely for greater caution.

IV. That religion, or the duty which we owe to our Creator, and the manner of discharging it, can be directed only by reason and conviction, and not by force and violence; and therefore all men have a natural, equal, and unalienable right to the exercise of religion according to the dictates of conscience; and that no particular religious sect or society ought to be favored or established, by law, in preference to others.

V. That the legislative, executive, and judiciary powers of government should be separate and distinct; and, that the members of the two first may be restrained from oppression, by feeling and participating the public burdens, they should, at fixed periods, be reduced to a private station, returned into the mass of the people, and the vacancies be supplied by certain and regular elections, in which all or any part of the former members to be eligible or ineligible, as the rules of the constitution of government and the laws shall direct.

VI. That elections of representatives in legislature ought to be free and frequent, and all men having sufficient evidence of permanent common interest with, and attachment to, the community, ought to have the right of suffrage; and no aid, charge, tax, or fee, can be set, rated, or levied, upon the people without their own consent, or that of their representatives so elected, nor can they be bound by any law to which they have not in like manner consented for the public good.

VII. That all power of suspending laws, or the execution of laws, by any authority, without the consent of the representatives of the people in the legislature, is injurious to their rights, and ought not to be exercised.

VIII. That, in all capital and criminal prosecutions, a man hath the right to demand the cause and nature of his accusation, to be confronted with the accusers and witnesses, to call for evidence, and be allowed counsel in his favor, and to a fair and speedy trial by an impartial jury in his vicinage, without whose unanimous consent he cannot be found guilty, (except in the government of the land and naval forces,) nor can he be compelled to give evidence against himself.

IX. That no freeman ought to be taken, imprisoned, or disseized of his freehold, liberties, privileges, or franchises, or outlawed, or exiled, or in any manner destroyed or deprived of his life, liberty, or property, but by the trial by jury, or by the law of the land.

X. That every freeman restrained of his liberty is entitled to a remedy, to inquire into the lawfulness thereof, and to remove the same if unlawful, and that such remedy ought not to be denied or delayed.

XI. That in controversies respecting property, and in suits between man and man, the ancient trial by jury, as hath been exercised by us and our ancestors, from the time whereof the memory of man is not to the contrary is one of the greatest securities to the rights of the people, and ought to remain sacred and inviolable.

XII. That every freeman ought to obtain right and justice, freely and without sale, completely and without denial, promptly and without delay; and that all establishments or regulations contravening these rights are oppressive and unjust.

XIII. That excessive bail ought not to be required, nor excessive fines imposed, nor cruel or unusual punishments inflicted.

XIV. That every person has a right to be secure from all unreasonable searches and seizures of his person, his papers, or his property; and therefore, that all warrants to search suspected places, to seize any person, his papers, or his property, without information upon oath or affirmation of sufficient cause, are grievous and oppressive; and that all general warrants (or such in which the place or person suspected are not particularly designated) are dangerous, and ought not to be granted.

XV. That the people have a right peaceably to assemble together to consult for their common good, or to instruct their representatives; and that every person has a right to petition or apply to the legislature for redress of grievances.

XVI. That the people have a right to freedom of speech, and of writing and publishing their sentiments. That freedom of the press is one of the greatest bulwarks of liberty, and ought not to be violated.

XVII. That the people have a right to keep and bear arms; that a well-regulated militia, including the body of the people capable of bearing arms, is the proper, natural, and safe defence of a free state; that the militia shall not be subject to martial law, except in time of war, rebellion, or insurrection; that standing armies, in time of peace, are dangerous to liberty, and ought not to be kept up, except in cases of necessity; and that, at all times, the military should be under strict subordination to the civil power; that, in time of peace, no soldier ought to be quartered in any house without the consent of the owner, and in time of war only by the civil magistrates, in such manner as the law directs.

XVIII. That any person religiously scrupulous of bearing arms ought to be exempted upon payment of an equivalent to employ another to bear arms in his stead.

Under these impressions, and declaring that the rights aforesaid cannot be abridged or violated, and that the explanations aforesaid are consistent with the said Constitution, and in confidence that the amendments hereafter mentioned will receive an early and mature consideration, and, conformably to the fifth article of said Constitution, speedily become a part thereof,—We, the said delegates, in the name and in the behalf of the people of the state of Rhode Island and Providence Plantations, do, by these presents, assent to and ratify the said Constitution. . . .

. . .

And the Convention do, in the name and behalf of the people of the state of Rhode Island and Providence Plantations, enjoin it upon their senators and representative or representatives, which may be elected to represent this state in Congress, to exert all their influence, and use all reasonable means, to obtain a ratification of the following amendments to the said Constitution, in the manner prescribed therein; and in all laws to be passed by the Congress in the mean time, to conform to the spirit of the said amendments, as far as the Constitution will admit.

Amendments

I. The United States shall guaranty to each state its sovereignty, freedom, and independence, and every power, jurisdiction, and right, which is not by this Constitution expressly delegated to the United States.

II. That Congress shall not alter, modify, or interfere in, the times, places, or manner, of holding elections for senators and representatives, or either of them, except when the legislature of any state shall neglect, refuse, or be disabled, by invasion or rebellion, to prescribe the same, or in case when the provision made by the state is so imperfect as that no consequent election is had, and then only until the legislature of such state shall make provision in the premises.

III. It is declared by the Convention, that the judicial power of the United States, in cases in which a state may be a party, does not extend to criminal prosecutions, or to authorize any suit by any person against a state; but, to remove all doubts or controversies respecting the same, that it be especially expressed, as a part of the Constitution of the United States, that Congress shall not, directly or indirectly, either by themselves or through the judiciary, interfere with any one of the states, in the redemption of paper money already emitted, and now in circulation, or in liquidating and discharging the public securities of any one state; that each and every state shall have the exclusive right of making such laws and regulations for the before-mentioned purpose as they shall think proper.

IV. That no amendments to the Constitution of the United States, hereafter to be made, pursuant to the fifth article, shall take effect, or become a part of the Constitution of the United States, after the year one thousand seven hundred and ninety-three, without the consent of eleven of the states heretofore united under the Confederation.

V. That the judicial powers of the United States shall extend to no possible case where the cause of action shall have originated before the ratification of this Constitution, except in disputes between states about their territory, disputes between persons claiming lands under grants of different states, and debts due to the United States.

VI. That no person shall be compelled to do military duty otherwise than by voluntary enlistment, except in cases of general invasion; any thing in the second paragraph of the sixth article of the Constitution, or any law made under the Constitution, to the contrary notwithstanding.

VII. That no capitation or poll tax shall ever be laid by Congress.

VIII. In cases of direct taxes, Congress shall first make requisitions on the several states to assess, levy, and pay, their respective proportions of such requisitions, in such way and manner as the legislatures of the several states shall judge best; and in case any state shall neglect or refuse to pay its proportion, pursuant to such requisition, then Congress may assess and levy such state's proportion, together with interest, at the rate of six per cent-per annum, from the time prescribed in such requisition.

IX. That Congress shall lay no direct taxes without the consent of the legislatures of three fourths of the states in the Union.

X. That the Journal of the proceedings of the Senate and House of Representatives shall be published as soon as conveniently may be, at least once in every year; except such parts thereof relating to treaties, alliances, or military operations, as in their judgment require secrecy.

XI. That regular statements of the receipts and expenditures of all public moneys shall be published at least once a year.

XII. As standing armies, in time of peace, are dangerous to liberty, and ought not to be kept up, except in cases of necessity, and as, at all times, the military should be under strict subordination to the civil power, that, therefore, no standing army or regular troops shall be raised or kept up in time of peace.

XIII. That no moneys be borrowed, on the credit of the United States, without the assent of two thirds of the senators and representatives present in each house.

XIV. That the Congress shall not declare war without the concurrence of two thirds of the senators and representatives present in each house.

XV. That the words "without the consent of Congress," in the seventh clause in the ninth section of the first article of the Constitution, be expunged.

XVI. That no judge of the Supreme Court of the United States shall hold any other office under the United States, or any of them; nor shall any officer appointed by Congress, or by the President and Senate of the United States, be permitted to hold any office under the appointment of any of the states.

XVII. As a traffic tending to establish or continue the slavery of any part of the human species is disgraceful to the cause of liberty and humanity, that Congress shall, as soon as may be, promote and establish such laws and regulations as may effectually prevent the importation of slaves of every description into the United States.

XVIII. That the state legislatures have power to recall, when they think it expedient, their federal senators, and to send others in their stead.

XIX. That Congress have power to establish a uniform rule of inhabitancy or settlement of the poor of the different states throughout the United States.

XX. That Congress erect no company with exclusive advantages of commerce.

XXI. That when two members shall move and call for the ayes and nays on any question, they shall be entered on the Journals of the houses respectively.

South Carolina[8]

. . .

And whereas it is essential to the preservation of the rights reserved to the several states, and the freedom of the people, under the operations of a general government, that the right of prescribing the manner, time, and places, of holding the elections to the federal legislature, should be forever—inseparably annexed to the sovereignty of the several states,—This Convention doth declare, that the same ought to remain, to all posterity, a perpetual and fundamental right in the local, exclusive of the interference of the general government, except in cases where the legislatures of the states shall refuse or neglect to perform and fulfil the same, according to the tenor of the said Constitution.

This Convention doth also declare, that no section or paragraph of the said Constitution warrants a construction that the states do not retain every power not expressly relinquished by them, and vested in the general government of the Union.

Resolved, That the general government of the United States ought never to impose direct taxes, *but* where the moneys arising from the duties, imports, and excise, are insufficient for the public exigencies, *nor then until* Congress shall have made a requisition upon the states to assess, levy, and pay, their respective proportions of such requisitions; and in case any state shall neglect or refuse to

[8] 4 Elliot's Debates 325.

pay its proportion, pursuant to such requisition, then Congress may assess and levy such state's proportion, together with interest thereon, at the rate of six per centum per annum, from the time of payment prescribed by such requisition.

Resolved, That the third section of the sixth article ought to be amended, by inserting the word "other" between the words "no" and "religious."

Resolved, That it be a standing instruction to all such delegates as may hereafter be elected to represent this state in the general government, to exert their utmost abilities and influence to effect an alteration of the Constitution, conformably to the aforegoing resolutions.

Virginia[9]

. . .

That there be a declaration or bill of rights asserting, and securing from encroachment, the essential and unalienable rights of the people, in some such manner as the following:—

1st. That there are certain natural rights, of which men, when they form a social compact, cannot deprive or divest their posterity; among which are the enjoyment of life and liberty, with the means of acquiring, possessing, and protecting property, and pursuing and obtaining happiness and safety.

2d. That all power is naturally invested in, and consequently derived from, the people; that magistrates therefore are their *trustees* and *agents,* at all times amenable to them.

3d. That government ought to be instituted for the common benefit, protection, and security of the people; and that the doctrine of non-resistance against arbitrary power and oppression is absurd, slavish, and destructive to the good and happiness of mankind.

4th. That no man or set of men are entitled to separate or exclusive public emoluments or privileges from the community, but in consideration of public services, which not being descendible, neither ought the offices of magistrate, legislator, or judge, or any other public office, to be hereditary.

5th. That the legislative, executive, and judicial powers of government should be separate and distinct; and, that the members of the two first may be restrained from oppression by feeling and participating the public burdens, they should, at fixed periods, be

[9] 3 Elliot's Debates 657–61.

reduced to a private station, return into the mass of the people, and the vacancies be supplied by certain and regular elections, in which all or any part of the former members to be eligible or ineligible, as the rules of the Constitution of government, and the laws, shall direct.

6th.   That the elections of representatives in the legislature ought to be free and frequent, and all men having sufficient evidence of permanent common interest with, and attachment to, the community, ought to have the right of suffrage; and no aid, charge, tax, or fee, can be set, rated, or levied, upon the people without their own consent, or that of their representatives, so elected; nor can they be bound by any law to which they have not, in like manner, assented, for the public good.

7th.   That all power of suspending laws, or the execution of laws, by any authority, without the consent of the representatives of the people in the legislature, is injurious to their rights, and ought not to be exercised.

8th.   That, in all criminal and capital prosecutions, a man hath a right to demand the cause and nature of his accusation, to be confronted with the accusers and witnesses, to call for evidence, and be allowed counsel in his favor, and to a fair and speedy trial by an impartial jury of his vicinage, without whose unanimous consent he cannot be found guilty, (except in the government of the land and naval forces;) nor can he be compelled to give evidence against himself.

9th.   That no freeman ought to be taken, imprisoned, or disseized of his freehold, liberties, privileges, or franchises, or outlawed, or exiled, or in any manner destroyed, or deprived of his life, liberty, or property, but by the law of the land.

10th.   That every freeman restrained of his liberty is entitled to a remedy, to inquire into the lawfulness thereof, and to remove the same, if unlawful, and that such remedy ought not to be denied nor delayed.

11th.   That, in controversies respecting property, and in suits between man and man, the ancient trial by jury is one of the greatest securities to the rights of the people, and to remain sacred and inviolable.

12th.   That every freeman ought to find a certain remedy, by recourse to the laws, for all injuries and wrongs he may receive in his person, property, or character. He ought to obtain right and justice freely, without sale, completely and without denial, promptly and without delay, and that all establishments or regulations contravening these rights are oppressive and unjust.

13th. That excessive bail ought not to be required, nor excessive fines imposed, nor cruel and unusual punishments inflicted.

14th. That every freeman has a right to be secure from all unreasonable searches and seizures of his person, his papers, and property; all warrants, therefore, to search suspected places, or seize any freeman, his papers, or property, without information on oath (or affirmation of a person religiously scrupulous of taking an oath) of legal and sufficient cause, are grievous and oppressive; and all general warrants to search suspected places, or to apprehend any suspected person, without specially naming or describing the place or person, are dangerous, and ought not to be granted.

15th. That the people have a right peaceably to assemble together to consult for the common good, or to instruct their representatives; and that every freeman has a right to petition or apply to the legislature for redress of grievances.

16th. That the people have a right to freedom of speech, and of writing and publishing their sentiments; that the freedom of the press is one of the greatest bulwarks of liberty, and ought not to be violated.

17th. That the people have a right to keep and bear arms; that a well-regulated militia, composed of the body of the people trained to arms, is the proper, natural, and safe defence of a free state; that standing armies, in time of peace, are dangerous to liberty, and therefore ought to be avoided, as far as the circumstances and protection of the community will admit; and that, in all cases, the military should be under strict subordination to, and governed by, the civil power.

18th. That no soldier in time of peace ought to be quartered in any house without the consent of the owner, and in time of war in such manner only as the law directs.

19th. That any person religiously scrupulous of bearing arms ought to be exempted, upon payment of an equivalent to employ another to bear arms in his stead.

20th. That religion, or the duty which we owe to our Creator, and the manner of discharging it, can be directed only by reason and conviction, not by force or violence; and therefore all men have an equal, natural, and unalienable right to the free exercise of religion, according to the dictates of conscience, and that no particular religious sect or society ought to be favored or established, by law, in preference to others."

Amendments to the Constitution

1st. That each state in the Union shall respectively retain every power, jurisdiction, and right, which is not by this Constitution delegated to the Congress of the United States, or to the departments of the federal government.

2d. That there shall be one representative for every thirty thousand according to the enumeration or census mentioned in the Constitution until the whole number of representatives amounts to two hundred; after which, that number shall be continued or increased, as Congress shall direct, upon the principles fixed in the Constitution, by apportioning the representatives of each state to some greater number of people, from time to time, as population increases.

3d. When the Congress shall lay direct taxes or excises, they shall immediately inform the executive power of each state, of the quota of such state, according to the census herein directed, which is proposed to be thereby raised; and if the legislature of any state shall pass a law which shall be effectual for raising such quota at the time required by Congress, the taxes and excises laid by Congress shall not be collected in such state.

4th. That the members of the Senate and House of Representatives shall be ineligible to, and incapable of holding, any civil office under the authority of the United States, during the time for which they shall respectively be elected.

5th. That the journals of the proceedings of the Senate and House of Representatives shall be published at least once in every year, except such parts thereof, relating to treaties, alliances, or military operations, as, in their judgment, require secrecy.

6th. That a regular statement and account of the receipts and expenditures of public money shall be published at least once a year.

7th. That no commercial treaty shall be ratified without the concurrence of two thirds of the whole number of the members of the Senate; and no treaty ceding, contracting, restraining, or suspending, the territorial rights or claims of the United States, or any of them, or their, or any of their rights or claims to fishing in the American seas, or navigating the American rivers, shall be made, but in cases of the most urgent and extreme necessity; nor shall any such treaty be ratified without the concurrence of three fourths of the whole number of the members of both houses respectively.

8th. That no navigation law, or law regulating commerce, shall be passed without the consent of two thirds of the members present, in both houses.

9th. That no standing army, or regular troops, shall be raised, or kept up, in time of peace, without the consent of two thirds of the members present, in both houses.

10th. That no soldier shall be enlisted for any longer term than four years, except in time of war, and then for no longer term than the continuance of the war.

11th. That each state respectively shall have the power to provide for organizing, arming, and disciplining its own militia, whensoever Congress shall omit or neglect to provide for the same. That the militia shall not be subject to martial law, except when in actual service, in time of war, invasion, or rebellion; and when not in the actual service of the United States, shall be subject only to such fines, penalties, and punishments, as shall be directed or inflicted by the laws of its own state.

12th. That the exclusive power of legislation given to Congress over the federal town and its adjacent district, and other places, purchased or to be purchased by Congress of any of the states, shall extend only to such regulations as respect the police and good government thereof.

13th. That no person shall be capable of being President of the United States for more than eight years in any term of sixteen years.

14th. That the judicial power of the United States shall be vested in one Supreme Court, and in such courts of admiralty as Congress may from time to time ordain and establish in any of the different states. The judicial power shall extend to all cases in law and equity arising under treaties made, or which shall be made, under the authority of the United States; to all cases affecting ambassadors, other foreign ministers, and consuls; to all cases of admiralty and maritime jurisdiction; to controversies to which the United States shall be a party; to controversies between two or more states, and between parties claiming lands under the grants of different states. In all cases affecting ambassadors, other foreign ministers, and consuls, and those in which a state shall be a party, the Supreme Court shall have original jurisdiction; in all other cases before mentioned, the Supreme Court shall have appellate jurisdiction, as to matters of law only, except in cases of equity, and of admiralty, and maritime jurisdiction, in which the Supreme Court shall have appellate jurisdiction both as to law and fact, with such exceptions and under such regulations as the Congress shall make; but the judicial power of the United States shall extend to no case where the cause of action shall have originated before the ratification of the Constitution, except in disputes between states about their territory, disputes between persons claiming lands under the grants of different states, and suits for debts due to the United States.

15th. That, in criminal prosecutions, no man shall be restrained in the exercise of the usual and accustomed right of challenging or excepting to the jury.

16th. That Congress shall not alter, modify, or interfere in the times, places, or manner of holding elections for senators and representatives, or either of them, except when the legislature of any state shall neglect, refuse, or be disabled, by invasion or rebellion, to prescribe the same.

17th. That those clauses which declare that Congress shall not exercise certain powers, be not interpreted, in any manner whatsoever, to extend the powers of Congress; but that they be construed either as making exceptions to the specified powers where this shall be the case, or otherwise, as inserted merely for greater caution.

18th. That the laws ascertaining the compensation of senators and representatives for their services, be postponed, in their operation, until after the election of representatives immediately succeeding the passing thereof; that excepted which shall first be passed on the subject.

19th. That some tribunal other than the Senate be provided for trying impeachments of senators.

20th. That the salary of a judge shall not be increased or diminished during his continuance in office, otherwise, than by general regulations of salary, which may take place on a revision of the subject at stated periods of not less than seven years, to commence from the time such salaries shall be first ascertained by Congress.

. . .

Appendix C: Justice Goldberg's Concurring Opinion in *Griswold v. Connecticut*

Mr. Justice **Goldberg,** whom the **Chief Justice** and Mr. Justice **Brennan** join, concurring.

I agree with the Court that Connecticut's birth-control law unconstitutionally intrudes upon the right of marital privacy, and I join in its opinion and judgment. Although I have not accepted the view that "due process" as used in the Fourteenth Amendment incorporates all of the first eight Amendments (see my concurring opinion in Pointer v. Texas, 380 U.S. 400, 410, 13 L. ed. 2d 923, 930, 85 S. Ct. 1065, and the dissenting opinion of Mr. Justice Brennan in Cohen v. Hurley, 366 U.S. 117, 154, 6 L. ed. 2d 156, 179, 81 S. Ct. 954), I do agree that the concept of liberty protects those personal rights that are fundamental, and is not confined to the specific terms of the Bill of Rights. My conclusion that the concept of liberty is not so restricted and that it embraces the right of marital privacy though that right is not mentioned explicitly in the Constitution[1] is

---

Reprinted from 381 U.S. 479, 486 (1965).

[1]My Brother Stewart dissents on the ground the he "can find no . . . general right of privacy in the Bill of Rights, in any other part of the Constitution, or in any case ever before decided by this Court." *Post,* at 542. He would require a more explicit guarantee that the one which the Court derives from several constitutional amendments. This Court, however, has never held that the Bill of Rights or the Fourteenth Amendment protects only those rights that the Constitution specifically mentions by name. *See, e.g.,* Bolling v. Sharpe, 347 U.S. 497, 98 L. ed. 884, 74 S. Ct. 693; Aptheker v. Secretary of State, 378 U.S. 500, 12 L. ed. 2d 992, 84 S. Ct. 1659; Kent v. Dulles, 357 U.S. 116, 2 L. ed. 2d 1204, 78 S. Ct. 1113; Carrington v. Rash, 380 U.S. 89, 96, 13 L. ed. 2d 675, 680, 85 S. Ct. 775; Schware v. Board of Bar Examiners, 353 U.S. 232, 1 L. ed. 2d 796, 77 S. Ct. 752, 64 ALR2d 288; NAACP v. Alabama, 360 U.S. 240, 3 L. ed. 2d 1205, 79 S. Ct. 1001; Pierce v. Society of Sisters, 268 U.S. 510, 69 L. ed. 1070, 45 S. Ct. 571, 39 ALR 468; Meyer v. Nebraska, 262 U.S. 390, 67 L. ed. 1042, 43 S. Ct. 625, 29 ALR 1446. To the contrary, this Court, for example, in Bolling v. Sharpe, *supra,* while recognizing that the Fifth Amendment does not contain the "explicit safeguard" of an equal protection clause, *id.,* at 499, 98 L. ed. at 886,

supported both by numerous decisions of this Court, referred to in the Court's opinion, and by the language and history of the Ninth Amendment. In reaching the conclusion that the right of marital privacy is protected, as being within the protected penumbra of specific guarantees of the Bill of Rights, the Court refers to the Ninth Amendment, *ante,* at 515. I add these words to emphasize the relevance of that Amendment to the Court's holding.

The Court stated many years ago that the Due Process Clause protects those liberties that are "so rooted in the traditions and conscience of our people as to be ranked as fundamental." Snyder v. Massachusetts, 291 U.S. 97, 105, 78 L. ed. 674, 677, 54 S. Ct. 330, 90 ALR 575. In Gitlow v. New York, 268 U.S. 652, 666, 69 L. ed. 1138, 1145, 45 S. Ct. 625, the Court said:

> For present purposes we may and do assume that freedom of speech and of the press—which are protected by the First Amendment from abridgment by Congress—are among the *fundamental* personal rights and 'liberties' protected by the due process clause of the Fourteenth Amendment from impairment by the States [emphasis added].

And, in Meyer v. Nebraska, 262 U.S. 390, 399, 67 L. ed. 1042, 1045, 43 S. Ct. 625, 29 ALR 1446, the Court, referring to the Fourteenth Amendment, stated:

> While this Court has not attempted to define with exactness the liberty thus guaranteed, the term has received much consideration and some of the included things have been definitely stated. Without doubt, it denotes not merely freedom from bodily restraint but also [for example,] the right . . . to marry, establish a home and bring up children. . . .

This Court, in a series of decisions, has held that the Fourteenth Amendment absorbs and applies to the States those specifics of the first eight amendments which express fundamental personal rights.[2]

nevertheless derived an equal protection principle from that Amendment's Due Process Clause. And in Schware v. Board of Bar Examiners, *supra,* the Court held that the Fourteenth Amendment protects from arbitrary state action the right to pursue an occupation, such as the practice of law.

[2]*See, e.g.,* Chicago, B. & Q. R. Co. v. Chicago, 166 U.S. 226, 41 L. ed. 979, 17 S. Ct. 581; Gitlow v. New York, *supra;* Cantwell v. Connecticut, 310 U.S. 296, 84 L. ed. 1213, 60 S. Ct. 900, 128 ALR 1352; Wolf v. Colorado, 338 U.S. 25, 93 L. ed. 1782, 69 S. Ct. 1359; Robinson v. California, 370 U.S. 660, 8 L. ed. 2d 758, 82 S. Ct. 1417; Gideon v. Wainwright, 372 U.S. 335, 9 L. ed. 2d 799, 83 S. Ct. 792, 93 ALR2d 733; Malloy v. Hogan, 378 U.S. 1, 12 L. ed. 2d 653, 84 S. Ct. 1489; Pointer v. Texas, *supra;* Griffin v. California, 380 U.S. 609, 14 L. ed. 2d 106, 85 S. Ct. 1229.

The language and history of the Ninth Amendment reveal that the Framers of the Constitution believed that there are additional fundamental rights, protected from governmental infringement, which exist alongside those fundamental rights specifically mentioned in the first eight constitutional amendments.

The Ninth Amendment reads, "The enumeration in the Constitution, of certain rights, shall not be construed to deny or disparage others retained by the people." The Amendment is almost entirely the work of James Madison. It was introduced in Congress by him and passed the House and Senate with little or no debate and virtually no change in language. It was proffered to quiet expressed fears that a bill of specifically enumerated rights[3] could not be sufficiently broad to cover all essential rights and that the specific mention of certain rights would be interpreted as a denial that others were protected.[4]

In presenting the proposed Amendment, Madison said:

> It has been objected also against a bill of rights, that, by enumerating particular exceptions to the grant of power, it would disparage those rights which were not placed in that enumeration; and it might follow by implication, that those rights which were not

[3]Madison himself had previously pointed out the dangers of inaccuracy resulting from the fact that "no language is so copious as to supply words and phrases for every complex idea." The Federalist No. 37 at 236 (Cooke ed. 1961).

[4]Alexander Hamilton was opposed to a bill of rights on the ground that it was unnecessary because the Federal Government was a government of delegated powers and it was not granted the power to intrude upon fundamental personal rights. The Federalist No. 84 at 578–79 (Cooke ed. 1961). He also argued,

> I go further, and affirm that bills of rights, in the sense and in the extent in which they are contended for, are not only unnecessary in the proposed constitution, but would even be dangerous. They would contain various exceptions to powers which are not granted; and on this very account, would afford a colourable pretext to claim more than were granted. For why declare that things shall not be done which there is no power to do? Why for instance, should it be said, that the liberty of the press shall not be restrained, when no power is given by which restrictions may be imposed? I will not contend that such a provision would confer a regulating power; but it is evident that it would furnish, to men disposed to usurp, a plausible pretence for claiming that power.

Id., at 579.

The Ninth Amendment and the Tenth Amendment, which provides, "The powers not delegated to the United States by the Constitution, nor prohibited by it to the States, are reserved to the States respectively, or to the people," were apparently also designed in part to meet the above-quoted argument of Hamilton.

singled out, were intended to be assigned into the hands of the
General Government, and were consequently insecure. This is
one of the most plausible arguments I have ever heard urged
against the admission of a bill of rights into this system; but, I
conceive, that it may be guarded against. I have attempted it as
gentlemen may see by turning to the last clause of the fourth
resolution [the Ninth Amendment].

I Annals of Congress 439 (Gales & Seaton ed. 1834).

Mr. Justice Story wrote of this argument against a bill of rights
and the meaning of the Ninth Amendment:

In regard to . . . [a] suggestion, that the affirmance of certain
rights might disparage others, or might lead to argumentative
implications in favor of other powers, it might be sufficient to say
that such a course of reasoning could never be sustained upon
any solid basis. . . . But a conclusive answer is, that such an
attempt may be interdicted (as it has been) by a positive declaration
in such a bill of rights that the enumeration of certain rights shall
not be construed to deny or disparage others retained by the
people.

II Story, Commentaries on the Constitution of the United States
626–27 (5th ed. 1891).

He further stated, referring to the Ninth Amendment:

This clause was manifestly introduced to prevent any perverse or
ingenious misapplication of the well-known maxim, that an affirmation in particular cases implies a negation in all others; and, e
converso, that a negation in particular cases implies an affirmation
in all others.

Id., at 651.

These statements of Madison and Story make clear that the
Framers did not intend that the first eight amendments be construed
to exhaust the basic and fundamental rights which the Constitution
guaranteed to the people.[5]

---

[5]The Tenth Amendment similarly made clear that the States and the people
retained all those powers not expressly delegated to the Federal Government.

While this Court has had little occasion to interpret the Ninth Amendment,[6] "[i]t cannot be presumed that any clause in the constitution is intended to be without effect." Marbury v. Madison, 1 Cranch 137, 174, 2 L. ed. 60, 72. In interpreting the Constitution, "real effect should be given to all the words it uses." Myers v. United States, 272 U.S. 52, 151, 71 L. ed. 160, 180, 47 S. Ct. 21. The Ninth Amendment to the Constitution may be regarded by some as a recent discovery and may be forgotten by others, but since 1791 it has been a basic part of the Constitution which we are sworn to uphold. To hold that a right so basic and fundamental and so deeprooted in our society as the right of privacy in marriage may be infringed because that right is not guaranteed in so many words by the first eight amendments to the Constitution is to ignore the Ninth Amendment and to give it no effect whatsoever. Moreover, a judicial construction that this fundamental right is not protected by the Constitution because it is not mentioned in explicit terms by one of the first eight amendments or elsewhere in the Constitution would violate the Ninth Amendment, which specifically states that "[t]he enumeration in the Constitution, of certain rights, shall not be *construed* to deny or disparage others retained by the people." (Emphasis added.)

[6]This Amendment has been referred to as "The Forgotten Ninth Amendment," in a book with that title by Bennett B. Patterson (1955). Other commentary on the Ninth Amendment includes Redlich, Are There "Certain Rights . . . Retained by the People"? 37 N.Y.U. L. Rev. 787 (1962), and Kelsey, The Ninth Amendment of the Federal Constitution, 11 Ind. L.J. 309 (1936). As far as I am aware, until today this Court has referred to the Ninth Amendment only in United Public Workers v. Mitchell, 330 U.S. 75, 94–95, 91 L. ed. 754, 769, 770, 67 S. Ct. 556; Tennessee Electric Power Co. v. TVA, 306 U.S. 118, 143–44, 83 L. ed. 543, 552, 553, 59 S. Ct. 366; and Ashwander v. TVA, 297 U.S. 288, 330–31, 80 L. ed. 688, 702, 703, 56 S. Ct. 466. *See also* Calder v. Bull, 3 Dall. 386, 388, 1 L. ed. 648, 649; Loan Assn. v. Topeka, 20 Wall. 655, 662–63, 22 L. ed. 455, 461.

In United Public Workers v. Mitchell, *supra* 330 U.S. at 94–95, 91 L. ed. at 770, the Court stated:

> We accept appellants' contention that the nature of political rights reserved to the people by the Ninth and Tenth Amendments [is] involved. The right claimed as inviolate may be stated as the right of a citizen to act as a party official or worker to further his own political views. Thus we have a measure of interference by the Hatch Act and the Rules with what otherwise would be the freedom of the civil servant under the First, Ninth and Tenth Amendments. And, if we look upon due process as a guaranteed of freedom in those fields, there is a corresponding impairment of that right under the Fifth Amendment.

A dissenting opinion suggests that my interpretation of the Ninth Amendment somehow "broaden[s] the powers of this Court." *Post*, at 536. With all due respect, I believe that it misses the import of what I am saying. I do not take the position of my Brother Black in his dissent in Adamson v. California, 332 U.S. 46, 68, 91 L. ed. 1903, 1917, 67 S. Ct. 1672, 171 ALR 1223, that the entire Bill of Rights is incorporated in the Fourteenth Amendment, and I do not mean to imply that the Ninth Amendment is applied against the States by the Fourteenth. Nor do I mean to state that the Ninth Amendment constitutes an independent source of rights protected from infringement by either the States or the Federal Government. Rather, the Ninth Amendment shows a belief of the Constitution's authors that fundamental rights exist that are not expressly enumerated in the first eight amendments and an intent that the list of rights included there not be deemed exhaustive. As any student of this Court's opinions knows, this Court has held, often unanimously, that the Fifth and Fourteenth Amendments protect certain fundamental personal liberties from abridgment by the Federal Government or the States. *See, e.g.,* Bolling v. Sharpe, 347 U.S. 497, 98 L. ed. 884, 74 S. Ct. 693; Aptheker v. Secretary of State, 378 U.S. 500, 12 L. ed. 2d 992, 84 S. Ct. 1659; Kent v. Dulles, 357 U.S. 116, 2 L. ed. 2d 1204, 78 S. Ct. 1113; Cantwell v. Connecticut, 310 U.S. 296, 84 L. ed. 1213, 60 S. Ct. 900, 128 ALR 1352; NAACP v. Alabama, 357 U.S. 449, 2 L. ed. 2d 1488, 78 S. Ct. 1163; Gideon v. Wainwright, 372 U.S. 335, 9 L. ed. 2d 799, 83 S. Ct. 792, 93 ALR2d 733; New York Times Co. v. Sullivan, 376 U.S. 254, 11 L. ed. 2d 686, 84 S. Ct. 710, 95 ALR2d 1412. The Ninth Amendment simply shows the intent of the Constitution's authors that other fundamental personal rights should not be denied such protection or disparaged in any other way simply because they are not specifically listed in the first eight constitutional amendments. I do not see how this broadens the authority of the Court; rather it serves to support what this Court has been doing in protecting fundamental rights.

Nor am I turning somersaults with history in arguing that the Ninth Amendment is relevant in a case dealing with a *State's* infringement of a fundamental right. While the Ninth Amendment—and indeed the entire Bill of Rights—originally concerned restrictions upon *federal* power, the subsequently enacted Fourteenth Amendment prohibits the States as well from abridging fundamental personal liberties. And, the Ninth Amendment, in indicating that not all such liberties are specifically mentioned in the first eight amendments, is surely relevant in showing the existence of other fundamental personal rights, now protected from state, as well as federal, infringement. In sum, the Ninth Amendment simply lends strong support to the view that the "liberty" protected by the Fifth and Fourteenth Amendments from infringement by the Federal Government or the States is not restricted to rights specifically mentioned in the first eight amendments. Cf. United Public Workers v. Mitchell, 330 U.S. 75, 94–95, 91 L. ed. 754, 769, 770, 67 S. Ct. 556.

In determining which rights are fundamental, judges are not left at large to decide cases in light of their personal and private notions. Rather, they must look to the "traditions and [collective] conscience of our people" to determine whether a principle is "so rooted [there] . . . as to be ranked as fundamental." Snyder v. Massachusetts, 291 U.S. 97, 105, 78 L. ed. 674, 677, 54 S. Ct. 330, 90 ALR 575. The inquiry is whether a right involved "is of such a character that it cannot be denied without violating those 'fundamental principles of liberty and justice which lie at the base of all our civil and political institutions'. . . ." Powell v. Alabama, 287, U.S. 45, 67, 77 L. ed. 158, 169, 53 S. Ct. 55, 84 ALR 527. "Liberty" also "gains content from the emanations of . . . specific [constitutional] guarantees" and "from experience with the requirements of a free society." Poe v. Ullman, 367, U.S. 497, 517, 6 L. ed. 2d 989, 1004, 81 S. Ct. 1752 (dissenting opinion of Mr. Justice Douglas).[7]

I agree fully with the Court that, applying these tests, the right of privacy is a fundamental personal right, emanating "from the totality of the constitutional scheme under which we live." Id., at 521, 6 L. ed. 2d at 1006. Mr. Justice Brandeis, dissenting in Olmstead

---

[7]In light of the tests enunciated in these cases it cannot be said that a judge's responsibility to determine whether a right is basic and fundamental in this sense vests him with unrestricted personal discretion. In fact, a hesitancy to allow too broad a discretion was a substantial reason leading me to conclude in Pointer v. Texas, supra, 380 U.S. at 413–14, 13 L. ed. 2d at 931, 932, that those rights absorbed by the Fourteenth Amendment and applied to the States because they are fundamental apply with equal force and to the same extent against both federal and state governments. In Pointer I said that the contrary view would require

this Court to make the extremely subjective and excessively discretionary determination as to whether a practice, forbidden the Federal Government by a fundamental constitutional guarantee, is as viewed in the factual circumstances surrounding each individual case, sufficiently repugnant to the notion of due process as to be forbidden the States.

Id., at 413, 13 L. ed. 2d at 932.

v. United States, 277 U.S. 438, 478, 72 L. ed. 944, 956, 48 S. Ct. 564, 66 ALR 376, comprehensively summarized the principles underlying the Constitution's guarantees of privacy:

> The protection guaranteed by the [Fourth and Fifth] Amendments is much broader in scope. The makers of our Constitution undertook to secure conditions favorable to the pursuit of happiness. They recognized the significance of man's spiritual nature, of his feelings and of his intellect. They knew that only a part of the pain, pleasure and satisfactions of life are to be found in material things. They sought to protect Americans in their beliefs, their thoughts, their emotions and their sensations. They conferred, as against the Government, the right to be let alone—the most comprehensive of rights and the right most valued by civilized men.

The Connecticut statutes here involved deal with a particularly important and sensitive area of privacy—that of the marital relation and the marital home. This Court recognized in Meyer v. Nebraska, *supra*, that the right "to marry, establish a home and bring up children" was an essential part of the liberty guaranteed by the Fourteenth Amendment. 262 U.S. at 399, 67 L. ed. at 1045, 29 ALR 1446. In Pierce v. Society of Sisters, 268 U.S. 510, 69 L. ed. 1070, 45 S. Ct. 571, 39 ALR 468, the Court held unconstitutional an Oregon Act which forbade parents from sending their children to private schools because such an act "unreasonably interferes with the liberty of parents and guardians to direct the upbringing and education of children under their control." 268 U.S. at 534–35, 69 L. ed. at 1078, 39 ALR 468. As this Court said in Prince v. Massachusetts, 321 U.S. 158, at 166, 88 L. ed. 645, at 652, 64 S. Ct. 438, the *Meyer* and *Pierce* decisions "have respected the private realm of family life which the state cannot enter."

I agree with Mr. Justice Harlan's statement in his dissenting opinion in Poe v. Ullman, 367 U.S. 497, 551–52, 6 L. ed. 2d 989, 1024, 81 S. Ct. 1752:

> Certainly the safeguarding of the home does not follow merely from the sanctity of property rights. The home derives its pre-eminence as the seat of family life. And the integrity of that life is something so fundamental that it has been found to draw to its protection the principles of more than one explicitly granted Constitutional right. . . . Of this whole "private realm of family life" it is difficult to imagine what is more private and intimate than a husband and wife's marital relations.

The entire fabric of the Constitution and the purposes that clearly underlie its specific guarantees demonstrate that the rights to marital privacy and to marry and raise a family are of similar order and magnitude as the fundamental rights specifically protected. Although the Constitution does not speak in so many words of the right of privacy in marriage, I cannot believe that it offers these fundamental rights no protection. The fact that no particular provision of the Constitution explicitly forbids the State from disrupting the traditional relation of the family—a relation as old and as fundamental as our entire civilization—surely does not show that the Government was meant to have the power to do so. Rather, as the Ninth Amendment expressly recognizes, there are fundamental personal rights such as this one, which are protected from abridgment by the Government though not specifically mentioned in the Constitution.

My Brother Stewart, while characterizing the Connecticut birth-control law as "an uncommonly silly law," *post*, at 540, would nevertheless let it stand on the ground that it is not for the courts to " 'substitute their social and economic beliefs for the judgment of legislative bodies, who are elected to pass laws.' " *Post*, at 541. Elsewhere, I have stated that

[w]hile I quite agree with Mr. Justice Brandeis that . . . "a . . . State may . . . serve as a laboratory; and try novel social and economic experiments," New State Ice Co. v. Liebmann, 285 U.S. 262, 280, 311, 76 L. ed. 747, 754, 771, 52 S. Ct. 371 (dissenting opinion), I do not believe that this includes the power to experiment with the fundamental liberties of citizens. . . .[8]

The vice of the dissenters' views is that it would permit such experimentation by the States in the area of the fundamental personal rights of its citizens. I cannot agree that the Constitution grants such power either to the States or to the Federal Government.

The logic of the dissents would sanction federal or state legislation that seems to me even more plainly unconstitutional than the statute before us. Surely the Government, absent a showing of compelling subordinating state interest, could not decree that all husbands and wives must be sterilized after two children have been

---

[8]Pointer v. Texas, *supra*, 380 U.S. at 413, 13 L. ed. 2d at 932. *See also* the discussion of my Brother Douglas, Poe v. Ullman, *supra*, 367 U.S. at 517–18, 6 L. ed. 2d at 1004 (dissenting opinion).

born to them. Yet by their reasoning such an invasion of marital privacy would not be subject to constitutional challenge because, while it might be "silly," no provision of the Constitution specifically prevents the Government from curtailing the marital right to bear children and raise a family. While it may shock some of my Brethren that the Court today holds that the Constitution protects the right of marital privacy, in my view it is far more shocking to believe that the personal liberty guaranteed by the Constitution does not include protection against such totalitarian limitation of family size, which is at complete variance with our constitutional concepts. Yet, if upon a showing of a slender basis of rationality, a law outlawing voluntary birth control by married persons is valid, then, by the same reasoning, a law requiring compulsory birth control also would seem to be valid. In my view, however, both types of law would unjustifiably intrude upon rights of marital privacy which are constitutionally protected.

In a long series of cases this Court has held that where fundamental personal liberties are involved, they may not be abridged by the States simply on a showing that a regulatory statute has some rational relationship to the effectuation of a proper state purpose. "Where there is a significant encroachment upon personal liberty, the State may prevail only upon showing a subordinating interest which is compelling," Bates v. Little Rock, 361 U.S. 516, 524, 4 L. ed. 2d 480, 486, 80 S. Ct. 412. The law must be shown "necessary, and not merely rationally related, to the accomplishment of a permissible state policy." McLaughlin v. Florida, 379 U.S. 184, 196, 13 L. ed. 2d 222, 231, 85 S. Ct. 283. See Schneider v. State, 308 U.S. 147, 161, 84 L. ed. 155, 164, 60 S. Ct. 146.

Although the Connecticut birth-control law obviously encroaches upon a fundamental personal liberty, the State does not show that the law serves any "subordinating [state] interest which is compelling" or that it is "necessary . . . to the accomplishment of a permissible state policy." The State, at most, argues that there is some rational relation between this statute and what is admittedly a legitimate subject of state concern—the discouraging of extramarital relations. It says that preventing the use of birth-control devices by married persons helps prevent the indulgence by some in such extra-marital relations. The rationality of this justification is dubious, particularly in light of the admitted widespread availability to all persons in the State of Connecticut, unmarried as well as married, of birth-control devices for the prevention of disease, as distinguished from the prevention of conception. *See* Tileston v. Ullman, 129 Conn. 84, 26 A2d 582. But, in any event, it is clear that the state interest in safeguarding marital fidelity can be served by a more discriminately tailored statute, which does not, like the present one, sweep unnecessarily broadly, reaching far beyond the evil sought to be dealt with and intruding upon the privacy of all married couples. *See* Aptheker v. Secretary of State, 378 U.S. 500, 514, 12 L. ed. 2d 992, 1001, 84 S. Ct. 1659; NAACP v. Alabama, 377 U.S. 288, 307–08, 12 L. ed. 2d 325, 338, 84 S. Ct. 1302; McLaughlin v. Florida, *supra*, 379 U.S. at 196, 13 L. ed. 2d at 231. Here, as elsewhere, "[p]recision of regulation must be the touchstone in an area so closely touching our most precious freedoms." NAACP v. Button, 371 U.S. 415, 438, 9 L. ed. 2d 405, 83 S. Ct. 328. The State of Connecticut does have statutes, the constitutionality of which is beyond doubt, which prohibit adultery and fornication. *See* Conn. Gen. Stat. §§ 53–218, 53–219 et seq. These statutes demonstrate that means for achieving the same basic purpose of protecting marital fidelity are available to Connecticut without the need to "invade the area of protected freedoms." NAACP v. Alabama, *supra*, 377 U.S. at 307, 12 L. ed. 2d at 338. *See* McLaughlin v. Florida, *supra*, 379 U.S. at 196, 13 L. ed. 2d at 231.

Finally, it should be said of the Court's holding today that it in no way interferes with a State's proper regulation of sexual promiscuity or misconduct. As my Brother Harlan so well stated in his dissenting opinion in Poe v. Ullman, *supra*, 367 U.S. at 553, 6 L. ed. 2d at 1025:

> Adultery, homosexuality and the like are sexual intimacies which the State forbids . . . but the intimacy of husband and wife is necessarily an essential and accepted feature of the institution of marriage, an institution which the State not only must allow, but which always and in every age it has fostered and protected. It is one thing when the State exerts its power either to forbid extra-marital sexuality . . . or to say who may marry, but it is quite another when, having acknowledged a marriage and the intimacies inherent in it, it undertakes to regulate by means of the criminal law the details of that intimacy.

In sum, I believe that the right of privacy in the marital relation is fundamental and basic—a personal right "retained by the people" within the meaning of the Ninth Amendment. Connecticut cannot constitutionally abridge this fundamental right, which is protected by the Fourteenth Amendment from infringement by the States. I agree with the Court that petitioners' convictions must therefore be reversed.

Bibliography on the Ninth Amendment

Books

*Bennett B. Patterson, The Forgotten Ninth Amendment (1955).
Mark N. Goodman, The Ninth Amendment: History, Interpretation, and Meaning (1981).

Symposium

Symposium on Interpreting the Ninth Amendment, 64 Chi.-Kent L. Rev. 37–268 (R. Barnett ed. 1988):

Randy E. Barnett, *Foreword: The Ninth Amendment and Constitutional Legitimacy.*

Morris S. Arnold, *Doing More Than Remembering the Ninth Amendment.*

Sotirios A. Barber, *The Ninth Amendment: Inkblot or Another Hard Nut to Crack.*

Thomas C. Grey, *The Uses of an Unwritten Constitution.*

Sanford Levinson, *Constitutional Rhetoric and the Ninth Amendment.*

Michael W. McConnell, *A Moral Realist Defense of Constitutional Democracy.*

Stephen Macedo, *Reasons, Rhetoric, and the Ninth Amendment: A Comment on Sanford Levinson.*

Andrzej Rapaczynski, *The Ninth Amendment and the Unwritten Constitution: The Problems of Constitutional Interpretation.*

Lawrence G. Sager, *You Can Raise the First, Hide Behind the Fourth, and Plead the Fifth. But What on Earth Can You Do with the Ninth Amendment?*

Commentary on the Symposium on Interpreting the Ninth Amendment, 64 Chi.-Kent L. Rev. 981-1014 (1988):

Karl M. Maltz, *Unenumerated Rights and Originalist Methodology: A Comment on the Ninth Amendment Symposium.*

Calvin R. Massey, *Antifederalism and the Ninth Amendment.*

Suzanna Sherry, *The Ninth Amendment: Righting an Unwritten Constitution.*

---

*Reprinted or excerpted in this volume.

Monographs

U.S. Department of Justice, Office of Legal Policy, Wrong Turns on the Road to Judicial Activism: The Ninth Amendment and Privileges or Immunities Clause (September 15, 1987).

Articles

Floyd Abrams, What Are the Rights Guaranteed by the Ninth Amendment? 53 A.B.A. J. 1033 (November 1967).

_____, The Ninth Amendment and the Protection of Unenumerated Rights, 11 Harv. J. L. & Pub. Pol'y 93 (1988).

*Randy E. Barnett, Reconceiving the Ninth Amendment, 74 Corn. L. Rev. 1 (1988) [revised version appears as the Introduction to this volume].

_____, Two Conceptions of the Ninth Amendment, 12 Harv. J. of L. & Pub. Pol'y 23 (1989).

_____, Foreword: Unenumerated Constitutional Rights and the Rule of Law, 14 Harv. J. L. & Pub. Pol'y 615 (1991).

_____, The Ninth Amendment, in The Oxford Companion to the Supreme Court of the United States (K. Hall ed. forthcoming 1992).

*Raoul Berger, The Ninth Amendment, 66 Cornell L. Rev. 1 (1980).

_____, The Ninth Amendment: The Beckoning Mirage, 42 Rutgers L. Rev. 951 (1990).

William O. Bertlesman, The Ninth Amendment and Due Process of Law—Toward a Viable Theory of Unenumerated Rights, 37 U. Cin. L. Rev. 777 (1968).

*Charles L. Black, Jr., On Reading and Using the Ninth Amendment, in Power and Policy in Quest of Law: Essays in Honor of Eugene Victor Rostow 187 (M. McDougal & W. N. Reisman eds. 1985).

Joseph L. Call, Federalism and the Ninth Amendment, 64 Dick. L. Rev. 121 (1960).

Francis Canavan, Judicial Power and the Ninth Amendment, 22 Intercollegiate Review, Spring 1987, at 25.

*Russell L. Caplan, The History and Meaning of the Ninth Amendment, 42 Va. L. Rev. 223 (1983).

Michael Conant, Antimonopoly Tradition Under the Ninth and Fourteenth Amendments: Slaughter-House Cases Re-Examined, 31 Emory L.J. 785 (1982).

Charles J. Cooper, Limited Government and Individual Liberty: The Ninth Amendment's Forgotten Lessons, 4 J. Law & Pol. 63 (1987).

Leslie W. Dunbar, *James Madison and the Ninth Amendment*, 69 Va. L. Rev. 627 (1956).

Mitchell Franklin, *The Relation of the Fifth, Ninth and Fourteenth Amendments to the Third Constitution*, 4 How. L. Rev. 170 (1958).

_____ , *The Ninth Amendment as Civil Law Method and Its Implications for Republican Form of Government: Griswold v. Connecticut; South Carolina v. Katzenbach*, 40 Tul. L. Rev. 487 (1966).

John P. Kaminski, *Restoring the Declaration of Independence: Natural Rights and the Ninth Amendment*, in The Bill of Rights (J. Kukla ed. 1987).

*Knowlton H. Kelsey, *The Ninth Amendment of the Federal Constitution*, 11 Ind. L.J. 309 (1936).

Irvin M. Kent, *Under the Ninth Amendment What Rights Are the "Others Retained by the People"?* 29 Fed. B.J. 219 (1970).

Gerald Kirven, *Under the Ninth Amendment, What Rights Are the "Others Retained by the People"?* 14 S.D.L. Rev. 80 (1969).

Luis Kutner, *The Neglected Ninth Amendment: The "Other Rights" Retained by the People*, 51 Marq. L. Rev. 121 (1968).

Leonard W. Levy, *The Ninth Amendment: Unenumerated Rights*, in Original Intent and the Framers' Constitution (1988).

*Calvin R. Massey, *Federalism and Fundamental Rights: The Ninth Amendment*, 38 Hastings L.J. 305 (1987).

_____ , *The Anti-Federalist Ninth Amendment and Its Implications for State Constitutional Law*, 1990 Wis. L. Rev. 1229.

Thomas B. McAffee, *The Original Meaning of the Ninth Amendment*, 90 Colum. L. Rev. 1215 (1990).

*Simeon C. R. McIntosh, *On Reading the Ninth Amendment: A Reply to Raoul Berger*, 28 How. L. Rev. 913 (1985).

Lawrence Mitchell, *The Ninth Amendment and the "Jurisprudence of Original Intention,"* 74 Geo. L.J. 1719 (1987).

Terence J. Moore, *The Ninth Amendment—Its Origins and Meaning*, 7 New Eng. L. Rev. 215 (1972).

Jordon J. Paust, *Human Rights and the Ninth Amendment: A New Form of Guarantee*, 60 Cornell L. Rev. 231 (1975).

*Norman Redlich, *Are There "Certain Rights . . . Retained by the People"?* 37 N.Y.U. L. Rev. 787 (1962).

_____ , *The Ninth Amendment*, in 3 The Encyclopedia of the American Constitution 1316–20 (L. Levy ed. 1982).

_____ , *The Ninth Amendment as a Constitutional Prism*, 12 Harv. J. of L. & Pub. Pol'y 23 (1989).

RIGHTS RETAINED BY THE PEOPLE

Lyman Rhoades & Rodney R. Patula, *The Ninth Amendment: A Survey of Theory and Practice in the Federal Courts Since Griswold v. Connecticut*, 50 Den. L. Rev. 153 (1973).

A. F. Ringold, *The History of the Enactment of the Ninth Amendment and Its Recent Development*, 8 Tulsa L.J. 1 (1972).

Thomas E. Towe, *Natural Law and Ninth Amendment*, 2 Pepperdine L. Rev. 1 (1968).

*Eugene M. Van Loan III, *Natural Rights and the Ninth Amendment*, 2 B.U.L. Rev. 1 (1968).

Gerald Watson, *The Ninth Amendment: Source of a Substantive Right to Privacy*, 19 J. Marshall L. Rev. 959 (1986).

Notes, Comments, and Reviews

Larry Alexander, *The Rights Retained by the People* (book review), 7 Const. Comm. 396 (1990).

Harold H. Boles, *Constitutional Law—Ninth Amendment—Right of Marital Privacy Violated by Connecticut's Anti-Birth-Control Law*, 40 Tul. L. Rev. 418 (1966).

Comment, *Constitutional Law—Abortions: Abortions as a Ninth Amendment Right*, 46 Wash. L. Rev. 565 (1971).

Gary L. Gardner, *The Ninth Amendment*, 30 Alb. L. Rev. 89 (1966).

George E. Garvey, *Unenumerated Rights—Substantive Due Process, The Ninth Amendment, and John Stuart Mill*, 1971 Wis. L. Rev. 922 (1971).

James F. Kelley, *The Uncertain Renaissance of the Ninth Amendment*, 33 U. Chi. L. Rev. 814 (1966).

Mark A. Koral, *Ninth Amendment Vindication of Unenumerated Fundamental Rights*, 42 Temp. L.Q. 48 (1968).

Jerry K. Levy, *Constitutional Law—A Refreshing Approach to the Right of Privacy—The Ninth Amendment*, 5 Washburn L.J. 286 (1966).

Geoffrey G. Slaughter, *The Ninth Amendment's Role in the Evolution of Fundamental Rights Jurisprudence*, 64 Ind. L. J. 97 (1988).

David K. Sutelan, *The Ninth Amendment: Guidepost to Fundamental Rights*, 8 Wm. & Mary L. Rev. 101 (1966).

Thomas R. Vickerman, *The Ninth Amendment*, 11 S.D. L. Rev. 172 (1966).

Note, *Griswold v. Connecticut: Peripheral Rights and Rights Retained by the People Under the Ninth Amendment*, 40 Conn. B. J. 704 (1966).

Selected Books Discussing the Ninth Amendment

H. Abraham, Freedom and the Court 72–88 (1982).

C. Black, Jr., Decision According to Law 43–83 (1981).

R. Bork, The Tempting of America: The Political Seduction of the Law, 183–185 (1990).

P. Brest, The Processes of Constitutional Decisionmaking: Cases and Materials 70–78 (1975).

H. Chase & C. Ducat, Constitutional Interpretation: Cases—Essays—Materials 1119 (1974).

E. Corwin, The Constitution and What It Means Today 440–42 (14th ed. 1978).

W. Duer, Constitutional Jurisprudence of the United States 269 (1844).

*J. Ely, Democracy and Distrust 34–41 (1980).

F. A. Hayek, The Constitution of Liberty 186 (1960).

P. Kurland & R. Lerner, eds., 5 The Founders' Constitution 388–400 (1987).

L. Levy, Original Intent and the Framers' Constitution 267–283 (1988).

J. Story, 2 Commentaries on the Constitution of the United States 624–25 (4th ed., T. Cooley ed. 1873).

L. Tribe, American Constitutional Law 774–777, 962–963 (2d ed. 1988).

Selected Articles Discussing the Ninth Amendment

Raoul Berger, Ely's "Theory of Judicial Review," 42 Ohio St. L.J. 87, 116–19 (1981).

Hugo L. Black, The Bill of Rights, 35 N.Y.U. L. Rev. 865, 871 (1960).

*Edward S. Corwin, The "Higher Law" Background of American Constitutional Law" (pt. 1), 42 Harv. L. Rev. 149, 152–53 (1928) (pt. 2 is at 365).

Forum: Equal Protection and the Burger Court (comments of Professors Choper, Forrester, Gunther & Sullivan), 2 Hastings Const. L.Q. 645, 679 (1975).

John J. Gibbons, Keynote Address, Symposium on Constitutional Adjudication and Democratic Theory, 56 N.Y.U. L. Rev. 260, 270–73 (1981).

Thomas C. Grey, Do We Have an Unwritten Constitution? 27 Stan. L. Rev. 703, 709 & 716 (1975).

Alfred H. Kelly, Clio and the Court: An Illicit Love Affair, 1965 Sup. Ct. Rev. 119, 14955.

Earl M. Maltz, Federalism and the Fourteenth Amendment: A Comment on Democracy and Distrust, 42 Ohio St. L.J. 209, 209 n.7 (1981).

Henry P. Monaghan, *Our Perfect Constitution*, 56 N.Y.U. L. Rev. 353, 36567 (1981).

Jordon J. Paust, *Human Dignity as a Constitutional Right: A Jurisprudentially Based Inquiry into Criteria and Content*, 27 How. L.J. 145, 220–22 (1984).

Michael J. Perry, *Interpretivism, Freedom of Expression, and Equal Protection*, 42 Ohio St. L.J. 261, 27073 (1981).

O. John Rogge, *Unenumerated Rights*, 47 Calif. L. Rev. 787 (1959).

Jeff Rosen, *Was the Flag Burning Amendment Unconstitutional?* 100 Yale L.J. 1073 (1991).

Suzanna Sherry, *The Founders' Unwritten Constitution*, 54 U. Chi. L. Rev. 1127, 1162–66 (1987).

William Van Alstyne, *Slouching Toward Bethlehem with the Ninth Amendment* (book review), 91 Yale L.J. 207 (1981).

Case Index

Adams v. Tanner, 244 U.S. 590 (1917), 169, 170

Adamson v. California, 332 U.S. 46 (1947), 131, 132, 133, 152, 392

Adkins v. Children's Hospital, 261 U.S. 525 (1923), 136

Afroyim v. Rusk, 387 U.S. 253 (1967), 172

Alcorta v. Texas, 355 U.S. 28 (1957), 135

Allen v. State Bd. of Elections, 393 U.S. 544 (1969), 265

Aptheker v. Secretary of State, 347 U.S. 500 (1964), 172, 387, 392, 397

Ashwander v. TVA, 297 U.S. 288 (1936), 149, 191, 244, 291, 391

Bailey v. Drexel Furniture Co., 259 U.S. 20 (1922), 171

Baker v. Carr, 369 U.S. 186 (1962), 174

Barbier v. Connolly, 113 U.S. 27 (1885), 169, 253

Barenblatt v. United States, 360 U.S. 109 (1959), 15

Barron v. Baltimore, 32 U.S. 242 (1833), 110, 139, 176, 187–88, 200, 209, 293, 319

Bates v. Little Rock, 361 U.S. 516 (1960), 396

Betts v. Brady, 316 U.S. 455 (1942), 131, 176

Blake v. McClung, 172 U. S. 239 (1898), 151

Boddie v. Connecticut, 401 U.S. 371 (1971), 251

Bolling v. Sharpe, 347 U.S. 497 (1954), 47, 136, 184–85, 211, 387, 392

Bonham's Case, 8 Coke Rep.107 (1610), 77, 80, 86, 187

Bowers v. Hardwick, 106 S. Ct. 2841 (1986), 323–32

Boyd v. United States, 116 U.S. 616 (1886), 321, 257

Bradwell v. Illinois, 83 U.S. 130 (1872), 2883

Branzburg v. Hayes, 408 U.S. 665 (1972), 246

Braunfield v. Brown, 366 U.S. 599 (1961), 130

Brown v. Board of Education, 349 U.S. 294 (1955), 170, 174, 239, 249

Brown v. Gerdes, 321 U.S. 178 (1944), 314

Brown v. Maryland, 25 U.S. 419 (1827), 170

Brown v. Walker, 161 U.S. 600 (1896), 98

Buck v. Bell, 274 U.S. 200 (1927), 143, 144

Buckley v. Valeo, 424 U.S. 1 (1976), 246

Burns v. Swenson, 430 F.2d 771 (8th Cir. 1970), 192

Bute v. Illinois, 333 U.S. 640 (1948), 149

Calder v. Bull, 3 U.S. 386 (1798), 115, 122, 283, 302, 391

Cantwell v. Connecticut, 310 U.S. 296 (1940), 170, 176, 388, 392

Carey v. Population Servs. Int'l, 431 U.S. 678 (1977), 327

Carrington v. Rash, 380 U.S. 89 (1965), 387

Carter v. Carter Coal Co., 298 U.S. 238 (1936), 137

Case v. Bowles, 327 U.S. 92 (1946), 141

Cawley v. United States, 232 F.2d 443 (2d Cir. 1959), 217

Champion v. Ames, 188 U.S. 321 (1903), 171

Chicago B.& Q. R.R. Co. v. Chicago, 166 U.S. 226 (1897), 176, 316, 388

Chicago R.I. & P. Ry. v. United States, 284 U.S. 80 (1931), 136

Chisholm v. Georgia, 2 U.S. 419 (1793), 317

405

City of New York v. Miln, 36 U.S. 102 (1837), 326

Clark v. Allen, 331 U.S. 503 (1947), 307

Cohen v. Hurley, 366 U.S. 117 (1961), 387

Cohens v. Virginia, 19 U.S. 264 (1821), 96

Coleman v. Miller, 307 U.S. 433 (1939), 307

Collector v. Day, 78 U.S. 113 (1871), 171

Connecticut v. Buxton, CR-5654, Conn. Cir. Ct. (1962), 129

Connecticut v. Griswold, CR-5653, Conn. Cir. Ct. (1962), 129

Coppage v. Kansas, 236 U.S. 1 (1915), 169, 170

Crandall v. Nevada, 73 U.S. 35 (1867), 145–46

Day-Brite Lighting, Inc. v. Missouri, 342 U.S. 421 (1952), 130, 173

DeJonge v. Oregon, 299 U.S. 353 (1937), 176

Dennis v. United States, 341 U.S. 494 (1951), 15, 173

Doe v. Bolton, 410 U.S. 179 (1973), 192, 246, 247, 321, 324

Downes v. Bidwell, 182 U.S. 244 (1901), 258

Dred Scott v. Sandford, 60 U.S. 393 (1857), 149, 187, 291, 244

Dronenburg v. Zeck, 746 F.2d 1579 (D.C.Cir. 1984), 239

Duncan v. Louisiana, 391 U.S. 145 (1968), 316

Edwards v. California, 314 U.S. 160 (1941), 146, 326

Eilenbecker v. District Court of Plymouth County, 134 U.S. 31 (1890), 114, 208, 284

Eisenstadt v. Baird, 405 U.S. 438 (1972), 324, 327

Elkins v. United States, 364 U.S. 206 (1960), 176

Employees v. Missouri Pub. Health & Welfare Dep't, 411 U.S. 279 (1973), 317

Erie R.R. v. Tompkins, 304 U.S. 64 (1938), 266

Everson v. Board of Education, 330 U.S. 1 (1947), 176

Ex parte Grossman, 267 U.S. 87 (1925), 281

Ex parte McCardle, 74 U.S. 506 (1868), 300

Ex parte Virginia, 100 U.S. 339 (1880), 171

Fallowfield Township v. Marlborough Township, 1 U.S. 32 (1776), 326

Ferguson v. Skrupa, 372 U.S. 726 (1963), 170

Fiske v. Kansas, 274 U.S. 380 (1927), 316

Fletcher v. Peck, 10 U.S. 87 (1810), 283

Fox v. State of Ohio, 46 U.S. 410 (1847), 110

Freeman v. Flake, 405 U.S. 1032 (1972), 192, 246

Garcia v. San Antonio Metro. Transit Auth., 105 S. Ct. 1005 (1985), 307

Gibbons v. Ogden, 22 U.S. 1 (1824), 253

Giboney v. Empire Storage & Ice Co., 336 U.S. 490 (1949), 137

Gideon v. Wainwright, 372 U.S. 335 (1963), 176, 316, 388, 392

Gitlow v. New York, 268 U.S. 652 (1925), 176, 202, 388

Griffin v. California, 380 U.S. 609 (1965), 388

Griffin v. Illinois, 351 U.S. 12 (1956), 185

Griswold v. Connecticut, 381 U.S. 479 (1965), 2, 150, 151, 167, 170, 172, 173, 174, 177, 179, 185, 191, 192, 198, 217, 219, 221, 222, 227, 233–34, 244, 247, 279, 284, 289, 290, 291, 293, 302, 321, 324, 327, 387–98

Grosjean v. American Press Co., 297 U.S. 233 (1936), 182

Hammer v. Dagenhart, 247 U.S. 251 (1918), 141, 171

Hans v. Louisiana, 134 U.S. 1 (1890), 317

Harisiades v. Shaughnessy, 342 U.S. 580 (1952), 173

Harper v. Virginia State Board of Elections, 383 U.S. 663 (1966), 185, 320

Hawaii v. Mankichi, 190 U.S. 197 (1903), 217, 258

Hawkins v. Barney's Lessee, 30 U.S. 457 (1831), 258

Heart of Atlanta Motel v. United States, 379 U.S. 241 (1964), 171

Helvering v. Davis, 301 U.S. 619 (1937), 171

Herbert v. Louisiana, 272 U.S. 312 (1926), 177

Hoke v. United States, 227 U.S. 308 (1913), 149

Holden v. Hardy, 169 U.S. 366 (1898), 169

Holmes v. Jennison, 39 U.S. 540 (1840), 96, 199, 279

Home Bldg. & Loan Ass'n v. Blaisdell, 290 U.S. 398 (1934), 172

Hood and Sons, Inc. v. Du Mond, 336 U.S. 525 (1949), 170

Hopkins Federal Savings and Loan Ass'n v. Cleary, 296 U.S. 315 (1915), 171

Humphrey's Ex'r v. United States, 295 U.S. 602 (1935), 172

Hurtado v. California, 110 U.S. 516 (1884), 176

In re Debs, 158 U.S. 564 (1895), 171

In re Kemmler, 136 U.S. 436 (1890), 176

In re Oliver, 333 U.S. 257 (1948), 135, 316

In re Rahrer, 140 U.S. 545 (1891), 173

International Ass'n of Machinists v. Street, 367 U.S. 740 (1961), 173

Jacobson v. Massachusetts, 197 U.S. 11 (1905), 169

Jay Burns Baking Co. v. Bryan, 264 U.S. 504 (1924), 173

Johnson v. United States, 163 F. 30 (1st Cir. 1908), 217

Katzenbach v. McClung, 379 U.S. 294 (1964), 149–50, 171

Katzenbach v. Morgan, 384 U.S. 641 (1966), 171

Kent v. Dulles, 357 U.S. 116 (1958), 136, 173, 387, 392

Ker v. California, 374 U.S. 23 (1963), 176

Klopfer v. North Carolina, 386 U.S. 213 (1967), 176, 316

Knowlton v. Moore, 178 U.S. 41 (1900), 96, 151

Kohl v. United States, 91 U.S. 372 (1876), 100

Korematsu v. United States, 323 U.S. 214 (1944), 171

Lambert v. California, 355 U.S. 257 (1957), 135

Lamont v. Postmaster General, 381 U.S. 301 (1965), 9, 28, 172

Lane County v. Oregon, 74 U.S. 71 (1868), 265

Lanza v. New York, 370 U.S. 139 (1962), 130

Legal Tender Cases, 79 U.S. 457 (1871), 171

Leisy v. Hardin, 135 U.S. 100 (1890), 173

Lessee of Livingston v. Moore, 32 U.S. 469, 7 Pet. 469 (1833), 111–12, 114, 244, 291, 293

Lincoln Federal Labor Union v. Northwestern Iron & Metal Co., 366 U.S. 420 (1961), 130

Live-stock Dealers' & Butchers Ass'n v. Crescent City Live-stock Landing & Slaughterhouse Co., 15 F. Cas. 649 (C.C.La. 1870), 203

Loan Ass'n v. Topeka, 87 U.S. 655 (1874), 283, 302, 391

Lochner v. New York, 198 U.S. 45 (1905), 129, 145, 169, 170, 202, 300

Louisville Joint Stock Land Bank v. Radford, 295 U.S. 587 (1935), 106

Loving v. Virginia, 388 U.S. 1 (1967), 323, 326, 331

Lubin v. Panish, 415 U.S. 709 (1974), 246

Ludecke v. Watkins, 335 U.S. 160 (1948), 307

Luther v. Borden, 48 U.S. 1 (1849), 307, 317

McCollom v. Board of Education, 333 U.S. 203 (1948), 170
McCulloch v. Maryland, 17 U.S. 316 (1819), 170, 174, 271, 279, 286, 306, 319
McCurdy v. United States, 246 U.S. 263 (1918), 149
McGautha v. California, 402 U.S. 183 (1971), 246
McGowan v. Maryland, 366 U.S. 420 (1961), 130
McLaughlin v. Florida, 379 U.S. 184 (1964), 396, 397
McLean v. Arkansas, 211 U.S. 539 (1909), 169
Malloy v. Hogan, 378 U.S. 1 (1964), 176, 388
Mapp v. Ohio, 367 U.S. 443 (1961), 130, 132
Marbury v. Madison, 5 U.S. 137 (1803), 1, 151, 304–5, 391
Martin v. Hunter's Lessee, 14 U.S. 304 (1816), 207
Massachusetts v. Mellon, 262 U.S. 447 (1923), 105
Maxwell v. Dow, 176 U.S. 581 (1900), 176
Meyer v. Nebraska, 262 U.S. 390 (1923), 134, 321, 387, 388, 394
Moore v. City of East Cleveland, 431 U.S. 494 (1977), 324, 325
Moore v. United States, 91 U.S. 270 (1875), 281
Murray's Lessee v. Hoboken Land and Improvement Co., 59 U.S. 272 (1855), 281, 317
Myers v. United States, 272 U.S. 52 (1926), 96, 151, 391

NAACP v. Alabama, 360 U.S. 240 (1958), 176, 387, 392, 397
NAACP v. Button, 371 U.S. 415 (1963), 397
Near v. Minnesota, 283 U.S. 697 (1931), 176
New State Ice Co. v. Liebmann, 285 U.S. 262 (1932), 395

New York Times Company v. Sullivan, 376 U.S. 254 (1964), 170, 392
New York v. Miln, 36 U.S. 102 (1837), 253
New York v. United States, 326 U.S. 572 (1946), 172
NLRB v. Friedman-Harry Marks Clothing Co., 301 U.S. 58 (1937), 150
NLRB v. Jones and Laughlin Steel Corp., 301 U.S. 1 (1937), 171
Norman v. Baltimore & Ohio R.R., 294 U.S. 240 (1935), 171
Northwestern Elec. Co. v. Federal Power Comm'n, 321 U.S. 119 (1944), 141

Ogden v. Saunders, 25 U.S. 213 (1827), 96, 258, 283
Oklahoma v. Post, 715 F.2d 1105 (1986), 327
Olff v. East Side Union High School Dist., 404 U.S. 1042 (1972), 191, 246
Olmstead v. United States, 277 U.S. 438 (1928), 289, 321, 393–94
Olsen v. Nebraska Ex Rel. Western Reverence & Bond Ass'n, 313 U.S. 236 (1941), 170
Oregon v. Mitchell, 400 U.S. 112 (1970), 217
Osborn v. United States, 385 U.S. 323 (1966), 151, 246

Palko v. Connecticut, 302 U.S. 319 (1937), 176, 177, 284, 324
Palmer v. Thompson, 403 U.S. 217 (1971), 246
Pennhurst State School & Hospital v. Halderman, 465 U.S. 89 (1985), 317
Pennsylvania v. Nelson, 350 U.S. 497 (1956), 170
Pierce v. Society of Sisters, 268 U.S. 510 (1925), 321–22, 387, 394
Planned Parenthood v. Danforth, 428 U.S. 52 (1976), 246
Poe v. Ullman, 367 U.S. 497 (1961), 128, 131, 132, 134, 137, 142, 143, 329, 330, 393, 394, 395, 397
Pointer v. Texas, 380 U.S. 400 (1961), 176, 316, 387, 388, 393, 395

Pollack v. Farmers' Loan & Trust Co., 158 U.S. 601 (1895), 172

Powell v. Alabama, 287 U.S. 45 (1932), 393

Presser v. Illinois, 116 U.S. 252 (1886), 176

Prigg v. Pennsylvania, 41 U.S. 539 (1842), 171

Prince v. Massachusetts, 321 U.S. 158 (1944), 323, 394

Prudential Ins. Co. of America v. Cheek, 259 U.S. 530 (1922), 176

Railroad Retirement Board v. Alton R.R., 295 U.S. 330 (1935), 136, 137

Reynolds v. Sims, 377 U.S. 533 (1964), 170, 320

Richmond Newspapers Inc. v. Virginia, 448 U.S. 555 (1980), 2, 47, 246

Roberts v. United States Jaycees, 468 U.S. 609 (1984), 326

Robertson v. Baldwin, 165 U.S. 275 (1897), 98, 281

Robinson v. California, 370 U.S. 660 (1962), 176, 388

Roe v. Wade, 410 U.S. 113 (1973), 246, 289, 321, 324, 327

Roosevelt v. Mever, 68 U.S. 512 (1863), 149

Rosenblatt v. Baer, 383 U.S. 75 (1966), 151

Roth v. United States, 354 U.S. 476 (1957), 149, 243, 291

Savings and Loan Association v. Topeka, 87 U.S. 686 (1875), 115, 122

Schecter Poultry Corp. v. United States, 295 U.S. 495 (1935), 137, 172

Schneider v. Rusk, 377 U.S. 163 (1964), 172

Schneider v. State of New Jersey, 308 U.S. 147 (1939), 396

Schware v. Bd. of Bar Examiners, 353 U.S. 232 (1957), 387, 388

Semayne's Case. 5 Co. Rep. 91 (K.B. 1605), 321

Shapiro v. Thompson, 394 U.S. 618 (1969), 320, 326

Singer v. United States, 380 U.S. 24 (1965), 149

Skinner v. Oklahoma, 316 U.S. 535 (1942), 134, 143, 170, 323

Slagle v. Ohio, 366 U.S. 259 (1961), 150

Slaughter-House Cases, 83 U.S. 36 (1872), 48, 283, 288, 302

Smith v. Alabama, 124 U.S. 465 (1888), 265

Smythe v. Fiske, 90 U.S. 374 (1874), 217

Snyder v. Massachusetts, 291 U.S. 97 (1934), 177, 388, 393

South Carolina v. Katzenbach, 383 U.S. 301 (1966), 171

Southern Pacific Co. v. Jensen, 244 U.S. 205 (1917), 170

Stanley v. Georgia, 394 U.S. 557 (1969), 327

Stanley v. Illinois, 405 U.S. 645 (1972), 246

Stanton v. Baltic Mining Co., 240 U.S. 103 (1916), 172

State v. Abellano, 50 Hawaii 384 (1968), 247

State v. Nelson, 126 Conn. 412 (1940), 128, 290

Steward Machine Co. v. Davis, 301 U.S. 548 (1937), 171

Steward v. Kahn, 78 U.S. 493 (1870), 171

Swift v. Tyson, 41 U.S. 1 (1842), 266

Tanner v. Armco Steel Corp., 340 F. Supp. 532 (S.D. Tex. 1962), 192

Tennessee Elec. Power Co. v. TVA, 306 U.S. 118 (1939), 149, 244, 291, 391

Terret v. Taylor, 13 U.S. 43 (1815), 283

Texas v. White, 74 U.S. 700 (1868), 263

Thornburgh v. American College of Obstetricians and Gynecologists, 106 S.Ct. 2169 (1986), 323–34

Thornhill v. Alabama, 310 U.S. 88 (1940), 137

Tileson v. Ullman, 129 Conn. 84 (1943), 397

Time, Inc. v. Hill, 385 U.S. 374 (1967), 289

Trop. v. Dulles, 356 U.S. 86 (1958), 172, 173

Trustees of Dartmouth College v. Woodward, 17 U.S. 518 (1819), 170

Twining v. New Jersey, 211 U.S. 78 (1908), 131, 132, 176

Tyson & Brother v. Banton, 273 U.S. 418 (1927), 170

United Pub. Workers v. Mitchell, 330 U.S. 75 (1947), 5, 8, 15, 142, 149, 172, 191, 243–44, 284, 286, 291, 293, 312, 391, 393
United States v. Barnett, 376 U.S. 681 (1964), 150
United States v. Brown, 381 U.S. 437 (1965), 172
United States v. Butler, 80 L. ed. 287 (1936), 105, 137, 141, 171
United States v. Cardiff, 344 U.S. 174 (1952), 172
United States v. Carolene Products Co., 304 U.S. 144 (1938), 284
United States v. C.I.O., 335 U.S. 106 (1948), 149
United States v. Cruikshank, 92 U.S. 542 (1876), 176
United States v. Darby, 312 U.S. 100 (1941), 141, 171, 172, 207
United States v. E.C. Knight Co., 156 U.S. 19 (1895), 288
United States v. Guest, 383 U.S. 745 (1966), 171
United States v. Orito, 413 U.S. 139 (1973), 192
United States v. Sanchez, 340 U.S. 42 (1950), 171
United States v. Sullivan, 332 U.S. 689 (1948), 171
United States v. Uhl, 436 F.2d 773 (9th Cir. 1970), 192
United States v. Wong Kim Ark, 169 U.S. 649, (1898), 281

United States v. Worrall, 2 U.S. 384 (1798), 265
Upper Dublin Overseers of the Poor v. Germantown Overseers of the Poor, 2 U.S. 213 (1793), 326

Walker v. Sauvinet, 92 U.S. 90 (1875), 176
Washington v. Texas, 388 U.S. 14 (1967), 176, 316
Weeks v. United States, 232 U.S. 383 (1914), 176
West Coast Hotel Co. v. Parrish, 300 U.S. 379 (1937), 136, 170
West v. Louisiana, 194 U.S. 258 (1904), 176
West Virginia State Bd. of Educ. v. Barnette, 319 U.S. 624 (1943), 130
Whalen v. Wade, 429 U.S. 589 (1977), 289
Wheaton v. Peters, 33 U.S. 591 (1834), 265
Wickard v. Filburn, 317 U.S. 111 (1942), 171
Williams v. Board of Education, 388 F.Supp. 93 (S.D.W.Va. 1975), 192
Wolf v. Colorado, 388 U.S. 25 (1949), 388
Woods v. Cloyd W. Miller Co., 333 U.S. 138 (1948), 149, 171, 243, 291
Writs of Assistance Case (Mass. 1761), 80

Yick Wo v. Hopkins, 118 U.S. 356 (1885), 320
Youngstown Sheet and Tube Co. v. Sawyer, 343 U.S. 579 (1952), 171, 172

General Index

Acton, Baron, 86
Adams, John: on natural rights, 83; on Otis' argument for independence, 80–82; on retained rights, 108
Adams, John Quincy, 68
American Revolution, 83–84
Antifederalists: and demand for guarantees of continued importance of states' laws, 262–63, 281; requirement for a bill of rights, 157–58, 266; *See also* Madison, James; State-based rights
Articles of Confederation: state and individual rights under, 256–59

Bentham, Jeremy, 97
Berger, Raoul, 9, 16; on judicial review, 23; on Ninth Amendment rights, 221, 305–6
Bill of Rights: functions of, 23; issued from distrust of federal and state governments, 195–96, 208; not applicable to the states, 195; power-constraint mechanism of, 17, 184; question of applicability to states of, 223; *See also* Antifederalists; Federalists; Madison, James
Birth control cases, Connecticut: and right of privacy, 394–98; invalidation of, 127, 130–35, 244–45, 291; judicial review of, 128–30
Black, Charles, 35, 43; on judicial review, 25; on Ninth Amendment, 247
Black, Justice Hugo L., 179, 185, 205; on enumerated rights, 198; opinion in birth control cases, 129, 132–34
Blackmun, Justice Harry: interpretation of rights under due process clause, 325–26; on woman's right of free choice in pregnancy, 327–28
Blackstone's *Commentaries*: classification of rights of Englishmen, 98;

importance of ideas of legislative sovereignty, 87–89, 97
Bork, Robert, 192
Brandeis, Justice Louis D., 289
Brennan, Justice William, 17; opinion in birth control cases, 129, 132–33; opinion in *Griswold*, 191, 245, 291
Burke, Edmund, 86, 97
Burke, Thomas: amendment to proposed Articles of Confederation, 255–56

Calvinism, 73–74
Camden, Lord, 86
Chatham, Lord, 86
Clergy in colonial America, 78–80
Coke, Sir Edward: comparison with Locke, 75; ideas blended with Locke, 82; influence in American colonies of, 76, 81
Colonies, American: political and philosophical influences on, 76–91, 303–4
Common law: arguments for inclusion in Constitution, 268–70; Madison's interpretation of, 265–66; uses of principles of, 41–42
Congress approves Ninth Amendment and Bill of Rights, 279–81
Constitution: effect of amended, 27; relation of Ninth Amendment to structure of, 28–29; supremacy and legality of, 69–71
Constitutional law, American: influence of Locke on, 71–72
Constitutional presumption: in amendments to Constitution, 41–44, 48
Constitutional rights: power-constraining functions of, 14–15, 17; rights-powers and power-constraint conceptions of, 3, 6–9, 8–10, 13–20
Constraints: to limit judicial action, 45–

49; *See also* Power-constraint conception

Constructive method: to interpret unenumerated or retained rights, 37–39

Contraception. *See* Birth control cases, Connecticut

Cooley, Thomas: on right of privacy, 321

Cover, Robert: on interpretation of Constitution, 217–18

Declaration of Independence, 84, 90; statement of rights in, 109–10

Declaration of Rights, Maryland (1776), 249

Declaratory Act of 1766, 86–87

Dickinson, John: proposed Article III of Articles of Confederation, 254–56

Douglas, Justice William O.: opinion in birth control cases, 132–35, 142; opinion in *Griswold*, 150, 191, 244–45; on possible rights under Ninth Amendment, 246

Duane, James, 83

Due process clause: interpretation of, 202, 204; and selective absorption or incorporation, 176–77, 203–4; use in right of privacy cases, 322–26

Ely, John Hart, 16, 32; on Ninth Amendment, 211–16, 247, 300–301

Enumerated rights, 4–5, 14, 232; concerns about, 181–83, 197–98; constraints concerning scope of, 47–49; derivation from state law of, 281–82; inclusion of retained rights in, 18–19; protection by courts of, 30–31; similarity to unenumerated rights, 232; *See also* Bill of Rights; Constitutional rights; Unenumerated rights

Fairman, Charles, 203

Federal government: distrust by Framers of, 193–95; effect of activities on state-based rights, 287–90;

expansion of powers of, 19, 171; limitations on powers imposed by Constitution before and after amendment, 14–15, 17, 26–27; proposed remedies for expansion of powers of, 30–31; Supreme Court construction of powers of, 170–73

Federalism: Ninth Amendment as keystone of, 336; *See also* Antifederalists; Articles of Confederation; Right of self-government

Federalists: argument against a bill of rights, 4–5, 13, 155–58, 260–61; against judicial review based on unenumerated rights, 20; reason for supporting rights-powers conception, 9, 11–13

Fifth Amendment: due process under, 204

First Amendment: presumption in favor of free speech, 42

Founders. *See* Framers

Fourteenth Amendment: application to states of rights in first eight amendments, 388; due process under, 317; effect of Privileges and Immunities Clause under, 48; and selective absorption or incorporation into, 176–77, 203–4, 210–11; use to interpret individual rights cases, 137–44; *See also* Due process clause

Framers: belief in natural rights, 33; distinction between natural and civil (or positive) rights by, 309–14; distrust of new federal government, 193–94; interpretation of enumerated and retained rights by, 118–19, 269

Frankfurter, Justice Felix, 186; opinion in birth control cases, 128–29

Fuller, Lon, 39, 174

Galloway, Joseph, 83, 253–54

Gerry, Elbridge, 153–54; on enumerated rights, 14; on powers of federal government, 195

Goldberg, Justice Arthur J., 198–99; interpretation of Ninth Amendment by, 2, 200–201, 205, 221, 389–98; opinion in *Griswold* of, 2, 150, 191–92, 245, 291, 387; use of Ninth Amendment by, 191–92

Guarantee clause: enforcement of state law through, 317–18

Hamilton, Alexander: on common law and individual state laws, 264; opposition to a bill of rights, 5, 11–12, 100, 156, 261–62, 304; on protection of retained rights, 262–63; on retained rights, 197

Harlan, Justice John Marshall: on Framers' intent for Fourteenth Amendment, 217; opinion in birth control cases, 129, 130–31, 133–34

Henry, Patrick: on importance of a bill of rights, 154–55, 157, 267–69; influence of clergy on, 79–80; on natural rights, 83; writes Fourth Resolution of Virginia Stamp Act, 252–53

Hichborn, Benjamin, 90

Hobbes, Thomas, 88, 89, 302

Hohfeld, W. H.: definition of rights, 228–29

Individual rights: according to Locke, 71; proposed use of Ninth and Tenth Amendments to interpret, 137–44; theory of, 107–9

Jackson, Rep.: opposition to a bill of rights, 116

Jefferson, Thomas, 45–46; advocacy of a bill of rights, 100–101, 154; on independence of colonies, 84; on limiting power, 194; on retained rights, 196; in support of Ninth Amendment, 224

Judicial decisions: based on doctrine of due process, 322–23; bypass of Ninth Amendment in, 103, 110–12; concerning right of privacy using Ninth Amendment argument, 328–34

Judicial review: criteria for individual rights in, 144–47; criteria in rights cases for, 224–26; escape of guarantee clause from, 317–18; of

legislation, 41; in unenumerated rights cases, 20–31; See also Birth control cases

Justinian, 69–70

Kelsey, Knowlton H., 109, 122–23

Kent, Chancellor James, 98, 101

King, Rufus: on right of state to change its constitution, 270, 313

Kutler, Stanley, 216

Labor theory of value: Locke's and Smith's use of, 72–73

Law of nature: support of and opposition to, 83

Lee, Richard Bland, 68

Lee, Richard Henry, 254

Legislative power: defined by Locke, 251; idea of limits to, 23–24, 86–87; Locke's specific limits to, 71–72

Legislative sovereignty doctrine, 86–91

Liberty: Blackstone's concept of natural, 87–88; concept of, 345–46; interpretation of, 201–2; Ninth Amendment as protection of, 113; presumption in Ninth Amendment of individual, 41–42; support by Ninth Amendment for concept of, 387–88; in theory of American government, 107–8

Locke, John: definition of political power, 251; ideas blended with Coke's, 82; ideas on natural law, 71; influence in American colonies of, 77–79; natural law-social contract theory of, 250–51; on property (labor theory of value), 72–73; on public good and executive prerogative, 74–75, 251; social contract theory of, 302–3

Lusky, Louis, 216

Macedo, Steven, 42

Maclay, William, 69

Madison, James: on abuse of federal and state power, 15, 194–96; on a bill of rights, 33–34, 159–61, 180–81, 275–

76, 305; on common law of states, 265–66, 270–71; on Constitution, 329; on constitutional rights, 3–4; on danger of enumerated rights, 12, 198; on effect of Bill of Rights in Constitution, 199–200; ideas of procedural and structural rights, 298; on natural rights, 318; on Necessary and Proper Clause, 16–17; Ninth Amendment draft, 175–76, 276–81; on Ninth Amendment use, 164–69, 305–7; as originator of Ninth Amendment, 2–4, 158, 296; on proposed amendments as a bill of rights, 51–63, 117, 274–76; reasons for adding rights' amendments to Constitution, 51–53, 56–63, 195–96; on retained rights, 20–21, 161, 197, 221–22; rights-powers interpretation of Ninth Amendment, 18–19, 193; on unamended Constitution, 26–27

Mansfield, Earl of, 86, 88
Marshall, Chief Justice John, 151, 170, 175
Martin, Luther, 258
Mason, George, 153–54; on importance of a bill of rights, 267–68
Massachusetts: proposed amendments to Constitution, 353–54
Massachusetts Circular Letter of 1768, 82
Massey, Calvin, 25
Milton, John, 87
Murphy, Justice: opinion in birth control case, 132, 135, 142

Natural law, 186
Natural, or inherent, rights, 318–20; defined, 96–97; as defined by Ninth Amendment, 107, 330–31; Framers' belief in, 33; John Adams on, 83; right of privacy as, 321–28; theory of, 162–63
Necessary and Proper Clause, 16–17; implied powers of, 30
New Hampshire: proposed amendments to Constitution, 354–56
New York: proposed amendments to Constitution, 99, 272, 356–64
Nicholas, George: on common law, 269
Ninth Amendment: cases using, 243–44; derivation and development of,

293–98, 332–33; purpose and meaning of, 248, 281–87, 316; reason for adoption of, 33–34; and selective absorption, 176–77
North Carolina: proposed amendments to Constitution, 364–70

Originalist method: to interpret unenumerated or retained rights, 35–37
Otis, James: influence on revolutionary ideas, 80–81; pamphlet on self-government, 251–52

Paine, Thomas: on convening Continental Conference, 67
Parliament: doctrine of legislative limits, 86–87
Patterson, Bennett: on Ninth Amendment, 205–9
Pennsylvania: proposed amendments to Constitution, 273, 370–73
Positive or civil rights: effect of federal government activity on state-based, 287–90; sources of, 309–10; of state-based Ninth Amendment interpretation, 314–17; and supremacy clause, 311–18, 335
Pound, Roscoe: on retained rights, 205
Power-constraint conception: of constitutional rights, 3, 13–20
Powers: divided from rights in Ninth and Tenth Amendments, 93–94, 297–98; enumerated in Constitution, 4–6; *See also* Federal government
Precedent, 41
Presumptive method: to interpret unenumerated or retained rights, 39–44
Privacy: as constitutional right, 245–46; Goldberg's interpretation of right of, 245, 393; interpretation of right of, 104; right in Ninth Amendment of, 321, 328–34; right of, 104, 125, 288, 321–28; *See also* Unenumerated rights
Procedural rights: example of unenumerated, 47
Property rights, 72–73, 105
Public good, 74

Quincy, Josiah, 69

Randolph, Edmund, 154; on common law, 269–70; opposition to Ninth Amendment, 277–79
Redlich, Norman: on Ninth Amendment, 208, 209–11
Reed, Justice Stanley F.: interpretation of Ninth Amendment, 5–6, 7
Rehnquist, Chief Justice William: position on use of due process clause, 328
Retained rights: enumeration of, 94–96; interpretations of, 196–97; relation to Ninth Amendment and Constitution, 31–34; stated in Ninth Amendment, 93, 107, 114–15; See also Unenumerated rights
Rhode Island: proposed amendments to Constitution, 99, 373–79
Right of privacy, 125
Right of self-government: retained by states, 251–59
Rights: concept of, 227–41; effect of enumeration of, 12; existence in Ninth Amendment of federal, 247–48; Framers' distinction between natural and civil (or positive), 309–11; identification of human, 94–96, 104–6; Madison's conception of, 298; protection by Ninth Amendment of positive and natural, 310–18; separated from powers in Ninth and Tenth Amendments, 297–98; See also Constitutional rights; Enumerated rights; Individual rights; Liberty; Natural, or inherent, rights; Positive, or civil, rights; Retained rights; Unenumerated rights
Rights independent of government. See Retained rights; Unenumerated rights
Rights-powers conception: advantages of, 6; of constitutional rights, 3; effect on Ninth Amendment of, 2–3, 8–10; effect on retained rights with government expansion, 19; objection to interpretation of Ninth Amendment using, 6–9; See also Power-constraint conception; Powers

Sherman, Roger: draft of Bill of Rights, 351–52
Smith, Adam: perception of public good, 74–75; use of labor theory of value, 73
Social contract theories: of Hobbes and Locke, 302–3
South Carolina: proposed amendments to Constitution, 99, 379–80
Spencer, Samuel: support for a bill of rights by, 266–67
State-based rights. See Positive, or civil, rights; Ninth Amendment
States: interpretation of powers of, 169–70; Ninth Amendment as protection of liberty from government of, 113–20; as protector by law of individual liberty, 287; as repository of information on unenumerated rights, 264–65; retention of right of self-government, 251–59; rights incorporated in constitutions of, 36
Stevens, Justice John Paul: position on use of due process clause, 328
Stewart, Justice Potter, 192–93; opinion in birth control cases, 129; opinion in Griswold, 192–93
Story, Justice Joseph: advocacy for a bill of rights, 101; on Ninth Amendment, 102–3
Sullivan, John: on colonists' rights, 254
Supremacy clause: and interpretation of state-based rights, 311–13
Supreme Court: interpretation of Ninth Amendment, 2–3, 111, 172; invalidation of state law in Griswold; as protector of individual liberty, 119–20, 173–76; See also Rights-powers conception

Tenth Amendment: complementary to and combined with Ninth Amendment, 93–94; language of, 6, 8; purpose and meaning of, 94, 284–87, 297
Trumbull, Sen. Lyman, 203

Unenumerated rights, 4–5, 232, 248; concerns about, 181–83, 197–98;

constraints to limit scope of, 45–49; constructive method to interpret, 37–39, 47–49; effect when using rights-powers or power-constraint conception, 3; equality with enumerated rights of, 41–42, 338; examples of, 120–22; Hamilton's argument against, 262–63; judicial review of, 20; originalist method to interpret, 31–37; presumptive method to interpret, 39–47; protection by courts of, 30–31; question of judicial review of, 20–31; rights-preserving function of, 25–29; as rights retained by the states, 281–82; similarity to enumerated rights, 232; subject to interpretation at state level, 264–65

Virginia: declaration of rights in constitution of, 85–86, 109; proposed amendments to federal Constitution, 35–36, 98, 271–72, 380–85
Virginia Stamp Act Resolutions, 252–53

Warren, Chief Justice Earl: on due process clause, 211; opinion in *Griswold*, 191, 245, 291
Washington, George: on Framers' intent, 118–19; on retained rights, 196
Wellington, Harry, 184
White, Justice Byron: interpretation of rights under due process clause, 324–25, 326; position on use of due process clause, 328
Whitefield, George, 79
Wilson, James: opposition to a bill of rights, 5, 13–14, 155–57, 260–61, 304; on rights, 36–37, 39–40